HIDDEN IN PLAIN SIGHT

Contributions of Aboriginal Peoples to Canadian Identity and Culture
Volume 2

Edited by Cora J. Voyageur, David R. Newhouse, and Dan Beavon

Hidden in Plain Sight highlights the extraordinary contributions made by Aboriginal peoples to Canadian society. This volume, like its acclaimed predecessor, traces the efforts of Aboriginal people to collectively improve their lives and those of other Canadians. Together, the volumes serve as a powerful affirmation of Aboriginal peoples' ability to transcend a long history of violent persecution, displacement, and cultural disruption.

In this second volume, scholars and other experts pay tribute to the enduring influence of Aboriginal peoples on Canadian economic and community development, environmental initiatives, education, politics, and arts and culture. Included are profiles of many notable individuals, such as singer-songwriter and educator Buffy Sainte-Marie, politician Elijah Harper, entrepreneur Dave Tuccaro, and musician Robbie Robertson. Engaging and informative, both volumes of *Hidden in Plain Sight* enrich and broaden our understanding of Aboriginal and Canadian history, while providing inspiration for generations to come.

CORA J. VOYAGEUR is an associate professor in the Department of Sociology at the University of Calgary.

DAVID R. NEWHOUSE is the Chair and an associate professor in the Department of Indigenous Studies at Trent University.

DAN BEAVON is the past director of Strategic Research and Analysis for Indian and Northern Affairs Canada.

Hidden in Plain Sight

Contributions of Aboriginal Peoples to Canadian Identity and Culture

Volume 2

Edited by

CORA J. VOYAGEUR
DAVID R. NEWHOUSE
DAN BEAVON

UNIVERSITY OF TORONTO PRESS
Toronto Buffalo London

© University of Toronto Press 2011
Toronto Buffalo London
www.utppublishing.com
Printed in Canada

ISBN 978-1-4426-4074-0 (cloth)
ISBN 978-1-4426-1012-5 (paper)

Printed on acid-free, 100% post-consumer recycled paper with
vegetable-based inks.

Library and Archives Canada Cataloguing in Publication

Hidden in plain sight : contributions of Aboriginal peoples to Canadian
identity and culture / edited by Cora Voyageur, David Newhouse,
Daniel Beavon.

ISBN 0-8020-8800-7 (bound : v. 1).   ISBN 0-8020-8581-4 (pbk. : v. 1).
ISBN 978-0-8020-8581-8 (pbk. : v. 1)   ISBN 978-1-4426-4074-0 (bound : v. 2).
ISBN 978-1-4426-1012-5 (pbk. : v. 2)

1. Canada – Civilization – Indian influences.   2. Native peoples – Canada –
Biography.   3. Native peoples – Canada – History.   4. Canada – Biography.
I. Voyageur, Cora Jane, 1956– II. Newhouse, David   III. Beavon, Daniel J.K.

E78.C2H487 2005   971.004'97   C2005-901134-3

Every attempt has been made to identify and credit sources for photographs.
The publisher would appreciate receiving information as to any inaccuracies in
the credits for subsequent editions.

University of Toronto Press acknowledges the financial assistance to its
publishing program of the Canada Council for the Arts and the Ontario Arts
Council.

 Canada Council   Conseil des Arts
for the Arts   du Canada   ONTARIO ARTS COUNCIL
CONSEIL DES ARTS DE L'ONTARIO

University of Toronto Press acknowledges the financial support of the
Government of Canada through the Canada Book Fund for its publishing
activities.

Contents

PART 4: POLITICS AND NORTHERN POWER

PART 5: ARTS AND CULTURE

PART 6: CONCLUSION

Acknowledgments

This book would not have been completed without the untiring efforts of many people. First, it would not exist without the contributions of the representatives of federal government departments and national Aboriginal organizations who served on the committee that provided advice and ideas on how to shape the project, as well as suggestions on which topics to include. Among these individuals were Sharon Jeannottee, Pierre Beaudreau, Vivian Gray, Glen Morrison, Peter Williamson, Gail Valaskakis, Christina Delguste, Melissa Lazore, Ryan Moran, and Rebecca McPhail. Second, the initial call for papers and the selection of authors was coordinated by Maurice Obonsawin. Third, two summer students, Christine Armstrong and Valerie Green, did considerable background research and coordinated the work of the various authors. Fourth, staff members of the Strategic Research Directorate, Indian and Northern Affairs Canada, contributed significant time and effort to this project; they include John Clement, Paula Sanders, Cynthia Davidson, Beverlee Moore, Marc Fonda, Beth Dunning, and Jodi Bruhn. Finally, we would like to thank the contributors and the students from Dr Cora Voyageur's classes at the University of Calgary who prepared the short biographies of famous Aboriginal people included in the book. We are indebted to all the individuals mentioned above for their support and assistance.

Most important, however, is the fact that this book could not have been written without the thousands of Aboriginal people who have worked tirelessly, ceaselessly, and continuously over the centuries to create better lives for future generations.

Contributors

Feruza Abdjalieva holds a bachelor of arts in interdisciplinary studies from the University of British Columbia. She has been assisting Rob VanWynsberghe on the research of the impacts of the 2010 Winter Olympic Games on the host region and city. She is a prospective law student with an interest in human rights and criminal law.

Jo-ann Archibald (Q'um Q'um Xiiem) is from the Stó:lō Nation, in southern British Columbia. She is the associate dean for Indigenous education and a professor in education at the University of British Columbia. At UBC, Archibald also held the positions of supervisor of the Native Indian Teacher Education Program from 1985 to 1992 and the director of the First Nations House of Learning from 1993 to 2001. Her research interests include Indigenous storywork and oral tradition, Indigenous knowledge systems, Indigenous methodology, teacher education, and higher education. Archibald received a National Aboriginal Achievement Award in 2000.

Dan Beavon is the past director of the Strategic Research and Analysis Directorate, Indian and Northern Affairs Canada (INAC). He has published dozens of research articles and many books on Aboriginal issues. He is also affiliated with the University of Western Ontario as an adjunct research professor in sociology. Beavon is the 2008 winner of the Gold Medal Award, which is awarded to only one scientist or researcher each year by the Professional Institute of the Public Service of Canada. This award acknowledges his outstanding scientific work that has led to the improvement and enhancement of public well-being.

Nick Bernard has been involved in Aboriginal studies at the Faculté des sciences sociales, Université Laval, since 1992, first as a research assistant and now as a research coordinator. He was also editorial coordinator of the collective work entitled *Le Nord: Habitants et mutations*, published in the Atlas historique du Québec collection (2001). He is the co-editor of *Arctic Food Security*, published by Canadian Circumpolar Institute Press.

Andrée Caron holds a master's degree in sociology. She is the executive director of databases for the Comparative Aboriginal Condition project housed at Université Laval. Caron set up ArcticStat, a statistical databank containing socio-economic indicators that covers the circumpolar Arctic region, which includes eight countries. She has co-authored papers, such as 'Economic Systems in the Arctic Human Development Report,' that employ ArcticStat data. She is currently associated with the Chaire de recherche du Canada sur la condition autochtone comparée at Université Laval (Quebec).

Wanda Dalla Costa is an architect with Dalla Costa Design Group Inc., a company specializing in culturally responsive and ecologically sustainable design projects for First Nations communities. She holds a master's degree in architecture from the Faculty of Environmental Design (University of Calgary, 2001) and a bachelor of arts in sociology/Native studies (University of Alberta, 1991); she is currently completing a master's degree in design research in urban policy and planning at the Southern California Institute of Architecture (2011). Dalla Costa is a member of the Saddle Lake First Nation in Alberta and currently resides in Calgary and Los Angeles.

Gérard Duhaime is a full professor of sociology at Université Laval and has been chairholder of the Canada Research Chair on Comparative Aboriginal Condition since 2002. He is the former elected president of the International Arctic Social Sciences Association, member of the International Polar Year Planning Committee appointed by the International Council for Science, director of the SLiCA-Canada research program in collaboration with the Canadian national and regional Inuit associations, and leader of ArcticStat.org and Nunivaat Program. He is the author of several books and papers in the fields of economic sociology specially related to the circumpolar Arctic (*Arctic Food Security*, 2008; *The Economy of the Circumpolar Arctic*, 2006; *Le Nord: Habitants et mutations*, 2001; *De l'Igloo au HLM*, 1985). Duhaime served as senior scientific advisor at the University of Lapland and as adjunct professor with the Canadian Circumpolar Institute at the University of Alberta. He holds a doctorate in sociology (economic sociology) and a master's degree in political science (policy analysis).

Sean Edwards has a master's degree in political science (public policy) from Simon Fraser University and works as a policy analyst. His research interests explore how and why public policy is created and the roles that individuals play in the policymaking process.

R. Wesley Heber is a full professor of Indigenous studies at the First Nations University of Canada. He holds an honours undergraduate degree in anthropology from Saint Mary's University, a master's degree in environmental studies from Dalhousie University, and a doctorate in anthropology from the University of Manitoba. Heber has been teaching anthropology and Indigenous studies for twenty-five years and has been at the First Nations University since 1991. During his formative years, between 1959 and 1962, he was an employee of the Hudson's Bay Company, working as a fur trader in their northern stores department.

Dean Jacobs was elected chief of the Walpole Island First Nation (WIFN) in June 2004. He was a member of the International Joint Commission's Council of Great Lakes Research Managers and the Ontario Round Table on Environment and Economy. Jacobs also served six elected terms on the WIFN Council of Three Fires. In addition, he is a former board member of the Ontario Heritage Foundation, Ontario Historical Society, and the Premier's Council. He is a recipient of an honorary doctorate in public service from Bowling Green State University.

P. Whitney Lackenbauer is associate professor and chair of history at St Jerome's University in the University of Waterloo. He has travelled extensively with the Canadian Rangers in the North over the last decade and is a frequent commentator on Arctic sovereignty and security issues. He has authored, co-authored, or edited more than a dozen books, including *Arctic Front: Defending Canada in the Far North,* which won the 2009 Donner Prize for the best Canadian book on public policy.

Laurie Meijer Drees is co-chair of the Department of First Nations Studies at Vancouver Island University (VIU) in Nanaimo. For the past two years she has held the position of teaching scholar, Indigenous knowledge and Aboriginal education, for VIU. She has also taught at the University of Saskatchewan, the First Nations University of Canada, and the University of Alaska-Fairbanks. Meijer Drees's research interests include First Nations political history and the history of Indian health services as related to Indigenous knowledge and oral histories.

David R. Newhouse is Onondaga from the Six Nations of the Grand River community near Brantford, Ontario. He is chair of the Department of Indigenous Studies and associate professor in business administration at Trent University. Newhouse teaches in the graduate Community Economic Development Program at Concordia University and was the IMC Canada–University of Saskatchewan Aboriginal Scholar in Residence. His research interests are focused on the way in which Aboriginal traditional thought and Western thought are coming together and creating modern Aboriginal societies. His current exploration is on the use of Indigenous knowledge in Canadian society.

Andrew Nurse teaches Canadian studies at Mount Allison University. His scholarly works include the edited collections (with Raymond Blake) *Trajectories of Rural Life* and *Beyond National Dreams*. He lives in Sackville, New Brunswick, with his wife, Mary Ellen, and their children, Hayden and Bryn.

Leanna Parker is a doctoral candidate in resource sociology and Native studies at the University of Alberta. Her primary research interest is Indigenous peoples' involvement in commercial economies. Her dissertation research compares Indigenous peoples' participation in the Canadian fur trade with Maori participation in the whaling industry of nineteenth-century New Zealand. Her past academic work compared economic and labour relations in the Canadian fur trade and the northern Australian cattle industry.

J. Douglas Rabb is professor emeritus at Lakehead University in Thunder Bay, Ontario. He has a doctorate from Queen's University. With Ojibwa philosopher Dennis McPherson he has co-authored a number of articles on Native philosophy as well as the book *Indian from the Inside* (second, revised, and extended edition: McFarland). With J. Michael Richardson he published *The Existential Joss Whedon: Evil and Human Freedom in 'Buffy the Vampire Slayer,' 'Angel,' 'Firefly,' and 'Serenity'* (McFarland, 2007) and 'Reavers and Redskins: Creating the Frontier Savage' in *Investigating 'Firefly' and 'Serenity': Science Fiction on the Frontier* (ed. R. Wilcox and T. Cochran, I.B. Tauris, 2008).

William Shead is a member of the Peguis First Nation in Manitoba. He served in the Canadian Navy and retired as a lieutenant commander. He was mayor of Selkirk, Manitoba, from 1980 to 1983, the Prairie regional director general for Veterans Affairs Canada from 1986 to 1992, and the chief executive officer of the Aboriginal Centre of Winnipeg from 1993 to 1996. Now that Shead has retired, his volunteer activities include serving as the chair of the Aboriginal Centre of Winnipeg, the vice-chair of the Centre for Aboriginal Human Resource Development, and a member of the board of directors of the National Aboriginal Achievement Foundation, the Aboriginal Aerospace Initiative, and the Winnipeg Symphony Orchestra.

Georges E. Sioui is coordinator of the Aboriginal Studies Program at the University of Ottawa, a position he has held since January 2004. He received his doctorate in history from Université Laval in 1991. In May 1990, Sioui and his four brothers obtained a landmark victory in the Supreme Court of Canada (the 'Sioui Case') over territorial and traditional land-use rights. His *Histoires de Kanatha: Vues et contées / Histories of Kanatha: Seen and Told*, based on his national and international presentations, was published by the University of Ottawa Press in 2008. Sioui has also authored two land-mark books on Aboriginal history and philosophy: *For an Amerindian Autohistory* (McGill-Queen's University Press, 1992) and *Huron-Wendat: The Heritage of the Circle* (UBC Press and Michigan State University Press, 1999).

David A. Smith is a faculty librarian and doctoral candidate in history at the University of Saskatchewan. He was a member of the editorial board, a contributing author, and a photographic researcher for *A Stó:lō–Coast Salish Historical Atlas*. Smith has recently authored articles in the *American Indian Culture and Research Journal*, *Journal of American Culture*, *Native Studies Review*, *Partnership*, and *South Dakota History*. His work has been honoured with awards from the Western Writers of America in 2009 and the American Culture Association in 2010. He resides in Saskatoon with his wife, Yumiko, and their two daughters, Emily and Rachel.

Frank J. Tough is an associate dean (research) and professor of Native studies at the University of Alberta, as well as a historical geographer adjunct to the university's Department of Rural Economy. He recently benefited from a sojourn as an academic visitor to the Department of Economic History at the London School of Economics. Tough published *As Their Natural Resources Fail: Native People and the Economic History of Northern Manitoba, 1870–1930* (UBC Press), which received two book awards. His research and publishing relate to several themes, including Native economic history, natural resource management, and treaty and Aboriginal rights. Specifically, he has published articles and chapters on the transfer of Rupertsland, the economic policies of the Department of Indian Affairs after 1870, Indian economic behaviour, the demise of Native fisheries, Indian treaties, the Natural Resources Transfer Agreement, and Métis scrip.

Rob VanWynsberghe is an assistant professor in the Department of Educational Studies at the University of British Columbia in Vancouver. His research expertise lies in sustainability and the related areas of social movements and capacity building. Among other topics his research looks at how catalytic interventions, such as mega-events, impact local communities and how curricula and pedagogy foster learning about and contributing to social movements. Current research projects include a study of the impacts of the 2010 Winter Olympic Games, with a specific interest in social leveraging and planned legacies. In addition, he is conducting action research on classroom features in sustainability programming. VanWynsberghe has published articles most recently in *Cities, International Journal of Urban and Regional Research, Canadian Journal of Education*, and *International Journal of Qualitative Methods*.

Edwinna von Baeyer has written on many aspects of Canadian history, from architecture to landscape history. She has published three books and numerous articles on Canadian cultural landscapes. Her contributions to Canadian landscape history were recognized by the Ontario Heritage Foundation's awarding of a certificate of achievement in 2005. Von Baeyer's latest book is *Down the Garden Path: A Guide for Researching the History of a Garden or Landscape*. She writes and edits on a wide range of subjects, including forestry, international development, the Internet, and Canadian history.

Cora J. Voyageur is an associate professor of sociology at the University of Calgary. Her research explores the Aboriginal experience in Canada, including leadership, employment, community and economic development, women's issues, and health. She has published more than forty academic papers and has written more than thirty commissioned research reports. Voyageur is the author of the books *Firekeepers of the 21st Century: Women Chiefs in Canada* and *My Heroes Have Always Been Indians: Contributions of Alberta's Indigenous Peoples*. She is co-editor of *Hidden in Plain Sight: Contributions of Aboriginal Peoples to Canadian Identity and Culture*, volumes 1 and 2. Voyageur is currently working on manuscripts about Aboriginal leadership in Canada and the position of Aboriginal women in Canada. She is a member of the Athabasca Chipewyan First Nation from northern Alberta.

Brian Wright-McLeod (Dakota-Anishinabe) is the author of *The Encyclopedia of Native Music* (University of Arizona Press, 2005) and executive producer of the companion box set *The Soundtrack of a People* (EMI Music Canada). With diplomas in journalism and graphic design, he began working as a music journalist in 1979. His work as a Native rights activist took him across North America, where he participated in many ceremonies and learned much about the history of Native music, culture, and rights. These experiences formed the basis of much of his work in radio since 1984, featuring music, interviews, live in-studio performances, and special programming for CKLN, Sirius Satellite Radio, CBC Radio in Toronto, and BBC Radio in London. A former board member of the Native American Journalists Association, Wright-McLeod also served as chair for the Aboriginal music category for the Juno Awards (Canadian Academy of Recording Arts and Sciences) and helped establish the Native Grammy category for the National Academy of Recording Arts and Sciences in 2000. In 2010 the Smithsonian's National Museum of the American Indian created the contemporary Native music exhibit *Up Where We Belong* based on his *Encyclopedia of Native Music*. Wright-McLeod was also the lead consultant for Library and Archives Canada's Native music site, 'Aboriginal Sound Recordings: Music and Song.' His lifelong work in music has culminated in the development of the Native Music Research Institute, a library and living archive of Native music and culture. In addition to working as a consultant for television and documentary film producers, he writes a monthly Native music column for *News from Indian Country* while working on new book, film, and media projects.

HIDDEN IN PLAIN SIGHT

Contributions of Aboriginal Peoples to Canadian Identity and Culture
Volume 2

Introduction

CORA J. VOYAGEUR, DAVID R. NEWHOUSE, AND
DAN BEAVON

There should be positive recognition by everyone of the unique contributions
of Indian culture to Canadian life.

           − The Red Paper[1]

It is easier to make people cry than it is to make them laugh. This is a truism
in theatre, and there are equivalent truisms in other sectors of society. In the
academic sector, for instance, it might be said that it is easier to deconstruct
the old than it is to construct the new. In policy development and implementation one might say something similar: it is easier to focus on past
failures than it is to meet current needs. In other words, often a focus on the
negative seems sharper than a vision of the positive. *Hidden in Plain Sight,
Volume 2*, seeks to help change this situation.

During the late 1990s the government of Canada became increasingly
interested in what was termed *social cohesion*. Members of the Social Cohesion Research Network identified and pursued at least two lines of inves-
tigation, one focusing on the negative concept of *fault lines* and the other
on the positive notion of *what binds people together*. The purpose of the first
and second volumes of *Hidden in Plain Sight* is to focus on the positive
contributions that Aboriginal peoples have brought to Canadian society.
In so doing, it becomes evident that Aboriginal contributions help to bind
together Canadian society, regardless of the numerous fault lines that have
been created between Aboriginal peoples and Canada in history, policy,
and circumstance.

Stories that have been told about the relationship of North America's
early European immigrants to its original inhabitants often include a
theme of *reciprocity*. Many Indigenous groups claim that reciprocity is
one of several core cultural values and is foundational to the continuance
of human life. The concept of reciprocity has been found to be common
to every culture and manifests the ethical underpinnings of the informal

exchange of goods and labour within a society. It is the basis of most non-market economies.

At least three forms of reciprocity are discussed in cultural anthropology. *Generalized reciprocity* is said to be much the same as uninhibited sharing or giving. It provides the giver a sense of satisfaction and the social closeness that is fostered by gift giving. *Symmetrical reciprocity* occurs when someone gives something to someone else with the expectation of a fair and tangible return at some undefined future date. This expectation of repayment is based on a moderate degree of trust. It is also controlled through social consequence; 'moochers,' those who expect gifts but who never give one in return, are soon recognized and find it increasingly difficult to receive favours. *Negative reciprocity*, more commonly known as barter, is an informal system of exchange that can involve a minimum amount of trust and a maximum degree of social distance, which is to say that even strangers can barter. In non-industrial societies this form of reciprocity was used to establish friendly relations between or among different groups. It is often just a first step in the development of a long-term relationship.

In the study of ethics and world religions, reciprocity is recognizable through the phrase *the golden rule*. A key element for people attempting to live by this rule is to treat all people, not just members of his or her in-group, with consideration and respect. This formalized approach to relationships has been found to be a common principle in most religions throughout the world, and it is common within traditional Aboriginal spirituality and practices.

One of the most striking examples of a formalized system of reciprocity among Aboriginal peoples is the potlatch. The potlatch is a highly complex event that has been practised for thousands of years and is most commonly associated with the First Nations located on the Pacific Northwest coast of Canada and the United States. It usually involves a ceremony that is used to celebrate rites of passages, such as births, puberty, weddings, and funerals, and to honour the deceased. While potlatch practices vary among nations, communities, and individuals, they generally involve music, dance, feasting, theatrics, and spiritual ceremonies.

The potlatch involves exchanges in the economic, political, and social realms. Through it the relations within and between clans, villages, and nations, as well as with the spiritual world, are observed, and they are reinforced by the redistribution of wealth. From a purely instrumental perspective, the potlatch has been used to raise the status of a community or a family. In these cultures, unlike the European preference, status is not determined by possession of resources; rather, status is earned by *giving away* resources, which leads to reciprocity when prominent guests hold their own potlatch. Holding a potlatch is a means of enhancing one's reputation and validating social rank; prestige increases with the generosity evidenced in the potlatch in terms of the value of the goods given away. At the urging of missionaries and government agents the potlatch was made illegal in Canada in 1884[2] and a few years later in the United States. The missionaries claimed that the potlatch was 'demonic' and 'satanic,' and the government agents considered it to be wasteful, unproductive, and injurious. As was often the case in these situations, the potlatch continued to be practised outside of the gaze of Europeans. In effect, it went underground. While there are recorded instances of the potlatch going 'wild,' in the sense that the hosts 'bankrupted' themselves or that the goods were destroyed following the ceremony, this more negative side to the potlatch is considered to be rare. What was more likely the case is that the ban resulted from a misunderstanding on the part of Europeans about the potlatch. One can easily imagine the confusion that was felt when a nascent capitalistic world view based on the accumulation of goods was confronted by a world view based on generosity, reciprocity, and distribution.

The potlatch ban was lifted in Canada in 1951, sixteen years after the United States had lifted its ban. Leading up to this decision were numerous petitions to the Canadian government to remove the law prohibiting a custom that is now seen to be no worse than Christmas; the latter has roots in the pre-Christian pagan communities of northern Europe and also emphasizes gift giving. It was fortunate that the ban on potlatch was lifted because it helped restore millennia of cultural practice, a practice that provides an alternate perspective on the world and the ways in which different peoples can interact and live well together. Rather than being limited to a capitalist vision of a world founded on negative reciprocity or barter (that is, involving a minimum of trust and a maximum of social distance), the potlatch can be taken as a symbol of both symmetrical and generalized reciprocity (that is, gift giving with or without expectations of a tangible return at some undefined date). This reciprocity is the sort of activity that binds different communities together. It has a world view based on greater levels of trust, sharing, and social closeness. It is one that assumes and tries to live by the golden rule.

The potlatch is not perfect, to be sure. Some commentators might point out that it emanated from the rank-ordered societies on the northwest coast and had as one of its principal purposes the recognition and reinforcement of social gradations within communities. Such commentators might, thus, find the potlatch to be a curious choice for a controlling metaphor in the twenty-first century. This aspect of the potlatch is not our focus. It would indeed be utopian if there were no form of social stratification in human societies. This book and its writers recognize that the relations between Aboriginal Canadians and mainstream society are, indeed, unequal; there are class structures and social stratification in Canada that are maintained by political, social, economic, cultural, and other interests. Nevertheless, we still believe that all persons in any society espousing democracy have the potential to contribute and make a difference.

For this reason, the potlatch can be seen as a metaphor to convey the purpose of the *Hidden in Plain Sight* volumes. It helps to place in context, for example, the stories we tell about ourselves and the ways in which those stories may or may not conflict. It puts into perspective the interplay between the stories about fault lines and the experiences that help to bind peoples together. It demonstrates the reciprocity that is a key element in human and social interaction, even across hierarchies. The potlatch informs us that sharing makes the diverse community of Canada stronger, potentially more cohesive, more viable, and more effective in innovating to meet the coming challenges of the twenty-first century. It also points to the issues of inequality that need to be addressed as Canadian society moves forward.

The Production Process

The origin of this book took place in 1999 when the editors decided to break away from the entrenched impression of Aboriginal peoples in Canada as poor, problem ridden, and unable to adapt to contemporary society. We wanted to help the country take a step in the direction of raising Aboriginals' social position in Canada, by putting a spotlight on both their historical and their current contributions to Canadian society. The *Hidden in Plain Sight* books show Aboriginal peoples in a more positive light. We offer you a new story.

As editors, we were overwhelmed at many points in the creation of these books. The first instance was the response to our call for papers. The initial call yielded approximately fifty submissions from writers across Canada. The quantity of papers and the variety of topics were too numerous for just one book. We knew we had enough quality material for at least two books. The subjects of the papers we received ranged from the influence of Aboriginal peoples on everyday matters, like furniture design and dog breeding, to the contribution of the ironworkers who built many American skyscrapers.

It was not our intention to be overly sentimental or romantic about the Aboriginal peoples' impact on Canadian society. We did not have to be. We were able to amass a strong collection of papers that clearly articulated evidence of Aboriginal peoples' contribution to Canadian society, while adhering to the demands of academic culture. Our manuscripts have undergone the blind peer review process that is the basis of academic publishing. Telling the Aboriginal story does not have to be divorced from academic rigour.

Hidden in Plain Sight: Volume 1

In the first volume a wide array of authors explored seven categories including treaties, arts and media, literature, justice, culture and identity, sports, the military, and an overview. Its contributors included Gerald McMaster, curator of the Aboriginal exhibit at the Smithsonian Institution in Washington, DC; his article explored the contributions of contemporary Aboriginal artists to the Canadian art world. Humorist and writer Drew Hayden Taylor highlighted the *permitted humour* within the Aboriginal community and the uniqueness of the Aboriginal sense of humour. Leading Aboriginal justice researcher Carole LaPrairie investigated the involvement of Aboriginal people in the Canadian justice system. Media scholar Valerie Alia looked at the significance of naming in the Inuit culture. In the sports world, Métis author and the curator of the Plains exhibit at the Canadian Museum of Civilization, Morgan Baillargeon, explored the involvement of Aboriginals in rodeos. Treaties and Aboriginal government relations between the end of the Second World War and the new millennium were the topic of Michael Cassidy's paper. Bruce W. Hodgins and Bryan Poirier wrote about the canoe and the kayak and their link to Canadian identity and culture.

The profiles included in *Hidden in Plain Sight: Volume 1* included actor and politician Chief Dan George, a sixth-generation chief of the Squamish First Nation of Burrard Inlet, British Columbia, from 1951 to 1963; he turned to acting in the late 1960s when he played Old Lodge Skins in *Little Big Man*, which starred Dustin Hoffman. The man called the father of Ojibwa art, Norval Morrisseau, was also profiled; his artistic style and impressive body of work have gained him the reputation as being one of the most accomplished painters in Canadian history. Also included was a short biography on Jeannette Armstrong, an accomplished writer, publisher, and civil rights activist; since beginning work at the En'owkin Centre in 1978, she has become one of the most influential writers in contemporary Aboriginal literature. Theytus Books, an Aboriginal-owned and -operated publishing house, is also located at the centre.

Volume 1 was released by University of Toronto Press in the summer of 2005, and it was enthusiastically received by the public. In our quest to distribute this book as widely as possible it was sent to all schools located on Indian reserves, to friendship centres across Canada, and to government departments. The first book launch was held at the International Indigenous

Librarian Conference in Regina, Saskatchewan, in September. A second was held at the Museum of Civilization in Gatineau, Quebec, in October, which was attended by approximately one hundred and fifty authors, government officials, and members of the Aboriginal community.

Hidden in Plain Sight: Volume 2

As mentioned earlier, Aboriginal people have made a variety of contributions to many aspects of everyday life, and *Hidden in Plain Sight: Volume 2* continues the story of these contributions. In five parts, the book contains articles and profiles of accomplished Aboriginal individuals. The mix of modern and historical topics includes economic and community development, the environment, education, politics and northern power, and arts and culture. Volume 2 concludes with an overview of the post-colonial situation in Canada.

The first section addresses the topic of economic and community development and covers well over a century of Aboriginal contributions. R. Wesley Heber's work, covering the early fur trade, serves to document the vital role that Aboriginal people played in sustaining Canada's fledgling economy, and the origins of a reciprocal partnership between Aboriginal and non-Aboriginal peoples. Continuing past Confederation, Frank Tough offers a historical analysis of Aboriginal labour in northern Manitoba from 1870 to 1915. Carrying the story of Aboriginal contributions to Canada's economy on into the twentieth century, freelance writer Edwinna von Baeyer discusses the invaluable role played by generations of Mohawk high steelworkers as they built the modern cityscapes of Canada and the United States; in the same historical vein, Leanna Parker explores labour relations in the Rupertsland fur trade.

The second section of the book deals with Aboriginal influence on Canadian environmental policy. The impact of Aboriginal people on northern Canadian mining practices is told by Gérard Duhaime, Nick Bernard, and Andrée Caron. Looking further south, the second article, by Rob Van-Wynsberghe, Sean Edwards, Dean Jacobs, and Feruza Abdjalieva, examines the issue of environmental policy affecting the people of Walpole Island.

The third section, 'Education,' examines an issue that is often surrounded by negativity in the Aboriginal context. Education has long been heralded as a necessary component of Aboriginal well-being, but the topic also serves to bring back memories of negative experiences during the shameful period of residential schools. In this book, however, the positive influences that Aboriginal people have had on education and Canadian thought are explored. The first article, by Jo-ann Archibald, discusses the way in which the teaching practices of British Columbia elders have been incorporated into school curricula in the form of 'Storywork.' Not only have Aboriginal contributions affected methods of learning, but they have also had a decisive impact on how Canadians, both Aboriginal and non-Aboriginal, think. For example, Douglas Rabb and Georges Sioui explore the Aboriginal influence on Canadian philosophy and identity, respectively. In this section Andrew Nurse and David Smith detail the impact of Aboriginal oral history and mapping on Canadian historiography and geography.

Of all the sections in the book, the fourth, on politics and northern power, is arguably the most pertinent to current Aboriginal issues in Canada. Laurie Meijer Drees tackles the issue of recent Aboriginal contributions to Canadian politics and government in her article 'White Paper / Red Paper: Aboriginal Contributions to Canadian Politics and Government.' Then we find ourselves above the treeline and into the land of the North where P. Whitney Lackenbauer delves into the issue of Canadian sovereignty and the vital contributions made by members of the Canadian Rangers, a largely Aboriginal military force dedicated to serving and protecting Canada's North.

Finally, the fifth section explores the magnificent contributions that Aboriginal people in Canada have made to the arts and culture and the ways in which those contributions have positively affected Canada's international prestige. Beginning with the urban renewal catalysed by Aboriginal culture, William Shead documents the history of Winnipeg's Aboriginal Centre. Building on this, architect Wanda Dalla Costa details the contributions of Aboriginal culture, noting how Aboriginal art and history have fused with steel, rock, wood, and glass to produce inherently Canadian architecture found across the nation; such edifices include the Museum of Anthropology at the University of British Columbia in Vancouver; the Canadian Museum of Civilization in Gatineau, Quebec; and the Seabird Island School in Agassiz, British Columbia. Next, Brian Wright-McLeod explores the contributions of Aboriginal musical artists who have taken Canada, and the world, by storm.

Once again, the profiles of prominent Aboriginal people in this book have been completed by Cora Voyageur's sociology students at the University of Calgary. They portray an array of contemporary and historical Aboriginal individuals who continue to build on previous contributions by undertaking new and innovative projects. In the section on economic and community development we profile John Charles Bernard, an Aboriginal information technology expert; Dave Tuccaro, founder of the National Aboriginal Business Association; the late James (Ed) Williams, developer of self-sustaining economies in his community; and Dorothy Grant, a Haida fashion designer who creates 'wearable art.'

Profiled in the section on the environment are Cindy Kenny-Gilday, an environmental activist working in the Northwest Territories who was nominated for a Nobel Prize for her work in exposing the environmental disaster caused by uranium mining near the village of Deline, otherwise known as the Village of Widows; Matthew Coon Come, a well-known politician and activist; and Nellie Cournoyea, a community activist and politician who strove to gain a viable deal for northern Aboriginal people.

In the section on education we profile the late educator and historical writer Olive Dickason; Verna Kirkness, a pioneer in advancing Aboriginal education; and Marlene Brant Castellano, who made significant contributions that led to the establishment of Native studies as a discipline in Canadian universities. We also include profiles of Buffy Sainte-Marie, who is an educator as well as an internationally recognized musician; Malcolm King, a professor of medicine and a champion for Aboriginal health; and Marie Battiste, a Mi'kmaq educator well known for her work in revitalizing the Mi'kmaq language.

In the section on Aboriginal political contributions and northern power we profile such individuals as Thelma Chalifoux, a contemporary Métis politician who was a member of the Canadian Senate; and Elijah Harper, well known for his role in the Meech Lake Accord. In considering the North, we profile Paul Okalik, the first premier of Nunavut; Susan Aglukark, singer and songwriter; and Rosemarie Kuptana, politician, broadcaster, and writer.

Continuing with Aboriginal contributions to the arts and culture, we offer profiles of Robbie Robertson, the creator of pop music classics like *The Night They Drove Old Dixie Down* and *The Weight*; Tantoo Cardinal, a well known actress who has starred in many notable productions; Alex Janvier, a Dene Suline artist and educator; Gil Cardinal, a Métis film-maker, director, and producer; Maria Campbell, one of Canada's best-known Métis authors; and Alanis Obomsawin, a documentary film-maker and activist. In the conclusion our final profile is politician Georges Erasmus.

As the chapters and profiles in both volumes of *Hidden in Plain Sight* show, the contributions made by Aboriginal peoples to Canadian identity and culture must not be overlooked like so many blades of grass. Each element making up both the literal and figurative environments that encircle us is essential to our individual and collective well-being. One of the basic tenets of many Aboriginal philosophies, regardless of location, is the interconnection of all things that surround us. This perspective underscores the importance of relationship, generosity, and reciprocity. It also emphasizes consideration and respect for all living beings. What we, the editors and the many authors who have contributed to these volumes, hope to bring to light are precisely these sorts of interconnections and relationships. It is never too late to recognize that the ever-present contributions of Canada's Aboriginal peoples help to ensure the viability and health of the Canadian social environment. We must recognize that together we are stronger than when we are apart. It is never too late to recognize the relationships that bind us together.

Notes

1 The Red Paper, Indian Association of Alberta, Citizens Plus (Edmonton: Indian Association of Alberta, 1970), 5.
2 An Act Further to Amend 'The Indian Act, 1880,' S.C. 1984 (47 Vict), c. 27, s.3.

PART 1

ECONOMIC AND COMMUNITY DEVELOPMENT

Aboriginal People and the Fur Trade

R. WESLEY HEBER

In writing this chapter on the history of the fur trade in Canada and the role of Aboriginal people in that enterprise, I have drawn mostly on secondary sources, supported by a teaching career in Indigenous studies at the First Nations University of Canada, as well as a formative experience serving with the Hudson's Bay Company as a fur trader in its northern stores from 1959 to 1962. While the chapter is a sketch of the history of the trade, it is also intended to acknowledge the role that Aboriginal people have had in the development of Canada.

Introduction

The fur trade in North America, which can be characterized as an exchange of European manufactured goods and commodities for Aboriginal-produced pelts and country produce, is generally seen to have begun with the first contact between Europeans and Aboriginal people. However, the fur trade should be viewed in its broader context as a system of social exchange encompassing a set of relations between Aboriginal nations, pre- and post-European contact. These relations involved a wide range of social and cultural interactions that helped to promote and sustain economic interactions.

This chapter outlines Indigenous trade prior to the arrival of Europeans in order to provide a framework for subsequent Aboriginal-European trade relations. It also shows how early European traders were obliged to accommodate themselves to Aboriginal trading practices in order to succeed and, indeed, to survive in North America. Four historic types of trade will be reviewed: Indigenous, early-contact, coastal, and inland. The objective is to show how the Aboriginal people's control over trade and trade relations changed at different times and under different circumstances and how the European trade priorities subsequently evolved. Finally, any portrayal of the fur trade in Canada must address the history of First Nations along with the contributions, hardships, sacrifices, and visions in the reality that is Canada today. This chapter provides an opportunity to reflect on the history of the fur trade and on the part played by the ancestors of many of the Aboriginal people of Canada.

Indigenous Trade

Before contact with Europeans, Aboriginal trading systems and trade networks flourished across the continent as a means of intertribal and interregional exchange. Primary, secondary, and tertiary trade centres were spread across the continent, some functioning as seasonal rendezvous points and others as permanent trade settlements. These trade centres were connected by a vast network of trade routes across the continent to facilitate the flow of material goods as well as ideas, customs, languages, and traditions from one people to another. Some nations, such as the Mandan of the Missouri Plains, specialized in trade. Through trade alliances, Aboriginal peoples could share tribal territories and resources, support allies, and restrain enemies.

The fur trade in pre-contact America was only one aspect of a varied and integrated economic system (Heber 2005, 249). Knowledge of Indigenous trade is part of oral traditions, and trade goods are part of the archaeological record (McMillan 1988). It is likely that any item that people desired, yet did not have, would have been valued in trade. Surplus materials or specialized goods often became items for trade. Through diffusion, trade items along with the innovations they encouraged became part of exchange. For example, agriculture spread from Central America as far north as the St Lawrence Valley where the Three Sisters of corn, beans, and squash became the basis for village settlement among the Wyandot (Huron) and Iroquois nations. Agricultural products were in turn traded for scarce commodities, such as fur, with the northern Algonquian-speaking peoples of the northeastern woodlands. Wild rice from Lake Michigan and Lake of the Woods country could be produced in surplus quantities (Vennum 1988) and was a valued commodity in trade. Soapstone from the Ohio River Valley was prized for pipe bowls and, along with tobacco, became a common feature of trade across the continent (Paper 1988). Likewise, pipestone was traded from its source in northern Saskatchewan at Pipe Stone Lake (Wapaweka, in Cree) near La Ronge (Cuthand 1997). Copper, mined on the north shore of Lake Superior, was used to manufacture projectile points, knives, fish hooks, awls, pendants, and beads, all of which are often found in ancient burial sites throughout the St Lawrence Valley (McMillan 1988). Native copper mined along the Coppermine River of the central Arctic and at White River Mountain in the Yukon was used in the manufacture of tools and ceremonial items (Jenness 1977, 111). These goods were dispersed by trade diffusion over great distances throughout the northwest to nations of the Pacific coast. Silver was mined north of Lake Superior and used in ornamental objects found in the region (McMillan 1988). The extent of Indigenous trade across the continent is evidenced by conch shells from the Gulf of Mexico found in deposits in southern Ontario, fifteen hundred kilometres north of their source. These and other trade goods of ancient times are most often found in association with burial sites, many dating back six thousand years or more. In more recent times, trade goods have been found in association with the settlement sites of those people who had taken up permanent village life (McMillan 1988, 57; Morrison and Wilson 1986, 41).

Trade is also a common means of social and cultural exchange between nations. Through trade networks and trading relations, neighbouring tribes formed social and political alliances, which were often established and sustained through marriage ties and kinship connections. In addition, trade often promotes military alliances, as well as being an avenue for negotiating peace. Trade is thus a means of integrating nations and defining tribal territories and of promoting the international flow of a range of material goods from one people to another. Moreover, trade promotes the spread of knowledge, beliefs, and cultural practices through cross-cultural contact and cultural diffusion. Through trade, Aboriginal peoples throughout North America were interconnected and thereby shared many features of their cultures across national (tribal) borders and across the continent. While Aboriginal groupings are culturally diverse, there are cultural and linguistic features that cross tribal boundaries, and these survive today as common cultural expressions among different Indian societies. Trade also brings about cultural change, spreading new objects and ideas between and among peoples. An example of trade-induced cultural change is the distribution of the horse from Central America to the northern plains after the Spanish had introduced horses to the continent in the mid-sixteenth century. The arrival of the horse in the northern plains by the mid-eighteenth century, along with the exchange of related technology, brought about a cultural revolution among the Plains tribes, a revolution that affected all future trade relationships among the Indian peoples of the Plains.

Under some conditions, Indigenous trade in North America used currency. Among the Gwich'in for example, shell beads were not only an object of trade but also a currency of exchange (Jenness 1977, 114). In other areas, a barter system of trade was common, whereby goods were exchanged based on their relative value. Europeans involved in the early fur trade in North America were obliged to adopt the barter system. It had evolved into a credit system in the Canadian fur trade by the early twentieth century (Ray 1984).

Finally, trade was the impetus for the European expansion that began in the late fifteenth century. The desire for access to the rich and exotic trade goods of the Orient brought European explorers to North America, where they encountered people who were accustomed to trade, and they began a long association founded on their common trade interests.

Early-Contact Trade

When Aboriginal people in North America first encountered Europeans landing on their shores, the initial contact experience usually involved trade. The earliest recorded trade interaction is found in the Norse sagas, the oral history of those Scandinavians who had established settlements in southwestern Greenland by AD 1000 (Kehoe 1992) and journeyed west across the Davis Strait to Labrador and Newfoundland in search of green-er pastures and timber. There they met the Aboriginal people whom they called Skraelings (from *skraelingjar* meaning 'small or withered') (Dickason 1992, 87). The Aboriginal people came in their skin-boats, and the motion of their staves or paddles was sun-wise, likely as a sign of peace, 'and they began trading together' (McGee 1974, 2). The Norsemen were especially interested in trading for sable or marten fur and for walrus tusks and wal-rus hides (Kehoe 1992, 241–2). Norse trade with the Aboriginal peoples of North America ended in the mid-fifteenth century, when the Norsemen deserted their Greenland settlements and returned to Iceland.

During the following century Aboriginal people along the east coast of North America came into frequent contact with European fishermen and whalers primarily from Portugal, France, and England, and they continued to trade furs for European goods. This type of independent seasonal trade likely continued even while more formal systems of trade were being estab-lished by European powers through royal chartered trading companies.

The establishment of chartered trading companies by the British and the French in the sixteenth and seventeenth centuries was carried out as a prerogative of the reigning monarchs. Often the king or queen, along with relatives, held majority shares in chartered trading companies. In 1670 a roy-al charter was issued by King Charles II of England, granting an exclusive trade territory to 'the Governor and Company of Adventurers of England Trading into Hudson Bay' (the Hudson's Bay Company). The Hudson's Bay Company (HBC) held rights to trade, to make treaties, and to defend the territory of Rupertsland, a territory that extended from Labrador in the east to the Great Lakes in the south, and westward to the Rocky Mountains.

In 1686 the Compagnie du Nord was founded by French royal charter to supplant the Hudson's Bay Company's monopoly over trade on Hudson Bay. Other European monarchs also granted charters for trade in America, including the Russian tsar, Paul I, whose royal charter of 1799 established the Russian American Trading Company for trade into Alaska. Many of these trading companies operated with a dual purpose: trade and exploration. Often the profits of trade were used to further the ambitions of foreign exploration, especially the discovery of a commercial route to the Orient.

Before the arrival of the Europeans, many Aboriginal nations were involved in trade as middlemen, facilitating the exchange of goods with neighbouring Aboriginal nations. The Mi'kmaq, for example, had a long history of trade and had been middlemen in pre-contact trade between northern hunters, including the Montagnais, and southern agriculturists, such as the Iroquois. They continued their middleman role in post-contact trade with the French (Dickason 1992). Other Aboriginal nations controlled the interior trade, acting as middlemen in early exchanges with Europeans by trading from coastal settlements as well as managing interior trade networks. The Montagnais at Tadoussac, at the mouth of the Saguenay River, controlled much of the trade from James Bay. The Wyandot (Huron) at Stadacona on the St Lawrence River controlled trade from the south and west as far as the Great Lakes. Throughout the second half of the sixteenth century, European ships made use of these Amerindian seaports to engage in a coastal trade that was under the control of Indian people. Dickason (1992, 104) notes that at the time as many as fifty ships were at anchor in Tadoussac harbour and that an estimated one thousand ships were trading along the east coast and the Gulf of St Lawrence each season. Many of these ships were part of European fishing fleets, and many of these fishermen were also engaged in trade. This early European contact trade was extensive, though limited to seasonal interactions on the coast. For example, in 1580 it was reported that four hundred ships visited Newfoundland to process cod on shore (Kehoe 1992, 244), and Aboriginal people likely took advantage of the fishermen's presence to trade.

Coastal Trade

During the early period of trade contact, many coastal Aboriginal nations were able to keep the Europeans out of the interior and thereby retain their control over the fur trade. The Huron, for example, retained their monopoly by keeping the French from the upper St Lawrence River and by having trade alliances with other Algonquian groups (Heidenreich and Ray 1976, 17). By the middle of the seventeenth century the French had moved inland from the St Lawrence Valley, and the Huron lost their middleman role in the fur trade (Heidenreich and Ray 1976, 7). On the west coast many Aboriginal nations, including the Tsimshian, Tlingit, and Kwagiulth, controlled inland trade networks well into the nineteenth century (Dickason 1992, 210).

The British royal charter of 1670 that established the Hudson's Bay Company granted an exclusive territory for trade that covered all the lands whose rivers drained into Hudson Bay and Hudson Strait. Soon trading posts were set up at the mouths of all the major rivers flowing into Hudson and James bays. In this manner the British were attempting to cut off the French drive inland through the Great Lakes, by providing alternate trading sites for the Indian nations of the northwest. The trade on Hudson Bay affected especially the Cree who controlled much of the inland trade by operating as middlemen to other Indian nations, including their Assiniboine and Blackfoot allies of the eastern and western plains. The primary trading centre on Hudson Bay was located at the mouth of the Nelson and Hayes rivers, which provided access to coastal trade for Indians from the northern plains and the northwest via the Saskatchewan River and Lake Winnipeg. Here the HBC established its primary trading fort of York Factory, followed in 1694 by the French who built Fort Bourbon on the nearby Hayes River (Heber 1989, 96). In 1688, the HBC first built a trading post, Fort Prince of Wales, at the mouth of the New Severn (Churchill) River, but it was abandoned the following year; it was rebuilt in 1717 specifically for the Dene or 'Northern Indian' trade (Rich 1948, 35; Heber 1989, 96). Trading posts were also set up at the mouths of the Severn, Albany, Moose, and Charles rivers, not only by the British under the Hudson's Bay Company but also at various times by the French and by independent traders out of New England and New France. At times, several trading concerns would build their posts at the same river mouth, each trying to gain an advantage over the regional fur market. This provided the Indian people with options in trade, an advantage that forced the Europeans to be fair in their dealings. Otherwise the Indian traders would simply take their furs to the competing trading post next door or down the coast.

In the late spring, as the interior rivers and lakes became free of ice, Indian traders travelled towards the coast, their canoes loaded down with winter furs. These trading gangs usually consisted of a number of men under a local leader. The leaders were recognized by the factors of the trading companies as prominent Indian men in charge of the interior trading networks. They were seen as capable and effective middlemen, spreading the trade among their own people and allied Indian nations. The European traders referred to them as trading captains, or 'Captains of the River,' and gave them special treatment, including a suit of clothing referred to as the 'Captains Outfit' (Ray 1998, 139) in order to acknowledge their authority over their Indian bands. Most of the trade in fur was carried out between the factors of the trading post and the trading captains, including the exchange of gifts and pipe ceremonies to initiate trade, and trade negotiations. Generally, in a large trading establishment such as York Factory, only the trading captain was invited onto the trading floor, while all others were obliged to trade through a 'hole in the wall' or window of the warehouse. In this way, any attempts by HBC employees to conduct a clandestine trade were curtailed.

The Aboriginal traders did not remain long at the coast, because the summer travel season was short and demanded a rapid turnaround at the trading posts on the bay. Furthermore, the Indians were likely anxious to return to their homes and resume their seasonal round of hunting and trapping and, for some, extend their inland trade networks for the following year. The European traders did not encourage the Indians to tarry at the coast as they then would be obliged to share their food, which was often in short supply. Some Indian men remained at the coast as hunters and provisioners for the trading posts. Eventually, some of these men brought their families and remained for more than one season, working for the European traders before returning to their home territory. The Aboriginal people who remained on the coast working for the trading companies became known as 'Home Guard' Indians (Heber 1989, 93). The Home Guard hunters helped to provision the trading posts and were crucial to the Europeans' survival when the posts ran out of food, which could happen if the supply ships from Europe failed to arrive. At such times the Europeans became dependent upon the Aboriginal hunters. At other times, when the Aboriginal people who had come to the coast to trade became stranded because of an early freeze, the company stores supported them for the winter. The need for good relations between Aboriginal people and European traders during the coastal period of the fur trade was crucial to both parties, and mutual support was one way of retaining good relations. Traders' support of Aboriginal people was also a way of encouraging loyalty to the trading company. However, trade rivalries within the Hudson's Bay Company and between European traders existed from the earliest stages of the fur trade (Yerbury 1986, 19). These rivalries were well understood by Indian traders, who were not above exploiting European greed and turning it to their own advantage. Carol Judd (1984, 84) presents one such case of an Indian middleman trading at Moose Factory who, according to the HBC factor, 'plays a sure card, trades his goods at Albany, and then comes here under the pretence of being captain of this river.'

Eventually, Home Guard populations of mixed European and Indian ancestry came to live around and work at the trading posts. The people of mixed Scottish and Indian ancestry came to be known as 'Hudson Bay Métis,' 'Rupertslanders,' or 'Halfbreeds.' After 1776, when Hudson's Bay traders moved inland, many of the Halfbreed men worked on the York boats, shipping trade goods to inland posts.

During the coastal period of the fur trade Aboriginal traders could always choose the European traders with which to deal. If they felt there was an advantage in dealing with the French over the British or with free traders over company traders, they made those choices. Aboriginal nations were also able to choose their allies. When England and France were at war or when they signed treaties of peace, Aboriginal nations consequently had new opportunities to create alliances in trade.

One way that Aboriginal nations and individual Aboriginal traders created or solidified alliances with trading companies or with individual European traders was through marriage. No European women resided on the shores of Hudson Bay during the coastal period of the fur trade, and many of the European traders married or developed liaisons with Aboriginal women. Often these women came from the Home Guard population. When European traders returned to their home country, they left behind their women and children. These women, with their mixed-blood children, returned to their people or were taken over by another European trader, or were left with one. This practice of giving over one's Aboriginal mate to another European trader was known as 'turning off' (Van Kirk 1993, 49–50). While the policy of the Hudson's Bay Company at the time was one of non-fraternization or non-interaction between employees and Aboriginal women, evidence of such relationships was often erased from company records (Thistle 1986, 16) and was therefore unknown or ignored by company officials in London.

The Aboriginal women who became attached to European traders were of great benefit to the fur trade as they introduced the traders to their language, culture, home territory, and people. Often these women of the fur trade acted as interpreters, guides, and teachers, as well as companions, and they became intermediaries between their European mates and their own people. Through association with their Aboriginal relatives, many European traders adopted Aboriginal customs and trade habits (Thistle 1986, 39). In some instances, alliances were forged between Aboriginal nations and trading companies through marriages between prominent and respected Aboriginal families and European traders. At other times, Aboriginal leaders adopted prominent traders in order to forge a good trade relationship either with the English or with the French. For example, Pierre-Esprit Radisson and his brother-in-law, Médard Chouart des Groseilliers, French traders out of Montreal who were primarily responsible for drawing the English into the fur trade on Hudson Bay, were both adopted by the Cree at Port Nelson in 1683 (Thistle 1986). During the early days of the coastal trade on Hudson Bay, Europeans made efforts to explore the interior of the country and make themselves known to other Aboriginal nations in order to draw those nations into the fur trade. In 1688, Henry Kelsey was sent from York Factory on Hudson Bay northward to try to contact the Dene (Chipewyan), whom the Europeans at that time referred to as the 'Dogside Nation' (Kelsey 1929, xxiv) or as 'Northern Indians.' Later, in 1690, a group of Western Woodland Cree conducted Kelsey inland to their home territory west of Lake Winnipeg and introduced him to their allies, the Assiniboine people. In 1715, the Chipewyan folk heroine, Thanadelthur, at the request of the Hudson's Bay Company governor at York Factory, James Knight, conducted William Stewart, a company trader, to a meeting with her people in the vicinity of Great Slave Lake; she subsequently drew the Dene into the coastal trade (Heber 1989; Johnson 1952). In 1717, the HBC built a post at the mouth of the Churchill River for trade with the Dene, which in turn provided the Dene coastal traders with a degree of security from raids by their enemies, the Cree.

From 1769 to 1772, just prior to the movement of the trading posts inland to the northwest, the Hudson's Bay Company explorer Samuel Hearne, guided by the Chipewyan Matonabbee, visited the country north and west of Hudson Bay and contacted many of the Dene nations within their homelands. Since the time of Henry Kelsey, the HBC had been very interested in the Dene, not only to draw them into the fur trade but also to mine the 'yellow metal' that was reported to be found in their country (Yerbury 1986, 24) and that the Europeans believed to be gold (Johnson 1952, 43).

The trade on Hudson Bay was conducted without any form of currency; instead, it was facilitated by the use of a barter system in which fur was exchanged for goods and country produce. However, the HBC did set an official standard of trade and a comparative standard of trade each year (Heidenreich and Ray 1976, 76) in order to promote consistency in all its trading posts. These standards of value were based on the concept of 'made beaver' (MB), that is, the value of the prepared skin of an adult beaver in prime condition. In this way, all HBC trading posts retained the same accounting system for all trade goods, but they did not necessarily follow the standard.

The following table gives some examples of exchange rates under the

Example of Hudson's Bay Company Accounts, Fort Prince of Wales, 1723

The Comparative	Standard of Trade	Standard of Trade
1 Parchet Moose (hide) as...2MB	Beads Value att 1 gr...3MB	Guns Value att 1 pr...16MB
1 Ditto Buffalo as ...2MB	Kettle Value att 1 ea...2MB	Guns Worme att 2 pr...1MB
1 Drest Moose as ...2MB	Powder Value att...11/2MB*	Gloves 1 pr...1MB
1 Quiquihatch (wolverine)...2MB	Shoes Value att 2 pr...1MB	Hatchetts at 1 pr...11/2MB
1 Wolf as...2MB	Tobacco Briz att1 lb...3MB*	Ice Chisells att 1 pr...11/2MB
1 Bear as...2MB	Ditto Leaf att 1 lb...11/2MB*	Knives Value att 1 pr...1MB
1 Black Fox as...3MB	Ditto Role att 1 lb...11/2MB*	Looking Glases 1 pr...11/2MB
1 Gray Fox as...2MB	Vermilien 1oz. yr...11/2MB*	Needles Value att 6 pr...1MB
1 Red Fox as...1MB	Thread Value att ?...2MB*	Nett Lines Value att 1 pr...1MB
2 White Fox as...1MB	Brandy att 1 gallon...4MB	Powder Hornes att 1 pr...11/2MB
1 Catt (lynx) as...1MB	Bays att ?...2MB*	Rings Plain att 3 pr...1MB
2 Otters as...1MB	Broad Clothe ?...4MB*	Scrapers Value att 1 pr...1MB
1 Cubb (mink) as...1MB	Blanketts att ?...?MB*	Scissor? Value att 1 pr...1MB*
2 Deer Skins as...1MB	Duffles Value att...?MB*	Spoons/? att 1 pr...1MB
2 Wichusk (muskrat) as...1MB	Flannell att 1 yard ?...2MB*	Shirt White att 1 pr...4MB
3 Martins as...1MB	Gartering att 1 ?...1MB*	Shirt Blue at 1 pr...3MB
10 lbs. Feathers...1MB	Club Blades att 4 pr...1MB*	Stockings Red att 1 pr...3MB
	Bayenetts att 1 pr...1MB	Ditto Coulerd att 1 pr...4MB
	Buttons att 4 gr...1MB*	Tobacco Tongs at 1 pr...1MB
	Combs Ivory att 1 gr...2MB	Twine 1 Scain att...11/2MB
	Fish Hooks att 5 pr...1MB	Sword Blades att 1 pr...1MB
	Fire Steels att 2 pr...1MB	Hawks Bells att 6 pr...1MB
	Flints Value att 10 pr...1MB	Shoes Value att 1 pr...3MB

Source: HBC Archives 1722–3. Note: The standard of value was based on the concept of 'made beaver' (MB).

trade standard of made beaver. The comparative value of fur is given in the left column, and the standard value in MB for trade goods is given in the centre and right columns. Note that several animal species are given the Cree names as these animals were likely unknown in Europe and had no English equivalent. Also note that the original Hudson's Bay Company accounts (HBC Archives 1722–3) are in part difficult to read. Any questionable interpretations are indicated by a question mark, and where any entry is copied as incomplete an asterisk follows it. Spellings, as much as possible, are original.

It should be noted that brandy is listed as a trade item, which indicates that alcohol was used in trade prior to the movement of the traders inland in the 1770s.

One contentious issue of the fur trade was the HBC traders' practice of overcharging for trade goods by using a markup or 'overplus' system, which has been called the factor's standard or the double standard. Through overplus the trader increased profits by giving short measure in trade goods (Ray and Freeman 1978). While overplus may not have been a stated policy of the HBC, it was a way for individual post factors and the company to overcome losses. Examples of losses and unforeseen expenses included the damage to trade goods in shipping, the cost of ceremonial gift giving, the salary paid for work done by local employees at the trading posts, or the increased expenses of shipping during times of war. However, the use of overplus by the traders was limited, for if Aboriginal customers believed they were being cheated or if the price of trade goods rose too much, the customers usually had the option of trading at another post or with another trading company. As Arthur Ray (1978) suggests, overplus was subject to negotiations between factors and Aboriginals during the bargaining process.

Inland Trade

The coastal period of trade on Hudson Bay, like that of the east coast trade, continued for over one hundred years. However, by the 1770s several factors external to the fur trade, along with continued European expansion into the northwest, resulted in rapid development of an inland trade. In 1763 the French, under the Treaty of Paris, ceded their North American territorial claims to the British. In 1776 the American Revolution resulted in the British loss of the thirteen colonies and in the declaration of American independence. The effect of these events on the fur trade was the end of French-controlled chartered companies in America, a flourishing of independent free traders operating out of Montreal, and restricted access by

American traders to the British northwest. The independent traders out of Montreal were primarily Scots, who along with their French or Métis coureurs de bois pushed the trade inland to the northwest. They set up trading posts along the major rivers west of the Great Lakes and Lake Winnipeg to the Rocky Mountains and north down the Mackenzie River to the Arctic Ocean. Many of these Canadian pedlars came together in 1774 to form the North West Company (NWC). The movement of the NWC prompted the HBC to follow and establish inland trading posts in competition.

The rapid spread of trading posts into the interior of the continent had several consequences for Aboriginal people. The first was the intrusion of Europeans into Aboriginal territory and their impact on the ancient Indigenous trading system. Part of the loss to this system was the end of the control by middlemen and individual Indian nations over the inland trade. Once trading posts were established along the inland waterways, the Indian people had direct access to European or Canadian trade and could carry out their own trade negotiations; however, not all trappers were good traders. The result was the individualization of the Aboriginal economy and the undermining of the collective economic action previously represented by trading chiefs. Moreover, those Aboriginal nations that had traditionally held the role of middlemen in trade between neighbouring nations were no longer able to carry out that important economic and political function with their inland allies. In this way, European inland trade signalled the end of Aboriginal control over the fur trade.

Furthermore, the inland trade devastated the health of Aboriginal people. As soon as European traders moved inland, European diseases spread rapidly among the Aboriginal populations of the interior. In the east, smallpox began to appear among the Montagnais by 1635, and one-half to two-thirds of the Huron died from the disease between 1639 and 1640 (Heidenreich and Ray 1976, 28). On Hudson Bay the spread of European diseases was curtailed as long as the European traders remained isolated at the coast. From 1670 to 1770 direct contact with Aboriginal people was limited, often to that between captains of the river and company factors. However, after 1770, inland trading posts were supplied annually by boat brigades from the coast, and any infectious disease brought in from Europe was rapidly transported, along with the trade goods, into the interior. The effects were devastating, especially for people who had no natural immunity or who had had no previous contact with these European diseases. Samuel Hearne (1934, 200) gives a description of the effects of the 1780–1 smallpox epidemic that swept through the western subarctic soon after British and Canadian traders had moved into the country: 'Since this Journal was written (1769–

1772), the Northern Indians [read Chipewyan], by annually visiting their Southern friends, the Athapuscaow Indians [read Cree], have contracted the small-pox, which has carried off nine-tenths of them.' The effects of unfamiliar diseases on the Aboriginal people were greatest with initial contact. The impact of some diseases was reduced over time through natural immunization and through the introduction of vaccination. For example, when a means of vaccination against smallpox was discovered in the mid-nineteenth century, HBC traders were trained in the procedure for its use in the Canadian West. With the decline of the buffalo and the establishment of the reserve system, the general condition of the Aboriginal populations on the northern plains was such that increased poverty had contributed to the spread of disease (Lux 2001).

The second devastating impact of the inland fur trade was the introduction of alcohol as a trade item. During the early period of coastal trade in the east, the French had forbidden the use of alcohol in trade (Heidenreich and Ray 1976, 27). As long as the European traders were located on the coast, the use of alcohol in trade had a temporary and minimal effect on Indian people. However, once the trading companies moved inland, extreme competition developed, and the greed for control of trade by both the HBC and the NWC prompted the spread of trade in alcohol. The profits from alcohol were great because the pure alcohol that had been transported inland was liberally watered down. However, this trade in alcohol did not last, as it was detrimental to fur production and therefore worked against trade profits (Innis 1984, 272–3).

The extreme competition continued between the NWC and the HBC until 1821, when the two companies amalgamated. However, this only came about after years of hostility and violence, with traders often wearing each other down in order to control trade in a region. These hostilities reached a climax at Red River in 1816 with the Battle of Seven Oaks, in which NWC traders rebelled against the HBC's attempts at monopoly over the northwest fur trade and access to the buffalo of the Plains. Buffalo and the trade in pemmican, a preserved food made from buffalo meat and fat mixed with berries and stored in the sewed-up buffalo hides, had become an important part of the fur trade, especially for the Métis people of Red River. Inland trading posts were supplied with pemmican to sustain the posts through the long winters and to support the crews of the boat brigades in their journeys to and from the coast.

The brigades of York boats continued to transport supplies for the inland trading posts. The boatmen, who were often Hudson Bay Métis, towed and poled the heavy York boats inland up the rivers, portaging around rapids and waterfalls and carrying double packs or 'pieces' of ninety pounds each.

They delivered the trade goods and supplies to inland posts throughout the northwest, returning down river in the fall with the annual harvest of fur for shipment to the European markets. The requirements for a single York boat brigade were considerable, typically consisting of '8 new Boats of 28 feet Keel (storing 80 pieces); 3,500 lbs. Grease; 150 Bales Dried Meat, 90 lb. each; 450 Bags (Common) Pemmican, 90 lb. each; 100 Pairs tracking shoes; 30 Leather Tents; 500 Buffalo Tongues' (Morton 1973, 696).

The fur trade continued to be the means of supporting exploration and the search for a viable trade route to the Orient. In the early nineteenth century HBC traders and explorers crossed over the mountains from the Mackenzie River district to establish a new trade district in the Pacific Northwest called New Caledonia (Morton 1973, 705–6), thereby coming into contact with the Russian traders of the Russian American Fur Company from Alaska and the American traders from the south. They moved down the rivers to the Pacific coast, not only to expand the fur trade but also to extend their knowledge of the route to the Pacific Ocean. With the arrival of the fur trade on the Pacific coast, Indian nations were drawn into an international trade in otter pelts, as these were in great demand in the expanding trade with China. The British traders had now achieved their task of connecting European trade with the Orient.

The fur trade in Canada had evolved out of an Indigenous trading system, through a coastal trade period, to an inland network of over two hundred trading posts extending from the Atlantic to the Pacific. The Hudson's Bay Company had given up much of its claim to the northwest by selling its chartered rights to the government of Canada and, by the early twentieth century, was facing increasing competition from free traders, who were growing in number, and the expanding Revillon Trading and Northern Trading companies (Keighley 1989; Ray 1990). When fur prices increased after the First World War many non-Aboriginals took up trapping, and Aboriginal trappers faced growing competition in a declining industry (Tough 1996). By the middle of the century the northern economy that had been built on fur began to collapse, owing to reduced animal populations, government interventions in animal conservation, fur-trapping regulations, and the increased cost of outfitting trappers and hunters (Ray 1990). Finally, the animal rights movement, combined with government pressures under a federal policy of 'Roads to Resources,' ended trapping as an economic option for many Aboriginal people. Today, the HBC trading posts have been taken over by the Northern Stores Company, and many trading posts of the interior have been closed. However, the fur trade remains subject to fashion, and as fashions change, the demand for fur may bring about a revival of the fur trade in Canada.

Conclusion

The culture of a people, along with the identity, is tied to a common heritage and way of life that connects the past to the present and to the future.
For many Aboriginal people of Canada, the tradition of hunting and gathering sustained the fur trade for over five hundred years. The hunting and
gathering way of life integrates people with the land, the animals, and the
seasons, producing an economy that is based on seasonality, diversity, and
opportunity. It also supports a philosophy of life that acknowledges spiritual relations with all things and connects the people to the land and to their
ancestors. Today, that philosophy is part of a cultural revival and is a source
of renewed identity for many Aboriginal people of Canada. The land is the
foundation of Aboriginal cultural heritage, and the fur trade is a significant
part of that heritage

However, there is a dark side to the fur trade and its decline. Wherever
Europeans moved inland to promulgate the trade, there followed conflict,
disease, and disruption. Once the Aboriginal people had lost control over
the trade, they became clients to trading companies and ever more dependent on those companies for their well-being. With the decline of the fur
trade, first in the east, then on the northern plains, and finally in the boreal
forests of the northwest and Pacific regions, collapse of the fur industry
meant collapse of the local economy and a new dependency on government. The fur trade, in all its complex history, has been both a boon and a
bane to Aboriginal people. It is part of a people's past and, as such, continues to influence the present. The fur trade may be recognized as a vehicle
that helped to sustain the cultural heritage of many Aboriginal people and
played a major role in the development of Canada.

Bibliography

Cuthand, Stan. 1997. Interview with Cree elder by author. Saskatoon, Canada.

Dickason, Olive Patricia. 1992. *Canada's First Nations: A History of Founding Peoples
    from Earliest Times*. Toronto: McClelland and Stewart.

Hudson's Bay Company Archives. 1722–3. HBC B. 42/ds/3.

Hearne, Samuel. 1934. *Journals of Samuel Hearne and Philip Turnor between the Years
    1774 and 1792*. Edited by J.B. Tyrrell. Toronto: Champlain Society 21.

Heber, Robert Wesley. 1989. *Chipewyan Ethno-Adaptations: Identity Expression for
    Chipewyan Indians of Northern Saskatchewan*. PhD diss., University of Manitoba.

– 2005. Indigenous knowledge, resources use, and the Dene of northern Saskatch-
    ewan. *Canadian Journal of Development Studies* 26 (2): 247–56.

Heidenreich, Conrad E., and Arthur J. Ray. 1976. *The Early Fur Trades: A Study in Cultural Interaction*. Toronto: McClelland and Stewart.

Innis, Harold A. 1984. *The Fur Trade in Canada*. Toronto: University of Toronto Press.

Jenness, Diamond. 1977. *The Indians of Canada*. Toronto: University of Toronto Press.

Johnson, Alice M. 1952. Ambassadress of peace. *The Beaver* 283 (Dec. 1952): 42–5.

Judd, Carol M. 1984. Sakie, Esquawenoe, and the foundation of a dual-native tradition at Moose Factory. In *The Subarctic Fur Trade*, ed. Shepard Krech, 81–98. Vancouver: University of British Columbia Press.

Kehoe, Alice B. 1992. *North American Indians: A Comprehensive Account*. Englewood Cliffs, NJ: Prentice Hall.

Keighley, Sydney Augustus. 1989. *Trader, Tripper, Trapper: The Life of a Bay Man*. Winnipeg: Rupert's Land Research Centre.

Kelsey, Henry. 1929. *The Kelsey Papers*. Edited by Arthur C. Doughty and Chester Martin. Ottawa: King's Printer.

Lux, Maureen K. 2001. *Medicine That Walks: Disease, Medicine, and Canadian Plains Native People, 1880–1940*. Toronto: University of Toronto Press.

McGee, Harold F. 1974. *The Native Peoples of Atlantic Canada: A Reader in Regional Ethnic Relations*. Toronto: McClelland and Stewart.

McMillan, Alan D. 1988. *Native Peoples and Cultures of Canada: An Anthropological Overview*. Toronto: Douglas and McIntyre.

Morrison, Bruce R., and C. Roderick Wilson, eds. 1986. *Native Peoples: The Canadian Experience*. Toronto: McClelland and Stewart.

Morton, Arthur S. 1973. *A History of the Canadian West to 1870–71*. Toronto: University of Toronto Press.

Paper, Jordan. 1988. *Offering Smoke: Sacred Pipe and the Native American Religion*. Moscow, ID: University of Idaho Press.

Ray, Arthur J. 1978. Competition and conservation in the early subarctic fur trade. *Ethnohistory* 25(4): 347–57.

– 1984. Periodic shortages, native welfare, and the Hudson's Bay Company, 1670–1870. In *The Subarctic Fur Trade: Native Social and Economic Adaptations*, ed. Shepard Krech, 1–19. Vancouver: University of British Columbia Press.

– 1990. *The Canadian Fur Trade in the Industrial Age*. Toronto: University of Toronto Press.

– 1998. *Indians in the Fur Trade*. Toronto: University of Toronto Press.

Ray, Arthur J., and Donald Freeman. 1978. *Give Us Good Measure: An Economic Analysis of Relations between the Indians and the Hudson's Bay Company before 1763*. Toronto: University of Toronto Press.

Rich, Edwin E. 1948. Copy-book of letters outward &c, begins 29 May, 1680, ends 5 July, 1687. London: Hudson's Bay Record Society.

Thistle, Paul C. 1986. *Indian-European Trade Relations in the Lower Saskatchewan River Region to 1840*. Winnipeg: University of Manitoba Press.

Tough, Frank. 1996. *As Their Natural Resources Fail: Native Peoples and the Economic History of Northern Manitoba, 1870–1930.* Vancouver: University of British Columbia.

Van Kirk, Sylvia. 1993. *Many Tender Ties: Women in Fur Trade Society in Western Canada, 1670–1870.* Winnipeg: Watson and Dwyer.

Vennum, Thomas, Jr. 1988. *Wild Rice and the Ojibway People.* St Paul: Minnesota Historical Society Press.

Yerbury, J.C. 1986. *The Subarctic Indians and the Fur trade, 1680–1860.* Vancouver: University of British Columbia Press.

Profile of John Charles Bernard (1961–)

Maliseet, Software Developer, and Businessman

John Bernard was born on 10 June 1961 in Boston, Massachusetts, to a non-Aboriginal mother, Margaret Elizabeth DiMaggio, and a Mi'kmaq father, Robert Stewart Bernard.[1] Bernard Sr suffered racial discrimination in the United States, causing him to move his family back to the Madawaska Maliseet reserve near Edmundston, New Brunswick.

Bernard attended the University of New Brunswick, where he intended to study law but instead graduated with a bachelor of arts in English in 1984.[2] The following year he earned a microcomputer and microprocessor management diploma through a correspondence course from NRI in Washington, DC.[3] Bernard believes that his interest in computers came from a Tandy programmable calculator that he bought for a second-year university calculus course. After graduation he worked as a senior systems operator for both Health Canada and Indian and Northern Affairs Canada.[4]

In 1992 Bernard and the information technology (IT) training company he founded, Aboriginal Informatics Services, joined Systems Interface, a non-Aboriginal IT firm in Ottawa.[5] In 1996 he and the other partners launched an Aboriginal subsidiary called Donna Cona. The subsidiary's focus was serving the Aboriginal community by designing IT systems for First Nations and by training Aboriginals in systems management. Later Donna Cona proposed to develop and implement the technical architecture for Nunavut's government. This project became Canada's first satellite-based IT infrastructure. Aware of the shortage of Aboriginal peoples in the field of information technology, Bernard has since dedicated his efforts through university lectures towards promoting informatics careers for Aboriginal youth.[6]

In 1997 John Bernard received a Deputy Minister's Award in recognition of the technical support offered by his firm to the Department of Indian and Northern Affairs during the 1998 ice storm.[7] He is also the recipient of the 2000 National Aboriginal Achievement Award in Business and Commerce. Later that year he was given a 'Top 40 under 40' award by the *Globe and Mail* for Donna Cona's installation of wireless communications for the government of Nunavut.[8] Donna Cona also received the Progressive Aborig-

John Charles Bernard.

inal Relations Silver Award in February 2001 for its commitment to working proactively with Aboriginal people, businesses, and communities.[9]

JOCELYN OBREITER

Notes

1 Lumley, *Who's Who in Canada* (Toronto: University of Toronto Press, 2003).
2 Ibid.
3 J. Stackhouse, 'The wireless warrior's digital dream,' *Globe and Mail*, 10 December 2001.
4 Lumley, *Who's Who in Canada*.
5 Stackhouse, 'The wireless warrior's digital dream.'
6 Joan Taillon, 'John Bernard: Chance for change on reserves,' *Windspeaker*, April 2000, 14.
7 Ibid.
8 Lumley, *Who's Who in Canada*.
9 Taillon, 'John Bernard,' 14.

'In the Midst of Plenty and Comfort': The Contribution of the Native Labour of the Lake Winnipeg Region during an Era of Economic Growth, ca 1870–1915

FRANK J. TOUGH

The economic landscape of the Lake Winnipeg region underwent a significant modification when, early in the post-Treaty period, the forces of frontier capitalism dislocated the mercantile fur trade. Sawmills, steamboat harbours, and fish camps sprang up alongside well-established trading posts and missions. Native labour was crucial in these economic changes. By providing alternate incomes and employment, new resource industries influenced the relationship between Indians and the Hudson's Bay Company (HBC). In 1885 and 1886 the value of HBC fur production amounted to $67,679; in contrast, the value of fish and lumber production for this region was $155,113, thereby indicating that these new industries were able to establish a commercial significance very quickly (Tough 1996, 351).[1] An export market for freshwater fish, the beginnings of a lumbering (that is, forest products) industry, and the establishment of steamboat transportation drew upon local resources and Native labour. In October 1888, the *Manitoba Daily Press* proudly announced that 'in fish, lumber, ties and cord wood, the export trade from Lake Winnipeg at the close of the present season will exceed $300,000.' Furthermore, the newspaper drew attention to this northern region by informing its readers that 'considering the infancy of the lumber and fish trade a great future awaits this northern section of Manitoba.' Significantly, this report did not ignore the employment effects of growth: 'It is estimated that in the lumber, fisheries and in the boats six hundred men, white people and Indians have found employment this year' (*Manitoba Daily Press* 1888). By 1895 lumber from the Lake Winnipeg region represented 40 per cent of Manitoba production (Canada 1896, 49). Clearly, the part of northern Manitoba that centred around Lake Winnipeg was an important resource hinterland, and Native labour was a contributing element in the regional economy. Both regional (Manitoba) and long-distance (United States) markets consumed the resources of the Lake Winnipeg region. In commercial terms, new resource industries rapidly dwarfed a system that had been arduously created over the preceding two hundred years.

The fundamental purpose of the fur trade – the creation of wealth through the production, exchange, and export of a commodity – seems to have been missed by many social scientists who persist in characterizing Native economies as essentially subsistence in nature.[2] During the mature fur trade (1821–70) many resources and labour demands were generated in order to sustain an expansive network of posts that were linked by a labour-intensive transport system. To sustain the fur industry, labour was needed to provision (by gardening, fishing, and hunting) the posts and the York boat brigades, as well as to obtain wood for boats, buildings, and heating. Within Rupertsland,[3] the large posts drew upon not only a variety of local resources to sustain operations but also locally produced goods, such as pemmican (an internal staple), which were transferred between regions. Interregional flows of commodities were an important part of the HBC system. Hence, Native participation in the fur trade was not limited to the discretionary trading of the occasional fur; instead, Natives sustained the system by provisioning posts (with meat and fish), supplying labour for a variety of tasks on a contract or temporary basis, and carrying out the exhausting York boat work, which moved cargoes of trade goods and fur packs through a vast country. While money was not in general circulation in the HBC territory prior to 1870, exchange was based on the widely appreciated, centuries-old, made-beaver standard (Ray and Freeman 1978).[4] By 1870 a wide variety of both essential and discretionary trade goods were being purchased by Natives. These purchases should also be regarded as essential capital and consumption inputs to the Native economy.[5]

The staple thesis has provided a number of insights into the history of the Canadian economy. Although fur was one of the first national staples produced by Native people, these same people are seen as being outside of the economic development of the country.[6] The ethnographic label *hunters and gatherers* is not a concept that opens up the possibility of Native people playing a role in economic history. Not only did Native people contribute to the economic structure that laid the foundation for the Canadian nation state, but they also played a role in other staple economies that followed in the wake of the fur trade's heyday (Knight [1978] 1996).

Until recently, the assertion by social scientists that Native economies remained subsistence based – despite decades of participation in a mercantile fur trade, and the historical existence of wage labour – had the effect of negating the contribution of Native peoples to the Canadian economy.[7] It has been assumed that Native participation in the Canadian economy was limited to the fur trade and that the demise of the fur trade brought about economic irrelevance for Native people.[8] This chapter will draw attention to some of the economic changes that occurred following the surrender of the HBC's claim to Rupertsland, the subsequent transfer of this vast territory to the Dominion of Canada, and the signing of the first numbered Indian treaties (Ray, Miller, and Tough 2000, 45–129). A re-evaluation of some of the assumptions about the Native economy, which have been popularized by social scientists, will follow a recounting of the Native participation in the new resource industries of northern Manitoba. The portrayal of the Native economy was a highly effective contribution to the debate regarding northern development; however, the model of the Native economy simplified certain aspects of the political economy of the north and offered little predictive insights about economic change, post–land claims.

The expansion of steamboating, commercial fishing operations, and saw mills was essentially a northward thrust into a region centred on the lakes of Manitoba, Winnipegosis, and Winnipeg (as can be seen in the figure 'Transportation and staples in Manitoba, 1870–1915'). Although new commercial entities competed with the Hudson's Bay Company, the fur trade had laid down the basics for such a commercial expansion. Along with a system of posts linked by transportation, the fur trade ushered in an economy in which many natural products were commodified and a system of exchange based on the made beaver was prevalent. Thus, by the time new commercial forces arrived, the buying and the selling of pelts, meat, fish, and, most significantly, labour and services were not alien concepts to the local inhabitants.

Given the absence of a resident European labour force, which could not have been created without the added costs of importing and sustaining it in a seasonal economy, frontier industries employed Native labour. This local labour was attractive for several reasons. Natives held many of the skills relevant to these new industries and, because these industries were seasonal in nature, the social overhead costs were not the responsibility of the frontier capitalists. The Natives' ability to live off the land, along with the relief and treaty payments from the Department of Indian Affairs, meant that a pure capitalist labour market was not needed in order to engage local Native labour. In fact, fish stations, sawmills, and steamboat harbours were often located near Indian reserves, in part, to take advantage of labour pools.

In 1870 the Hudson's Bay Company decided to replace the York boats labour with steam power for the Lake Winnipeg and Saskatchewan River segments of its transportation system (HBCA 1870). Investment in boats, terminals, harbours, and fuelling stations was not based entirely on the handling of long-distance freight, the prospects of which were limited after the completion of a transcontinental railway in 1885; rather, these facilities

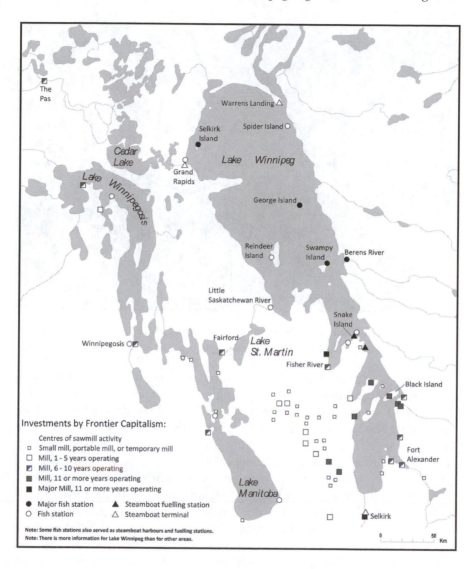

Transportation and staples in Manitoba, 1870–1915. Tough (1996). By permission of UBC Press.

Steamboat *Grand Rapids* at Black River, Lake Winnipeg, 1929. Sailboats were used for fishing. Archives of Manitoba, ON451.

were part of a system to extract local resources. Lake Winnipeg region was something of a transportation backwater because steamboats were not displaced by railways. Initially, the HBC encouraged the development of the Northwest Navigation Company, but eventually Captain William Robinson secured control over this steamboating firm, a nascent lumbering industry, and the fish business. Regional transport needs, along with the lumber and fish industries, made Robinson's steamboat enterprise viable for decades.

Although the HBC had introduced steam power in order to reduce its vulnerability with Native labour, this new, more capital-intensive form of transport did not completely displace Natives. An increase in the volume of freight and the need for fuel stimulated a demand for labour and created a demand for local resources. The historical record indicates that Natives had a presence in this new form of transport. In 1915, H.A. Bayfield noted that on the Nelson River 'the half breed skipper of the tug showed remarkable skill in handling his boat in the intricate waterway' (Bayfield 1915). On Lake Winnipeg one Indian held the rank of master on a large steamer, and another Indian held the same position on a smaller steamer (Canada 1907, 81). Native crews predominated on the steamboats on the lower Saskatchewan River (Cumberland House to Grand Rapids) (Barris 1977). The expansion of steamboating after 1885 resulted in some employment for Natives

– both as skilled labour (pilots) and general labour (deck hands, wharf and warehouse workers, and cordwood cutters).

While the expansion of export-oriented commercial fishing on lakes Manitoba, Winnipegosis, and Winnipeg generated concern and opposition to fishing companies, Natives were also an important source of labour for this industry.[9] Participation in the fishing industry provided another source of trade goods. In 1886, Fisheries Inspector A. McQueen described this trade: 'There were upwards of one hundred Indians engaged [in] fishing, who traded their fish for flour, bacon, tea, tobacco, twine, clothing &c., supplied from two stores doing a thriving trade in this locality' (Canada 1887, 318). In 1884, for the Brokenhead Band at the south end of Lake Winnipeg, trade was vigorous: 'As the fish was good, men from Winnipeg came and bought the fish from them at their door, giving fair prices[;] they were therefore comparatively comfortable throughout the year' (Canada 1885, 54). For the Sandy Bay Indians on Lake Manitoba, 'in the winter time they get a ready sale at good prices for all whitefish and pike they take' (Canada 1886, 50). Petite-Nation fish traders obtained fish from Indian families; however, some of the traders were specifically employed by the larger companies.

In short order, commercial fishing spread northward along the shores of the large lake and into the drainage of the Saskatchewan and Nelson rivers. This expansion was driven largely by a pursuit of the high-valued sturgeon and its caviar. By 1900, commercial operations had reached the Playgreen Lake and Nelson River fisheries near Norway House. An annual report for the HBC observed that 'employment in the neighbor hood [sic] of Norway House post is so abundant that several families of Indians have come up from Interior posts to settle' (HBCA 1900). In fact, the movement of Natives out of northeastern Manitoba, which had stagnated under the old fur trade regime, was a major demographic shift.[10]

With respect to sturgeon fisheries, as a matter of policy, fisheries officials favoured the licensing of local residents. Fisheries Inspector La Touche Tupper explained the way in which Native labour was incorporated into commercial fishing: 'I only licensed residents, and near the Indian reserves at Berens River, Bloodvien, I only issued to the Indians of the reserve, much to their benefit and satisfaction' (Canada 1899a, 208). Of the 180 sturgeon licences issued for the Nelson River in 1903, all but four went to Natives (Canada 1904, 205). Agency Inspector McColl reported in 1900: 'I found the Indians of the Norway House Band scattered for seventy miles around Playgreen Lake busily engaged in fishing for sturgeon. They also make a comfortable livelihood at the fisheries, having caught about ten thousand sturgeon and over a hundred thousand whitefish' (Canada 1901a, 108). Just north of Norway House, McColl reported that 'the Indians of Cross Lake

Indian Agency Inspector J. Semmens at Spider Island, a fish station on Lake Winnipeg, 1910. Archives of Manitoba, A.V. Thomas Collection 166, N8240.

Band are doing a thriving business of fishing for sturgeon and whitefish this season' (Canada 1901b, 108). Relative to other commercial fish species, the value of sturgeon, and more particularly, the market price for caviar, escalated in this period. The price of a 135 lb. keg of caviar increased from $9 to $12 in 1885, and to $100 by 1899 (Houston 1987, 182).[11] To compare with other sources of cash income, a special report on lake sturgeon noted that 'a female sturgeon with roe is worth more than a beaver, for the roe is worth over 50 cents per pound, and a ripe fish may yield 20 pounds' (Canada 1905a, xii). In terms of effort and return, fishing for sturgeon was a more 'rational' choice than was trapping for beaver.

    Indian participation in the lumbering industry is well documented. Indian Agency Inspector E. McColl reported on the Fisher River reserve in 1883: 'From fifty to seventy-five Indians are employed at the three saw-mills in the vicinity of the reserve, and receive from $25 to $30 a month' (Canada 1884). Indian Agent A. McKay explained the benefits of this new economic development:

> The success of the band is, however, in a measure due to their having three lumbering mills in the vicinity of their reserve, where they are able to get work as lumber men, sawyer, &c., at which, I am told, they are very good, and if required of them, they could run the mills themselves without the aid of white men. These lumbering companies have rendered great assistance to

the band, they pay them good wages, sell them lumber and goods cheap, and often teach and aid them with their gardens. The majority of the men are able to do carpenter work, such as building houses and boats, making furniture, &c. (Canada 1889, 80)

Similarly, Methodist minister Fred Stevens noted that with the appearance of the lumbering industry the Fisher River Indians 'soon adapted themselves to this kind of work and became expert lumberjacks' (UCCA 1939–54, 3). Stevens recorded that William Robinson, the leading frontier capitalist of the Lake Winnipeg region, had told him that 'I have employed Scots from Glengarry, French Canadians from Quebec, Swedes from Sweden and all kins [kinds] of lumberjacks, but the Fisher River Indians are better than any others' (UCCA 1939–54, 3). Reverend Young observed at Fort Alexander that only three Canadians worked at the mill, which worked day and night, and that 'Indians were engaged in the most intricate portions of the work, feeding the saws, working with machine like quickness and precision' (Church Missionary Society Fonds 1882). From these observations, it would seem that Natives were not merely involved in bush work but were also engaged in the more skilled, production-line type of employment.

The lumbering industry involved a number of reserves. Indian Agent S.J. Jackson noted that a number of young men of the Hollow Water Band worked in the logging camps during the winter and that 'they are valued by the lumber companies and are in great demand' (Canada 1905b, 114). When H.A. Bayfield visited the Bad Throat River Band, he observed that 'a large gang of half breed and Indians were working' at the mill (Bayfield 1899, 3). In 1909, after a mill had been established at Black River, Inspector of Indian Agencies J. Semmens stated: 'These people, who have long looked for employment, have found themselves in *the midst of plenty and comfort*' (emphasis added; Canada 1910, 115). Along with lumber, railroad ties, and steamboat cordwood, additional demands were generated for Native labour. According to the observation of travellers, missionaries, and Indian Affairs officials, Natives provided skilled and general labour for the lumbering industry.

As fisheries, lumbering, and steamboats involved complementary activities, the organization of capital in these industries was closely interrelated. Grand Rapids, at the mouth of the Saskatchewan River, was a minor post in the fur trade era; however, with the changes to the regional economy brought by frontier capitalism, Grand Rapids took on new significance. Clergyman J. Sinclair noted that no other place on the lower Saskatchewan River 'has so many advantages as Grand Rapids[;] a man can earn a dollar every day all the year round' (CMS 1893). Summer employment involved fishing and working on steamboats and wharves, and in the winter five thousand tons of ice were stored in the icehouse for the summer fishing season and four hundred cords of wood were cut. However, such an advantage was not permanent, as Indian Agent C.C. Calverley explained in 1909: 'Before the railroads traversed the west this was a very important place, most of the freight for the west went through it, but now all has changed and these Indians have to rely on their hunting, fishing and trapping' (Canada 1910, 103). In the same year, for the Poplar River Band on the east shore of Lake Winnipeg, Calverley wrote: 'At least $5,000 can be made by this band in cutting wood, putting up ice and fishing for the fish companies.'[12] These staple industries were not purely extractive; income-generating ancillary activities were created – fishing stations required ice, and steamboats were fuelled by cordwood. These inputs created a demand for local labour and, in turn, generated incomes. Nonetheless, changes in the demand for a staple or in the transport systems would have an impact on local economies.

Commercial fishing, lumbering, and steamboating were key sources of income. However, farm labour and commercialized gathering contributed to a more diversified regional economy. Indian Agent Swinford described the Manitowapah Agency in 1900:

> A lot of money is earned by the Indians of all the reserves at fishing during the winter, there is also a good deal earned at hunting, trapping, digging senega-root [Seneca root], picking berries and working as boatmen on the lakes. Many of them work for settlers during haying, harvest and threshing time; others work at the saw-mill at Winnipegosis, and in the lumber woods, and this year a number have been working at the big government canal at Fairford River. A few are still skilled at building boats and birch bark canoes, and make money at it; others are good at making snow-shoes, light sleighs (jumpers), flat sleighs and such like; but there is one thing they can all do the year round, so that they never want for food, and that is, catch fish. (Canada 1901b, 88)

Similarly, in 1898, McColl recorded that many of the Indians of the Clande-boye Agency were 'employed as voyageurs, guides to tourists, at fisheries, lumber camps and saw-mills, cutting cordwood, hunting, &c., while others are farming, stocking-raising and hay-cutting, from all of which they make a comfortable living' (Canada 1899b, 72). Seneca root, berries, and dead-wood were also marketable commodities, which required labour to collect. McColl reported that the Indians 'gather tons of huckleberries, raspberries, Saskatoon berries, cranberries and strawberries, which are in constant demand in the market' and that 'thousands of cords of wood are annually sold at Selkirk, and a large quantity of hay is also disposed of to dealers, which nets them a handsome amount' (Canada 1900, 77). In 1905, Inspector of Indian Agencies Semmens summed up the demand for labour: 'The fish companies, the mill-owners, travelers and explorers and steamboat-owners, all seek for help from our native population. Only when dissatisfied do they look elsewhere' (Canada 1906, 99).

A variety of economic activities engaged the talents of Indians as the old mercantile fur trade gave way to new market forces. Owing to a lack of agriculture potential, new economic forces created a demand for labour in a region largely ignored by economic history. The diversification of the regional economy is summarized in the figure 'Band and reserve economies in Manitoba, ca 1900.' The economic landscape is considerably more varied than that shaped by the fur trade. In contrast to the view that a marginal and depressing economic existence universally followed the treaties between the Crown and Indian nations, in the Prairie provinces a variety of means of optioning a livelihood were pursued in a region that was experiencing economic growth.[13]

Despite a dismissive scepticism about certain categories of archival records, especially with respect to income data, the observations of Native participation in a robust economy made by Indian agents cannot be dismissed simply as government deception.[14] Descriptions of the economic conditions and activities of Natives can be found in the business records of the Hudson's Bay Company. Understandably, local HBC officials had to take note of the redirection of Native labour from the fur production to the new frontier resource industries. In 1883, Norway House Chief Factor R. Ross recognized an emerging problem for a company that was well acquainted with the advantages of having a monopoly relationship with Native producers: 'A new disturbing element is now beginning to be felt in this business of this district through the establishment of saw mills and lumbering operations … [A] good many of … [the] Indians are giving up hunting and are going to work in the lumber camps.' The situation was serious enough that Ross urged 'a remodeling of our system of business without further delay' (HBCA 1883). The company's inspection report for 1887 recorded that 'the Indians at St. Peters are spoken of as being amongst the best and most prosperous in the Country,' and Lake Winnipeg Indians 'appear also to be well off; in addition to hunting, there being employment at the Lumber Camps[,] Saw mills and at Fishing' (HBCA 1887b). In effect, the internal business records of the HBC provide external verification of the observations made by Indian Affairs officials.

Alternate sources of income for the Indians had an impact on the HBC's operations. In 1889 it was noted that the Berens River Indians 'appear to be comparatively well off. Many of them are employed by the fishing cos.

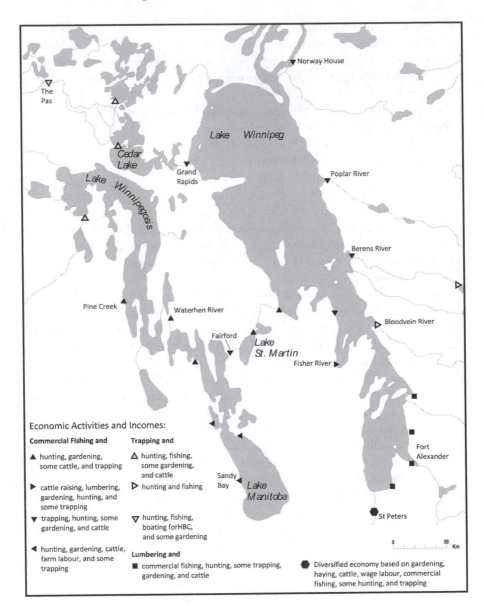

Band and reserve economies in Manitoba, ca 1900. CSP, 1899–1900, 'Indian Affairs.'

Fishing station at Matheson Island, Lake Winnipeg, 1924. Archives of Manitoba.

[companies] on Swampy Island and other points in the neighborhood. Are lazy as hunters' (HBCA 1889). Similarly, for the post at Manitoba House: 'The Indian hunt [trapping or fur production] at this place is not much at its best as the greater part of the Furs are caught by half-breeds; the Indians are getting lazy and indolent, in fact those on the Reserves are useless; there are only one or two families that follow the old style of hunting, that is camping out and moving from one place to another' (HBCA 1891a). In 1891, the HBC's inspection report for Fairford indicated the problems that the company faced: 'All Treaty Indians owing to furs being scarce a large portion of their time is devoted to fishing for the produce of which a good market is provided by dealers in the settlement and other points along the lake – not industrious' (HBCA 1891b). Similarly, in the same year, the Berens River Indians were described thus: 'The Indians are comparatively well off. Many of them do not hunt furs in winter, but are employed in fishing. Said to be lazy as hunters' (HBCA 1891c). Later, the 1905 inspection report for Fort Alexander noted that 'the Indians are taking themselves more and more to lumbering, fishing and other such work in preference to hunting'

(HBCA 1905). References to increased 'laziness' and 'indolence' indicate a frustration at the lack of Indian commitment to traditional fur production. In fact, production from new resource industries required hard work.

Fur prices remained low until 1900.[15] Despite the cultural appropriateness of the traditional economy,[16] Natives were not held to the production of fur when higher incomes could be earned by other means. In 1887, Chief Factor Belanger recognized that wage labour provided more security than trapping because 'very few of them would risk the uncertainty and undertake the fatigue of hunting expeditions without which very few furs are to be obtained as fur-bearing animals are very scarce' (HBCA 1887a). The assumed proclivity towards the traditional economy cannot explain what might have motivated Indians to participate in new resource industries, even at the expense of their long-term relationship with the HBC.[17] In fact, forgoing the higher incomes of new industries for the sake of traditional economy would be irrational from the point of view of neoclassical economics.

The injection of cash income into the regional economy was significant.[18] In 1899, McColl estimated that 'Captain Robinson pays annually upwards of $40,000 to the Indians in my inspectorate for lumbering, cutting cordwood, making ties, working on steamboats, and at the fisheries' (Canada 1900, 106). Natives were generally paid on the basis of how much they produced, but time wages were also paid. They were paid in money; earlier on, however, payment in kind or in trade was common. In 1886, Indian Agent A.M. Muckle recorded that digging Seneca root earned '$1 to $3 a day, in trade … in fact the whole business with Indians is in trade; when they have anything to sell they take flour, dry goods and groceries for it and very seldom receive cash' (Canada 1888, 54). In 1901, Inspector McColl provided evidence that a certain prosperity had been achieved: 'I found the Indians in better condition than they have been at any time during my twenty-four years among them. This was owing to the prosperous condition of the fishing industry and the extensive lumber interests of Captain Robinson, of Selkirk, with either of which industries nearly every Indian is more or less intimately connected, and from which he draws an ever-increasing yearly revenue' (Canada 1902, 77). An element of prosperity, or at least the absence of chronic destitution, was evident in this time period. While low fur prices and scarcity of fur-bearing animals combined to push Indians from the traditional economy, there is little doubt that new industries were able to pull Indians to seasonal labour markets.

In the 1870s a treaty payment of five dollars per person was a significant source of family cash income.[19] With employment available in the resource sector, the Indian Affairs annual report for 1882 noted that not all the annuities had been collected by members of the Hollow Water Band, because

Fishing station at Black River, Lake Winnipeg, 1929. The fish plant, dock, steamboat, cordwood, wooden fish boxes, sail boats, and gill net rack are outcomes of investment by frontier capitalists and Native labour. Archives of Manitoba, N20857.

those 'employed at the reserve in Mr. Dick's saw mill, refused to go after theirs [annuities], stating that the amount received was not worth the time lost in going after it' (Canada 1883, 141). Such an observation indicates that some sort of equation of time and money was guiding behaviour and that the opportunity cost of meeting the Indian agent in order to collect the annual five-dollar treaty payment had been considered. In this instance, the band members' relationship with the employer eclipsed their relationship with the Crown, because they postponed collection of the treaty payment in order to work.

An account of the economic history of Natives of the Lake Winnipeg region may simply serve to fill some gaps in our historical understanding of a particular and perhaps unique region; it may also help balance the overwhelming academic fascination with the history of Indian policy. The involvement of Native people in the frontier capitalism of Lake Winnipeg region was not a unique experience. Some long-standing awareness has acknowledged that the Mohawk were sought-after ironworkers who built many landmark projects (Mitchell 1959). In other regions Native people played contributing roles in regional economies (High 1994; Lutz 1992; Wien 1986).

In 1978, Rolf Knight's pioneering study, *Indians at Work*, provided a compelling rationale for understanding Native labour history, and, in contrast to romantic constructs of the role of Indian peoples in Canadian history, he stressed: 'But the pride of most Indian people might better be served by appreciating their real history and contributions. One might remind people that Indian workers also dug the mines, worked the canneries and mills, laid miles of railway and did a hundred other jobs. They helped lay the bases of many regional economies. That is well worth being proud of' (Knight [1978] 1996). Knight suggested that 'Indian people in some regions have been more intimately and longer involved in industrial wage work than many Euro-Canadians from rural area' (7).[20] By describing their roles as loggers, farmers, farm labourers, cowboys, teamsters, commercial fishermen, cannery workers, longshoremen, freighters, mine labourers, and coal trimmers, Knight identified important historical contributions made by Indians to the development of British Columbia. In this sense, the experience with work in the Lake Winnipeg region has a correspondence to that of the west coast. Subsequent research has demonstrated the involvement of Indian people in the frontier economies of British Columbia.[21] In particular, Lutz (2008) challenged the view that Indians were irrelevant to history, and he confirmed the central point of Knight's findings in *Indians at Work*.[22]

Consideration of the economic contributions that Native people have made can also generate other insights. Again with respect to BC labour history, Yale Belanger (2006) has identified both the role that Aboriginal people played in the union movement and the importance of this political experience to their land struggle (227–58). In *Neighbours and Networks: The Blood Tribe in the Southern Alberta Economy, 1884–1939*, Keith Regular provides an interesting description of the Blood economy (land, credit, hay, coal, and sugar beets) and challenges the view that reserve economies were necessarily isolated or irrelevant. The state's support of migrant Native labourers for southern Alberta's sugar-beet industry following the Second World War was explained by Ron Laliberte (2006). His study demonstrates the merits of considering social policies as lived experience in contrast to the largely redundant academic commentaries concerning the flawed Indian Act and unimplemented treaty rights.[23] In a significant and original contribution Robin Jarvis Brownlie (2008) demonstrated a relationship between the enfranchisement of Mohawk and Anishinabe women and their involvement with wage employment. Nonetheless, Aboriginal economic and labour history receive little notice in academia.

Significantly, Cree and Ojibwa participation in frontier capitalism in the late 1800s and early 1900s may serve to challenge generalizations held by some social scientists about the nature of the traditional economy and the roles that Native people played in regional economies. The numerous observations concerning Native participation in the frontier resources of the Lake Winnipeg region are not easily reconciled with George and

Preston's (1987) assertion that 'the [West Main] Cree's cultural aversion to wage work provided fertile ground for Indian-European misunderstanding.'[24] Accordingly, the conflict in the 1970s over land claims was 'in essence cultural, a continuing clash between two forms of rationality, one European, the other Indian' (447).[25] George and Preston further argued that the differing underlying principles of rationality complicated contemporary European-Indian relations (448). Such assertions appear to contradict the effort to obtain insights about Indian-white relations by employing formal economics.[26] The aversion to wage work and the conflicting forms of rationality are concepts that can be challenged from the perspective of economic history.

In the past some social scientists even employed mode-of-production terminology to describe the Native economy. However, the significance of market relations – in effect, participation in a world system – was virtually ignored. In the course of the development of the fur trade a traditional Native economy was forged out of coherence between commercial and subsistence activities, which were linked and interdependent.[27] In contrast to the field-based social scientists of that era, K.J. Rea (1968) argued a fundamentally different understanding of the problem: 'The recent economic problems of the native population of the north have been the consequence of the markets and technology of the twentieth century impinging not upon a primitive native economy, but upon a native economy which had adapted all too thoroughly to the markets and the technology of the nineteenth century' (322–3).[28] Owing to the fact that he noted the problems of market relations in the traditional economy, Rea characterized the problem in entirely different terms than did most of the other social scientists. An emphasis on subsistence meant that cash income problems (such as low fur prices) – that is, the vulnerabilities of the total Native economy to market relations – could be downplayed. By giving heavy weight to the subsistence sector, one could ignore the economic and political problems of market integration inherent in the commercial sector. Moreover the characterization of the traditional Native economy as essentially subsistence-based not only lacked empirical validity but also created a judicial risk by inferring that there is no significant commercial content to treaty and Aboriginal rights. The legal argument that treaty and Aboriginal rights might concern commercial rights entails an intellectual struggle against the subsistence stereotype of ethnography, and the case was best advanced legally by employment of the business records of the Hudson's Bay Company archives (Ray 1995).

In 1913, towards the end of a period of economic growth, the Reverend F. Stevens explained the reason traditional employers (missionaries and the HBC) were unable to afford Native labour in the Norway House area after labour markets had shifted northward: 'In the North there was a boom on ... The Hudson's [sic] Bay Railway was under construction. Survey parties were working. Prospectors were seeking gold. All the Indians were earning high wages. Some Indians were lighting their pipes with one-dollar bills. Gramophones and jam were everywhere. Missionary stipends remained the usual starvation rates. They [missionaries] could not compete in the labour market' (UCCA 1939–54, 44). Increased consumption, made possible by rising wage rates, affected the long-established connections with missionaries. Certainly, market imperatives overshadowed the existing understandings of relationships between missionaries, HBC traders, and Indians.

Market relations were an important force in shaping the regional economy, as evidenced by the willingness of frontier capitalists to employ Native people and to invest near Indian reserves, the large migration out of the stagnant fur country of northeastern Manitoba to the buoyant commercial fishing opportunities at the north end of Lake Winnipeg, the redirection of labour from trapping to new activities, and the calculation of the opportunity costs of collecting treaty annuities. Participation, as seasonal labourers and autonomous producers in the new economic activities brought by frontier capitalism, required a certain detachment from the traditional Native economy and fur production for the Hudson's Bay Company. Evidently, an adequate supply of labour was provided to new resource industries, and this required shifting efforts away from the traditional economy. Whether or not academics chose to ignore it, the contribution that Natives made to the economic history of the Lake Winnipeg region is significant. The development of labour and minor commodity markets in the Lake Winnipeg region, initiated by new forms of resource capitalism, challenges the view that communal subsistence (enhanced by resource-rent royalties) is the only historically appropriate economic strategy available to Aboriginal communities.

Acknowledgments

An earlier version of this chapter was presented as a paper, entitled 'In the Midst of Plenty and Comfort': Native Labor and the Traditional Economy in an Era of Economic Growth in Northern Manitoba, ca. 1870–1915, at the XIII International Economic History Conference, International Economic History Association, Buenos Aires, in July 2002. I appreciate Peter J. Usher's commentary on an early draft of the chapter.

Notes

1 For the purpose of this analysis, the Lake Winnipeg region includes Lakes Winnipeg, Manitoba, and Winnipegosis and bands extending from Cross Lake to
   Sandy Bay. For an overview history of the region, see Mochoruk (2004).

2 Among many of the social scientists supporting the political and traditional
   strengths of the established economy, no distinction was made between the
   subsistence activities in an economy governed by use values and the same
   sort of 'subsistence' activities that served to keep low the production costs of a
   mercantile company's operations. The conceptualization of a Native economy
   in northern Canada in the 1970s was based on the use of mode-of-production
   phraseology, the staple thesis, twentieth-century salvage ethnography, and contemporary field observations. In my view, this model of the Native economy
   was erroneously projected back into the classic fur trade. For an understanding
   of the ways in which many social scientists conceptualized the Native economy, see Berger (1977). For an insightful retrospective analysis of the Berger
   report, see Usher (1993).

3 Rupertsland had been granted to the HBC in 1670 by royal charter and was
   part of the Hudson Bay Company territory. Much of the Canadian subarctic
   was part of Rupertsland.

4 A made beaver (MB) was the unit of exchange based on the ideal prime beaver.
   This unit not only served to price pelts, skins, provisions, trade goods, and
   wages but was also the basis of post accounting records. The MB could be converted to English sterling currency.

5 For an elaboration of fur trade economics, see Tough (1996).

6 For the initial formulation of the staple theory, see Innis ([1930] 1970), although
   historian Michael Bliss proclaimed some two decades ago that *The Fur Trade in
   Canada* 'is no longer worth reading' (1987, 588). However, fur was not the first
   regional staple. From the Gulf of the St Lawrence, whales and cod became the
   first staple exports (Innis 1940).

7 Neither Steinbring (1981, 244–55) nor Brown and Peers (1988, 135–51) acknowledged the active role that the Ojibwa played in the frontier industries of the
   Lake Winnipeg region.

8 For a lengthy review of the rather limited literature on Native economic history
   see Tough (2005, 26–66).

9 With respect to Indian opposition to commercial fishing see Tough (1984,
   303–19) and Canada (1887).

10 In fact, 318 Indian individuals were known to have migrated from the York
   Factory and Island Lake districts between 1885 and 1908 to Norway House
   and Cross Lake. Moreover, Half-breed land-scrip applications made at Norway
   House and Cross Lake indicate the migration of 57 individuals from northeast-

ern Manitoba to Norway House or Cross Lake (Canada. Department of Indian and Northern Affairs 1908).

11 In a certain sense, the choice of sturgeon over beaver would have been hypothetical since the seasonal harvesting of each product did not conflict.

12 With a population of 149, the annuity payments for 1909 can be estimated to total $785, and thus cutting wood, putting up ice, and fishing, which earned $5,000, is a relatively significant source of cash income (Canada 1910, 103).

13 Buckley briefly described the situation in the transition period for the Prairie provinces, and she was attentive to the fact that it was less dire in the bush and parklands than in the grassland region. However, she did not acknowledge the economic growth in the Lake Winnipeg region. Her explanation of the economic difficulties focuses on failed government policies. See Buckley (1992, 28–66).

14 Such a view was expressed by High (1994, 23–39; 1996, 243–64).

15 For price data see Tough (1996, 310–17). For an account of the changing organization of the industry and the movement of prices see Ray (1990).

16 For two studies concerning the importance of the traditional land-based economy see Rushforth (1977) and Asch (1977).

17 However, the view exists that Native participation in the wage economy was selective, voluntary, and only done to strengthen traditions. See High (1996, 263).

18 For further evidence of participation in a more diverse economy see Tough (1992, 95–146).

19 Annuities of the first and second treaties were raised from three to five dollars (per person) in 1875. Annuities of the fifth treaty were five dollars. The terms of the treaties can be found in Morris (1880). For an explanation of the importance of annuities to the traditional economy, see Ray, Miller, and Tough (2000).

20 However, see Carlson (1996) for an important review of the second edition of *Indians at Work*.

21 With respect to the importance of an economic diversification see Burrows (1986). However, readers should appreciate that the viewpoint that Indians contributed to the development of British Columbia following the fur trade, which was forcefully articulated by Knight, was rejected in no uncertain terms by Fisher (1992), who stated in self-defence, 'In fact, Knight modifies nothing because he proves nothing' (xix). An account of the development of 'irrelevance' is a central theme in Miller ([1989] 2000).

22 Lutz (2008) has also claimed that the attraction to the wage economy was essentially a 'cultural' opportunity because participation in the wage economy enhanced potlatch ceremonies.

23 However, Laliberte (2006) ignores the literature on Native economic and labour history.

24 George and Preston (1987) contradicted the integrity of their own argument

when they noted that, in the first instance, very little paid fur-trade employment was available to which the Cree could be averse and that, in the second,
the Cree gravitated to the railways in search of jobs.

25 It is hard to appreciate how a Native assertion of a property right or of a desire
to benefit from modernization could be beyond the realm of European rationality.

26 A forceful case for employing economics in the history of Indian-white relations was made by Trosper (1988).

27 The assumptions about subsistence and the dichotomy between subsistence
and commercial activities are discussed more fully in Tough (1996, 14–43).

28 For an understanding of the ways in which subsistence activities were not
autonomous from the dynamics of the commercial sector see Ray (1984, 1–20).

Bibliography

Asch, Michael. 1977. The Dene economy. In *Dene Nation: The Colony Within*, ed. Mel
Watkins, 47–61. Toronto: University of Toronto Press.

Barris, Theodore. 1977. *Fire Canoe: Prairie Steamboat Days Revisited*. Toronto: McClelland and Stewart.

Bayfield, H.A. 1899. Lake Winnipeg trip. MG1 B25, 3. Winnipeg: Archives of Manitoba.

– 1915. Diary and photographs of a trip from Winnipeg to Port Nelson, May 27 to
June 22. MG1 B24, 7. Winnipeg: Archives of Manitoba.

Belanger, Yale D. 2006. Seeking a seat at the table: A brief history of Indian political
organizing in Canada, 1870–1951. PhD diss., Trent University.

Berger, Thomas. 1977. *Northern Frontier, Northern Homeland: The Report of the Mackenzie Valley Pipeline Inquiry*. Vol. 1. Ottawa: Minister of Supply and Services.

Bliss, Michael. 1987. *Northern Enterprise: Five Centuries of Canadian Business*.
Toronto: McClelland and Stewart.

Brown, Jennifer S.H., and Laura L. Peers. 1988. The Chippewa and their neighbors:
A critical review. In *The Chippewa and Their Neighbors: A Study in Ethnohistory*, ed.
Harold Hickerson. Rev. ed. Prospect Heights, IL: Waveland Press.

Brownlie, Robin Jarvis. 2008. 'Living the same as the white people': Mohawk and
Anishinabe women's labour in Southern Ontario, 1920–1940. *Labour/Le Travail*,
no. 61 (Spring): 41–68.

Buckley, Helen. 1992. *From Wooden Ploughs to Welfare: Why Indian Policy Failed in the
Prairie Provinces*. Montreal: McGill-Queen's University Press.

Burrows, James K. 1986. 'A much-needed class of labour': The economy and
income of the Interior Southern Plateau Indians, 1897–1910. *BC Studies*, no. 71:
27–46.

Carlson, Keith. 1996. Indians at work. *Native Studies Review* 11 (1): 147–51.

Canada. Department of Indian and Northern Affairs. 1908. Government of Canada Files: Annuity paylists. RG15, vols. 709, 990, 1042, 1043, 1063, 1067, 1348, 1361, 1365, 1367. Ottawa: Library and Archives Canada.

Canada. Parliament. House of Commons. 1883. Annual report for the Department of Indian Affairs, 1882. *Sessional Papers*, no. 5. Ottawa: Queen's Printer.

– 1884. Annual report for the Department of Indian Affairs, 1883. *Sessional Papers*, no. 4. Ottawa: Queen's Printer.

– 1885. Annual report for the Department of Indian Affairs, 1884. *Sessional Papers*, no. 3. Ottawa: Queen's Printer.

– 1886. Annual report for the Department of Indian Affairs, 1885. *Sessional Papers*, no. 4. Ottawa: Queen's Printer.

– 1887. Annual report for the Department of Marine and Fishers, 1886. *Sessional Papers*, no. 16. Ottawa: Queen's Printer.

– 1888. Annual report for the Department of Indian Affairs, 1887. *Sessional Papers*, no. 15. Ottawa: Queen's Printer.

– 1889. Annual report for the Department of Indian Affairs, 1888. *Sessional Papers*, no. 16. Ottawa: Queen's Printer.

– 1896. Annual report for the Department of the Interior, 1895. *Sessional Papers*, no. 13. Ottawa: Queen's Printer.

– 1899a. Annual report for the Department of Marine and Fishers, 1898. *Sessional Papers*, no. 11A. Ottawa: Queen's Printer.

– 1899b. Annual report for the Department of Indian Affairs, 1898. *Sessional Papers*, no. 14. Ottawa: Queen's Printer.

– 1900. Annual report for the Department of Indian Affairs, 1899. *Sessional Papers*, no. 14. Ottawa: Queen's Printer.

– 1901a. Annual report for the Department of Indian Affairs, 1901. *Sessional Papers*, no. 27. Ottawa: Queen's Printer.

– 1901b. Annual report for the Department of Indian Affairs, 1900. *Sessional Papers*, no. 27. Ottawa: Queen's Printer.

– 1902. Annual report for the Department of Indian Affairs, 1901. *Sessional Papers*, no. 27. Ottawa: Queen's Printer.

– 1904. Annual report for the Department of Marine and Fishers, 1903. *Sessional Papers*, no. 22. Ottawa: Queen's Printer.

– 1905a. Annual report for the Department of Marine and Fishers, 1904. Special appended report: Canadian sturgeon and caviar industries (1904, E.E. Prince). *Sessional Papers*, no. 22. Ottawa: Queen's Printer.

– 1905b. Annual report for the Department of Indian Affairs, 1904. *Sessional papers*, no. 27. Ottawa: Queen's Printer.

– 1906. Annual report for the Department of Indian Affairs, 1905. *Sessional Papers*, no. 27. Ottawa: Queen's Printer.

– 1907. Annual report for the Department of Indian Affairs, 1906. *Sessional Papers,* no. 27. Ottawa: Queen's Printer.

– 1910. Annual report for the Department of Indian Affairs, 1909. *Sessional Papers,* no. 27. Ottawa: Queen's Printer.

Church Missionary Society Fonds (CMS). 1882. MG17-B2, R10977-0-1-E, microfilm reel A-110, 8 April. Ottawa: Library and Archives Canada.

– 1893. MG17-B2, R10977-0-1-E, microfilm reel A-118, 4 July.

Fisher, Robin. 1992. *Contact and Conflict: Indian-European Relations in British Columbia, 1774–1890.* 2nd ed. Vancouver: University of British Columbia Press.

George, Peter J., and Richard J. Preston. 1987. Going in between: The impact of European technology on the work patterns of West Main Cree of Northern Ontario. *Journal of Economic History* 47 (2): 456.

High, Steven. 1994. Responding to white encroachment: The Robinson-Superior Ojibwa and the capitalist labour economy, 1880–1914. *Thunder Bay Historical Museum Society Papers and Records,* 22:23–39.

– 1996. Native wage labour and independent production during the 'era of irrelevance.' *Labour/Le Travail,* no. 37 (Spring): 243–64.

Houston, J.J. 1987. Status of the Lake Sturgeon, *Acipenser fulvescens,* in Canada. *Canadian Field-Naturalists* 101 (2): 182.

Hudson's Bay Company Archives (HBCA). 1870. A.11/51 (August 1), fol. 100. Winnipeg: Archives of Manitoba.

– 1883. B.154/b/11 (January 3). Winnipeg: Archives of Manitoba.

– 1887a. B.49/e/13, fol. 1. Winnipeg: Archives of Manitoba.

– 1887b. D.25/2, fol. 69. Winnipeg: Archives of Manitoba.

– 1889. D.25/6, fol. 173. Winnipeg: Archives of Manitoba.

– 1891a. A.74/1, fol. 140–41. Winnipeg: Archives of Manitoba.

– 1891b. D.25/13, fol. 236. Winnipeg: Archives of Manitoba.

– 1891c. D.25/13, fol. 297. Winnipeg: Archives of Manitoba.

– 1900. A.74/9, fol. 22. Winnipeg: Archives of Manitoba.

– 1905. A.12/FT 322/1 (a), fol. 173. Winnipeg: Archives of Manitoba.

Innis, Harold. (1930) 1970. *The Fur Trade in Canada: An Introduction to Canadian Economic History.* Toronto: University of Toronto Press.

– 1940. *The Cod Fisheries.* New Haven, CT: Yale University Press.

Knight, Rolf. (1978) 1996. *Indians at Work: An Informal History of Native Labour in British Columbia, 1848–1930.* 2nd ed. Vancouver: New Star Books.

Laliberte, Ron. 2006. The 'grab-a-hoe' Indians: The Canadian state and the procurement of Aboriginal labour for the Southern Alberta sugar beet industry. *Prairie Forum* 31 (2): 305–24.

Lutz, John. 1992. After the fur trade: The aboriginal labouring class of British Columbia, 1849–1890. *Journal of Canadian Historical Association* 3: 69–93.

– 2008. *Makúk: A New History of Aboriginal-White Relations.* Vancouver: UBC Press.

Manitoba Daily Press. 1888. 8 October.

Miller, J.R. (1989) 2000. *Skyscrapers Hide the Heavens: A History of Indian-White Relations in Canada*. 3rd ed. Toronto: University of Toronto Press.

Mitchell, Joseph. 1959. The Mohawks in high steel. In *Apologies to the Iroquois*, ed. Edmond Wilson, 3–36. New York: Farrar, Straus, and Cudahy.

Mochoruk, Jim. 2004. *Formidable Heritage: Manitoba's North and the Cost of Development*. Winnipeg: University of Manitoba Press.

Morris, Alexander. 1880. *The Treaties of Canada with the Indians of Manitoba and the North-West Territories*. Toronto: Belfords, Clarke, and Company.

Ray, Arthur J. 1984. Periodic shortages, native welfare, and the Hudson's Bay Company, 1670–1930. In *The Subarctic Fur Trade: Native Social and Economic Adaptations*, ed. Shepard Krech III, 1–20. Vancouver: University of British Columbia Press.

– 1990. *The Canadian Fur Trade in the Industrial Age*. Toronto: University of Toronto Press.

– 1995. Commentary on the economic history of the Treaty 8 area. *Native Studies Review* 10 (2): 169–95.

Ray, Arthur J., and Donald B. Freeman. 1978. *'Give Us Good Measure': An Economic Analysis of Relations between Indians and the Hudson's Bay Company before 1763*. Toronto: University of Toronto Press.

Ray, Arthur J., Jim Miller, and Frank Tough. 2000. *Bounty and Benevolence: A History of Saskatchewan Treaties*. Montreal: McGill-Queen's University Press.

Rea, K.J. 1968. *Political Economy of the Canadian North: An Interpretation of the Course of Development in the Northern Territories of Canada to the Early 1960s*. Toronto: University of Toronto Press.

Regular, W. Keith. 2008. *Neighbours and Networks: The Blood Tribe in the Southern Alberta Economy, 1884–1939*. Calgary: University of Calgary Press.

Rushforth, Scott. 1977. Country food. In *Dene Nation: The Colony Within*, ed. Mel Watkins, 32–46. Toronto: University of Toronto Press.

Steinbring, Jack H. 1981. Saulteaux of Lake Winnipeg. In *Subarctic*, vol. 6 of *Handbook of North American Indians*, vol. ed. June Helm, ed. William C. Sturtevant, 244–55. Washington, DC: Smithsonian Institution.

Tough, Frank. 1984. The establishment of a commercial fishing industry and the demise of Native fisheries in Northern Manitoba. *Canadian Journal of Native Studies* 4 (2): 303–19.

– 1992. Regional analysis of Indian aggregate income, Northern Manitoba: 1896–1935. *Canadian Journal of Native Studies* 12 (1): 95–146.

– 1996. *'As Their Natural Resources Fail': Native Peoples and the Economic History of Northern Manitoba, 1870–1930*. Vancouver: University of British Columbia Press.

– 2005. From the 'original affluent society' to the 'unjust society': A review of economic history in Canada. *Journal of Aboriginal Economic Development* 4 (2): 26–66.

Trosper, Ronald L. 1988. The other discipline: Economics and American Indian history. In *New Directions in American Indian History*, ed. Colin G. Calloway, 199–222. Norman, OK: University of Oklahoma Press.

United Church of Canada Archives (UCCA). Frederich George Stevens fonds. 1939–54. Autobiography of the Rev. Frederich G. Stevens. Toronto: United Church of Canada.

Usher, Peter J. 1993. Northern development, impact assessment, and social change. In *Anthropology, Public Policy, and Native Peoples in Canada*, ed. Noel Dyck and James B. Waldram, 98–130. Montreal: McGill-Queen's University Press.

Wien, Fred. 1986. *Rebuilding the Economic Base of Indian Communities: The Micmac in Nova Scotia*. Montreal: Institute for Research on Public Policy.

Profile of David Gabriel Tuccaro (1959–)

Cree, Entrepreneur, and Business Consultant

David Gabriel Tuccaro grew up as a member of the Mikisew Cree First Nation on the shores of Lake Athabasca in Fort Chipewyan, Alberta. He was one of nine children born to Gabriel and Terese (Mercredi) Tuccaro. He attended high school at Grandin College in Fort Smith, Northwest Territories, because Bishop Piche School in Fort Chipewyan only included kindergarten and Grades 1 to 9. In an interview Tuccaro admitted that he never excelled at academics and only attained the minimum necessary to ensure that he could play collegiate sports.[1] His philosophy paid off when, in his last year at Grandin College, he won a gold medal at the Arctic Winter Games.

Tuccaro graduated from high school in 1976, but he did not continue his formal education. He believed that Grade 12 was 'good enough' to get a job. Early in his career he worked in construction, operated heavy equipment, and also drove a taxi. However, such jobs did not sufficiently satisfy his desire to be his own boss.[2] This desire led David Tuccaro to become one of the best-known and successful Aboriginal business owners in western Canada. He currently employs more than 350 people through his various businesses,[3] and he owns and controls Tuccaro Inc., a company that finances property rentals and commercial development. He is also president of Aboriginal Global Investments, Aboriginal Technical Services, TUC's Contracting, and Neegan Development Corporation Ltd., whose activities range from market investment to environmental engineering to earth moving with heavy equipment.[4]

Tuccaro applies a consistent philosophy to all of his businesses: 'to create opportunities for Aboriginal people at every level of employment.'[5] His companies share the goal of ensuring that 80 per cent of their employees are Aboriginal.[6] He not only supports educational and training initiatives to make certain his staff is fully qualified but also encourages other Aboriginal people to become entrepreneurs.[7]

Dave Tuccaro. Photo courtesy of Greg Halinda Photography.

Mr Tuccaro is also very active with his message of self-determination, taking it to regional high schools, where he is known to teach, 'Don't listen to those who say you won't succeed … A lot of times people quit one day before they [would reach] success.'[8] Currently, Tuccaro's pet project involves establishing a private boarding school for Aboriginal students from northern Alberta. The proposed school has been tentatively named the Leadership Academy, and it plans to offer a blend of academic and business courses, while providing mentorship from business and cultural leaders. Tuccaro is working with businesses in the Fort McMurray area to help cover the costs because he judges that federal or provincial school-funding transfers will not completely cover them.[9]

One of Tuccaro's greatest accomplishments was the creation of the National Aboriginal Business Association (NABA) in 1996. NABA is a not-for-profit business association, which recognizes that creating sustainable Aboriginal enterprises is critical to economic growth.[10] The goal of its president, Tuccaro, is to oversee and promote the members' involvement in bulk purchases as a way of saving on the cost of doing business.[11] His leadership and business prowess have not gone unnoticed. For example, David Tuccaro was included in the *Financial Post Magazine*'s 'Top 40 under 40' in April 1998.[12] The following year he received a National Aboriginal Achievement Award for his contribution to business and commerce.[13] In 2000 he was named one of 'Alberta's 50 Most Influential People' by *Venture Magazine*.

Mr Tuccaro's volunteer activities include sitting on the boards of the Regional Health Authority and the Alberta Chamber of Resources. He spearheaded the formation of the Northeastern Alberta Aboriginal Business Association (NAABA),[14] sat as a director of the National Aboriginal Achievement Foundation, and co-chaired the 2004 Arctic Winter Games Committee.[15] With such a successful and demanding career, Tuccaro makes sure he takes time off to enjoy spending time with his family, fishing, and golf.

JOCELYN OBREITER

Notes

1 Joan Black, 'David Tuccaro: Creating opportunities for others motivates businessman,' *Windspeaker*, 1999, http://www.thefreelibrary.com/Wind+Speaker/1999/April/1-p5678.

2 Ibid.

3 Northern News Service Online, 'Conference encourages local business in NWT,' http://nnsl.com/northern-news-services/stories/papers/oct29_07biz.html (accessed 27 January 2011).

4 Black, 'David Tuccaro.'

5 National Aboriginal Business Association, 'David Tuccaro,' 2003, http://www.thefreelibrary.com/Creating+opportunities+for+others+motivates+businessman%3A+David...-a030540173.

6 Ibid.

7 Ibid.

8 Ibid.

9 Kevin Libin, 'Rethinking the reserve,' *National Post*, 7 February 2008, http://www.nationtalk.ca/modules/news/article.php?storyid=6333.

10 Ibid.

11 Ibid.
12 Staff Writer, 'Top 40 under 40: Reflections on the quality of leadership,' *Financial Post Magazine*, April 1998, 18–36.
13 Staff Writer, 'Neegan president wins aboriginal business award,' *Edmonton Journal*, March 1999, 1.
14 Ibid.
15 Ibid.

Profile of James Edward (Ed) Williams (1948–2010)

Potawatomi, Politician, and Businessman

James Edward (Ed) Williams was born on 10 November 1948 in French River, Ontario. He was one of seven children born to Percy Williams and Florence Williams (née Agowissa). His first language was Ojibwa, and he learned English only after starting school at the one-room schoolhouse located a mile from his home. After completing Grade 12 at Parry Sound High School in 1970, Williams earned a journeyman machinist certificate at Conestoga College.[1] He worked as a machinist and lived away from his community until the early 1980s.

In 1982 Williams moved his family back to the Moose Deer Point First Nation, a community located in the Muskoka region of Ontario, about two hours' drive north of Toronto. Upon his return to the reserve, he quickly recognized that economic development opportunities could be derived from the reserve's location on Georgian Bay. For example, while managing the community's marina, Williams saw a demand for boat slips, and he helped the marina to nearly double in size, from 120 boat slips to 225.[2] He was also able to capitalize on the increased need for winter storage facilities for boats and other recreational vehicles. This facility grew to provide services for more than two hundred clients.[3]

In addition to expanding or establishing economically viable enterprises in the community, Williams involved himself in band politics. Within one year after moving back to the reserve, he was elected to the office of chief. Williams completed nine consecutive terms (over eighteen years) as chief of Moose Deer Point First Nation. Under his leadership the reserve continued to pursue economic development ventures that provided employment for community members and joint ventures with investors. For example, a major accomplishment under Williams's leadership was the creation of Niigon (Ojibwa: 'for the future') Technologies Limited, in partnership with Robert Schad of Husky Injection Molding Systems Ltd. This joint venture resulted in the first injection molding company in Canada under First Nations ownership. It received the Ontario Aboriginal Partnership Recog-

Ed Williams. Courtesy of Tracy Hendricks.

nition Award.[4] The company manufactured computer, electronic, and automobile parts as well as medical equipment, creating seventy local jobs.[5] The job-creation aspect of this venture was significant in light of the community's 70 and 30 per cent unemployment rates during the winter and the summer months respectively.[6] Until the creation of Niigon, Moose Deer Point had relied solely on the marina to provide employment for tribal members.

Niigon's corporate philosophy promotes environmentalism. For example, its building has a number of environmentally friendly features, such as natural lighting through skylights, natural ventilation, radiant floor heating, and photovoltaic cells on the roof that provide power to the building.[7] Williams wanted to create employment opportunities for the First Nations people of Moose Deer Point, and he laid the foundation for a future based on a self-sustaining economy.[8] All of Niigon's profits are administered by Moose Deer Point's chief and council. Business proceeds are used to increase the reserve's housing and to provide health and education programming for its residents.[9]

Ed Williams lived at the Moose Deer Point First Nation with his wife, children, and grandchildren. He enjoyed fishing, playing golf, and doting on his grandchildren.[10] He passed away in 2010.

HOLLY BAUER

Notes

1 Personal correspondence with Ed Williams, 7 October 2004.
2 http://www.anishinabek.ca/news.asp.
3 Personal correspondence with Ed Williams, 7 October 2004.
4 Margo Little, 'Moose Deer Point First Nation receives partnership recognition,' *Windspeaker* 11 (1987): 30.
5 Michael Lagault, 'Building from the ground up: A few hours north of Toronto, the Moose Deer Point First Nation will soon be opening the first aboriginal-owned injection molding company in Canada,' *Canadian Plastics* 59, no. 7: 23–4.
6 Ibid.
7 Ibid.
8 Ontario Ministry of Aboriginal Affairs, 'Aboriginal sustainable community project a first for Canada,' http://www.aboriginalaffairs.gov.on.ca/english/news/archives/news_000602.asp.
9 Kelly Louiseize, 'Manufacturer adopts global position for success,' *Northern Ontario Business* 22, no. 11: 1C.
10 Personal correspondence with Ed Williams, 7 October 2004.

Walking Tall:
Mohawk Ironworkers

EDWINNA VON BAEYER

Mohawk ironworkers from Kahnawake have written their legacy in steel. With their sweat, blood, and, sometimes, their lives they helped to create the modern North American skyline of skyscrapers, massive bridges, and other high structures. They have worked the high steel since the late 1800s, putting together by hand the massive frameworks of these structures. They are the men you see walking along narrow steel beams, manhandling huge, swinging girders into place, and bolting them together – all at dizzying heights, often without a safety line.

The Mohawk ironworkers' contribution to Kahnawake,[1] the Aboriginal community, Canada, and the United States has been significant and a continuing source of pride. Beyond helping build our modern cities, as the first Indian ironworkers in North America they have also cleared the path for other First Nations into a tough profession, through their solid reputation and pride in their work. They have broken the stereotype of 'Indian' and forced society to pay attention to 'the urban Indian as people who weren't doing basketwork' (Baylis 2002, 2.29). In fact, Richard Hill believes that the Kahnawake ironworkers even created the category of urban Indian (Hill 1987, 27). In addition, they found a profession that suited their culture and helped to economically develop Kahnawake. They also contributed to Mohawk sovereignty and recognition of Aboriginal rights. Ironworkers put their lives on the line during the Oka crisis of 1990. Many left jobs and returned to the community in order to support it and help protect their land. Some ironworkers, such as 'Lasagna' (Ronald Cross) and 'Spudwrench' (Randy Horne), even joined the more militant Mohawk Warrior encampment (Cross and Sévigny 1994, 80).[2]

Mohawk ironworkers have been called many things: 'skywalkers,' 'cowboys of the skies,' 'hot shots of the construction world,' 'daredevils,' and 'heroes,' especially following their rescue and clean-up efforts after the September 2001 terrorist attack on New York's World Trade Center. They have always been regarded as belonging to a class apart from other ironworkers, even though they are not, in numbers, the dominant group. Today ironworkers come from a broad cross-section of the North American population, including other First Nations.[3] However, the Mohawk ironworker has captured the public's imagination for decades – in Canadian school curricula, the media, and museum exhibits. As one Mohawk ironworker noted, 'ask anyone and they'll tell ya, those Indians are darn good ironworkers' (National Film Board of Canada 1965). The profession is still highly valued in the Mohawk community. Ironworkers are looked up to for doing a tough, dangerous job at high personal cost: long periods away from home, injury, physical disability, and sometimes death.

Breaking the Myth

The media have often romanticized Mohawk ironworkers, saying that they are born with perfect balance and great agility and without fear of heights. However, Mohawk ironworkers deny this myth. On the job, Mohawks fall and are injured at about the same rate as non-Aboriginal ironworkers. As one ironworker put it, 'we're not born with magnets on our feet' (Egan 2002, A3). Another ironworker explained further: 'We have as much fear as the next guy. The difference is that we deal with it better. We also have the experience of the old timers to follow and the responsibility to lead the younger guys. There is pride in walking iron' (Elmes and Prasad 2002, 13).

   The work itself is not romantic: death or injury is only a misstep away. One must be constantly careful, yet work as rapidly as possible to stay on schedule. The work is hard, often done in extremes of weather. Income fluctuates with the cycle of building – 'feast or famine,' according to Reaghen Tarbell, wife of a present-day ironworker.

Reflecting Mohawk Culture

Yet, ironworking has attracted Mohawk men since the late 1800s. Economics have played a large role in this attraction. Jobs were scarce in Kahnawake, as they were in most Native communities in the mid to late 1800s. The income from ironworking has greatly contributed to Kahnawake's economic independence and prosperity.[4] Ironworking is also a good cultural fit. Alex McComber, a retired ironworker, says that construction is in his blood. Iroquois[5] call themselves *hodinoso:ni* (they build longhouses). For centuries the Mohawk were renowned for their superbly built towns, which could be quite extensive, featuring double palisaded walls, dozens of large longhouses, and defensive catwalks (Hill 1987, 12).

Cooperative labour and hard work were traditional values in the community as was their sense of freedom and adventure. From the 1700s to the 1820s, Mohawks participated in the fur trade as expert canoeists (Mitchell [1949] 1960). This reputation even took some Mohawks to Egypt where they ferried British troops up the Nile River in 1884–5 to help free General Gordon, who was being held captive in the Sudan (*Canadian Encyclopedia* 2001).

Long absences from home are still an accepted way of life for men. In the past they were often off hunting and fishing, waging war, and participating in diplomatic missions, for example. Men later worked away from home as loggers and voyageurs and as entertainers in Wild West shows. Running the community and its families has been traditionally left to the women, as befits the Mohawk matrilineal social structure. One ironworker's wife explained that she 'took care of everything' during her long marriage (National Public Radio 2002).

Ironworking provides income, adrenaline-raising adventure, pride in one's work, building skills, and a challenging combination of physical and mental skills. Ironworking also confers power on the ironworker: the work at great heights and the structures themselves are power symbols. Working at great heights also puts the worker in a place of spirit: 'When you're up in the air, sometimes you have to call on an eagle, when it gets windy, or if it's raining or you have to work on ice. The eagle is closest to the Creator, and when the Mohawk builds a skyscraper, he is close to the Creator' (Garcia 2002).

David Blanchard, an ethnohistorian, believes that ironwork has symbolic meaning for the community. Ironwork personifies the meaning of 'real work,' which is highly regarded in the community. Becoming an ironworker, he believes, is a rite of passage – a young man's transition from boyhood to manhood – symbolized by strapping on his ironworking tool belt for the first time. Ironworking tools are often passed down to the next generation. Ironworking also links the worker to his past. As Blanchard further notes, 'the Mohawk are conscious of the fact that by working the high steel, they are acting out their own history' (Blanchard 1983). This history is kept alive by swapping stories about big jobs, retired ironworkers' experiences, and ingenious solutions for a construction problem; ancestors who were legendary ironworkers, as well as the stories, emphasize the Mohawk role in building North America (Blanchard 1983, 52–8). For example, James Jacobs, an ironworker apprentice, heard stories from his foreman who had worked with Jacobs' grandfather. The stories have also drawn young men into the profession over the years: 'Weekends when they came home all they talked about was the jobs they was on, what they were doing, where they were traveling. It was great. Specially when you started working yourself. You could almost do the job, you were talking so much about it when you were a kid. You knew what the hell to do, no one really had to tell you' (National Public Radio 2002).

An Ironworker's Profile

James Jacobs sums up the timeless qualities that characterize a good iron-worker: 'I'm not afraid of heights, I'm a quick learner. As soon as they show me something, I can do it immediately. I like a lot of physical work. This job will make you or break you. I like that challenge. You get to climb, and there are a lot of risks. But you can't be a crybaby – don't whine. That is number one. You have to accept the job for what it is. The more you try, the more respect you earn.'[6]

An ironworker needs to be physically fit and must have a good sense of balance to walk across three-inch, six-inch, and twelve-inch beams – what Louis Stacey, who has been an ironworker for twenty-three years, calls 'a sidewalk.' Ironworkers carry heavy loads and often climb nine-metre-high steel columns. An ability to perform hard work in all kinds of weather is a must. Ironworkers should have a high degree of technical skill and be able to make quick, independent decisions, using what Richard Hill calls 'Injun-nuity.' Ironworkers must be able to read blueprints, tie a variety of rope knots, and know the most efficient way to use their equipment, tools, and supplies (Hill 1987, 46).

Ironworkers do many types of jobs. They assemble the cranes and der-ricks that move structural steel and other materials and equipment (U.S. Department of Labor 2004). They also install metal interior fittings, such as stairways, or set steel reinforcing bars and tie them together with wire before concrete walls or floors are cast. Some ironworkers work in the shop, fabricating pieces of steel, cast iron, and aluminum, as needed (Hill 1987, 32).

In the past the most prestigious, the most 'macho,' and the highest-paid jobs were done by four-man riveting gangs, which consisted of a riveter, a man who heated the rivets and tossed them to two other men, who ham-mered the red-hot rivets in place. However, with the replacement of rivets by high-strength steel bolts, today the prestigious jobs are done by the con-nectors, members of the raising gangs who bolt together steel columns, beams, and girders. These men are always taking calculated risks to get the steel up in a dangerous environment where 'steel beams wobble like linguine when the wind blows, and incoming beams can whirl like kites and crush body parts' (Kilgannon 2002, 14WC.4). Here teamwork is often a matter of life and death; each member of a gang has a strong sense of responsibility for the other. The connectors direct swinging steel beams, which are dangling from cranes, into place and use driftpins or the handle of a spud wrench to align the holes in the steel with the holes in the framework – all the while wearing tool belts that sometimes weigh 32 kilograms (U.S. Department of Labor 2004). Using high-tension bolts, which are afterwards welded into place, they connect the beams. James Jacobs describes the allure of connecting: 'Connectors are very well respected. Being in a business that's already dangerous and doing the most dangerous part of it, shows a lot of who you are, your character. To be a good connector, you must have the guts to do it. You are not tied up all the time. You are on the edge. Once it's up, you're part of the building – you're the guy who connected the beams – there's a lot of pride involved.'[7] There has always been competition between raising gangs, as Louis Stacey notes, 'to see who's working faster, setting more steel. However, you wind up at the top where both gangs have to work together, so it's more of a pride thing than an actual winner. Everyone knows what the score is. The whole job at the end is the winner – we all put it together.'[8]

A good job is defined in many ways – by good pay, a long run, difficulty, or challenge. One ironworker reminisced about a job doing repairs on the vertical cables of the Brooklyn Bridge: 'There were thousands of clamps to put on. We were hanging like spiders in a web. It was a good job' (National Film Board of Canada 1997).

The First Mohawk Ironworkers

It all began with curiosity in 1850 when the Grand Trunk Railway started building an iron railroad bridge, called Victoria Bridge, across the St Lawrence River near Montreal, about three kilometres from Kahnawake. Local Mohawks were hired as day labourers to quarry stone on their land[9] and transport it by boat to the bridge site. To get a closer look at how the bridge was being constructed, they often climbed onto the top girders. Their surefootedness and lack of fear impressed company officials so much that they hired a group of Mohawks and began training them.

The ironworkers never looked back. For the next fifty years Mohawks were steadily employed by the Canadian Pacific Railway and the Grand Trunk Railway. They built bridges near Montreal, Ottawa, and Quebec City as well as at logging camps, quarries, and over ravines in the Laurentians (Blanchard 1983, 44). Black Bridge, which they helped build near Kahnawake in 1886, still has special significance for the community. On this particular job a few Mohawk were picked out and, for the first time, trained in riveting; 'it turned out that putting riveting tools in their hands was like putting ham with eggs' (Hill 1987, 18). Black Bridge also has significance for generations of young Mohawks who test their skill and courage on high steel by climbing up onto its girders (Rasenberger 2004, 167). Louis Stacey laughs when he relates how he was one of the very few Kahnawake boys to fall off this bridge while testing himself: 'I broke both my arms but told my mother I'd fallen out of a tree.'[10]

As more Kahnawake men entered the profession, they began making up their own gangs, with members often related by blood (Blanchard 1983, 45). By 1887 there were more than fifty Mohawks, mostly in riveting gangs, working on the Sault Ste Marie bridge between Michigan and Ontario. One ironworker described the on-the-job training that became an ironworking tradition: 'The Indian boys turned the Soo Bridge into a college for themselves. They way they worked it, as soon as one apprentice was trained, they'd send back to the reservation for another one. By and by, there'd be enough men for a new Indian gang. When the new gang was organized, there'd be a shuffle-up – a couple of men from the old gangs would go into the new gang and a couple of the new men would go into the old gangs ... They taught us the sharing, the idea of giving someone else the opportunity. When you're given a gift, you pass it back on freely to another' (Elmes and Prasad 2002, 14). Many present-day ironworkers carry the family names of these pioneer ironworkers, such as McComber, Stacey, Horne, Jacobs, Diabo, Williams, Rice, Beauvais, Lahacte, Phillips, and Tarbell.

By 1900 the Kahnawake Mohawks had established a solid reputation as skilled ironworkers. With the founding of the ironworkers' union (International Association of Bridge and Structural Iron Workers of America) in 1896, the hourly pay scale and safety standards began to rise. As local branches formed, Mohawk ironworkers joined them. Even today, the majority of Kahnawake ironworkers belong to locals 711 in Montreal, 361 in Brooklyn, or 40 in Manhattan. Membership often followed family lines; for example, Ronald Cross ('Lasagna,' a Mohawk warrior in the Oka crisis) was a third-generation Mohawk ironworker in Local 361 (Cross and Sévigny 1994, 73).

One factor that did not change with unionization was the ultimate reality of the ironworker's life – death on the job. The first Mohawk ironworker to be killed was Joe Diabo, who fell from the Sault Ste Marie bridge in 1888 (Hill 1987, 18). By 1890, ironworking was called one of the most dangerous professions in North America, having the highest accident and mortality rate of all the construction trades. An ironworker slogan in the early 1900s said it all: 'We don't die, we are killed' (Rasenberger 2004, 57).

Even today, most deaths are caused by falling. In fact, it took decades before simple safety measures were enforced. These measures included wearing hard hats and safety goggles; planking floors as the framework rose so that if a worker fell into the building, he would not plummet to the ground; hanging safety nets under bridges and along the sides of buildings; and having ironworkers 'tie off' when they are doing especially hazardous work.

The worst disaster for the community occurred after seventy Mohawk ironworkers were hired to work on the Quebec bridge near Quebec City. It was to have a centre span of 1,600 feet, an engineering challenge for the times. However, the design engineer's load-bearing calculations were wrong. On 29 August 1907 the south arm collapsed, and ninety-six men were killed, thirty-three of whom were Mohawk. On that day, twenty-four women became widows and fifty-six children became fatherless in Kahnawake. Two large iron crosses, which still stand, honour these iron-workers. Many of their graves are marked with small steel-beam crosses.

The personal toll and the economic toll were horrendous. The women of the community demanded that ironworkers not work in such large numbers on the same project ever again. Their voices carried great weight. Richard Hill (1987, 22) dates the practice of 'booming out' (travelling great distances to find work, leaving their families behind) from that time.

Bridges and Skyscrapers

Surprisingly, the tragedy of the Quebec bridge attracted Mohawk men even more to ironworking: 'It made them take pride in themselves that they could do such dangerous work.' By 1915, out of 651 working-age men in Kahnawake, 587 belonged to the ironworkers' union – a huge increase from 1907 (Rasenberger 2004, 158).

The great era of bridge and skyscraper construction had begun with the birth of the modern skyscraper in Chicago in 1884–5. Technological advances in manufacturing iron and steel had paved the way for higher structures. Steel replaced iron because steel was eight times stronger and made construction faster and less expensive (Hill 1987, 34). The steel frame-work became self-supporting. It could be built higher and was independent of load-bearing external masonry walls (Kalman 1994, 571). As well, the invention of the hydraulic elevator in the late 1850s allowed architects to design higher buildings and gave construction crews the means to work on them.

Jobs increased in Canada and the United States, especially in Montreal, Toronto, Boston, Detroit, New York, and Chicago as these cities began to grow – not only in population but also in the number and the height of their buildings. Mohawk ironworkers were there, in the forefront, to help change the North American skyline. As more and more skyscrapers and bridges were built, the reputation of Mohawk ironworkers also rose. This solid reputation helped pave the way for other First Nations to enter the profession.

Booming Out

The first Mohawk ironworker from Kahnawake 'boomed out' to New York City in 1912. By 1920 three gangs of Mohawks were working in the city, which had become the focus of ironworking jobs. As well, the union pay scale there was the highest in North America (Hill 1987, 27).

It was the golden age of the skyscraper. In the previous decade half of all the skyscrapers built in the United States were constructed in New York (Rasenberger 2004, 197). Companies, such as Bethlehem Steel, and architects competed with their rivals to build the tallest building. It was the Progressive Era, symbolized by the grandeur and power of skyscrapers and massive, high bridges: 'This lust for height was seen as a triumph of the human spirit over nature, and a symbol of corporate dominance over the urban landscape' (Hill 1987, 35).

Some early Mohawk ironworkers travelled throughout North America, 'seeking rush jobs that offer unlimited overtime at double pay … A gang may work in half a dozen widely separated cities in a single year … Several foremen who have had years of experience with Caughnawagas believe they roam because they can't help doing so, it is a passion, and that their search for more overtime is just an excuse' (Mitchell [1949]1960, 21). The names of the buildings and bridges on which they worked read like the *Who's Who* of the rise of the twentieth-century city, through to the 1990s: Empire State Building, Dominion Express Building in Montreal, Golden Gate Bridge, Rainbow Bridge, Toronto-Dominion Centre in Toronto, Rockefeller Center, CN Tower, Verrazano-Narrows Bridge, and World Trade Center, plus thousands of lesser-known hospitals, stadiums, and apartment buildings. An ironworker once noted that 'almost all of New York above the 20 story level has been built by Mohawks' (Hill 1987, 36) and that nearly every tall building and bridge in Montreal had Mohawk ironworkers on it (Montgomery 2001, A6).

However, by the 1920s, working in the United States had begun to be problematic. Many Mohawks were deported or denied access to jobs. In 1926 Paul Diabo from Kahnawake had been working on the Philadelphia-Camden bridge over the Delaware River when he was forcibly deported. The Mohawks decided to fight the case, basing their defence on the 'fact that the Iroquois considered themselves to be "North American" citizens, not subject to the U.S. or Canadian definitions of citizenship' (Hill 1987, 28).

Mohawk riveter Joseph Jocks on Golden Gate Bridge, San Francisco, 1936. Photo courtesy of Kanien'kehá:ka Onkwawén:na Raotitióhkwa Collection; donated by Joseph Jocks.

Peter Rice (front centre) with a group of ironworkers, 1936. Photo courtesy of
Kanien'kehá:ka Onkwawén:na Raotitióhkwa Collection; donated by Joseph Jocks.

The case was based on the Jay Treaty of 1794 and the Treaty of Ghent, which guaranteed Mohawks the right of free passage at the border. The Mohawks won their case, which was later interpreted as one of the important milestones 'in defining the sovereign status of the Six Nations' (Hill 1987, 29).[11]

The Depression was hard, even though ironworking was one of the best ways for someone in the community to earn a living during those difficult times. Alex McComber remembers 'riding the rails like a hobo' in the early 1930s, looking for work in Detroit.[12] However, sixty Kahnawake ironworkers were denied jobs on federally funded relief projects in the United States. When the Mohawks prepared to fight this issue in the courts, the American government backed down and allowed those men to be hired.

By this time, Mohawk ironworkers were competing almost equally with others in the 'white man's world': 'construction companies sought out Indian ironworkers and treated them well with a lot of good jobs. Iroquois men were called upon for the most dangerous jobs, for the most difficult situations, and the Ironworker became a symbol of Indian manhood' (Hill 1987, 30).

Orvis Diabo, in 1949, underlined this pride by noting that he had 'heated a million rivets' in his day, working on buildings and bridges in seventeen states: 'When they talk about the men that built this country, one of the men they mean is me' (Mitchell [1949] 1960, 28). Although it has been estimated that Mohawks have never numbered more than 15 per cent of the iron-workers in New York (Rasenberger 2004, 161), they are a cohesive group. Some say that they find it easier to work with another Mohawk: 'You knew each other from home; you knew how the other men worked, and you knew their quirks of personality and wasted little time in cultural translation. But it was also true ... that you pushed yourself hard when you work with other Mohawks. In a Mohawk gang, your pride was on the line; you cared what your fellow Mohawks thought of you in a way that you did not of non-Indians. They're not expecting you to be the best you can be ... You can float a little. But if you work with guys from home, everybody expects you to be the best. You want to make them proud' (Rasenberger 2004, 116).

An Enclave in Brooklyn

By the late 1920s some Mohawk ironworkers had established homes for their families in New York, mostly in the Brooklyn neighbourhood of north Gowanus. By the 1940s there were four hundred Mohawks living in the area, which some residents called 'Downtown Caughnawaga' (Kennedy 1996, 29). 'It was always so nice,' reminisces an ironworker, 'because the whole building was just family, just Mohawks ... All the doors to all the apartments were open and you could go into any of them.' The Nevins Bar and Grill (nick-

Group of Mohawk ironworkers, North Vermont Bridge, November 1953. Left to right: Joe Jocks, Joe Horn, Joey Stacey, Louis Beauvais, Greg Splicer. Photo courtesy of Kanien'kehá:ka Onkwawén:na Raotitióhkwa Collection; donated by Louis Beauvais.

named the Wigwam) was a favourite hang-out; it was like 'Grand Central for Mohawk Indians … People sometimes picked their mail up there. They got rides back to the reservation there. They found out about jobs there.' In the early 1950s there was a sign over the Wigwam's entrance reading 'The Greatest Iron Workers in the World Pass Thru These Doors' (29).

So many Mohawks were attending nearby Cuyler Presbyterian Church by the 1930s that the pastor, Dr David Cory, even learned to speak Mohawk. He held a monthly service in Mohawk and, together with two Mohawk women, translated the Gospel of Luke and a hymnal into the language (Conly 1952, 142).

However, by 1960 there were few Mohawks left in the neighbourhood. Many had retired back to Kahnawake, including Alex McComber, and others (such as Reaghen Tarbell's family) had moved back because of the rising crime rate in Brooklyn. They did not want to raise their children there.

Group of Mohawk ironworkers. Left to right (standing): Chuck Sky, Percy Skye, Wallace Montour. Photo courtesy of Kanien'kehá:ka Onkwawén:na Raotitióhkwa Collection; donated by Agnes Pelisle.

The Commute

For those ironworkers who decided not to live in New York, but in Kahnawake, and who worked in other eastern American cities, the week-end commute between Kahnawake and the job became a fixture in their lives. It was hard, noted a retired ironworker; 'if there was work here, we'd take it … You don't want to leave your family, everything that goes with home' (National Public Radio 2002). Another said he always counted 'the sleeps' until he returned home (National Film Board of Canada 1997).

As soon as work finished on Friday afternoons, the men would begin the long drive back to Kahnawake, sharing rides, gas costs, and stories. The drive was nearly twelve hours long until the last 276 kilometres of the New York State Thruway (Interstate 87) were built to the Canadian border in 1967, upon which the drive was shortened by half. One iron-worker said, 'When you travel with other guys, yeah … coming back on a Friday is enjoyable. The stories are good all the way home' (National Public Radio 2002).

Returning on Sunday was another story: 'A lot of times it's really quiet in the car. I know how I am on Sunday afternoon. You get lonesome before you even leave.' An ironworker's wife named Rosie said, 'In this house on Sunday, I generally cook. I'll make something that the boys will like, like this weekend I'll make them corn bread and steak. And they'll eat and then they'll go to sleep around 7:00. I kiss him goodbye when he goes down, and then he'll wake up around midnight … and he's gone' (National Public Radio 2002).

The Effect on the Community

Ironworking has shaped not only the rhythm of the week but also family relationships. Randy Horne said that the time he worked on the World Trade Center was the 'most time I ever spent with my father one-on-one. I never really knew him. He was always away providing for his family. I learned to know him on the job. My father put me in the game, start bolting up right away.' Rosie observed that out of forty-two years of marriage her husband and she 'lived together as man and wife for only ten. The rest of the time he was always gone' (National Public Radio 2002).

Ironworkers had another profound and quite different effect on the community. In the past many of the ironworkers, who had often worked in all-Mohawk groups, had used the Mohawk language on the job, which helped preserve it. The language grew to meet the demands of the work because the Mohawk vocabulary did not include words for ironworking (Language among the Mohawk skywalkers 2001). Some older ironworkers laugh about having had to make up new words on the spot for different tools or for equipment (Radz 2001, C8). Today Mohawk is not used as often on the job, because many younger men do not know the language very well and many work in mixed crews.

Family finances are also shaped by the frequent 'rest periods' between jobs. Reaghen Tarbell remembers her grandmother saying to her mother, 'Around Christmas it gets really hard, so save your money.'[13] In fact, during lean times her grandmother went out to work as a welder in a New York shipyard.

The number of Mohawks becoming ironworkers began to decline during the construction slump of 1975 to 1980. The 'glamour' of working in New

York had faded a bit, the cost of travelling and living away from home was increasing, and there were more job and career opportunities to choose from at home. By 1987 only about 60 per cent of the Mohawk men in Kahnawake were ironworkers.[14]

The World Trade Center

Pride in one's work has been a constant refrain throughout Mohawk history. In the recent past one of the most famous examples to which Mohawk ironworkers would point with pride was the World Trade Center. Between 150 and 200 Mohawk ironworkers, out of 500 ironworkers on the project, worked on the site. One ironworker reminisced, 'They told me it's going to go up to 110 floors. I said, "I want to get on that building!"' (National Public Radio 2002). The terrorist attacks in September 2001 had a powerful affect on the Mohawk ironworkers who had worked on the towers or whose fathers, cousins, or uncles had. One ironworker sadly noted, 'When I seen that antenna go down on the north tower, my heart just sank with it, you know. I worked on that building. And I explained to my son that I was on there. And I don't know. It was just that emptiness when they went down' (National Public Radio 2002).

Mohawk ironworkers were among the first on the scene to try to help move the twisted steel to search for victims. They knew how to handle steel so it could be removed safely. 'The first day I walked into ground zero it was such an emotional event for all ironworkers all going in there together' (Garcia 2002). Many worked nearly around the clock in those early days. 'Our people were carrying ceremonial tobacco and they made silent prayers,' a Mohawk ironworker said. 'They asked for forgiveness from the spirits of the dead who wander until they're released' (Garcia 2002). In 2002 the ironworkers were honoured as heroes when the exhibit *Booming Out: Mohawk Ironworkers Build New York* opened on 25 April 2002. New York City mayor Michael Bloomberg proclaimed that day to be Mohawk Ironworkers Day.[15]

The Future of Ironworking

In Canada, ironworker apprenticeship programs were formalized in the mid to late 1960s. Various programs from the 1980s onward were developed to increase the number of trained Aboriginal ironworkers. According to Jacques DuBois, business manager of Montreal Local 711, more women are entering the apprenticeship program every year. Between 1999 and 2004 this local trained four groups of Native men and women. In 2004, Local 361 in Brooklyn recruited sixty men into its apprenticeship program. With pay scales reaching seventy-nine dollars an hour (including benefits) in Local 40 in Manhattan, there has never been a shortage of people applying, although many ironworker fathers try to dissuade their children from entering the trade.

The old ways are changing. There is now mandatory safety training, as well as more safety standards that, according to some ironworkers, hinder the speed of the work. Louis Stacey observes that today one must work 'the safest way and the fastest way. However, the safest way is the slowest way – but you must make both of these work to the benefit of the contractor – if the company makes money, you will make money.'[16]

In addition, the construction materials for tall buildings are changing. More structural concrete is being used, which limits the work of ironworkers. However, polymer-based structural elements are in development. Stronger than steel, they will still need to be assembled using some traditional ironworking skills. Retraining will be required, but one believes that Mohawk ironworkers will be up to this new challenge. Nor, judging by James Jacobs' feelings, will there be a shortage of young men who want to test themselves against one of the most demanding, and one of the most rewarding, jobs in the industry. As Louis Stacey observes, 'when I drive by buildings I help put up or my friends helped on, I feel pride, that I was part of that and to know that job had Mohawks on it.'[17]

Acknowledgments

I would like to thank the many people who took the time to explain ironworking, unions, and the history of Mohawk ironworking to me. I could not have written this paper without their help. Foremost, my great thanks go to Louis Stacey for his invaluable help. As well, I would like to thank Jacques DuBois, James Jacobs, Alex McComber, Martin Loft, Richard O'Kane, Reaghen Tarbell, and Bob Walsh.

Notes

1 Kahnawake is ten kilometres southwest of Montreal on the St Lawrence River on about 4,811 hectares of land. In 2009 the population was estimated to be about 7,556 people (Indian and Northern Affairs website, http://www.ainc-inac.gc.ca/ai/scr/qc/aqc/prof/Kahnawake-eng.asp/.

2 When Cross was asked which was more dangerous, doing ironwork or being

a warrior during the Oka crisis, he said, 'Defying the "white people's" laws holds the greater hazard.' He died of a heart attack on his first ironworking job after being released from prison in 1999.

3 For example, many Newfoundlanders have boomed out over the past century. Conception Harbour is famous for producing generations of ironworkers.

4 Martin Loft, Public Program Supervisor, Kanien'kehaka Raotitiohkwa Cultural Center, Kahnawake, telephone interview by the author, 26 November 2004.

5 The Mohawk Nation was part of the Six Nations Iroquois, who in turn were part of the group that anthropologists classify as Northeastern Woodlands.

6 James Jacobs, telephone interview by the author, 3 December 2004.

7 Ibid.

8 Louis Stacey, interview by the author, 6 December 2004.

9 Mohawks had already been contributing to building Canada by supplying the stone needed in the construction boom of the times.

10 Stacey, interview, 6 December 2004.

11 However, Canada does not recognize this ruling.

12 Alex McComber, telephone interview by the author, 29 November 2004.

13 Reaghen Tarbell, telephone interview by the author, 4 December 2004.

14 It was estimated in the late 1980s that there were seven thousand Indian iron-workers across North America.

15 Many of these rescue workers are still suffering from respiratory problems owing to the toxic gases and dust that they inhaled while doing the job.

16 Stacey, interview by author, 6 December 2004.

17 Ibid.

Bibliography

Baylis, Sarah. 2002. An image welded to the skyline. *New York Times*, 7 July, p. 2.29.

Blanchard, David. 1983. High Steel! The Kahnawake Mohawk and the high construction trade. *Journal of Ethnic Studies* 11 (2): 41–60.

Booming Out: Mohawk Ironworkers Build New York. 2002. Smithsonian National Museum of the American Indian. http://www.sites.si.edu/exhibitions/exhibits/archived_exhibitions/booming/main.htm.

Cherry, Mike. 1974. *On High Steel: The Education of an Ironworker.* New York: Quadrangle Press.

Conly, Robert L. 1952. The Mohawks scrape the sky. *National Geographic Magazine,* July, 133–42.

Cross, Ronald, and Hélène Sévigny. 1994. *Lasagna.* Vancouver: Talonbooks.

Egan, Kelly. 2002. The natives who built New York. *Ottawa Citizen,* 28 August, p. A3.

Elmes, Michael B., and Pushkala Prasad. Circa 2002. Resisting in high places: A study of First Nation Mohawk ironworkers. http://group.aomonline.org/cms/Meetings/Seattle/PDF/12362.pdf.

Garcia, Maria. 2002. Dance honors courage of the steelworkers. *Windspeaker*, June. http://goliath.ecnext.com/coms2/gi_0199-1757919/Dance-honors-courage-of-the.html.

Hill, Richard. 1987. *Skywalkers: A History of Indian Ironworkers.* Brantford, ON: Woodland Indian Cultural Centre.

International Society of Bridge, Structural, Ornamental, and Reinforcing Iron Workers. About the ironworkers: History. http://www.ironworkers.org/about/history.aspx.

Kalman, Hal. 1994. *History of Canadian Architecture.* Vol. 2. Toronto: Oxford University Press.

Kennedy, Randy. 1996. An Indian community flourished and faded in a section of Brooklyn. *New York Times*, 12 December, p. 29.

Kilgannon, Corey. 2002. Athletes in the sky wrestle high steel. *New York Times*, 15 September, p. 14WC.4.

Language among the Mohawk skywalkers. 2001. Episode 1, *Finding Our Talk.* Written and directed by Paul M. Rickard. Mushkeg Media Inc. Video recording.

Mitchell, Joseph. [1949] 1960. The Mohawks in high steel. In *Apologies to the Iroquois*, ed. Edmond Wilson. New York: Farrar, Strauss and Cudahy.

Mohawk. 2000. In *Canadian Encyclopaedia 2001.* Toronto: McClelland and Stewart.

Montgomery, Sue. 2001. Farewell to an ironworker. *Montreal Gazette*, 9 July, p. A6.

National Film Board of Canada. 1965. *High Steel.* Directed by Don Owen; produced by Julian Biggs. Video recording.

– 1997. *Spudwrench: Kahnawake Man.* Produced by Alanis Obomsawin. Video recording.

National Public Radio. 2002. Profile: Mohawk steelworkers who worked the World Trade Towers. In *All Things Considered*, 1 July. Radio script.

Rasenberger, Jim. 2004. *High Steel: The Daring Men Who Built the World's Greatest Skyline.* New York: Harper Collins.

Radz, Matt. 2001. Rising to language challenge. *Montreal Gazette*, 1 February, p. C8.

United States. Department of Labor. 2004. Structural and Reinforcing Iron and Metal Workers. Bureau of Labor Statistics Bulletin 2540. In *Occupational Outlook Handbook*, 2004–5 edition. Washington, DC: Department of Labor.

Profile of Dorothy Grant (1955–)

Haida, Fashion Designer, and Businesswoman

Dorothy Grant is a woman of many talents. She is an artist, fashion designer, businesswoman, and role model. She is best known for her 'wearable art,' clothing that can be both worn and displayed.[1] She has achieved domestic and international success, and her designs are popular with Aboriginals and non-Aboriginals alike.[2] Grant's designs are found in museums and art galleries throughout North America, and her business acumen has won accolades from various business communities.[3]

Dorothy Grant was born on 14 March 1955 in Hydaburg, Alaska.[4] She credits much of her success to her female relatives,[5] saying, 'Their sense of strength and identity as Haida women has impressed me since I was a little girl.'[6] She notes that female Haida elders are responsible for transferring culture to younger generations, a tradition that she continues by incorporating Haida imagery in her clothing designs and in her art.[7]

Grant began sewing as a teenager.[8] She apprenticed with Haida elder Florence Edenshaw-Davidson, who taught her Haida history and spruce-root basket weaving.[9] This experience increased Grant's appreciation of Haida traditions, and in 1977 she began making button blankets (ceremonial clothing worn at potlatches), a process she refers to as 'sculpting on cloth.'[10] She married Robert Davidson, a fellow Haida artist, with whom she collaborated artistically and hosted potlatches.[11]

In the late 1980s she attended a fashion design school in Vancouver, where her work gained attention.[12] For example, her *Raven Creation Tunic* was displayed at Expo '86 in Vancouver. The dress would later be transferred to the Canadian Museum of Civilization, along with another of her creations, the *Hummingbird Copper Panel Dress*.[13] Several of her other designs are owned by the National Gallery of Canada.[14]

In 1994 Grant opened a boutique in downtown Vancouver, where she sells items belonging to her labels, Feastwear and Dorothy Grant, as well as jewellery and limited edition, silk-screened prints.[15] Annual sales are near

Dorothy Grant (right). Photo courtesy of Terry Lusty.

the half-million-dollar mark.[16] Her clothing has been worn by former Minister of Indian Affairs Jane Stewart, Assembly of First Nations Grand Chief Phil Fontaine, Inuit singer Susan Aglukark,[17] and such media personalities as Robin Williams and Marie Osmond.[18]

Dorothy Grant has won many awards for her business savvy and for her artistic ability. In March 1993 she won the Best Professional Designer Award at the Winds of Change design competition, organized by the Canadian Council for Native Business.[19] She was conferred an honorary doctorate by the University of Northern British Columbia in 1998.[20] The following year she won the National Aboriginal Achievement Award in Business and Commerce[21] and was invited to participate in the Team Canada Mission to Japan.[22] She has displayed her collections at several museums including the Poeh Museum in Santa Fe in 2005 and the Vancouver Art Gallery in 2006.[23] Grant won the Individual Achievement Award from the British Columbia Aboriginal Business Awards in 2009.[24]

Dorothy Grant continues to operate her boutique and maintain her website, www.dorothygrant.com. She conducts speaking tours[25] and is considering expanding her business to include interior decorating.[26]

BRANDI DURDA

Notes

1 Margaret B. Blackman, 'Feastwear: Haida art goes couture,' *American Indian Art Magazine*, Autumn 1992, http://www.dorothygrant.com.
2 Blackman, 'Feastwear.'
3 Vesta Giles, 'Fashion designer: Dorothy Grant,' *Indian Artist*, Fall 1997.
4 Dorothy Grant, *Dorothy Grant Boutique*, http://www.dorothygrant.com.
5 Giles, 'Fashion designer.'
6 'Native designer makes art out of fashion,' *First Nations Drum*, December 1999, http://firstnationsdrum.com/1999/12/native-designer-makes-art-out-of-fashion (accessed 22 January 2011).
7 Blackman, 'Feastwear.'
8 Giles, 'Fashion designer.'
9 Dorothy Grant, http://www.dorothygrant.com.
10 Doreen Jensen and Polly Sargent, *Robes of Power, Totem Poles on Cloth* (University of British Columbia Press in association with the UBC Museum of Anthropology, 1986). http://www.dorothygrant.com.
11 Giles, 'Fashion designer.'
12 Dorothy Grant, http://www.dorothygrant.com.
13 http://www.dorothygrant.com/Exhibitions (accessed 27 January 2011).
14 Ibid.
15 'Native designer makes art out of fashion.'
16 Joan Black, 'Dorothy Grant: Making clothes for her sisters was beginning of great career,' *Windspeaker* April 1999, 14.
17 Indian and Northern Affairs Canada, 'Aboriginal peoples profiles artists: Dorothy Grant, fashion designer,' 31 December 2002.
18 Ibid.
19 Ibid.
20 Ibid.
21 Ibid.
22 Department of Foreign Affairs and International Trade, 'First Nations and Inuit art,' http://www.canadainternational.gc.ca/detroit/about-a_propos/first_nations-indien.aspx?lang=eng (accessed 27 January 2011).
23 http://www.dorothygrant.com/pr/bio.html (accessed 17 April 2009).
24 British Columbia Achievement Foundation, 'Two honoured with Aboriginal achievement award,' 26 January 2009, http://www.bcachievement.com/news/news.php?id=53.
25 Giles, 'Fashion designer.'
26 Black, 'Dorothy Grant.'

Labour Relations in the Rupertsland Fur Trade and the Formation of Métis Identity

LEANNA PARKER

The creation of a mixed-descent population is an experience common to most, if not all, colonized countries.[1] However, it is only in a few colonies that these mixed-descent populations have developed a distinct identity, separate from both the colonizers and the Indigenous peoples. In parts of Canada, especially the west, the mixed-descent population was formed as a result of interactions between Europeans and Indigenous peoples during the fur trade; these descendants developed a distinct identity and came to be known as the Métis. The question of the formation of Métis identity in Canada is one that has been contemplated by several scholars.[2] These scholars have taken various approaches to the question, many focusing solely on the social and political aspects of Métis history. While such approaches can be useful, they ignore the crucial influence of labour relations in the Rupertsland fur trade in the development and expression of a distinct Métis identity in western Canada.[3] The specific labour relations of the Rupertsland fur trade allowed a cohesiveness and an interconnectedness to develop between the Aboriginal labourers and their European employers that emphasized the interdependencies inherent in the industry.[4]

While these labour relations were an important catalyst for the development and expression of a distinct Métis identity, it is too simplistic to suggest that they alone encouraged such a phenomenon. Several external influences in the fur trade were also critical to this development. The four most important were the needs of the colonial employers regarding land tenure, the economic opportunities available to the people of mixed descent, the educational opportunities available to the people of mixed descent, and the length of time that these labour relations operated. Combined with the use of personal labour organization in the Rupertsland fur trade, these influences encouraged the development and expression of a distinct Métis identity in Canada.

Furthermore, when the economic roles of the Métis in Rupertsland, and by extension their identity, were threatened by external forces, the Métis elite were able to unite the mixed-descent population as a distinct people to protect their position in the region's society and to exert their own economic and political pressures. The struggles of the Métis that culminated in the Red River Rebellion of 1869–70 had a significant and lasting impact on the political and economic development of western Canada.

Labour Relations in the Rupertsland Fur Trade

Canada's economic history has been dominated by the exportation of raw materials and the importation of manufactured goods. The fur trade was one of the country's first important export industries. Although the fur trade was conducted on some level in almost every region of Canada, it was only in Rupertsland that the fur trade developed as a large-scale economic activity. In this region two main companies, the Hudson's Bay Company (HBC) and the North West Company (NWC), established and maintained a profitable trade until 1821, when they merged to form one company under the name of the Hudson's Bay Company. Although the trading companies operated under a mercantilist system in London,[5] the economic conditions that they faced in Rupertsland differed considerably from those being experienced in London at the time. As a result, the trading companies were forced to adjust their trading practices and their labour relations. The labour relations that were created under these conditions have been classified as 'personal labour organization' by Canadian economist H. Clare Pentland.[6]

Pentland argued that four basic economic conditions must exist in order for personal labour organization to develop – all of which were present in Rupertsland. The first economic condition is that there must be a scarcity of labourers. This condition was created in Rupertsland in two main ways: first, the fur-trading posts were far removed from any European settlements, and the HBC and the NWC were constantly struggling to find labourers from Europe or eastern Canada who were willing to relocate to such a remote, unsettled territory. Second, the fur companies required skilled labourers, which applied to both the European labourers working directly for the companies and the Aboriginal trappers and middlemen engaging in trade with the companies. The need for skilled labour restricted the number of potential workers available for employment with the fur companies.[7]

The second economic condition required for personal labour organization, identified by Pentland, is that the labourers should be able to hinder production by leaving their employment or by producing inferior-quality work. The European fur traders' lack of technical knowledge and experience in trapping made them dependent on the continual participation of the Aboriginal peoples in the trade. Thus, the Aboriginal peoples were in a position to disrupt trade and hinder production if they so chose – and they did choose to do so from time to time. For example, if trappers could not meet the needs of their families by trapping for the fur companies, they would stop trapping commercially and find new means to meet their needs (Ray 1984, 16–17; Innis 1956, 174). Also, Indian or Métis wage labourers who were engaged directly by the trading companies could interfere with the trade by deserting or refusing to work at an efficient pace (Judd 1980b, 311; Burley 1997, 156–93; Tough 1996, 54). Clearly, employees of the trading companies could interfere with production.

The third economic condition that Pentland identified as necessary for the creation of personal labour organization is an employer monopoly. Prior to 1821, several fur companies operated in Rupertsland. However, Rupertsland encompassed a vast territory, and the costs of transportation were considerable. Thus, direct competition between the companies was discouraged. The fur market was too unstable for companies to compete directly by offering higher wages and lower priced merchandise. Instead, they worked together to keep wages low and the costs of merchandise high by focusing on indirect forms of competition, such as maintaining personal relationships with employees and trappers and constantly seeking new individuals with whom to engage in trade. In this sense, the trading companies operated under oligopolistic conditions in much the same way as employers with a monopoly operate. Although the HBC enjoyed a brief monopoly after the 1821 merger, free traders and the American Fur Company began competing with the company, particularly in the Red River area.[8] Regardless of this competition, however, the high operating costs of the trading companies continued to keep direct competition to a minimum, and oligopolistic conditions remained.

The final economic condition identified by Pentland is that employers must use positive incentives to obtain satisfactory work from their employees. When commercial trading was first introduced to Rupertsland, the European traders soon discovered that the Aboriginal trappers did not respond to changes in the market in the same manner that European employees did. For example, when the fur companies were in a position to offer higher prices for prime pelts, they hoped that the trappers would respond by bringing in a greater number of pelts. However, this was not the case. Unlike the European capitalists, the Aboriginal trappers were not, in general, concerned with accumulating vast material wealth. As such, when the price of pelts was high, they could bring in fewer pelts to obtain the goods that they needed. Much to the frustration of the fur companies, when the price of pelts rose, the number of pelts returned to the post fell.[9] The European traders also discovered that they could not refuse to accept poorer quality pelts, which they could not sell on the European market; if they refused to trade for these pelts, the Aboriginal trappers were likely to stop trapping commercially (Innis 1956, 106; Ray and Freeman 1978, 155). As a result of these unique responses of the Aboriginal trappers to the market, the fur companies had to use positive incentives, instead of financial ones, in order to encourage them to bring in as many high-quality pelts as possible.

Such positive incentives included rewarding reliable trappers with gifts, gratuities, and promotions. For example, those Aboriginal trappers who provided the best-quality pelts or brought in the most followers were given commodities such as knives, gun flints, hooks, awls, needles, thread, and beads as rewards. Some of the best trappers and leaders were given the title 'trading captain' by the HBC and, as a result, were given preferential treatment in the hopes that their status within their bands would increase and even more trappers would follow their lead, thereby increasing the overall fur returns for the company (Innis 1956, 320; Ray 1974, 141; Ray and Freeman 1978, 228). In general, the HBC only hired Aboriginal men as labourers when they would not be engaged in trapping, and often hired only the most reliable trappers. The company hoped that these practices would encourage them to continue trapping when they were not employed (HBCA B.89/b/3, George Keith; Judd 1980b, 308; Ray 1984, 10).[10] The fur companies used such positive incentives to encourage the work ethics that they believed were necessary to sustain a profitable trade.

Pentland also argued that at times, when skilled labour and continuous employment was required, personal labour organization could develop more quickly. As discussed previously, the fur companies were required to hire (or trade with) individuals who had specific technical knowledge, and so, in this sense, the companies required skilled labourers. In general, Aboriginal trappers were engaged seasonally in the fur trade, not continuously; nevertheless, the economic conditions faced by the fur traders in Rupertsland were such that the companies established a system of personal labour organization in order to sustain a profitable trade.

Under standard capitalist labour systems, employees are responsible for their own social overhead costs. Social overhead costs are costs associated with providing for the physical survival of one's self and dependants. In most cases employees are expected to cover these costs through the wages they are paid. Under the system of personal labour organization, however, it is the employer who carries the social overhead costs of the employees. In this situation, the employer not only provides the employees with a wage but also provides other materials to help them meet their physical needs, in order for them to continue working (Pentland 1981, 29). As a result, both institutional and personal relationships develop between the employer and the employees. To ensure that personal labour organization runs efficiently, a system of hierarchy, status, and paternalism develops (Pentland 1959, 453).

In Rupertsland the fur companies carried the social overhead costs of both their European and their Aboriginal employees in several different ways. For example, some company employees were paid in kind. In other words, instead of receiving a cash wage, employees were given commodities such as clothing, blankets, tobacco, brandy, and any additional equipment needed to accomplish specific tasks (HBCA B.49/d/99, list of Indians; B.89/d/107, post expenses; B.89/d/145, general charges; B.89/d/198, credit to widow; B89/d/200a, list of twine; B.89/d/208, monthly issues; B.303/d/3a; account books; Innis 1956, 238–40). While other employees did receive cash wages, extra gratuities were often added, such as room and board and other equipment needed to perform certain tasks (HBCA B.89/d/150, account books; Judd 1980a, 128). The fur companies could minimize the amount of capital needed in Rupertsland by paying wages in this manner.

The Hudson's Bay Company in particular carried the social overhead costs of their Aboriginal employees also through the debt system and through relief. Aboriginal trappers needed specific supplies and equipment to spend a season trapping commercially. The HBC ensured that the trappers had this equipment at the start of each season by extending credit. Similarly, in years when fur populations were low, the HBC would write off bad debts to ensure that the trappers would continue trapping commercially (Ray 1990, 188–9; Tough 1992b, 403).

Relief and food were also provided to Aboriginal employees and their families during times of famine and hardship (HBCA B.89/b/3, Correspondence outwards; Judd 1980a, 130). As the following table demonstrates, nearly 22 per cent of the food provisions at the Il a la Crosse post in northwestern Saskatchewan were given to the families of HBC employees, indicating the importance of providing for the employees' dependants as a way to ensure that the men could continue their participation in the trade. Carrying the social overhead costs of their employees allowed the fur companies to preserve their labour force and maintain a continuous and profitable trade.

The debt system and the provision of relief and food encouraged the development of personal bonds and obligations between the employees and their employers, the fur companies. These bonds and obligations were important to the system of personal labour organization as they allowed the establishment of rigid occupational hierarchies and paternalistic manage-

Food expenditures (%), Il a la Crosse, 1875–80

	November 1875	December 1875	April 1876	August 1876*	April 1880	December 1880
Officers' mess	10.22	12.08	14.05	2.28 (*11.54*)	12.88	4.53
Servants	43.67	35.82	46.54	10.03 (*50.82*)	44.36	52.29
Servants' families	22.47	19.08	21.26	6.87 (*34.81*)	18.95	15.41
For voyages	9.11	3.53	4.47	80.27		4.40	12.69
Strangers	1.25	6.49	6.96	0.32 (*1.59*)	12.94	10.01
Sales	13.62	22.99	6.72	0.24 (*1.24*)	6.47	5.08

Source: HBCA (1875–6, 1880).
* The numbers in italics in this column indicate the percentage excluding the provisions sent on voyages.

ment techniques, which were necessary to ensure that the companies could still operate profitably.

In the Hudson's Bay Company the officers (for example, factors, chief traders, and clerks) occupied the upper echelon of the occupational hierarchy, while the servants (for example, boatmen, tradesmen, and general labourers) occupied the lower. The majority of HBC employees were in this servant class, and the Aboriginal employees generally remained at the very bottom of the hierarchy (Judd 1980b, 305; Ray 1984, 10).

After the merger of the HBC and the NWC in 1821, the occupational hierarchy became even more distinct. Prior to the merger, employees of mixed descent had considerable upward mobility within the trading companies. After 1821, the HBC introduced racial hiring practices such that ethnicity became an influential element in the determination of a servant's future. Only those mixed-descent men who had been educated outside of Rupertsland and whose fathers were prominent and active officers were able to achieve officer status themselves (Judd 1980b, 312). Thus, after the merger, ethnicity became increasingly influential in structuring the occupational hierarchies in the trading companies, and institutional racism was, in a sense, introduced to Rupertsland. As a result, there was a decline in the opportunities for employees of mixed descent to advance in the company.

The occupational hierarchies in the fur trade were emphasized by both a physical and a social separation between their various levels. A social separation was created through the status, prestige, and responsibility allotted to those individuals filling the upper echelons of the hierarchy. Separate living quarters for the officers, the servants, and the tradesmen created physical separation (Judd 1980a, 128; Burley 1997, 14–15). Additionally, Aboriginal trappers were kept physically separate from company employees, especially at HBC posts, by being required to trade through the 'hole-in-the-wall' (Ray and Freeman 1978, 58).[11] The one exception to this rule was the Aboriginal trading captains, who were allowed to enter the trading

room directly. In this sense, HBC officers imposed occupational stratification on the Aboriginal trappers as well.

Although initially the trading companies did not encourage families and
settlement in Rupertsland, over time they did begin to support controlled
settlement in certain regions. These settlements then became areas in which
the companies could find future employees and in which children could be
socialized to accept the occupational hierarchies in the fur trade; through
these measures the work force was stabilized. Most children who went on to
enter the fur trade achieved the same level of occupation and status as their
fathers had before them (Innis 1956, 161–3; Judd 1980b, 308). In this way the
organization of the fur trade was sustained for nearly two centuries.

The occupational hierarchies in the fur companies were maintained
through paternalistic management techniques. In order for the trade
to remain profitable, the officers had to win loyal service from the servant class, and such loyal service could only be won if they could establish
personal contacts with the servants while still maintaining their superior
status. Often the most effective manner to do this was to display paternal
interest in the employees and demonstrate superior intelligence and fair-
ness (Burley 1997, 202; Innis 1956, 248). Owing to the labour shortages and
other economic conditions in Rupertsland, the trading company employers could not rely on the legal authority of employment contracts alone to
encourage appropriate work habits. The labourers demanded fair treatment
and would not tolerate any abuses of the system by the officers (Burley
1997, 15). For example, both before and after the 1821 merger, HBC servants staged various strikes, acts of resistance, and protests. Some scholars
have suggested that these conflicts were mainly concerned with low wages
(Makahonuk 1988). Edith Burley, however, argues that while wage disputes
occurred occasionally between HBC officers and the men with whom they
were negotiating *new* employment contracts, wage disputes initiated by
employees who were already on contract were rare, especially after 1821
(Burley 1997, 202). Instead, the most serious disputes concerned working conditions and the treatment of the employees by the officers. Moreover, these disputes were not intended to threaten or challenge the overall
employment hierarchy imposed by the HBC. As Burley (1997) explains,
'there is also no indication that the company's workers were developing
what one might term a "modern" view of employment relations and starting to behave like modern workers bargaining over pay and benefits in a
capitalist system whose economic laws they had come to accept. Instead,
they continued to operate within a traditional framework and to see their
relationship with their employer as a moral one that was no mere monetary
transaction' (197). In this sense, HBC employees were not protesting the

hierarchical employment scheme itself; they were protesting the aspects of their treatment that contradicted their expectations of the paternal obligations of their employers.

In a similar manner, paternalism was used to 'shape' Aboriginal responses to the trade. Many traders spoke of the need to 'control' Aboriginal trappers with a 'firm hand.' For example, in a letter written at Fort Garry in 1822, Governor George Simpson commented, 'I have made it my study to examine the nature and character of Indians and however repugnant it may be to our feelings, I am convinced that they must be ruled with a rod of Iron to bring and keep them in a proper state of subordination, and the most certain way to effect this is by letting them feel their dependence upon us' (Innis 1956, 248). The firmness and strictness used with the Aboriginal trappers was an important part of the paternalistic management techniques used by the factors and traders. These techniques allowed the fur companies to establish a highly centralized organization that was crucial to the success of the fur trade. Company paternalism did not end when employees retired from the service. The Hudson's Bay Company extended special prices to retired servants, provided pensions, rehired destitute employees, and granted land in Red River.

After the period of intense competition that culminated in the merger of the HBC and the NWC, Governor Simpson attempted to reduce the costs of trade in several different ways. For example, he laid off a significant number of employees and closed the redundant posts. He also worked to reduce transportation costs by moving supplies between Red River and St Paul (instead of York Factory as had previously been the case) and by increasing the size of boats (Innis 1956, 292, 343; Judd 1980a, 130).

Simpson also introduced new hiring practices after the merger, mainly based on race and ethnicity. Although not entirely successful, he preferred to hire Canadians and Orcadians and to minimize the number of Scottish and Irish servants; however, there were often not enough competent men in Canada and the Orkney Islands to fill positions in the company. The new hiring practices had a significant impact on the men of mixed descent in the trade as well. Simpson believed that the Métis were lazy, disobedient, and worthy only of the lowest levels of employment. Thus, the career opportunities for Métis men declined steadily after 1821 (Burley 1997, 93–105; Judd 1980a, 130–4, 137, 145; Judd 1980b, 310–11).

Gradually the HBC began to implement changes after 1821 that allowed the company to reduce its need to cover the social overhead costs of its employees. As the settlement at Red River began to grow, it formed a labour pool from which the company could hire temporary employees as needed and which started to reduce the labour shortage that the company had always faced (Innis 1956, 309–10; Judd 1980a, 138). By the 1860s, personal labour organization was declining in the Rupertsland fur trade, although it would not entirely disappear until well into the twentieth century. The growth of the settlement at Red River and the increasing pressures exerted on the mixed-descent population there after the merger, however, had an important influence on the political development of this settlement and led, at least in part, to the events that culminated in the Red River resistance of 1869–70.

The Development and Expression of Métis Identity in Red River

The beginnings of a distinct and separate Métis identity were established when the mixed-descent population was given a unique and specialized economic role in the fur trade. Although the fur trade was conducted in several regions in Canada, it was in Rupertsland that the Métis first used their identity to protect their economic and political rights. Thus, the role of the Métis in the fur trade only partially explains the development and expression of their identity. In particular, there were four crucial factors beyond labour relations that encouraged this phenomenon.

The system of land tenure that existed in the Rupertsland fur trade differed significantly from the system of land tenure that was common to areas of large-scale agricultural settlement in other regions of Canada. Agricultural settlement required the agriculturalists to exercise complete control and ownership over the land. This requirement led, in part, to the belief that the Aboriginal peoples were 'in the way.' Racial segregation and stereotypical views of Aboriginal peoples as 'backward' and 'inferior' were developed to justify the displacement of Aboriginal peoples from the land. The attitudes and racism that developed in areas of widespread agricultural settlement severely limited the opportunities for Aboriginal peoples to participate in the economy. However, such was not the case in the Rupertsland fur trade.

Unlike agriculture, which involves the production of a commodity, the fur trade involved an exchange of commodities, albeit unequal. In other words, the European traders exchanged manufactured goods for the furs and the country products harvested by the Aboriginal peoples. As such, the trading companies did not have to enforce absolute land ownership in the same manner as did the agriculturalists, at least initially. Although the royal charter of 1670 provided the HBC with legal proprietorship of Rupertsland, the company did little to enforce this proprietorship and allowed the Aboriginal peoples to remain in at least partial control of the land (Burley 1997, 23–4; Bryce 1900, 12–19). Thus, even though attitudes

of European superiority existed in the Rupertsland fur trade, these attitudes were far less severe than in other regions of Canada, and opportunities for Aboriginal peoples to participate actively in the economy were
available.

The attitudes of the fur traders towards Aboriginal peoples, especially in comparison to those of other settlers, influenced the economic and
employment opportunities available to Aboriginal peoples in Rupertsland. Within the fur trade, men of mixed descent were often considered
more desirable for employment than were men of full Aboriginal descent,
at least prior to 1821. It was most common for men of mixed descent to
find positions in the lower ranks of the trading companies, especially the
HBC. Often, the mixed-descent men were hired as general labourers and
employed in constructing and navigating canoes, initiating trade with
Aboriginal trappers, acting as interpreters, and provisioning the posts.
However, some of the sons of prominent company officers were able to
advance relatively high in the employment hierarchy before 1821. Some
were even promoted to the position of trader at secondary posts. The men
who were promoted to these ranks were, in general, those whose fathers
were influential and wealthy enough to ensure that they received a formal
education (Giraud 1986, 334–5; Judd 1980b, 310).

The paternalistic management techniques that were used to maintain the
system of personal labour organization in the fur trade worked most efficiently when there was an education gap between employers and employees and as long as the employers could demonstrate a level of sophistication
well above that of their employees. In general, as the knowledge and skills
of the employees engaged in personal labour organization began to rise, so
too did the episodes of labour militancy and the creation of labour unions
(Pentland 1979, 22). In Rupertsland it was the mixed-descent sons of the
most influential fur traders who were educated formally and who were the
first to start closing the gap between employer and employee (Brown 1982,
59). It was also these mixed-descent men who began to accumulate capital,
prestige, and status in Rupertsland and who eventually led the struggles
against the Dominion of Canada.

The final external factor that influenced the development and expression
of a Métis identity in Canada was the length of time during which these
labour relations operated. While in other parts of Canada the colonial governments, and later the Dominion government, regulated and controlled the
Aboriginal population, in Rupertsland the only governing body for nearly
two centuries was the Hudson's Bay Company and, to a lesser extent, the
other trading companies. While the HBC did try to regulate its employees,
enforcement was not always effective. Thus the mixed-descent population

grew, relatively unimpeded by any formal regulations, and created an economic niche for itself. Over a significant period of time the mixed-descent people were able to develop a unique identity that was distinct from both the European and the Aboriginal populations in Rupertsland. Moreover, other peoples in Rupertsland recognized the mixed-descent people as a distinct group as well.

However, beginning in the mid-nineteenth century, as the personal labour organization of the early fur trade began to decline, the Métis who had been able to accumulate capital, prestige, and status began to lose their prominent positions within the fur trade. This shift led to a number of developments through which the Métis worked to protect their position within Rupertsland society, especially at Red River. At the same time that the HBC started to restructure the trade and phase out personal labour organization, the American fur market started to grow in importance. This new fur market interfered with the HBC monopoly in the Red River region, and a desire for free trade started to develop. As the HBC began to lose some of the fur traffic to the American markets, it responded by tightening its trade restrictions under the authority of its royal charter, arguing that trading outside of the company was, in fact, violating the law (Bumsted 1996, 32). To illustrate the point, in the spring of 1849 the HBC arrested four Métis men and charged them with illicitly trafficking in furs.

Guillaume Sayer was tried on 17 May 1849. Although he admitted his guilt, the HBC and the Council of Assiniboia did not have any means by which to enforce the court's decision, and, as such, he was not punished. Furthermore, the cases against the other three men were never brought to trial (Bumsted 1996, 32; Ross 1972, 373–6). This trial was an important event in the expression of the economic rights of the Red River Métis. While the HBC was trying to protect its failing trading monopoly, the Métis of Red River (particularly those involved in the commercial aspect of the fur trade) were interested in establishing free trade in an effort to improve their position within the trade, which had been declining since 1821. Thus, the inability of the HBC to enforce its regulations allowed the Métis to establish a de facto free trade in the Red River area and shift the balance of power slightly, such that they were in a better position to profit from the trade.

In the two decades that followed the Sayer trial the HBC continued to restructure the trade and phase out personal labour organization. While the company wanted to re-establish itself as a basic retail business and to stop covering the social overhead costs of its employees and the Aboriginal peoples in Rupertsland, it still recognized that the conditions in Rupertsland meant that the Aboriginal peoples did require assistance with their social overhead costs. As a result, at the end of the 1860s, the HBC negotiated a transfer of its proprietorship over Rupertsland to the Dominion of Canada and, in so doing, transferred the responsibility for carrying the social over-head costs of the people of the region from the company to the Canadian government (Tough 1992a, 241–3).

The deed of surrender was extremely favourable to the HBC and provided it with a £300,000 cash payment and a land grant of almost seven million acres. The deed also ensured that the company would not be responsible for paying for Aboriginal land claims or providing for the social welfare of Aboriginal peoples as they had prior to 1870 (Tough 1992a, 399–400). While the deed of surrender amply compensated the shareholders of the HBC, it undermined the already declining economic position of the Métis. With little left to lose and with a chance to protect their economic power and position in Rupertsland, some of the elite of the mixed-descent population decided to resist the unilateral decision of the HBC board of directors to transfer control over Rupertsland to the Dominion of Canada.

The majority of men who formed the Convention of Forty – the representatives of the Red River settlement who were responsible for drafting the list of rights that the Métis demanded as terms of reference for the entrance of Rupertsland to the Dominion of Canada – were members of the commercial and governing elite of Red River. For example, Louis Riel was the son of a respected free trader and had been educated as a lawyer; his mother's family were prominent landowners in Red River. James Ross was the son of the respected historian Alexander Ross and was an influential figure in Red River politics. John Sutherland became a senator after the resistance. Thomas Bunn was the son of Dr William Bunn. Alfred Boyd was an English merchant and became the first provincial secretary of Manitoba. Ambroise Lépine was the son of a prominent buffalo hunter. Charles Nolin was an educated farmer, trader, and merchant in Red River. John Black was a judge for the district of Assiniboia (Bumsted 1996, 311–12; Ens 1996, 130; Morton 1965, 6–12; Siggins 1994, 24).

Thus, it was predominantly members of the Red River elite who initiated the resistance. They were in the most advantageous positions not only to recognize the inequity of the HBC's actions but also to act upon it through the power and status they had achieved in Rupertsland society because of their economic positions, education, and experience. In this sense, then, the Métis resistance of 1869–70 was an attempt to shift the balance of power so that the London board of directors and the Dominion of Canada would not be the only ones to profit from the transfer. The leaders of the resistance wanted to ensure that a portion of the HBC's economic and political gains would remain in Rupertsland and become centred in Red River so that their prominent positions in this society might be protected or enhanced.

In order to gain popular support for their efforts to renegotiate the entrance of Rupertsland to Canada, some of the leaders emphasized their unique identity as mixed-descent people and their oppression (defined by their ancestry) at the hands of the new controlling interests of the HBC and Rupertsland. After considerable negotiations between the provisional government of Red River and the government of Canada, the Manitoba Act was passed in May 1870, and the province of Manitoba was admitted to the Dominion of Canada. Métis land rights were formally protected in this Act. Although ultimately the 1869–70 Métis resistance did not achieve lasting economic and political advantages for the people of mixed descent, it did succeed in solidifying a unique Métis identity that was, and continues to be, formally acknowledged by the Canadian government.

Conclusion

Although the personal labour organization that characterized the Rupertsland fur trade prior to the late 1860s laid the foundation for the development and expression of a Métis identity in Canada, there were four important and interrelated external factors that influenced this development, relating to land tenure, economic and employment opportunities, educational opportunities, and the duration of the labour relations. These external factors, together with the labour relations in the fur trade, provided the necessary conditions for the people of mixed descent in Red River to develop a distinct identity that they ultimately used to protect their interests in Rupertsland. The actions of the Métis in Red River had considerable influence on the political and economic development of western Canada.

Notes

1 This paper is based largely on a portion of the research that was conducted for a master's degree thesis: Leanna Parker (1999).

2 See for example, Devine (2004), Dickason (1982), Peterson (1982, 1985).

3 Rupertsland was the territory granted to the Hudson's Bay Company under

its royal charter of 1670. According to this document, Rupertsland included 'all those seas, streights [sic], and bays, rivers, lakes, creeks, and sounds, in whatsoever latitude they shall be, that lie within the entrance of the streights commonly called Hudson's Streights together, with all the lands, countries, and territories upon the coasts and confines of the seas, streights, bays, lakes, rivers, creeks, and sounds aforesaid, which are not now actually possessed by any of our subjects or by the subjects of any other Christian prince or State [sic]' (quoted in Bryce [1900, 15]). This territory came to include parts of what are now Ontario, Quebec, the Prairie provinces, and Nunavut.

4 For an alternative approach to fur trade history and Métis identity that focuses on the social and political relations, particularly with regard to women and family relationships, see Brown (1980) and Van Kirk (1980).

5 Mercantilism refers to an early form of capitalism that focused on the exchange of commodities. The system supported the spread of colonization as colonies were established to supply materials and become markets for their home nations.

6 This chapter is heavily reliant on Pentland's theory of personal labour organization because it best fits the economic and labour conditions of the Rupertsland fur trade (Pentland 1981, 60). Few scholars have made much use of economic and labour theory when considering the fur trade, with the notable exceptions of Innis (1956), Ray (1990, 188–202), and Ray and Freeman (1978). However, the limited use of such theory can, at times, lead to a more vague understanding of the complex economic and labour relations in the trade, especially between Aboriginal and non-Aboriginal peoples. As such, I make extensive use of Pentland's theory in order to ground my discussion of labour relations in the fur trade. A larger discussion of this theoretical issue can be found in the second chapter of my thesis (Parker 1999).

7 Although the Aboriginal trappers and middlemen were not employees in the formal sense of the term, the fur companies treated and responded to these men in the same manner that they treated and responded to their European employees; therefore, the Aboriginal men can, in essence, be considered employees (Innis 1956, 133–4).

8 The Red River Settlement was an important settlement area that developed during the fur trade. It was located at present-day Winnipeg, Manitoba.

9 This phenomenon is generally referred to as a *backward sloping supply curve*.

10 One exception at times were the mixed-descent sons who were hired more formally by the HBC and were not expected to trap (HBCA B.89/d/3, George Keith; Judd 1980b, 308; Ray 1984, 10).

11 As the name implies, trade was conducted through a hole that had been cut into the wall of the storage room where the trade goods were kept.

Bibliography

Brown, Jennifer S.H. 1980. *Strangers in Blood: Fur Trade Company Families in Indian Country*. Vancouver: University of British Columbia Press.
– 1982. Children of the early fur trades. In *Childhood and Family in Canadian History*, ed. Joy Parr, 44–68. Toronto: McClelland and Stewart.
Bryce, George. 1900. *The Remarkable History of the Hudson's Bay Company*. Toronto: W. Briggs.
Bumsted, J.M. 1996. *The Red River Rebellion*. Toronto: Watson and Dwyer.
Burley, Edith I. 1997. *Servants of the Honourable Company: Work, Discipline, and Conflict in the Hudson's Bay Company, 1770–1879*. Toronto: Oxford University Press.
Devine, Heather. 2004. *The People Who Own Themselves: Aboriginal Ethnogenesis in a Canadian Family, 1660–1900*. Calgary, AB: University of Calgary Press.
Dickason, Olive P. 1982. From 'One Nation' in the Northeast to 'New Nation' in the Northwest: A look at the emergence of the Métis. *American Indian Culture and Research Journal* 6 (2): 1–21.
Ens, Gerhard J. 1996. *Homeland to Hinterland: The Changing Worlds of the Red River Métis in the Nineteenth Century*. Toronto: University of Toronto Press.
Giraud, Marcel. 1986. *The Métis in the Canadian West*. Vol. 1. Trans. George Woodcock. Edmonton, AB: University of Alberta Press.
Hudson's Bay Company Archives (HBCA). Winnipeg: Archives of Manitoba.
– B.49/d/99 Cumberland House, list of Indians receiving ammunition for fowls, 1868.
– B.89/b/3 George Keith, letter dated 'Ile a la Crosse 31 May 1825.'
– B.89/b/3 Correspondence outwards, Ile a la Crosse, 6 April 1826.
– B.89/b/107 Ile a la Crosse, post expenses, 1875.
– B.89/d/145 Ile a la Crosse, general charges for English River District, 1870.
– B.89/d/150 Ile a la Crosse, account books, 1868–71.
– B.89/d/198 Ile a la Crosse, credit to widow Jourdain, 1876.
– B.89/d/199 Ile a la Crosse, account book, 1875–6.
– B.89/d/200a Ile a la Crosse, list of twine given out to net-makers 1875.
– B.89/d/208 Ile a la Crosse, monthly issues to engaged servants, 1877.
– B.89/d/231 Ile a la Crosse, account book, 1880.
– B.303/d/3a Lower Fort Garry, accounts books – general and blotter, 1861–2.
Innis, Harold A. 1956. *The Fur Trade in Canada: An Introduction to Canadian Economic History*. Rev. ed. Toronto: University of Toronto Press.
Judd, Carol M. 1980a. 'Mixt bands of many nations':1821–70. In *Old Trails and New Directions: Papers of the Third North American Fur Trade Conference*, ed. Carol M. Judd and Arthur J. Ray, 127–46. Toronto: University of Toronto Press.

– 1980b. Native labour and social stratification in the Hudson's Bay Company's Northern Department, 1770–1870. *Canadian Review of Sociology and Anthropology* 17 (4): 305–14.

Makahonuk, Glen. 1988. Wage-labour in the Northwest fur trade economy, 1760–1849. *Saskatchewan History* 41 (1): 1–17.

Morton, William Lewis. 1965. *Manitoba: The Birth of a Province*. Vol. 1. Altona, MB: Manitoba Record Society Publications.

Parker, Leanna. 1999. Paternalism and identity: The role of personal labour organization in the formation of group identity among the Métis in the Rupertsland fur trade and the Aboriginal people in the northern Australian cattle industry. Master's thesis, University of Saskatchewan, Native Studies department.

Pentland, H. Clare. 1959. The development of a capitalistic labour market in Canada. *Canadian Journal of Economics and Political Science* 25 (4): 450–61.

– 1979. The Canadian industrial relations system: Some formative factors. *Labour/ Le Travailleur* 4 (Fall): 9–23.

– 1981. *Labour and Capital in Canada, 1650–1860*. Ed. Paul Phillips. Toronto: James Lorimer.

Peterson, Jacqueline. 1982. Ethnogenesis: Settlement and growth of a 'New People' in the Great Lakes region, 1702–1815. *American Indian Culture and Research Journal* 6 (2): 23–64.

– 1985. Many roads to Red River: Métis genesis in the Great Lakes region, 1680–1815. In *The New Peoples: Being and Becoming Métis in North America*, ed. Jacqueline Peterson and Jennifer S.H. Brown, 37–71. Winnipeg: University of Manitoba Press.

Ray, Arthur J. 1974. *Indians in the Fur Trade: Their Role as Hunters, Trappers and Middlemen in the Lands Southwest of Hudson Bay, 1660–1870*. Toronto: University of Toronto Press.

– 1984. Periodic shortages, Native welfare and the Hudson's Bay Company, 1670–1930. In *The Subarctic Fur Trade: Native Social and Economic Advantages*, ed. Shepard Krech III, 1–20. Vancouver: University of British Columbia Press.

– 1990. The decline of paternalism in the Hudson's Bay Company fur trade, 1870–1945. In *Merchant Credit and Labour Strategies in Historical Perspective*, ed. Rosemary E. Ommer, 188–202. Fredericton, NB: Acadiensis Press.

Ray, Arthur J., and Donald Freeman. 1978. *'Give Us Good Measure:' An Economic Analysis of Relations between the Indians and the Hudson's Bay Company before 1763*. Toronto: University of Toronto Press.

Ross, Alexander. 1972. *The Red River Settlement: Its Rise, Progress, and Present State with Some Account of the Native Races and Its General History to the Present Day*. Edmonton, AB: Hurtig.

Siggins, Maggie. 1994. *Riel: A Life of Revolution*. Toronto: Harper Collins.

Tough, Frank. 1992a. Aboriginal rights versus the deed of surrender: The legal rights of Native peoples and Canada's acquisition of the Hudson's Bay Company territory. *Prairie Forum* 17 (2): 225–50.

– 1992b. Buying out the Bay: Aboriginal rights and the economic policies of the Department of Indian Affairs after 1870. In *The First Ones: Readings in Indian/ Native Studies*, ed. David R. Miller, Carl Beal, James Dempsey, and R. Wesley Heber, 398–406. Craven, SK: Saskatchewan Indian Federated College Press.

– 1996. '*As Their Natural Resources Fail:*' *Native Peoples and the Economic History of Northern Manitoba, 1870–1930*. Vancouver: University of British Columbia Press.

Van Kirk, Sylvia. 1980. '*Many Tender Ties': Women in Fur-Trade Society, 1670–1870*. Winnipeg: Watson and Dwyer.

PART 2

ENVIRONMENT

Profile of Cindy Kenny-Gilday (1954–)

Dene, Human Rights Activist, and Environmental Activist

The circumstances surrounding Cindy Kenny-Gilday's birth are unusual. Her family lived in Tulita, Northwest Territories, but she was born on an aeroplane that was transporting her expectant mother to the town of Norman Wells. Consequently, her birth certificate says she was born in Norman Wells in 1954. She is a member of the Treaty 11 Deline First Nation of the Northwest Territories.

Her father's decision to move the family to Fort Franklin (now Deline) would help chart the course of her life's work. A Dene community on the shore of Great Bear Lake, Deline was deeply affected by the resource companies operating in the area. Exploration and mining activities occupied lands that once sustained the Dene's traditional hunting and fishing lifestyle. The opening of the Eldorado mine in Port Radium in the 1930s had helped to transform this region of the north into a uranium-producing area. The demand for uranium grew with the invention of the atomic bomb. In fact, this mine produced the uranium that was used in the bombs dropped by the United States on Hiroshima and Nagasaki during the Second World War.[1] Although dropping the bombs was said to have ended the war, it had a devastating effect on Japanese people and changed the world forever.

The uranium mining activities in Deline also had a devastating effect on those living nearby. The Canadian government (which eventually took over operations of the Eldorado mine) paid all able-bodied Dene men to transport the bags of raw uranium ore on their back, for five dollars per day. The one-hundred-pound sacks of ore leaked uranium dust onto their clothes, hair, and skin. Many of these men later died of uranium-induced radiation illnesses such as lung, kidney, and colon cancers.[2]

Kenny-Gilday became aware of the widespread uranium contamination in the Great Bear Lake region. While working with the Dene Nation, she discovered the prevalence of former uranium mine workers dying of various forms of cancer. She also had personal experience with this phenom-

Cindy Kenny-Gilday. Photo courtesy of Terry Lusty.

enon, as both her father and her brother died of cancer in the 1970s. Owing to the uncharacteristic number of cancer deaths among the Dene men, Kenny-Gilday named Deline 'a village of widows.' She believes that the actions of the government and industry constitute a form of cultural geno-cide.[3] She argues that the death of the community's men threatens the tradi-tional values and customs of the Dene. Without the men, the elders' ability to pass on traditional culture and learning was lost.

In addition to her participation in the Uranium Contamination Project, Cindy Kenny-Gilday has been actively involved in environmental issues with Indigenous peoples around the world. She served as the international communications co-coordinator for Indigenous Survival International and was the chair of the International Union for Conservation of Nature's (IUCN's) World Conservation Union Task Force on Indigenous Peoples. She also co-chaired the national stakeholder forum for the National Round Table on Environment and Economy and produced a report called 'Aboriginal Communities and Non-renewable Resource Development in the North.' Kenny-Gilday was the moderator of the first United Nations conference on Aboriginal peoples and the environment.[4] She received the 1994 Aboriginal Achievement Award in recognition of her work on environmental and Aboriginal rights. She currently works as the Aboriginal relations manager for Diavik Diamond Mines in Yellowknife.[5]

KRISTA WHITEHEAD

Notes

1 Janice Tibbetts, 'Dene tell ministers story of "village of widows": Uranium used in Hiroshima, Nagasaki bombs continues to kill Deline Indians, committee hears,' *Edmonton Journal*, 12 June 1998.
2 Andrew Nikiforuk, 'Canada's deadly secret: 50 years on, the world's first uranium mine is still taking its toll on a northern community. Why didn't the federal government, the guardian of the Dene, tell them of the danger?' *The Gazette*, 19 April 1998.
3 Cindy Kenny-Gilday, 'A village of widows,' *Arctic Circle Online*, http://arcticcircle.uconn.edu/SEEJ/Mining/gilday.html (accessed on 24 May 2003).
4 Trent University. 'Honouring the knowledge of the land: A gathering of Aboriginal voices,' Trent University Indigenous Environmental Studies Program, 4 March 2002, http://www.trentu.ca/nativestudies/events/CindyKennyGilday.html (accessed on 24 May 2003).
5 http://www.naaf.ca/board.

Mining on Aboriginal Lands

GÉRARD DUHAIME, NICK BERNARD, AND
ANDRÉE CARON

For centuries, colonial powers considered the North to be a vast reservoir
of natural resources. The social importance of furs grew as the boundaries
of major cities were pushed into the cold latitudes of the North, in Europe
and in North America (Armstrong, Rogers, and Rowley 1978; Sugden
1982). For millennia, Aboriginal peoples had been using copper to make
tools and to trade by the time European explorers reached Canada's Coppermine River and then found gold at Fortymile River and in the Klondike
(1896). Major geological expeditions at the start of the twentieth century
discovered massive deposits of northern mineral resources and paved the
way for large-scale exploitation. Consequently the mining industry set up
operations throughout the circumpolar north, whether in America, Europe,
or Asia. During the twentieth century, uranium, gold, tungsten, lead, zinc,
and silver were intensively extracted from different locations throughout
Canada's northern latitudes. Starting with the last decade of the twentieth
century, mining activities focused on diamonds. Oil and gas from the northern territories and the Arctic Ocean, as well as the tar sands of certain western provinces, were also heavily exploited in order to feed the developed
world's greed for energy and resources.

In all of the Arctic, resource exploitation represented some US$60 billion
at purchasing power parity (PPP) in 2001 and up to US$62 billion at PPP in
2003. The mineral extraction sector was responsible for 28 per cent of the
total gross domestic product for the whole Arctic. It represented some 35
per cent of the Canadian Arctic's gross domestic product (Duhaime and
Caron 2006; Duhaime et al. 2004). The impact of mining on the environment is considerable and well documented, in particular by several Arctic Monitoring and Assessment Programme (AMAP) reports (2009, 2004a,
2004b, 2003, and 1997). However, environmental impacts are not the whole
story. The social risks of large-scale resource exploitation in the North are
also considerable, such as widespread pollution, economic boom-and-bust

cycles, and massive and temporary migration of workers into an Aboriginal environment. Nothing guarantees that social and environmental concerns will be weighed when resources are exploited, as past and contemporary cases demonstrate.

This chapter attempts to answer the following question: what are the conditions under which social concerns can change corporate practices so that the negative effects of mining development will be diminished and the positive effects will not have detrimental impacts? Based on a selection of cases on northern Canada, our study found that, among other factors, the active presence of Aboriginal organizations seems to be a key agent for change in corporate encounters with Aboriginal peoples.

Corporate Rationality and Society

Economic development requires that corporations, governments, and citizens (and their associations) in a given geopolitical area work together. These three social actors pursue their own interests in economic development activities, which they promote more or less effectively depending on their capacity. Numerous exchanges take place between these actors. What we are interested in here are the flows of influence (see the following figures).[1]

Each of these actors represents a set of realities, the complexity of which can only briefly be mentioned. For instance, the corporation is a legal entity that brings together capital, with a view to making profits. The government is an institution that redistributes resources levied from corporations and citizens. In our approach the citizens' associative world is the plural universe of unions, voluntary associations, and other institutions (non-governmental organizations and churches, for example). Citizen associations are created by groups of individual citizens in order to promote interests of some sort that are not necessarily supported by or may be at odds with government or corporate interests. As a matter of fact, the category of citizen associations (or associative society) includes a large spectrum of organizations, from grass roots local associations based upon volunteer work to professional interest groups using various experts. Canadian Aboriginal organizations fall under the category of the associative society.

The specific interest of the corporation is to make profits in order to redistribute them among its shareholders. To achieve this goal, the corporation endeavours to impose its interests and the means to attain them on the other two actors in question, namely the government and the citizen.[2] The government redistributes collectivized resources according to its perception of the common good. Concurrently, the corporation seeks to impose its

Interaction models between corporation, government, and associative society

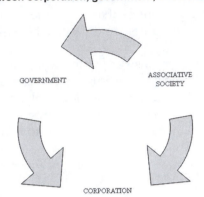

Note: Arrows represent flows of influence. In the 'neutral' model all arrows should be bi-directional. This figure illustrates the optimal conditions, under which associative society's concerns can be taken into consideration by corporations.

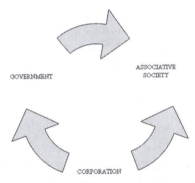

Note: This figure illustrates the worst conditions, under which associative society's concerns are not taken into consideration by corporations.

vision of the common good on the government. Neoliberal societies, such as Canada, have governments that endorse this corporate vision and seek to impose it on their citizens (see the first figure above).[3] The citizen participates in the interrelations between government and corporate interests in various ways: the individual citizen may simply contribute by a consenting silence, which allows the corporation and the government to pursue their own agenda without much constraint;[4] the individual citizen and citizens' associations may participate actively by indicating their preferences or claims, and they may endeavour to impose their interests[5] by impassioned representations, revolt, or rebellion (Bergeron 1977).

In this study we suggest that in the absence of explicit pressure brought to bear by associative society or by the government, corporations do not take social concerns into consideration.[6] Additionally, we suggest that associative society can impose its concerns on corporations by exerting pressure simultaneously on corporations and government.[7] We use the following approach to verify these assumptions: first, we highlight the importance of the mining industry in the northern economy as a whole by using statistical indicators; second, we examine the practices of mining companies in relation to the social environment by using comparative case studies. In both steps we focus especially on regions in northern Canada. Finally, the findings of these steps are discussed by comparing them to recent international research on mining on Aboriginal land worldwide.

The Mining Industry and Economic Activity

Resource exploitation shapes a large extent of the economy in the Canadian North. In all northern regions, resource exploitation (mainly minerals, gas, oil, and fisheries) is very important.[8] The primary sector, as it is known, is concentrated on non-renewable resource exploitation and creates between one-fifth and one-quarter of all economic activities in the Northwest Territories, Nunavut, and Nunavik, mainly through mining. The mineral sector in northern Canada is now of prime importance, and diamond mines are largely responsible for this. In 2003 the shipments of production from Canadian diamond mines exceeded $800 million, while the production value was estimated at more than $1,700 million, according to the preliminary estimate of the mineral production in Canada (see the following table).

The mineral extraction sector is not only important from a statistical standpoint. To a large extent, it is central because the formal economy revolves around it, and the government's presence is largely explained by this degree of impact on the formal economy. The Canadian militarization of the Arctic during the Second World War and the Cold War brought to the world's attention the material distress afflicting the Inuit, in particular following the sharp decline of the fur trade after the crash of 1929. In 1959 the Canadian government took responsibility for building permanent villages and for assuming the related recurrent operating costs. Coincidentally, the frantic growth in consumption in the 1960s and America's vulnerability to oil supplies from the Middle East, underscored by the 1973 oil crisis, intensified North America's appetite for Canada's northern mineral resources. However, the Aboriginal groups, who had started to organize at that time, opposed these plans. Basically, they wanted guaranteed access to the territory, use of the resources, and compensation for losses resulting from the planned resource exploitation. The Aboriginal groups called for a key seat at the political decision-making table inasmuch as their own affairs were

Mining in the Canadian North in percentage of the
gross domestic product of these regions and in 2001
Canadian dollars

	%	C$
Yukon Territories	4.86	51,100,000
Northwest Territories	24.08	585,400,000
Nunavut Territories	22.18	186,900,000
Nunavik	19.02	29,800,000
Labrador	15.29	n/a
Average	17.09	
Total		853 200 000

Sources: Statistics Canada, Duhaime, G. et al. *Nunavik Economy*
Notes: Data for Nunavik refer to 1998. GDP distribution
is given for the Yukon Territories, Northwest
Territories, Nunavut Territories, and Nunavik. Labour
force distribution is given for Labrador.

concerned. At the same time, the relevant public administration bodies were restructured, and growth ensued from several subsequent agreements: the James Bay and Northern Quebec Agreement (1975), the Northeastern Quebec Agreement (1978), the Inuvialuit Final Agreement (1984), the Nunavut Final Agreement (1993), and, more recently, the Labrador Inuit Final Agreement (1997).

Common Characteristics

An analysis of the practices of mining corporations in terms of their relations with the social environment reveals, first, that they have several traits in common. Second, it also shows that it is possible to distinguish between two different types of corporations: those that do not take social concerns into account and those that do take them into account, regardless of the source of their motivation.

Mining companies share some characteristics, aside from having the common objective of making profits. Contrary to expectations, all the corporations that concern us are huge, which can be illustrated easily with a few indicators. For example, such companies are responsible for a large share of the North's economic activity by making highly intensive use of capital, equipment, and machines of impressive size. In Schefferville, on the southern fringe of Nunavik, the abandoned facilities of the Iron Ore Company cover fifteen square kilometres. The profits of a single year of the Ekati diamond mine, in the Northwest Territories, for a second example, would be sufficient to pay all the public services intended for the entire population of Nunavik, namely some twelve thousand people spread out over fourteen villages on a territory that is 500,000 square kilometres in size. This includes but is not limited to education, health, social services, and subsidized housing.

The number of shareholders of these companies is often high. However, while the number of companies is relatively low, they are vertically integrated with one another. For instance, the Colomac mine in the Northwest Territories belongs to Royal Oak Mines, an American company that has some fifty thousand shareholders, 80 per cent of whom are American residents. Despite the large number of small shareholders, the number of people who make major decisions for these companies is limited: the head of the executive of the parent company and his immediate committee.

These companies invest in mining exploration operations. Such operations are sometimes very lengthy and can mobilize significant amounts of capital. When these explorations are successful, the companies then invest in mining operations by building the facilities required to extract and separate the ore in order to make it a marketable product and to facilitate its transport. The exploration that led to the development of the new nickel-copper complex located in Katiniq in northern Quebec, then owned by Falconbridge, extended over a period of twenty years; the investment required for the actual mining was spread out over many years and represents some $700 million, so the company reported.

All companies produce outputs. They create wealth, which is shared unequally between the actors involved: members of the board of directors and the executive, shareholders, employees, suppliers, government, and the institutions belonging to the surrounding society. They generate waste in the air (smoke containing non-degradable organic pollutants; heavy metals), on the ground (tailings; deposits of pollutants that have been carried by air), and in the water (deposits of pollutants that have been carried by air and transported by sea currents; tailing confinement ponds; leakage; and acid run-off). The effects of the pollutants are felt not only in the immediate area but also over very large distances since they are carried by major air and sea currents. Several kinds of pollutants enter the food chain and have harmful effects on living creatures, including humans. These pollutants eventually create disturbances in the human environment. The presence of the companies produces disturbances in mining towns as well. These centres are economically vulnerable to such companies and their activities. Indeed, most are based on a single industry, whose profitability is partly linked to world price-setting mechanisms; moreover, the communities become highly dependent on the efficiency and reliability of transportation

Smelter chimneys. Photo by Gérard Duhaime.

systems, which are often developed by these companies (Myers 2001; Notz-ke 1994). It needs to be noted, however, that the decisive factors underlying these investments, operations, and impacts differ from one corporation to the next, as was revealed by our comparative examination of corporate practices.

Corporations That Pay Little Attention to Social Concerns

Corporations that pay little attention to social concerns seek to maximize their profits by following market signals, which strictly dictate the relevance of investing and of reinvesting if the outlook is favourable (for example, according to the price of ore or the status of reserves), or of shutting down operations. Such corporations endeavour to keep their operating costs as low as possible, which includes avoiding wage increases, not treating waste, or neglecting to re-naturalize sites at the time of closure. These externality costs, as they are called in business language, are left up to public authorities. Such corporations tend to concentrate the wealth created into a few hands and, consequently, effect only a minimal redistribution of the wealth generated.

Numerous companies conduct mining exploration without having any concern for the environmental impact of this type of activity. In Nunavik, for instance, on a territory approximately 500,000 square kilometres in size, promoters abandoned some six hundred mining exploration sites between 1940 and 1975, some of them containing highly toxic chemical compound (Duhaime, Bernard, and Comtois 2005). This problem is not only extensive; some mining sites are intensely contaminated. Giant Mine in the Northwest Territories of Canada is one of them. Belonging to Royal Oak Mines, this underground mine was opened in 1948 and produced some 90,000 ounces of gold annually, for a total of 7.7 million ounces. The mine closed after the price of gold depreciated in the late 1990s, and its assets were sold. Giant Mine granted concessions to its employees following a bitter strike, during which production continued uninterrupted, except for the week after an underground explosion that resulted in the deaths of seven employees. With its closure, the mine left behind a huge environmental problem in the form of 250,000 tonnes of arsenic mixed in the tailings. The extent of the problem was such that government officials examined the possibility of exploiting the arsenic in some way in order to offset the costs of a clean-up that the industry did not want to assume and which fell to the Canadian taxpayers, as represented by the Department of Indian and Northern Affairs and the government of the Northwest Territories.

Numerous mines that opened during the period 1945–70 fall under this category. It was an era in which environmental questions, even less social impacts, were not yet on the agenda. At that time, the role played by civil society was minimal or none at all. As a matter of fact, governments of the time were also largely insensitive to these concerns. Moreover, associative society itself was not yet sufficiently organized to express its concerns and, in general, to have an impact over the ways, means, and goals of resource exploitation. This is the era that preceded the emergence of Aboriginal organizations as a political force in Canada. The environmental and social problems related to these northern mining operations are a dark collective legacy to which the mining industry contributed heavily.

Corporations That Pay More Attention to Social Concerns

Some companies pay more attention to social concerns, albeit their degree of attention is not necessarily very high; still, it is better than nothing. In theory, the factors underlying decision making about investments, operations, and impacts apply to these companies as well; according to corporate rationality, they seek to maximize profits, keep production costs down, reject externality costs, and so on. Yet, some of their practices differ. In what follows we examine two case studies to determine these practices and the conditions that make them possible, or even demand them.

Nanisivik Mine

Nanisivik Mine, located north of Baffin Island near Arctic Bay, has been in operation since 1976.[9] It is an underground zinc, lead, and silver mine. The extracted ore is transformed into a zinc concentrate containing lead and silver; it is then shipped by boat in four loads to blast furnaces in Europe. The mine is wholly owned by Breakwater Resources Ltd., which acquired it in 1996 for $2.5 million. Breakwater is active in exploration, development, and mining production in the Americas and North Africa and is among the world's biggest zinc producers. The head office of Breakwater Resources is located in Toronto. It also has offices in North Bay (Ontario), Rouyn-Noranda (Quebec), Joutel (Quebec), and Wenatchee (Washington), as well as at its mines in Honduras, Tunisia, and Chile. The main shareholder is Dundee Bancorp Inc., which owns 33.6 per cent of the shares.

In 1997 the Nanisivik mine had a record year, extracting 805,000 tonnes of ore. This resulted in a number of consequences. As the mine is located on Arctic territory, where the permafrost reaches considerable depth, it cannot be heated. The temperature remains at about −20°C all year round. Water is not used in the diamond drilling process, to avoid the permafrost's melting. Dry drilling techniques have been developed, and a sophisticated ventilation system is used to eliminate the ensuing dust (Allen 1998.). However, some Nanisivik residents lodged a complaint with the government of the Northwest Territories in 1997 concerning the high levels of dust and other environmental practices of the company.[10] The mine was closed in 2002 after the price of nickel hit a historic low point worldwide. At that time some two hundred workers, including thirty permanent residents of Arctic Bay, were employed at the Nanisivik mine. The industrial complex was partially dismantled, and a reclamation process occurred. Former mine infrastructure, such as harbour facilities and an airstrip, was upgraded as a consequence of the federal government's decision to create a permanent military installation on the site.

Katiniq Mine

The mine located at Katiniq in Nunavik is operated by the Raglan Mining Corporation.[11] It was originally owned by Falconbridge but now is integrated with Xstrata, one of the world's nickel giants along with Inco and Rao Norilsk. It is involved in the exploration, production, and refinement of nickel, copper, and cobalt, and its head office is located in Toronto.[12]

The extraction of ore at Katiniq Mine began in December 1997, at the same time as did the start-up of the concentrator. Approximately 3,700 tonnes of ore are processed each day, for an annual quantity of about 130,000 tonnes. The ore is transformed on site into a nickel-copper concentrate. The concentrate is transported by truck over 100 kilometres to Deception Bay, where vessels transport it to Quebec City. At Deception Bay, Xstrata is reusing a wharf that was built in the 1970s for an asbestos mine near Salluit. The navigation season lasts eight months, and at least six maritime trips are planned each year. The first load of nickel-copper concentrate was shipped in March 1998 on the MV *Arctic*.[13] Once in Quebec City, it is then transported by rail to the company's blast furnace in Sudbury for processing. The resulting matte (a mixture of metal and sulphurs) is shipped back to Quebec City by rail, where it is loaded on a vessel bound for Norway; there the metal receives a final stage of refinement. In 2003, once refined, the production of the Raglan mine totalled some 25,100 tonnes of nickel, 6,600 tonnes of copper, 380 tonnes of cobalt, as well as a small quantity of platinum and palladium.

Approximately 400 persons have been working at the Katiniq mine site since 1995. The number of employees has reached 700 in recent years as facilities have been upgraded and production has increased. Local Inuit people were hired during the development stage (66 Inuit, or 15 per cent of the manpower, in 1996) (George 1996b). In fact, the company made considerable efforts to involve the local Inuit communities of Salluit and Kangiqsujuaq. In 1995 Raglan Mining Corporation and Makivik Corporation (a not-for-profit organization that represents Inuit interests) signed the Raglan Agreement, which included clauses on compensation for the residents of these two neighbouring villages, hiring Inuit workers as a priority, training manpower, subcontracting to Inuit firms, and providing for environmental stakes (Phillips 1995). The agreement led to the establishment of manpower training programs for the populations of Salluit and Kangiqsujuaq. It also led to two instalments of $1 million being paid by the Raglan Corporation, the first in 1996 and the second at the time of production start-up in 1997, directly to the Inuit of the two villages. A third point in the agreement was the granting of a $60 million contract between Raglan and a joint-venture company for the development of open-pit mines on the property. Kiewit, a multinational construction company, invested $8 million in the joint venture and is entitled to 80 per cent of the earnings; the minority partner, Nunumviut Development Inc., invested $2 million and is entitled to 20 per cent of the earnings. Nunumviut was formed by the villages of Salluit and Kangiqsujuaq, and because it did not have the initial capital required, Makivik Corporation loaned 85 per cent of the amount, and Kativik Regional Development Council provided the remaining 15 per cent. The Department of Indian and Northern Affairs provided the loan guarantees under its Resource Access Negotiations Program (George 1996a).

Political Power and Corporate Practices

The two examples above reveal important common corporate traits, over and above those already mentioned. Indeed, in all reported cases the corporations agreed to change some of their practices to take into account the pressures from their social and political environments. The factors explaining this type of behaviour are limited in number. From a corporate perspective the incentives to change include the following: government regulations that allow the corporation to define the pace and the means of required changes; a profitable period that makes such changes more palatable; some economic benefits to the corporation itself; the willingness on the part of the government or associative society to enter into a partnership with the corporation; a cost-effective ecological approach; a flexible approach that makes it possible to define goals according to opportunities; and an informed public (Gunn 2001; see also Gunn 1995).

The changes made to the operations at the Nanisivik mine and to the plans at the time of its closure were imposed by pressure from associative society, exerted directly on the corporation and indirectly on the government. The gains were obtained during a period that was favourable for the company to maintain its profitability, where its investment was likely amortized, even though the subsequent drop in the price of base metals led to the mine's eventual closure. With regard to the Katiniq mine, the negotiation of agreements between Raglan and Makivik Corporation reveals a clear willingness on the part of associative society to enter into a partnership with the company, which had a lot to gain. Finally, changes to these mining companies' practices occurred at a time when legislation to protect Aboriginal rights (the Nunavut Final Agreement and the James Bay and Northern Quebec Agreement) and regulations to protect the environment (for example, the Canadian Environment Assessment and Review Process of 1973) existed.

Indeed, it seems that the basic difference between these cases and those that were mentioned earlier lies in the acquisition of significant political influence and power by Aboriginal organizations, owing to the territorial claim agreements that they succeeded in obtaining. These land-claims agreements resulted from a transformation of Canada's political culture, which was itself a response to the conditions in which the Inuit lived at the time. Moreover, the Inuit learned to use the tools of the contemporary world to their advantage, including representative democracy, negotiations, and corporate rationality. Equipped with the means put at their disposal by previous gains, they succeeded in applying the necessary pressure to impose some conditions on those companies that wished to exploit the resources on the territory for which the Aboriginal organizations were henceforth responsible. The process was not fundamentally different in Nanisivik. Here Indigenous peoples' complaints received attention only late in the twentieth century, when the Inuit of Nunavut acquired mastery over these same tools of influence and were preparing to exercise political power in 1999 through the creation of the new Territory of Nunavut.

Dynamics of Relations

It would seem, however, that the effectiveness of associative society in influencing corporate practices is neither final nor decisive. Indeed, relations between the actors in question continue over time as each remains concerned about its own interests. The objectives and the means at the disposal of the corporation are often much more coherent over the long term than are the objectives and the means used by the surrounding actors.

It must be noted that associative society is presented here in an overly simplified form as some sort of homogeneous whole. In fact, it is made up of a vast plurality of groups that are not organized according to a coherent and harmonized theoretical structure. The idea of associative society only has coherency in a theoretical framework; there is no single voice to express what could be considered an opinion of associative society as a totality. Moreover, the reality is that when facing huge corporations, associative society cannot hope to have the same resources at its disposal. Moreover, the state as a whole also is homogeneous only in theory; in practice, it is composed of a multiplicity of superimposed layers and parallel hierarchical lines that often ignore and occasionally contradict one another.

In this landscape who oversees corporate practices? The agreements entered into may have no effect if appropriate means of oversight are not implemented. In 1997, for instance, a typical year in the profitable business of mining, Nanisivik Mine employed approximately 190 persons, 18 per cent of whom were Inuit, out of a population of 350 in the entire community of Nanisivik. Yet, when the mine had opened in 1976, the owners had promised that 30 per cent of the workforce would be Inuit (Bourgeois 1997). The situation is nearly identical at the Katiniq mine: 15 to 18 per cent of the workforce was Inuit, although the agreement had specified that a minimum of 20 per cent of the total workforce should come from Inuit communities. In 2008 no more than 8 per cent of the employees were Inuit.[14]

These results can be (and are) interpreted in different ways. Corporations see them as tangible expressions of their efforts to implement the promises they made. Aboriginal groups denounce them as lower than what was agreed. To explain these results, numerous factors should be considered, including corporate commitment; various constraints associated with industrial work (Duhaime 1991), such as worker training for specific jobs, which require high and persistent investment; and shaky relations between non-Aboriginal workers and Inuit trainees and workers, including racial tensions, bad communication, and sexual harassment.[15] Nevertheless, the fact remains that provisions in the formal agreements were not completely fulfilled. It is not our goal to make a judgment, but importantly, in these contexts, it seems clear that pressure is needed to safeguard the interests of associative society in face of corporate free rein. Once they succeed in gaining benefits from such agreements, Aboriginal organizations play the role of watchdog, with the support of the press and other civil society institutions. This role is crucial in implementing provisions, in order to improve the results and to ask for supporting measures when the results are found to be unsatisfactory.

Can the watchful eye of public authorities re-establish some form of balance between the powerful mining companies and the less powerful associative society? It is not clear that this balance is attainable. Environmental regulations adopted in Canada and the United States call for impact studies but do not impose follow-up studies or corrective measures in cases where the actual consequences differ from the anticipated ones. Katiniq Mine is an example of such a situation. This mining operation anticipated positive impacts to the local social environment in the form of jobs, contracts, and mitigation measures designed to address negative impacts on the natural environment. In 2008 Xstrata delivered a $32.5 million profit-sharing payment to Makivik Corporation. Unfortunately it appears that this 'annual cash windfall' has led to several social disturbances within the recipient communities: a stratification between the newly well-to-do and those left behind; an increase in social problems such as overspending, bootlegging, substance abuse, and family violence; socio-economic stratification between the villages favoured by the agreement with the mining corporation and the other villages in the region. Consequently, these other communities see the agreement as a sort of denial of sharing, which is considered a basic value of Inuit culture and identity.

Finally, government-mediated settlements, between the interests of corporations and those of the actors in associative society, do not necessarily lead to a balance between them. It may tip the scales back in favour of the corporations, which occurs often in market economies that are dominated by the neoliberal credo. Privatization commonly leads to a reduction of corporate social and environmental obligations at the expense of society if the state does not step in to ensure compliance (Duhaime et al. 2001).

Discussion

Recent case studies involving mining operations throughout the Aboriginal world tend to confirm the above results and our theoretical perspective. For instance, Jenkins and Yakovleva (2006, 281) did a remarkable analysis of the ten top mining corporations in the world (including some we have just seen at play on Canadian Aboriginal lands, such as BHP Billiton, Barrick Gold, and Xstrata). They reviewed the way in which these mining corporations conducted performance reporting in relation to sustainability and social responsibility. The authors reached conclusions that are similar to ours. In their words, reporting practices are made of *leaders*, who are 'mature reporters,' and *laggards*, who are 'infant reporters.'

Around the world, relationships between transnational mining corporations, local and national governments, and local and national Aboriginal associations are consistent with those found in the Canadian cases. A further example is the case of Richards Bay Minerals (a Rio Tinto subsidiary) on Mbonambi land in South Africa. An analysis of this case brought Paul Kapelus to conclude, 'In order to promote their ultimate goal of profit maximization, firms will have to take into account the costs and benefits of addressing the concerns of each of these groups in the process, ignoring the interests and claims of some (e.g., small NGOs) and paying close attention to those of others (e.g., multilateral financial institutions)' (2002, 291). In other words, communities' expectations might be taken into consideration and lead to concrete actions if they represent a serious threat to the profitability of operations. As Katherine Anne Trebeck observed, 'some communities have been able to force their demands into corporate decision-making to the extent that recognizing and responding to community expectations becomes a prudent strategy in the company's self-interest' (2007, 542). In two cases – Century Mine (Rio Tinto), on Indigenous land near Doomadgee in Queensland, and Jabiluka (Energy Resources of Australia), near the Indigenous village of Mirras in the Northern Territory – Trebeck observed that this 'prudent strategy' was literally forced upon the mining companies by significant pressure tactics used by local communities, such as local sit-ins, blockades, and large protests in major cities (2007, 552, 554).

When pressure is not put on corporate shoulders, what motivation do they have for taking into account social concerns, and, more important, what motivation is there to actually take concrete actions as a response to these concerns? Without pressure from local citizen associations there are few incentives to move forward in a socially and environmentally responsible manner by mobilizing resources and developing adequate tools to address such concerns (Clark and Clark 1999, 196). This is what we observed in such cases as Giant Mine in the Northwest Territories and in the hundreds of abandoned mining exploration sites in Nunavik.

It is our contention that government has a role in mediating relations between corporations and associative society. This has also been observed by several others. For instance, government can define the legal obligations requiring corporations to address social concerns. Ideally, it may define a comprehensive framework for project development and monitoring post facto, for benefit-sharing agreements, and for mitigation programs. However, several cases studies prove that this ideal remains exceptional. For example, Marlin Mine (Gladis Gold), near Los Encuentros in Guatemala, delivered few local jobs and benefits, while heavily poisoning the local environment, in spite of a large body of regulations and the involvement of institutions at both national and international levels (Fulmer, Godoy, and Neff 2008). Fulmer, Godoy, and Neff argue that such legal tools are an ambiguous response to the needs of Indigenous communities because they do not have 'the combination of coherence, political will, and ability to ensure [the] compliance that would make a dependable source of rights protection' (2008, 113). The Marlin Mine case is a perfect example of the model represented in the second figure accompanying this chapter: while Indigenous farmers told government and corporate representatives that the mine was not welcome in their territories, the Guatemala president cited a need to protect investors' rights, and the project continued. In a subsequent blockade one opponent citizen was killed and sixteen others were arrested and charged with terrorism (Fulmer, Godoy, and Neff 2008, 91). In other words, a legal framework is no guarantee that social concerns will be adequately addressed. This is also our conclusion based on Canadian case studies.

However, the government's role as a mediator exists and, at least, has potential to ameliorate the situation. In Clark and Clark's (1999) and Trebeck's (2007) view, the government's role is to regulate the industry and to intervene in order to deal with inequities. Moreover, corporations themselves have few incentives to change their practices, and they are generally poorly equipped to deal with social developments or poverty alleviation (Downing 2002, 19).

The best means by which this mediator role could be implemented is through the deliberate actions of associative society. The cases of Century and Jabikula led Trebeck (2007, 557) to the conclusion that Indigenous communities 'are most effective in bringing leverage over mining companies when they impact upon profit,' using legislative or judiciary tools (for example, native title provisions, and civil rights) or, when such tools do not exist, by employing 'political mobilisation, engagement of influential supporters, blockades and other means to inflict delay.' Brett Clark (2002) comes to similar conclusions. In his view the Indigenous Environmental Movement provides a model of successful actions by associative society. What is remarkable about the movement is that it transcends ethnic borders and provides unity to this citizens' opposition in a way that parallels the transnational structure of the mining industry.

The deliberate action of associative society is not without paradox, however, as Kirsch (2007, 314) has shown in his examination of the case of Ok Tedi Mine (BHP Billiton) near the Yonggom people's village in Papua New Guinea. Such actions may lead to negotiation, which may then force a choice – or a trade-off – between environmental and social protection, on the one hand, and benefits, on the other. Cases of this nature are numerous, where associative society has embraced corporate business logic. Sometimes the tools at its disposal are so ineffectual that the associative society is forced to take whatever financial compensations are offered. This is the case of marginalized Indigenous groups (Taylor 2008, 123) and was also observed to be the case in the Canadian context.

Conclusion

While corporations once were at liberty to abandon hundreds of spoiled mining exploration sites in Nunavik and, in the process, create massive ecological threats on sites like the former Giant mine, they now enter agreements with Aboriginal organizations in order to clean up the waste of past operations and concede some social benefits. What happened during the last fifty years that brought about such changes in corporate practices?

The Canadian cases discussed above suggest one major conclusion, that the apparent change in the corporate practices of the mining industry active on Inuit territories was brought about by the fortification of Aboriginal associative society. This fortification includes the development of its organizational capacity in order that the society may successfully put its ecological, social, and cultural concerns on the public agenda. We can diagnose two processes that created this new responsiveness. The first was mobilization; the second was professionalization.

In the 1960s and especially the 1970s, a growing number of volunteer associations started to voice concerns for a safer environment in all respects: the air to be breathed, the water to be drunk, and the food to be eaten, for example. During this same period, Canadian Aboriginal associations multiplied in order to defend their views in the face of growing multinational corporate interest in northern natural resources. This organizational wave soon led to the definition of different territories in the North based on the Inuit's own views, above and beyond the official political division of the territories, throughout northern Canada, from the Inuvialuit region to Labrador. Ultimately, it led to different land claims being negotiated from that period onward.

Negotiations with a central government and multinational corporations forced the newly formed associations to engage in a process of professionalization. Like ecological interest groups, who had to base their concerns in scientific evidence in order to be heard in the public arena, Aboriginal groups had to support their land claims, as well as their demands on the industry, with credible expertise. Consequently, they gradually hired a number of experts, especially lawyers and natural scientists. Besides local associations, they created national organizations to lobby centres of influence more effectively. In other words, from grass-roots civic (and sometimes noisy) mobilization, based on local problems and concerns, were born sophisticated organizations that were characterized by expert management and that engaged high-profile politicians. Owing to this transformation of the public agenda, Aboriginal territories no longer could be seen only as vast reservoirs of natural resources that one could carelessly exploit in order to make a profit. While this point of view still persists, it is no longer 'the only game in town' and, one could argue, it is in decline. Canada's northern territories are now seen as carrying life – including human life and societies – that have to be respected, supported, and protected when necessary.

Ecological and Aboriginal concerns were not exclusive to Aboriginal organizations or to the North. Such concerns were also of growing importance throughout Canada. As mentioned, the Environmental Assessment and Review Process was adopted in Canada in 1973, and Aboriginal leaders were part of the discussions concerning constitutional changes in the 1980s. At the same time, environmental and human rights concerns reached international organizations: first, we saw the Stockholm Declaration made at the United Nations Conference on the Human Environment in 1972; and, second, the Working Group on Indigenous People was created under the United Nations Human Rights Commission in 1981 (Marantz 1996).

The evolution from mobilization to professionalization mentioned above was not exclusive to northern Canada. Such transformations were at play throughout Canada as a whole as well as in the United States, as demonstrated by Theda Skocpol (2003). What does this mean? First, it tells us that what happened on Canadian Aboriginal lands was not isolated from the world context. At the very least, it means that Aboriginal groups were deeply engaged in these developments and, at best, that their action contributed to these international changes.

Finally, the cases examined allow for theoretical considerations, which we would like to discuss briefly. The summary model presented here is valid for an analysis of this dynamic under certain basic conditions. First, it must be understood that it is a schema that requires considerable development, which would have to call on the resources of several scientific disciplines such as industrial and organizational sociology and political science. Indeed, the intrinsic complexity of the actions and the rationalities of each of the actors cannot be expressed so briefly without simplification. All simplification is by definition unsatisfactory when it involves reporting on reality itself. Such is the thanklessness of modelling.

With this caveat in place, we note that our model must incorporate spatial dimensions; one must consider that it operates simultaneously at the local, regional, national, and international levels. Thus the factors in question interact among these vertically linked geographic layers: the corporation can act at the local level, but it must answer to a parent company, which acts at the global level and which may choose to cease operations in a given geographical area when it deems that conditions there are not profitable, only to invest in a different geographical area. It is the same for the other actors: there are governing institutions that more or less interrelate at the local, regional, national, and international levels; there are citizens' institutions at each of these levels; and both government and civic association actors operate with vertical interrelations.

Our model also must carefully take into account the dynamic dimension of interrelations between the actors. Indeed, these interrelations involve a complex system of actions and reactions among the three generic actors involved. This is complicated all the more by the fact that, as was mentioned earlier, none of the actors involved is, in reality, a monolithic bloc; even the interests of local and global corporations differ. This fundamental characteristic of our model could also benefit from comparative studies, for example, on the behaviour in various social and political contexts and on the policies of corporations with simultaneous operations in several geographical regions. Almost all the mining companies in question have operations elsewhere than in the Canadian Arctic.

What conclusions, then, might be drawn from our examination of the mining industry's corporate practices on Aboriginal land? What conclusions could be derived from the observations made elsewhere in the Indigenous world by recent research that is consistent with the cases we have examined? One thing we can say: nothing will ever ensure that social concerns will be heard and addressed satisfactorily by corporations in the absence of sufficient pressure by associative society; nothing will ever ensure that government intervention will advance the inclusion of social concerns in the corporate plans; and, finally, nothing will ever ensure that the inclusion of social concerns will not have immediate effects or subsequent effects that run counter to those anticipated.

Inspired by corporate rationality, companies seek to bring about favourable conditions that will allow them to continue profitable operations. They take social concerns into account only when associative society clearly indicates the need to do so. By saying nothing, associative society helps to minimize the corporation's investment and operating costs and helps to maximize its profits. That is, silence is taken as consent to the interest of mining companies. In contrast, associative society maximizes its own interest by demanding that such companies take, for example, acceptable steps to reduce pollution, to maximize the positive impacts in the social environment, and to follow up on the actual impacts. In sum, corporations only react if they are prodded to do so. At any rate, they always have the possibility of not investing in a place if they believe that they cannot meet imposed social requirements while ensuring the profitability of their investment. During negotiations they undoubtedly will invest significant energy in highlighting the economic benefits of their activities and in reducing social requirements. This includes threats to postpone their investment or to make investments elsewhere since they know that mineral resources are never found at only one place. The world is their market.

Acknowledgments

This research was funded by the Social Sciences and Humanities Research Council of Canada and by the Canada Research Chairs Secretariat. The economic data on circumpolar north comes from ArcticStat, the main research infrastructure of the Canada Research Chair on Comparative Aboriginal Condition of Université Laval, which was created thanks to funds from the Canadian Foundation for Innovation.

Notes

1 These relations can be represented by models, equations, or charts. Typically in the equations the corporation is represented by the symbol C, the government G, and the associative society S. The flows of interest are represented by an arrow ($\rightarrow$). A chart model is presented in the figures accompanying this chapter.

2 (C → (G ⇆ S))

3 (C → G → S)

4 ((C ⇆ G) → S)

5 ((C ⇆ G) ← S)

6 (C → (G ⇆ S))

7 (C ← S) + (C ← G ← S)

8 With the exception of Finland, where the manufacture of communication technology plays a large role.

9 Breakwater Resources Ltd., *Annual Report 1997* and *First Quarter Interim Report, March 31, 1998*, http://www.breakwater.ca; Allen 1998; Bourgeois 1997; and Info-Mine, *Nanisivik Mine, Breakwater Resources*.

10 For more information on the project of military infrastructure see http://www.forces.gc.ca/site/Commun/ml-fe/article-fra.asp?id=5711 (accessed 19 November 2009). See also Bourgeois 1997.

11 Xstrata, http://www.xstrata.com/operation/raglan/ (accessed 19 November 2009); Falconbridge, *Annual Report 1996*, http://www.falconbridge.com; Info-Mine, *Raglan Mine; Globe and Mail* 1998; George 1996a; George 1996b; Phillips 1995; and Wilkin 1998.

12 *Globe and Mail* (1998).

13 Unused material and the machinery used to build the mine and the concentrator were brought back to Quebec City at the same time as the first shipment (Wilkin 1998).

14 *Nunatsiaq News*, 'A big cash windfall, murder, mayhem and much more' (Nunavik 2008 in review), January 2009. See also 'Raglan mine workforce short on Inuit,' 3 September 2004; 'Few Inuit working at Nunavik's Raglan Mine,' 11 November 2002; 'Raglan audit identifies concerns with Inuit training at mine,' 2 August 2002; and 'Training of Inuit stepped up at the Raglan mine,' 24 April 1998.

15 Ibid.

Bibliography

Allen, Don. 1998. Nanisivik, a different kind of mine. *Nunatsiaq News*, 20 March, p. 18.

Arctic Monitoring and Assessment Programme (AMAP). 1997. *Arctic Pollution Issues: A State of the Arctic Environmental Report*. Oslo: AMAP.

– 2003. Report from the AMAP conference and workshop: Impacts of POPs and mercury on Arctic environments and humans. Tromsø, 20–24 January. Norsk Polarinstitutt Internrapport Nr. 12, Tromsø.

– 2004a. AMAP assessment 2002: Heavy metals in the Arctic; Arctic Monitoring and Assessment Programme (AMAP). Oslo, Norway.

– 2004b. AMAP Assessment 2002: Persistent organic pollutants (POPs) in the Arctic; Arctic Monitoring and Assessment Programme (AMAP). Oslo, Norway.

– 2009. Arctic pollution 2009 (POPs, human health, radioactivity): Arctic Monitoring and Assessment Programme (AMAP). Oslo, Norway.

Armstrong, T., G. Rogers, and G. Rowley. 1978. *The Circumpolar North*. London: Methuen.

Bergeron, Gérard. 1977. *La gouverne politique*. Paris-La Haye: Mouton. Québec: Les Presses de l'Université Laval.

Bourgeois, Annette. 1997. Mine probe at Nanisivik to study environment practices. *Nunatsiaq News*, 25 April, pp. 1–2.

Breakwater Resources Ltd. 1997. *Annual Report 1997*. Investor package.

– 1998. *First Quarter Interim Report: March 31, 1998*. Investor package.

– Website: http//www.breakwater.ca.

Clark, A., and J. Cook Clark. 1999. The new reality of mineral development: Social and cultural issues in Asia and Pacific nations. *Resources Policy* 25 (3): 189–96.

Clark, B. 2002. The indigenous environmental movement in the United States: Transcending borders in struggles against mining, manufacturing, and the capitalist state. *Organization & Environment* 15 (4): 410–42.

Downing, T. 2002. Avoiding new poverty: Mining-induced displacement and resettlement. *Mining, Minerals, and Sustainable Development*, April, no. 58: 1–29.

Duhaime, Gérard. 1991. Le pluriel de l'Arctique : Travail salarié et rapports sociaux en zone périphérique. *Sociologie et Sociétés* 23 (2): 1131–280.

Duhaime, Gérard, Nick Bernard, and Robert Comtois. 2005. Inventory of abandoned mining exploration sites in Nunavik (Canada). *The Canadian Geographer/ Le géographe canadien* 49 (3): 260–71.

Duhaime, Gérard, and Andrée Caron. 2006. The economy of the circumpolar Arctic. In *The Economy of the North*, ed. Solveig Glomsrød and Iulie Aslaksen, 17–23. Oslo: Statistics Norway.

Duhaime, Gérard, Pierre Fréchette, and Véronique Robichaud. 1999. The economic structure of the Nunavik region (Canada): Changes and stability. Québec, Chaire de recherche du Canada sur la condition autochtone comparée. Collection recherche en ligne. http://www.chaireconditionautochtone.fss.ulaval.ca/ extranet/doc/103.pdf.

Duhaime, Gérard, André Lemelin, Vladimir Didyk, Oliver Goldsmith, Gorm Winther, Andrée Caron, Nick Bernard, and Anne Godmaire. 2004. Economic systems. In *Arctic Human Development Report*, ed. Young Oran and Niels Einarsson, 69–84. Reykjavik: Arctic Council.

Duhaime, Gérard, Alexandre Morin, Heather Myers, and Dominic St-Pierre. 2001. Inuit business ownership: Canadian experiences, Greenland challenges. *Inussuk, Arctic Research Journal*, 1: 193–210.

Falconbridge.1996. *Annual Report 1996*.
– Websites: http://www.falconbridge.com and http://www.falconbridge.ca/our_
business/nickel_raglan.html.
Fulmer, A., A. Godoy, and P. Neff. 2008. Indigenous rights, resistance, and the
law: Lessons from a Guatemalan mine. *Latin American Politics and Society* 50 (4):
91–121.
George, Jane. 1996a. Nunavik firms ink $60 million deal with Falconbridge. *Nunat-
siaq News*, 13 September, p. 13.
– 1996b. Raglan deal could mean good jobs for Inuit. *Nunatsiaq News*, 13 September, p.14.
Globe and Mail. 1998. Noranda raises stake in Falconbridge. 23 September, p. B14.
Gunn, John. 1995. *Restoration and Recovery of an Industrial Region*. New York:
Springer-Verlag.
– 2001. Environmental and social consequences of industrialisation: Community
driven restorations initiatives for industrial landscapes. Communication at
CAES and CASS Networks Joint Course, 16 September, Apatity (Russia).
Info-mine. n.d. *Nanisivik Mine, Breakwater Resources*. http://www. info-mine.com.
– n.d. *Raglan Mine*. http://www.info-mine.com.
Jenkins, H., and N. Yakovleva. 2006. Corporate social responsibility in the mining
industry: Exploring trends in social and environmental disclosure. *Journal of
Cleaner Production* 14 (3–4): 271–84.
Kapelus, P. 2002. Mining, corporate social responsibility and the 'community': The
case of Rio Tinto, Richards Bay Minerals and the Mbonambi. *Journal of Business
Ethics* 39 (3): 275–96.
Kirsch, S. 2007. Indigenous movements and the risks of counterglobalization:
Tracking the campaign against Papua New Guinea's Ok Tedi mine. *American
Ethnologist* 34 (2): 303–21.
Marantz, Denis. 1996. Questions touchant les droits des peoples autochtones dans
les instances internationals. In *Peuples ou populations; égalité, autonomie et autodé-
termination: Les enjeux de la Décennie international des populations autochtones*, 9–71.
Montreal: Centre international des droits de la personne et du développement
démocratique.
Myers, Heather. 2001. Changing environment, changing times: Environmental
issues and political action in the Canadian North. *Environment* 43 (6): 32–44.
Notzke, Claudia. 1994. Native people and environmental impact assessment. In
Aboriginal Peoples and Natural Resources in Canada, 263–98. North York, ON: Cap-
tus University Publications.
Phillips, Todd. 1995. $486 million Nunavik mine may create 400 jobs. *Nunatsiaq
News*, 10 February, p. 5.
Skocpol, Theda. 2003. *Diminished Democracy: From Membership to Management in
American Civic Life*. Norman: University of Oklahoma Press.

Sugden, D.E. 1982. *Arctic and Antarctic: Modern Geographical Synthesis*. Totowa, NJ: Barnes and Noble.

Taylor, J. 2008. Indigenous peoples and indicators of well-being: An Australian perspective on UNPFII global frameworks. *Centre for Aboriginal Economic Policy Research* 87 (1): 111–26.

Trebeck, K. 2007. Tools for the disempowered? Indigenous leverage over mining companies. *Australian Journal of Political Science* 42 (4): 541–62.

Wilkin, Dwane. 1998. Raglan mine makes small first shipment. *Nunatsiaq News*, 27 March, p. 15.

Profile of Matthew Coon Come (1956–)

Cree, Environmental Activist, and Politician

Mathew Coon Come was born on 13 April 1956 in a tent near Lake Mistassini, some nine hundred kilometres north of Montreal, Quebec.[1] His parents, Alfred and Harriet (née Etapp), were trappers. When he was a young boy he left his family for a decade-long stay at a series of residential schools in Moose Factory, Ontario, as well as in La Tuque and Hull, Quebec.[2] After graduating from Grade 12, Coon Come continued his education at Trent and McGill universities, where he studied political science, economics, and law.[3] He married Maryann Matoush in September 1976, and the couple subsequently had five children: Justus, Marilyn, Ryan, Sarah, and Emma.[4]

After completing his post-secondary studies, Coon Come returned to his people in the James Bay area of Quebec. He was chief of the Mistissini Cree from 1981 to 1986.[5] In 1987 Coon Come was elected Grand Chief of the Grand Council of the Crees and Chairman of the Cree Regional Authority. He was re-elected four times by the James Bay Cree people as their grand chief and has continuously demonstrated his commitment to their fundamental rights and their convictions.[6]

Coon Come wanted to protect and preserve Cree land. His commitment to his people resulted in the organization of and participation in various initiatives that can be described as environmental activism. For instance, he created local, national, and international coalitions of environmental, human rights, and tribal activists to stop the creation of the Great Whale hydroelectric project. The project, which was backed by the Quebec provincial government, would have devastated 'an environment already on the verge of ecological collapse.'[7] Under his leadership, these coalitions organized a canoe trip down the Hudson River to a well-attended press conference in New York City, where the Quebec Cree's concerns for their livelihood and territorial lands were expressed. The event initiated a public outcry, and eventually New York State cancelled its purchase contracts with Hydro-Québec. The following year the Great Whale hydroelectric

Matthew Coon Come. Photo courtesy of Canadian Press (Andrew Vaughan).

project was abandoned. Coon Come did not stop there. He eventually obtained a revenue-sharing contract with the Province of Quebec for all future natural resource projects on Cree land.[8] For his efforts, Coon Come was awarded the 1994 Goldman Prize, the equivalent of the Nobel Prize for environmental issues.

Coon Come's leadership skills were further highlighted prior to the 1995 Quebec referendum, when the Cree nation held its own referendum regarding secession. Members of the nation were asked whether or not the Grand Council of the Crees and their vast territories should consent to remain with Quebec if the province voted to separate from Canada. The Grand Council of the Crees voted overwhelmingly to remain within Canada if Quebec seceded, a decision that gained national attention.

Coon Come's dedication to and passion for the advancement of Aboriginal rights in Canada motivated him to run for National Chief of the Assembly of First Nations in 2000. Upon election, he was described as one of the most outspoken chiefs of the assembly. As promised, he forced Native issues onto the government's agenda.[9] However, he was defeated in his bid for re-election in 2003.

Matthew Coon Come has received many awards and accolades, including recognition as one of Maclean's 'Top 50 Power Brokers in Canada' in 1996.[10] He was also given a National Aboriginal Achievement Award in 1995, and Trent University conferred an honorary doctorate upon him in 1998.[11]

Currently, Coon Come lives with his wife and children in the James Bay area. They enjoy hunting, fishing, trapping, and gathering along the Coon Come trapline on traditional Cree land.

KRISTA WHITEHEAD

Notes

1 Barry Came, 'Coon Come fights separatists,' *Maclean's*, 27 February 1995.
2 Ibid.
3 Elizabeth Lumley (ed.), 'Matthew Coon Come,' in *Who's Who in Canada*, vol. 37 (Toronto: University of Toronto Press, 2002), 273.
4 Ibid.
5 Ibid.
6 'Dr. Matthew Coon Come – Biography,' http://www.cooncome.ca/biography. html (accessed 22 January 2011).
7 Canadian Press, 'Chief fears James Bay "disaster" will get worse,' *Edmonton Journal*, 2 February 1990.

8 Canadian News Facts, '(Matthew) Coon Come to lead AFN,' 1 July 2000: 6084, *CPI.Q* (accessed 26 January 2011).

9 Paul Barnsley, 'New chief for AFN (Matthew Coon Come),' *Windspeaker*, Aug. 2000:1, 12, *CPI.Q* (accessed 27 January 2011).

10 'Maclean's top 50 power brokers of 1996,' in *Historica: The Canadian Encyclopedia*, http://www.thecanadianencyclopedia.com/index.cfm (accessed 24 May 2003).

11 Lumley, 'Matthew Coon Come.'

Native Environmental Justice:
Duty to Consult and Walpole Island

ROBERT VANWYNSBERGHE, SEAN EDWARDS,
DEAN JACOBS, AND FERUZA ABDJALIEVA

> We the First Nations of Walpole Island Indian Territory have inhabited these lands since the beginning of time. With this occupation we have developed our own language, heritage and values ... in accordance with the Creator, mankind and nature. Through this relationship we possess the rights and freedom to determine our own path. We shall carry on these responsibilities as handed down to us by our Creator, our Elders, and ensure that future generations shall be entrusted with these sacred obligations.
> – 'Walpole Island Philosophy and Principles'

The Walpole Island First Nation is a band of 3,100 members consisting almost entirely of people from the Ottawa, Ojibwa, and Potawatomi nations. Of these, 2,300 members are permanent residents on Walpole Island. They live on the southern-most reserve in Canada, situated in the extreme northeastern corner of the mouth of the St Clair River, which runs south from Lake Huron in the Great Lakes chain. The island sits downriver from industrial, chemical, and sewage plants. It is located literally at the mouth, but figuratively at the kidney, of the St Clair River. Walpole is separated from the Canadian mainland by a swing bridge and from the American mainland by a ferry. However, due to their geographical location, current island residents and future generations are affected by the actions of those who are upstream, 'out in the world.'

For the last twenty years the Walpole Island community has actively opposed the environmental destruction of their land base and the harmful health effects of toxic discharge in the nearby St Clair River. Shoreline erosion, mercury contamination, dredging, thermal pollution, industrial air and water pollution, and human contamination of water resources are everyday realities. These external factors threaten the natural and human resources of the community. In keeping with its heritage the community resists these threats, based on an understanding of its 'responsibilities as an environmental steward and ... a keeper of the lands and waters' (Jacobs 2003, 81).

The focus of this chapter is to posit the merit expressed in the actions of the Walpole people in asserting their right to intervene and articulate the impacts of external decisions on their surroundings, based on their environmental principles and their ongoing relationship with the landscape. This right of intervention is a key principle of what we are calling Native environmental justice. It arises from the need for federal and provincial Native policy to be more responsive to the preferences and collective demands for the integrity of physical environments and to the health concerns as expressed by residents of First Nations. Any case of environmental injustice involving First Nations must be placed in its proper historical context. Any legislative infringement of an Aboriginal right or title must both accommodate the special fiduciary relationship between the Crown and First Nations groups and fulfil 'a compelling and substantial legislative objective' (Chartier 2001, 18–19). A shift towards Native environmental justice must involve the recognition of the importance of Native oral history, its admission at courts, and its pre-eminence in the First Nations way of life (Haluza-Delay 2007, 560).

Walpole Island has the potential to provide the template and, perhaps, the nexus for Native environmental justice. This may be accomplished by illuminating how and why environmental justice matters to Aboriginal people. Exploring the process of how, why, and when the Walpole Island First Nation confronts corporate toxic wastes in the waters surrounding the community provides a useful analytical framework for explaining a number of questions: What is environmental justice? What has it got to do with the recognition that modern society is bringing environmental destruction to Walpole Island? Could its tenets find their way into policy or activism? Do the actions taken by the Walpole Island residents reflect the principles of Native environmental justice?

Environmental Justice

The U.S. Environmental Protection Agency defines environmental justice as follows:

> [T]he fair treatment and meaningful involvement of all people regardless of race, color, national origin, or income with respect to the development, implementation, and enforcement of environmental laws, regulations, and policies. Fair treatment means that no group of people, including a racial, ethnic,

or socio-economic group, should bear a disproportionate share of the negative environmental consequences resulting from industrial, municipal, and commercial operations or the execution of federal, state, local, and tribal programs and policies. Meaningful involvement means that (1) potentially affected community residents have an appropriate opportunity to participate in decisions about a proposed activity that will affect their environment and/or health; (2) the public's contribution can influence the regulatory agency's decision; (3) the concerns of all participants involved will be considered in the decision making process; and (4) the decision makers seek out and facilitate the involvement of those potentially affected. (U.S. Environmental Protection Agency 2002)

Page (2007) comments that this definition of environmental justice is predicated on two independent but interconnected dimensions: distributive justice and procedural justice (616–17). Distributive justice is concerned with equitable protection from harm, whereas procedural justice addresses issues of equitable participation in decision-making processes – both are integral features of environmental justice.

For Walpole, race and place are seen as key factors in asking 'political questions about social power and justice' (Darnovsky 1992, 50), as are systems of production linked to 'pollution, pesticides and toxic wastes' (Darnovsky 1992, 16; Di Chiro 1992; Almeida 1994).

Walpole residents want meaningful involvement in decisions that affect them, consistent enforcement of existing environmental regulations, and substantial consideration on who bears the effects of toxins in the water. In fighting for these issues, residents often lack the institutional and financial capacity to match the pocketbook of those responsible for the toxic waste affecting their lives. This struggle involves intersecting issues of traditional territories, living conditions, and physical and cultural placement within the logic of colonialism, which has contributed to an 'outside' definition of what constitutes *the environment*: something that can merely be inhabited and ascribed monetary value. In terms of Walpole, it is not just the landscape; it is the waters that surround it, and even the 'uninhabitable lands,' such as marshes. For First Nations, water carries a distinctly cultural meaning – it is a sustaining life force that evokes reverence – and preservation of water is integral to their cultural identity (Mascarenhas 2007, 570). Caring in this way for the landscape motivates Native environmental activism (Jacobs 2003). This stewardship approach can be used as a framework for Native environmental justice.

The main historical factors in a Native environmental-justice framework are the outside challenges to traditional lands, substantial differences in approach to 'management,' and a world view that holds the land as a key part of history. To put things more forcefully, the Native environmental-justice framework draws on nothing less than historical alienation from land without consultation, genocidal attacks on what Krauss (1994, 267) calls 'Native American cultural identification, the experience of colonialism, and the imminent endangerment of their culture.'

For now, this framework highlights the relevance of communities that have served as literal dump sites for capital (Sachs 1995) – akin to what Bullard (1994, 17) describes as 'garbage imperialism' in black communities in the southern United States. Environmental justice is often site specific, as are the responses to the hazard.

In Walpole Island, we expand the concept of environmental justice to include the culture, history, and language of the First Nations, which shape their perceptions of the problems as well as their response to them. A workable conception of Native environmental justice cannot exist without a consolidated and consistent commitment of government bureaucracies to culturally sensitive treatment and the provision of access by Native peoples to legitimate participation in the environmental processes affecting them (Mascarenhas 2007, 573).

These points illustrate that Native environmental justice is not just social justice or equitable treatment. In relation to Walpole, the concerns are layered on top of a history wherein Aboriginal residents of the island were pushed to the margins of society and had their land base restricted and affected through the treaty process, or lack thereof. The members of Walpole Island have been marginalized at times, yet their advocacy, capacity building, and legal tools provide them with greater opportunities to affect the environmental status of other groups in similar situations. Particularly noteworthy is the manner in which Walpole Islanders' identification with the sustainability framework (based on culture and history) has been mobilized in the face of the distributed and subtle affects of things like cancer, contaminated water, and declining fish stocks.

The Walpole Case

Walpole Island's survival has been threatened by chemical spills and discharges into the waters that surround the community. The majority of the effluents released into the St Clair River originate from fifty-two industrial points dotting the St Clair shoreline. These comprise four electric thermal generating stations, thirty-four industries, and fourteen municipal waste-water treatment plants. The industrial facilities include petroleum refineries, organic and inorganic chemical manufacturers, paper companies, salt producers, and thermal electric generating facilities. Powerful multinational companies, such as Esso, Shell, and Dow, own them. Most of the companies rely on the St Clair for water needed in the refining process. From 1986 to 1992 these companies, as well as others, produced 550 chemical spills. Seventeen were severe enough to force Walpole Island's water treatment plant to shut down. On average, one hundred spills per year occurred between 1986 and 1992 (Lilliston 1992, 9). As a result, sediments along the Canadian shoreline of the St Clair River have been particularly contaminated with a variety of inorganic and organic materials from industrial, municipal, and non-point sources, including polychlorinated biphenyls (PCBs), oil, grease, and mercury. The presence of such contaminants lying on the bottom of the St Clair River is especially problematic for the residents of Walpole Island because sediment is responsible for the formation of the delta upon which Walpole rests and these chemicals work their way into the water supply, the fish, the wildlife, and the soil on which the people live, work, and eat. The results are numerous. Residents' claims include high cancer rates, earaches among children who swim, and tumours on the fish. Also unmistakable is the residents' change in behaviour: they are eating less fish and other wildlife, buying bottled water, and viewing their natural surroundings as sick and in pain.

Walpole's concerns are lodged in its asymmetrical relationship to powerful corporations. The residents witness the health impacts of the destruction of the physical environment, but the corporations are located outside of the community and often the country and they view the St Clair River as natural capital, something employed to facilitate the production process. Discharges of toxins into the river, accidental spills, increased water temperature, and poor air quality are direct impacts. These accepted impacts of the production process allow the companies to externalize the costs of the production process. The second-order impacts hit home as Walpole residents complain of health problems related to pollution.

It is necessary to go back over fifty years to judge the potential harm involved in living, working, and playing downriver to petrochemical facilities (Great Lakes Science Advisory Board 1993, 8). Assessing the presence of toxic substances in one part of the Great Lakes must be undertaken with the knowledge that the existence of toxins in the wider Great Lakes is potentially injurious to any other location in the system. Only 1 per cent of the water contained in the lakes exits the St Lawrence River. This means that the Great Lakes constitute an essentially closed system with little chance of either the dilution of pollutants or their effluence into the Atlantic. It may take more than a century to 'flush' the toxins. Consequently, the adage that pollution dilution is not a solution is appropriate; toxic contamination concerns must transcend immediate location and time.

The most perilous element of the existence of contaminated sediments is the potential impact of what the International Joint Commission calls persistent toxic substances. For Walpole Island residents, the existence of persistent toxic substances has labelled them a 'critical subpopulation' in the world of toxicology (Myers, Manno, and McDade 1995). As a particularly stable Great Lakes community composed of peoples who consume larger quantities of fish than do others, Walpole residents are at a greater risk of toxic contamination (Gilbertson 1985, 1682). This population is exposed to organochlorine compounds, such as PCBs and DDT, via the food chain. One study showed that the consumption of predator fish, such as trout and salmon, correlated with higher blood and tissue levels of PCBs. Consumption of Great Lakes fish has also been related to the presence of PCBs in breast milk and tissue among Mohawk women on the Akwesasne reserve along the St Lawrence River (Myers, Manno, and McDade 1995). The impact of PCBs was examined by testing infants born to women who had consumed Lake Michigan fish for a consistent period, while controlling for thirty-seven confounding variables. The results correlated with lower birth weights, shorter gestational periods, smaller head circumferences, and a variety of cognitive, motor, and behavioural deficits (International Joint Commission 1993b). These studies hint at the potential in utero injury to hormones, especially sex steroids, in the endocrine system and increases in testicular, bladder, and rectal cancer that cannot be separated from chemical pollutants (especially chlorinated hydrocarbons) that are poisoning the biosphere (International Joint Commission 1993).

Harm done by the chemical companies and their discharges is only a part of the larger process of commodification that erodes the everyday, experiential world of Walpole Island residents. In aiming to integrate the material in a way that Native environmental justice is relevant, one must examine the broader treatment of Native populations. Why is it acceptable for this community to absorb such physical, economic, and cultural impacts? Are these impacts a result of geographic location or historical accident or the result of a process that pushed the Indigenous people off their existing territory and onto Walpole Island reserve, outside the mainstream both socially and geographically, their welfare being trumped by the importance of business and jobs? Environmental scholars and activists propose that environmental and social inequities are inseparable, arguing that 'environmental justice is as much about civil rights, self-determination and power, as it is about the questions of health and environmental quality' (Mascarenhas 2007, 574).

To give but one current example, the Walpole community recently lost a fight to prevent the discharge of 3.5 billion litres (750 million gallons) of treated wastewater into the St Clair River at approximately fourteen kilometres (nine miles) upriver from Walpole Island. The wastewater has to be released as a condition of sale of the plant by International Chemical Industries of Canada to Terra International Canada. The water is held in ponds that encompass approximately 250 acres and is accompanied by an eighteen-metre (sixty-foot) gypsum by-product stack covering one hundred acres. This discharge is a response to an unsuccessful attempt to get rid of the wastewater using a filtration system. Filtering this discharge on site would have cost the company $25 million. Hence the overriding rationale for claiming that the water is not so toxic as to prevent it from being released into the river. The existing system allows the company to mitigate economic damage, by externalizing the costs of dealing with the waste products that it produced, and overlooks the environmental damage.

The shift towards market deregulation in Canada, and southern Ontario in particular, exacerbated historical disparities in the social, environmental, and communal well-being of First Nations. Substantial budgetary reductions at local and provincial levels, as well as the considerable restructuring of roles and the amendments to environmental legislation, preclude meaningful 'recognition [by state actors] of environmental injustice and participation in environmental regime' by First Nations groups. Deregulatory practice further frames environmental discourse in such a way as to marginalize and diminish spiritual and cultural Indigenous values, thus disengaging First Nations from their land and resources (Mascarenhas 2007, 567–8, 572).

Culturally speaking, the unrelenting drive for unfettered accumulation, commodifying the values of Native communities and Native people more generally, exacerbates the asymmetries of power and money. In this way, capital denies the importance of Walpole Island or Native values as tools for justice, by trivializing and homogenizing a diversity of perspectives. Native environmental justice argues for conserving Native human and land resources because these represent the preservation of diverse cultures composing part of human life. No distinction should be made between the goal of sustainable development and the goal of maintaining cultural diversity. What we are encouraging here is a framework for seeing the link between the survival of Native culture and the site-specific degradation that disproportionately has an impact on those less powerful. Government agencies need to reconcile the issues of First Nations environmental justice and cultural particularism. In so doing, it will become possible to move towards a unique appreciation of the distinct nature of the relationship of First Nations to the land and resources, thus adding a heretofore missing dimension of 'recognition' to the definition of environmental justice (Page 2007, 618, 625).

In putting forward this Native environmental-justice framework we appreciate that most individuals are no longer directly dependent on the land and that most see the environment in very concrete terms (as the place where individuals live and work), not as some abstract concept of nature. A pristine existence is not sought. However, in a world of many choices, individuals need to be able to make decisions consistent with their well-being. Native communities, as experienced victims of colonialism, racism, and capitalism, can offer a model for doing so.

Implications: Policy Context and History

Native environmental justice cannot be separated from the evolving legal status of Aboriginal rights and the effect that this has on policy. Native peoples in Canada have constitutionally guaranteed Aboriginal rights (Section 35[1], Constitution Act 1982). According to *Regina v. Van Der Peet* (1996), Aboriginal rights are practices, traditions, and customs central to the Aboriginal societies in North America that existed prior to contact with Europeans. As Valiante explains, the definition and use of these rights continues to change owing to ongoing legal challenges: 'because of their special status, the involvement of First Nations in the decisions that affect their entrenched rights is profoundly different from, and judged by a much higher standard than, any other type of public or stakeholder consultation. This requires a fundamental shift in government administrative procedures' (2002, 10).

Their inclusion in current discussions has been aided by legal and constitutional changes (Poelzer 2002, 88). This does not exempt them from the consequences of past policy decisions. As discussed later, Walpole Island has pursued intervener status and acted as a mouthpiece for surrounding communities, which are also subject to the environmental effects but are also more susceptible to economic harm if the companies cease operations. The willingness of businesses to change has involved a sustainability discourse, but this provides scant solace when it is understood that change can only happen if it serves the prime directive of economic efficiency while supplementing social legitimacy (MacDonald 2002, 83). The Walpole Island example alone attests that the first duty of businesses is to their shareholders and not the affected participants. However, this ought not to absolve businesses from the ethical responsibility to adopt 'communicative competencies' and engage in dialogue with Indigenous and minority groups in order to become conscientious interveners in disputes when they arise (Lane 2006, 389). Nonetheless, given the substantial costs often involved in pollution reduction, the bottom line often trumps environmental equity. However, policy has some encouraging aspects, as briefly outlined in this section.

The concrete implications of the rights-based dialogue in the Native environmental-justice framework lead to the question of what element of this rights-based discourse needs to be developed. Here the discussion of Native environmental justice is useful. LaDuke (1992) and Bryant (1995) offer the following descriptions of these rights and their ideal implication: 'It [the rights] refers to those cultural norms and values, rules, regulations, behaviors, policies, and decisions to support sustainable communities, where people can interact with confidence that their environment is safe, nurturing, and productive ... These are the communities where both cultural and biological diversity are respected and highly revered and where distributed justice prevails' (Bryant 1995, 5; LaDuke 1992).

Aboriginal rights provide a lever for policy change that is not available to other actors in the environmental-policy system. Therefore, settlement of land claims and movement towards reconciling coincident proprietary land-ownership claims are essential in meeting 'community aspirations' (Lane 2006, 391).

Poelzer argues that, owing to legal changes, governments must adapt to current political and administrative realities in order to fulfil their duty to consult (2002, 88). The courts have consistently held that the Crown is under a duty to consult 'when it proposes to engage in an action that threatens to interfere with existing Aboriginal or treaty rights recognized and affirmed by s.35(1) of the Constitution Act, 1982' (Lawrence and Macklem 2000, 252). Lawrence and Macklem argue that 'the reason why the duty to consult is failing to accomplish its purpose is because it has been widely misunderstood by parties, by counsel and by courts' (2000, 255).

The duty to consult is largely regarded as a legal requirement, but this characterization displaces emphasis from the duty's ex ante function – namely, engagement in meaningful dialogue as a measure to avoid litigation. Lawrence and Macklem propose that 'the duty requires the Crown to make good faith efforts to negotiate an agreement with [the] First Nation in question that translates Aboriginal interests adversely affected by the proposed Crown action into binding Aboriginal or treaty right' (2000, 255).

It has been proposed that the duty to consult is viewed differently by both the Crown and First Nations groups (Chartier 2001, 1). To many First Nations, the fulfilment of the duty entails the Crown's consulting them and gaining consent whenever it undertakes an action that could impact their rights. The Crown 'argues that the constitutional duty to consult is limited to cases in which an infringement of an aboriginal or treaty right has been proven' (Chartier 2001, 1). In *Regina v. Sparrow* the Supreme Court of Canada established a justificatory test 'which protects aboriginal rights while also permitting governments to legislate for legitimate purposes where the legislation is a justifiable infringement of those protected rights. The test must be used each time the Crown purports to infringe an aboriginal or treaty right' (Chartier 2001, 13–18).

The Sparrow test dictates that the First Nations group challenging an activity of the Crown must first establish a prima facie violation of its existing Aboriginal or treaty right. If a prima facie infringement has been established, then the onus shifts to the Crown to provide justification for the violation. The duty of the Crown to consult with First Nations has been interpreted as giving First Nations a blanket veto whenever exploitation of resources is concerned. But that is simply not the case. The scope of the consultation can range anywhere from minimal to substantial involvement of First Nations 'on a case-by-case basis' (Fenwick 2005, 40). Chartier argues that anything between these two extremes should constitute 'meaningful' consultation (2001, 69–71). Both the parameters and the practicalities of the duty have been articulated by Lawrence and Macklem (2000, 255–63). The difficulty has been the variability of circumstances from case to case, insomuch as a concrete elaboration of the specific guidelines for the duty is incredibly problematic. In *Haida Nation v. B.C. (Minister of Forests)* the Supreme Court articulated 'a general framework for the duty to consult and accommodate, where indicated, before Aboriginal title or rights claims have been decided' (Fenwick 2005, 40).

The possible implication for Walpole Island is that jurisprudence may grow to allow First Nations to prevent activities, such as chemical discharges, that would unduly affect an Aboriginal right like subsistence food fishery. 'By promoting negotiation over litigation, the duty [to consult] will foster … the reconciliation of the pre-existence of aboriginal societies with the sovereignty of the Crown' (Lawrence and Macklem 2000, 279).

Walpole residents face the problem of a limited commitment to implementation of environmental regulations at the provincial level. The shift to voluntary codes of conduct, cooperative enforcement, and regulation between business and government is an approach that is seeking to moderate behaviour instead of preventing it (VanNijnatten 2002; MacDonald 2002). This leaves Walpole residents still receiving toxic by-products of a modern society despite their involvement in the process. Even the province's environmental commissioner was alarmed by the pace and extent of this environmental deregulation. In 1998 he recommended that 'the ministry place a priority on pollution prevention rather than on pollution control – reducing the production of pollutants rather than focusing on minimizing environmental damage only after the pollutants are produced' (Environmental Commissioner of Ontario 1999). Lane emphasizes the importance of developing a comprehensive process of Indigenous participation in all facets of state planning (2006, 389). The presented framework would enable Indigenous groups to view the state as a medium rather than an adversary in asserting their claims.

Aside from standard techniques to influence policy, such as lobbying decision makers and holding media events and stakeholder consultations, Canadian legal changes have increased the First Nations' involvement in environmental policymaking. However, this alone may not achieve the desired ends of reducing toxic discharges into the water. Simpson argues that 'while the process is certainly important, researchers study process with the distribution primarily in mind – ultimately the goal of such studies is to understand the skewed distribution of hazard. A just process that allows everyone to participate will mean little if the distribution remains the same' (Simpson 1997, 2).

In this context, Walpole Island First Nation policies and guidelines have led to a proposed protocol for developing memorandums of understanding or impacts and benefits agreements. Through open consultation with Aboriginal peoples about proposed developments these memorandums may be obtained. The recognition of Walpole's land claims offers the First Nation an advisory role, while setting up a structure (that is, meetings, standards, resources, and definitions) for monitoring the firms that are discharging or spilling contaminants into the St Clair River. More important, it yields benefits, not only to those corporations that agree to them but to the environment that all must share and protect. This coincides with Aboriginal peoples' belief that they have a special responsibility to protect the environment for the generations to come. Some benefits include the following:

1 Creating a positive relationship between the corporation, Aboriginal leadership, and community members
2 Incorporating and enhancing a traditional ecological knowledge through
   (a) baseline environmental studies,
   (b) environmental monitoring protocols, and
   (c) development of mitigation measures
3 Initiating a partnership approach to resolving environmental problems during a project's construction and operation
4 Employing qualified First Nation members to work on the project
5 Establishing clear mechanisms for informing the Aboriginal community about the development
6 Enhancing the opportunities for Aboriginal businesses to supply goods and services to a proponent's project

In terms of Native environmental justice these benefits are only realized through the recognition of the critical importance of the duty to consult. Thus, Walpole needs to monitor and regulate the environmental performance of the industries. It needs regular information to ensure that industries are operating in accordance with Walpole Island's environmental requirements. As well, Walpole Island Heritage Centre needs to obtain disclosure from industry when an environmental incident occurs, such as an unplanned discharge to the St Clair River. It is not consistent with the duty to consult that Walpole Island First Nation should learn of such incidents casually and infrequently, even though this does happen on an ad hoc basis. The duty to consult needs to become a regular procedure. This requires reliable funding through a percentage of the fines collected for environmental offences. In time, Walpole will assume an investigative and prosecutorial function pertaining to industrial environmental performance, pursuant to locally applicable environmental laws. Finally, Walpole will become engaged more actively in the sentencing hearings that are held after charges have been laid and proven under federal and provincial legislation in court (that is, through victim impact statements).

In sum, the courts point out that governments must consult Canadian First Nations if their Aboriginal title (whether proven in court or not) or rights will be interfered by development decisions. The courts in British Columbia have extended this duty to consult to the corporations that are aware of Aboriginal title claims. Although the courts have had to steer governments and corporations in this direction, this movement can yield benefits to the Aboriginal peoples whose rights and title will be, or may be, negatively affected. Moreover, corporations choosing to embrace consultation as a means of enhancing the success of their project and limiting its negative environmental impacts may also receive benefits.

Aside from judicial involvement, propositions have arisen to expand the Native environmental-justice framework by synthesizing First Nations interests with the environmental movement, thus 'increasing the mobilization potential of the movement, as well as its scope, by linking environmental justice and resource protection' (Robinson et al. 2007, 580). By linking First Nations conservation concerns with the broader environmental issues of respective environmental organizations, there is an increased potential for a wider recognition of the significance of environmental justice. Furthermore, a greater mobilization potential is conducive to the greater possibility of collective participation in environmental planning initiatives (Robinson et al. 2007, 591). Robinson et al. hope that, '[by] linking[,] … the two frames – environmental justice and environmental protection – will both reinforce the core support for the movement and increase the number of new recruits, ensuring a sustained commitment to the movement's goals and increasing the likelihood of successful movement outcomes' (2007, 591–2).

To conclude, a lens is offered for viewing policy in Canada from a Native environmental-justice perspective that asks, would this policy dispropor-tionately affect one racial, ethnic, or socio-economic group? Does this poli-cy meaningfully involve the affected participants? Are the existing laws or regulations being fairly implemented? Does the policy accommodate and consult the First Nations involved?

In short, governments and proponents of development in Aboriginal ter-ritory need to start seeing meaningful and productive consultation with Aboriginal peoples much differently. Rather than fighting the idea of con-sulting with Aboriginal people, so that the duty is viewed as a cost with no benefits, this needs to become part of a process that can benefit all the par-ties involved, Aboriginal people and proponents alike.

Conclusion

Generally, the suggestion here is that environmental-justice activists and academics explore, connect, and learn from Walpole Island. Walpole is a site-specific case study of environmental injustices in the context of Native history. Overlaying these layers is an increasingly globalized economy that demands environmental deregulation. Native environmental-justice issues make race and place the factors, as well as the analytical tools, for the great-er politicalization of this important topic. In other places, VanWynsberghe (2001, 2002) has commented on these matters in spelling out Walpole Island residents' authentic and pragmatic employment of the sustainability dis-course as a way of increasing their negotiating power with external actors. Here, we have expanded this argument in locating this resistance to envi-ronmental damage in policies that recognize culture, tradition, and history. In doing so, we are suggesting that Walpole has taken another step in devel-oping a Native environmental-justice framework. The Walpole residents have used this framework to obtain intervener status regarding initiatives that affect them and to build capacity with the attendant duties and respon-sibilities. The upshot is that the Native environmental-justice approach is not just site specific but also cultural in the importance of the land and water to our day-to-day lives. It is an attempt to build capacity using the key tool of the duty to consult, as it is being imposed on external actors by current court decisions. It encourages the creation of radically new environ-mental discourse and activism in Native communities in Canada. The point is that the histories of colonialism and racism have created site-specific cen-tres of environmental degradation, and, in turn, this has created a new kind of environmental consciousness in places like Walpole. This consciousness has the potential to further challenge mainstream environmental organizations, and the politico-economic institutions that support them, in order to consider issues of race, class, and exclusion in their discussion of environmental issues.

Bibliography

Almeida, Paul. 1994. The network for environmental and economic justice in the Southwest: Interview with Richard Moore. *Capitalism, Nature and Socialism* 5: 21–54.

Bryant, Bunyon, ed. 1995. *Environmental Justice: Issues, Policies and Struggles*. Washington, DC: Island Press.

Bullard, Robert D., ed. 1994. *Unequal Protection: Environmental Justice and Communities of Color*. San Francisco: Sierra Club Books.

Canada. Constitution Act. 1982. Being Schedule B to the Canada Act 1982 (U.K.), 1982, c. 11. http://laws.justice.gc.ca/en/charter.

Chartier, Melanie. 2001. *The Crown's Duty to Consult with First Nations*. Vancouver: University of British Columbia.

Darnovsky, Marcy. 1992. Stories less told: Histories of U.S. environmentalism. *Socialist Review* 21: 11–54.

Di Chiro, Giovanna. 1992. Defining environmental justice: Women's voices and grassroots politics. *Socialist Review* 21: 93–130.

Environmental Commissioner of Ontario. 1999. Ontario Environmental Commissioner reports decline in environmental protection. http://www.eco.on.ca/eng/uploads/eng_pdfs/1999/99apr28.htm. See also http://translate.google.ca/translate?hl=en&sl=fr&u=http://www.eco.on.ca/french/newsrel/99apr28a.htm&ei=Kjw3TbySHpG-sAPKt5iBAw&sa=X&oi=translate&ct=result&resnum=1&ved=0CBsQ7gEwAA&prev=/search%3Fq%3Dhttp://www.eco.on.ca/english/newsrel/99apr28a.htm%26hl%3Den%26biw%3D1676%26bih%3D877%26prmd%3Divns.

Fenwick, Fred R. 2005. Supreme Court confirms duty to consult with Aboriginal peoples (in *Haida Nation v. British Columbia [Minister of Forests]*). *Law Now* 29 (5): 39–40.

Gilbertson, Michael. 1985. The Niagara labyrinth: The human ecology of producing organochlorine chemicals. *Canadian Journal of Fisheries and Aquatorial Science* 42: 1681–92.

Gilbertson, Michael, and R. Stephen Schneider. 1993. Causality: The missing link between science and policy. Preface to the special section on cause-effect linkages. *Journal of Great Lakes Research* 19: 720–1.

Great Lakes Science Advisory Board. 1993. *Report to the International Joint Commission*. Windsor, ON: International Joint Commission.

Haluza-Delay, Randolph. 2007. Environmental justice in Canada. *Local Environment* 12 (6): 557–64.

International Joint Commission. 1993a. *A Strategy for Virtual Elimination of Persistent Toxic Substances.* Vol. 1, *Report of the Virtual Elimination Task Force to the International Joint Commission*. Windsor, ON: International Joint Commission.

– 1993b. *A Strategy for Virtual Elimination of Persistent Toxic Substances.* Vol. 2, *Seven Reports to the Virtual Elimination Task Force*. Windsor, ON: International Joint Commission.

Jacobs, Dean. 2003. History of community strategies and activities on environmental issues of the Walpole Island First Nation within the Bkejwanong territory in the 1990s. Draft working paper.

Krauss, Celene. 1994. Women of color on the front line. In *Unequal Protection: Environmental Justice and Communities of Color*, ed. Robert D. Bullard, 256–71. San Francisco: Sierra Club Books.

LaDuke, Winona. 1992. Preface. In *Struggle for the Land: Indigenous Resistance in Genocide, Ecocide, and Contemporary North America*, by Ward Churchill. Toronto: Between the Lines.

Lane, Marcus B. 2006. The role of planning in achieving Indigenous land justice and community goals. *Land Use Policy* 23:385–94.

Lawrence, Sonia, and Patrick Macklem. 2000. From consultation to reconciliation: Aboriginal rights and the Crown's duty to consult. *The Canadian Bar Review* 79:252–79.

Lilliston, Ben. 1992. Island of poison. *Multinational Monitor*, September: 8–9.

MacDonald, Douglas. 2002. The business response to environmentalism. In *Canadian Environmental Policy: Context and Cases*, 3rd ed., ed. Deborah L. VanNijnatten and Robert Boardman, 66–86. Toronto: Oxford University Press.

Mascarenhas, Michael. 2007. Where the waters divide: First Nations, tainted water and environmental justice in Canada. *Local Environment* 12 (6): 565–77.

Myers, Sheila, Jack Manno, and Kimberly McDade. 1995. Great Lakes human health effects research in Canada and the United States: An overview of priorities and issues. *Great Lakes Research Review* 1:13–23.

Page, Justin. 2007. Salmon farming in First Nations' territories: A case of environmental injustice on Canada's west coast. *Local Environment* 12 (6): 613–26.

Poelzer, Greg. 2002. Aboriginal people and environmental policy in Canada: No longer at the margins of environmentalism. In *Canadian Environmental Policy: Context and Cases*, 2nd ed., ed. Deborah L. VanNijnatten and Robert Boardman, 87–106. Toronto: Oxford University Press.

Regina v. Van der Peet, [1996] 2 S.C.R. 507.

Robinson, Joanna L., D.B. Tindall, Erin Seldat, and Gabriela Pechlaner. 2007. Sup-

port for First Nations' land claims amongst members of the wilderness preservation movement: The potential for an environmental justice movement in British
Columbia. *Local Environment* 12 (6): 579–98.

Sachs, Aaron. 1995. *Eco-Justice: Linking Human Rights and the Environment*. Washington, DC: Worldwatch Institute.

Simpson, R. 1997. In pursuit of justice: Conceptualized and unstratified environment. Paper presented at the meeting of the American Sociological Association,
Toronto, Canada, August.

United States Environmental Protection Agency. 2002. Office of Enforcement and
Compliance Assurance. http://www.epa.gov/opptintr/tribal/pubs/Tribal-
Newsletter1of2.pdf.

Valiante, Marcia. 2002. Legal foundation of Canadian environmental policy:
Underlining our values in a shifting landscape. In *Canadian Environmental Policy:
Context and Cases*, 2nd ed., ed. Deborah L. VanNijnatten and Robert Boardman,
3–24. Toronto: Oxford University Press.

VanNijnatten, Deborah L. 2002. The bumpy journey ahead: Provincial environmental policies and national environmental standards. In *Canadian Environmental Policy: Context and Cases*, 2nd ed., ed. Deborah L. VanNijnatten and Robert
Boardman, 145–70. Toronto: Oxford University Press.

VanWynsberghe, Robert. 2001. The 'unfinished story': Narratively analyzing collective action frames in social movements. *Qualitative Inquiry* 7 (6): 733–44.

– 2002. *AlterNatives: Sustainability, Environmental Justice, and Collective Identity on
Walpole Island*. London: Allyn Bacon Press.

Profile of Nellie J. Cournoyea (1940–)

Inuvialuit, Politician, and Activist

Nellie J. Cournoyea is one of the most influential contemporary leaders of the Canadian North. She developed the necessary experience to thrive in today's Northern political environment as a result of having held various government positions and having had significant involvement in land-claim settlements.

Cournoyea was born in Aklavik, Northwest Territories, on 4 March 1940. She was the second of eleven children born to Maggie and Nels Hvatum.[1] During her childhood she lived a traditional life on the land. As a young adult she began her career as a broadcaster and manager for the Canadian Broadcasting Corporation in the Inuvik region.[2] However, her true passion was focused on community matters. For instance, in the 1970s she was leader of the Committee for Original People's' Entitlement, the group that negotiated the land claim for the Inuvialuit. When ratified, it resulted in the Inuvialuit receiving '$45 million and title to 91,000 square kilometers, including sub-surface rights to 13,000 sq. km.'[3] She later commented that this land-claim settlement was the highlight of her career.[4]

In 1979, Cournoyea left the Committee for Original Peoples' Entitlement to take a seat as the elected representative for Nunakput riding in the Northwest Territories legislature.[5] She held that position for sixteen years, and it provided a comprehensive understanding of a wide range of Northern issues. As a result of her combination of detailed knowledge and well-respected public image, Nellie J. Cournoyea was elected premier of the Northwest Territories in 1991. She was the first Aboriginal woman to be a premier in Canada, serving from 1991 to 1995.[6]

Other important leadership roles played by Cournoyea include particularly her involvement in the finalization of the Inuit Land Claims Agreement, which resulted in the creation of the Nunavut territory. When Cournoyea's term in office concluded in 1995, she left behind her legislative duties, but she did not leave the political arena altogether.

Nellie Cournoyea. Photo courtesy of Hans Blohm.

Today she serves as chair of the board and chief executive officer of Inuvialuit Regional Corporation – one of the most important positions in the Beaufort-Delta region.[7] The corporation has become increasingly important as oil and gas prices rise and more interest is shown in Northern resources. Cournoyea encourages involvement of the Inuvialuit as business partners working together to meet the growing needs of the industry. She is also head of Aboriginal Pipeline Group, which lobbies for greater control over the $3-billion to $4-billion pipeline that is planned for the Mackenzie Valley region.[8]

Cournoyea's contributions to the Aboriginal community were recognized in 1994 when she became one of the first recipients of the National Aboriginal Achievement Award for Public Service.[9] She has also been granted honorary degrees from the University of Toronto, Lakehead University, Carleton University, and the University of Lethbridge.[10] Other awards include the Woman of the Year Award from the Northwest Territories Native Women's Association and the Wallace Goose Award from Inuvialuit Regional Corporation.[11] In 2008 she was awarded the Northern Award by Governor General Michaëlle Jean.[12]

As Carol Howes, a journalist at the *National Post,* states, 'she is viewed as one of the toughest and most powerful leaders north of the Arctic Circle.'[13] Nellie J. Cournoyea continues to work for the betterment of Aboriginal people as well as for the Northwest Territories.

ALETA AMBROSE

Notes

1 Glen Korstrom, 'A woman of purpose: Nellie Cournoyea gets personal while she stays relevant,' *Northern News Service* (Yellowknife: Canarctic Publishing Ltd.), 17 August 1998.
2 'Nellie Cournoyea,' in *Who's Who of American Women* (New Jersey: Reed Publishing, 1993), 201.
3 Ed Struzik, 'A force of nature, a champion of her people: Nellie Cournoyea has never backed away from a fight – and she's had plenty in her life,' *Edmonton Journal*, 15 August 2001, A1.
4 Ibid.
5 Korstrom, 'A woman of purpose.'
6 'Nellie Cournoyea,' in *The Canadian Encyclopedia 2000 World Edition* (Toronto: McClelland and Stewart, 2000), 1.
7 Chris Varcoe, 'Natives look to Ottawa for pipeline financing,' *Calgary Herald*, 7 November 2001, D1.

8 Ed Struzik, 'The greening of Inuvik: As talk of pipelines escalates, Inuvik is juggling a booming economy with its corresponding influx of people and their needs,' *Calgary Herald*, 26 August 2001, B13.

9 National Aboriginal Achievement Foundation, 'National Aboriginal Achievement Awards 1994 recipients: Nellie Cournoyea,' http://www.naaf.ca/program/92 (accessed 26 January 2011).

10 http://www.collectionscanada.gc.ca/women/030001-1332-e.html.

11 Ibid.

12 Thomas Brodie, 'Nellie Cournoyea receives Northern Award,' Northern News Service, 21 April 2008, http://nnsl.com/northern-news-services/stories/papers/apr21_08awa.html (accessed 20 April 2009).

13 Carol Howes, 'Where the white north is deep with black gold: Inuvialuit hunger for recognition,' *National Post*, 9 December 2000, D5.

PART 3

EDUCATION

Profile of Olive Patricia Dickason (1920–2011)

Métis, Journalist, Historian, and Professor Emerita

The Métis have always stood with one foot in both worlds, straddling a cultural divide. Knowing this, it seems most fitting that a Manitoba-born Métis woman would build bridges of understanding between the Indigenous and non-Indigenous peoples of Canada. Indefatigable and youthful, the acclaimed historian and academic Olive Dickason managed to rewrite Canadian history while battling institutional ageism.[1] Her efforts in bridging cultures and generations within Canada were remarkable in reshaping the attitudes of Canadians.

Dickason was born in Winnipeg, Manitoba, in 1920 to a Métis mother, Phoebe Cote, and an English father, Frank Williamson.[2] Her background was as varied as her career path. As a child she began her studies in an oblate convent.[3] During the Great Depression, after her father had lost his banking job, her mother fed the family using her 'bush survival skills.' It was also her mother who persuaded Dickason to continue her studies through correspondence courses.[4] This encouragement would eventually lead to a university degree.[5] For the next twenty-four years Dickason worked as a journalist at various prominent newspapers including the *Globe and Mail*.[6]

Increasing awareness of her mixed heritage spurred Dickason to return to university and study history. Christopher Moore notes that Dickason's penchant for rewriting Canadian history was sparked by her indignation at the textbooks that cast Natives in a secondary role in the so-called discovery of Canada and, more insultingly, as 'savages.'[7] Her decision to pursue a graduate degree in Native history was questioned because 'the University [of Ottawa] in those days doubted that Aboriginal history was real history.'[8] Determined to give voice to her Native heritage, Dickason eventually graduated with a doctorate and thus the right to teach the seldom-heard Aboriginal side of Canadian history. Her battle had just begun.

In 1985 the University of Alberta informed the then 65-year-old Dickason that she was obliged to retire under the terms of her contract. Dickason

Olive Dickason. Reprinted with the permission of the *Edmonton Sun*.

replied, 'I am just getting started.'[9] She took the institution to court under the new Charter of Rights and Freedoms, and by the time a ruling was reached by the Supreme Court of Canada some seven years later, she was ready to retire of her own accord.[10]

Dickason took the historical establishment to task, using a powerful arsenal of words. Some of her more notable writings included *The Myth of the Savage* (1977) and the highly acclaimed *Canada's First Nations: A History of Founding Peoples from Earliest Times* (1992; now in its fourth edition). Although Dickason's mainstream accolades included the esteemed Order of Canada (1996), her proudest moment came when she was awarded the National Aboriginal Lifetime Achievement Award in 1997.[11] Her commitment to the truth initiated a genuine dialogue between the Native and the non-Native peoples of Canada, helping both sides to take those first steps together towards real understanding. Olive Dickason passed away in Ottawa in March, 2011.

YVONNE PRATT

Notes

1 'Olive Dickason: Woman who changed history wins lifetime achievement award,' *Windspeaker*, 1997, http://www.highbeam.com/doc/1G1-30452094.html.
2 Christopher B. Tower, 'Olive Patricia Dickason,' in *Notable Native Americans*, ed. Sharon Malinowski (New York: Gale Research, 1995), 124.
3 Fred Favel, 'Success by degree: Olive Patricia Dickason, CM, Ph.D., D.Litt., Professor Emeritus,' in *Transition (Portrait)* 8, no. 12 (April/May 1996): 1.
4 Tower, 'Olive Patricia Dickason.'
5 Favel, 'Success by degree.'
6 Tower, 'Olive Patricia Dickason.'
7 Christopher Moore, 'The first people of America,' *The Beaver: Exploring Canada's History* 72 (5): 53.
8 Ibid.
9 Ibid.
10 Elizabeth Lumley, ed., 'Dickason, Olive Patricia,' in *Canadian Who's Who*, vol. 35 (Toronto: University of Toronto Press, 2000).
11 National Aboriginal Achievement Awards, '1997 Lifetime Achievement: Dr. Olive Patricia Dickason,' http://www.naaf.ca/program/92.

Elders' Teachings about Indigenous Storywork for Education

JO-ANN ARCHIBALD (Q'UM Q'UM XIIEM)

In Aboriginal gatherings we start with prayerful thoughts and words. The late elder, Tsimilano (Vincent Stogan), of the Musqueam First Nations people of southwestern British Columbia would call us together and say:

> My dear ones,
> Form a circle and join hands in prayer. In joining hands, hold your left palm upward to reach back to grasp the teachings of the Ancestors. Hold your right palm downward to pass these teachings on to the younger generation. In this way, the teachings of the Ancestors continue, and the circle of human understanding and caring grows stronger.

Even though Tsimilano has passed to the Spirit World, I still hear his voice echo the important teaching of maintaining our cultural knowledge links. I continue to share his teaching with others. I have stood in many different circles of people, praying for guidance from the Creator, to help us make a better world for the younger and future generations. I speak from the traditions and experiences of the Coast Salish peoples of British Columbia, in particular the Stó:lō of the Lower Fraser River.[1] In many of these circles the elders of the Aboriginal communities share their perspectives, knowledge, and insights gained from many years of learning, teaching, and reflection. This chapter focuses on the impact of the storytelling teachings of the Stó:lō and Coast Salish Aboriginal elders on educational curricula.[2]

Elders possess wisdom and insight gained from their cultural knowledge and lived experience. Age is not the determining factor for achieving elder status. I have heard elders say that what matters is how an individual 'carries' herself or himself. They mean that an elder must treat cultural knowledge respectfully and demonstrate responsibility or care in the process of sharing it, or teaching it, with others. Aboriginal communities and organizations across Canada have various ways of identifying and working with elders, and their criteria may differ.

In Aboriginal communities and educational contexts we share the value of taking guidance and learning from elders who are Aboriginal knowledge holders. Elders are participating in Canadian educational systems as teachers and invited speakers. Sometimes they are hired to teach subjects such as Aboriginal language. At other times they come into educational contexts as resource persons to tell stories, to lead cultural workshops, to serve on advisory committees, and to say opening words and prayers for gatherings and meetings.[3] For many years elders have been involved in local curriculum-development projects. However, little has been written about how they carry out their leadership role and how they have been involved in this important educational endeavour. Canadian educational systems are enriched by the involvement of Aboriginal elders in schooling across the country. Elders are among our best storytellers, and they have knowledge about how we can effectively learn from cultural stories. Aboriginal stories and storytelling are finding their way into all levels of education today, and they are contributing significantly to the quality of educational curricula used in Canadian schools across the country.

I am fortunate to have learned from elders who have upheld and 'carried' their cultural responsibility by passing their teachings to others in ways that are mindful of cultural knowledge and protocols. I coined the term *storywork* as a result of my research and learning relationships with elders.[4] During a Stó:lō cultural gathering one of the organizing speakers tells the guests that it is time to start the (cultural) 'work.' When these words are spoken, we know that it is time to give serious attention to what is said and done. Storywork is about ways of making meaning or gaining insights from stories, whether they are traditional or from lived experience. With storywork, we get ourselves ready to engage in stories by practising the values of respect, responsibility, reverence, and reciprocity. Storywork is also about understanding the interrelatedness and synergy among the storyteller, the story, the listener, and the context in which the story is used. The 'wholistic' nature of stories is another element that will be described later. Humour also facilitates learning through stories, and the Trickster character is a fine example of this.

In British Columbia, Aboriginal cultures have Trickster characters such as Raven, Coyote, and Mink. In our stories the multifaceted Trickster changes form and shape. The forms may range from a human being to any element of nature to a more sacred form. The Trickster often gets into trouble by ignoring good teachings (such as sharing, caring, taking responsibility, and being fair) and letting negative traits (such as greed and envy) take over. Trickster's separation from the cultural teachings of the family, community, land, and nation provide many life lessons as he or she tries to reconnect to these teachings. Trickster is usually in motion, travelling and learning life lessons, and once in a while Trickster surprises us by using supernatural powers to help others. Do not be fooled by thinking that Trickster will use obvious 'tricks' to get his or her way. I have learned to value Trickster's humorous learning ways and the process-oriented nature of teaching and learning through Aboriginal stories.

What follows is a story that Eber Hampton, Chickasaw Nation, told a gathering of educators. He gave me permission to use this story and encouraged me to adapt it for storywork purposes.[5] I renamed the Trickster of this story Old Man Coyote because Coyote in all its forms has become my Trickster of learning and *Old Man Coyote* was calling out to be used as a name in this story.[6] In the background we hear Tsimilano (Vincent Stogan) say, 'My dear ones, the work is about to begin.'

> Old Man Coyote had just finished a long hard day of hunting. He decided to set up his camp for the night. After supper he sat by the fire and rubbed his tired feet from the long day's walk. He took his favourite moccasins out of his bag and noticed that there was a hole in the toe of one of them. He looked for his special bone needle to mend the moccasin but couldn't feel it in the bag. Old Man Coyote started to crawl on his hands and knees around the fire to see if he could see or feel the needle. Just then Owl flew by and landed next to Old Man Coyote and asked him what he was looking for. Old Man Coyote told Owl his problem. Owl said that he would help his friend look for the bone needle. After he had made one swoop around the area of the fire, he told Old Man Coyote that he didn't see the needle. Owl said that if it were around the fire, then he would have spotted it. He then asked Old Man Coyote where he last used the needle. Old Man Coyote said that he used it quite far away, somewhere in the northern direction, to mend his jacket. Then Owl asked him why he was searching for the needle around the campfire. Old Man Coyote said, 'Well, it's much easier to look for the needle here because the fire gives off such good light, and I can see much better here.'

I have behaved like Old Man Coyote many times, wanting to stay close to a cosy fire, continuing to think and act in ways that are comfortable, well known, and easy. But mentors like the Owl or the elders come into my life to remind me to actively seek the bone needle – or Aboriginal solutions for better education. The search for the bone needle may mean going back to the knowledge territories established by the Ancestors in order to transform traditional philosophies into current-day practice. It may mean going into the dark, to new, yet untravelled knowledge territories.

Walking Away from the Fire: Going Back to the Stó:lō Elders

From 1992 to 1996 I worked on my doctoral research about Indigenous storytelling. I was interested in elders' perspectives about the characteristics of stories and how stories could be used for high-quality education. My interest in Aboriginal curricula and stories stems from my teaching experience. When I began teaching in 1972, the study of Aboriginal culture was recommended for Grade 4 and Grade 10 social studies, and, at Grade 10, the problems of 'Indian' people were often discussed as a topic in these classes. At that time Aboriginal people were often portrayed negatively, our cultures were studied in piecemeal fashion, and we were not involved in curriculum development. My personal experience was reiterated by Werner, Connors, Aoki, and Dahlie's study (1977) that analysed the multicultural content of provincially prescribed social studies curricula across Canada. They classified the study of First Nations at the elementary-school level as 'museum and heritage,' and at the secondary school level as 'discipline and issues.' Both approaches tended to present Aboriginal people as objects of study, and their culture as relics of a past heritage. The few Aboriginal stories found in readers were presented as simple 'why' or aetiological myths with no cultural context; hence, they were often not regarded as quality learning resources. Certainly, any student learning about First Nations culture and people during this time period would not think that the First Nations contributed positively to Canadian culture and identity.

In 1974, in response to the lack of culturally appropriate curricula and the dismal portrayal of First Nations, the Stó:lō elders and staff of the Coqualeetza Cultural Centre, located in Sardis, British Columbia, decided that it was time for all children attending schools in the traditional territory of the Stó:lō people to learn about the culture of the Stó:lō from a Stó:lō perspective, through cultural curricula. They felt that non-Stó:lō children needed to learn about the ways in which the Stó:lō people had helped the early settlers to survive, how the Stó:lō had contributed to the development of British Columbia society, and about aspects of Stó:lō culture. They believed that Stó:lō children would benefit from this knowledge and that the cultural curriculum would positively influence the Stó:lō students' self-esteem. Another curriculum goal was to improve cultural understanding and relationships between Aboriginal and non-Aboriginal people.[7] The elders had already been active in a cultural revival initiative since the late 1960s, meeting on a weekly basis to document their First

Nations language – called Halq'eméylem – and their cultural knowledge. An elementary social studies curriculum, the *Stó:lō Sitel*,[8] was subsequently developed. The elders were the 'backbone' of the curriculum because the cultural content was based on their knowledge and their perspectives. A number of Stó:lō stories were documented and published as booklets, and teacher guidebooks were developed with complete unit and lesson plans. The elders took great care in determining the stories that were to be used for young children and in directing the curriculum staff in the ways to 'treat,' or teach with the stories.

During 1975–80, while I worked as a curriculum developer for *Stó:lō Sitel*, I was introduced to the various traditional stories told by the elders and by others with traditional cultural knowledge. However, at that time I did not fully appreciate the power of stories to engage learners in a wholistic[9] process of feeling, thinking, doing, and being. I was at the stage of realizing what Elder Ellen White, of the Snuneymuxw First Nation (at Nanaimo, Vancouver Island), called *surface learning*. There were times when I did not understand the stories being told or did not appreciate the core cultural teachings embedded in the stories. After being away for many years I returned to the Stó:lō elders because I was finally ready to learn more about the cultural core of stories and how to make meaning through stories.

Imagine that we are sitting in a circle with the elders and listening to them talk about why stories are important, what we should know about the characteristics of some stories, and how to teach or work with the story.

TILLIE GUTIERREZ: If a young person has a problem, often times the Elder gives them a story. The story does not give them all the answers. It shows them the way … Each person who hears a story feels and thinks for [herself or himself]. In the old days stories were told many times over. That's how the people learned to listen. The stories are often teachings about the way to live. The stories teach us to survive as human beings and how to respect, share and care for one another. (Law Courts Education Society 1994a, 8)

MARY LOU ANDREW: Stories were told when children were being taught how to sew, how to do laundry … in my childhood, my grandmother, my grandfather, always had stories … [when] walking through the fields[,] or if you went to gather fruit or food, or if you were just going from point a to point b, there was a story to be told about the area [its place name] or [a historical story of] what happened at that place. Sometimes it took a long time to get there. You got not only history about the place, the land; you were taught [other] lessons …. You got social studies … sometimes even science was thrown in, when you had to deal with herbs and medicines. You learned the importance of why you do something; like why you walked on a certain part of the pathway, so that you didn't destroy certain plants. (Archibald 2008, 73)

MARY USLICK: When our Ancestors talk about our mountains, our rivers, our trees, and our lakes, they got names for all these places ... The names of the mountains and everything was given by our Ancestors because it had a meaning ... it should be respected. That's how they teach the children about it. First of all, they must know the name of that mountain, why the old people call it that. Like Tamahi [Mountain]. We give our offering, we face it, that's where the sun comes out. These children have to learn to respect these [teachings] and then they will teach their children our stories. They will know the names of our mountains, the rivers ... Those are the kind of stories that the old people tell so the children will remember those things. (Archibald 2008, 73–4)

ROY POINT: The way our people were taught ... went by our old people ... At bedtime, when the little ones were ready to go to sleep, they had a story for everything that had to be taught to that young one. Usually [the story] came out when something that little one done, that needed to be taught ... for instance, a little boy went into stealing ... then my grandfather would have a story for that ... The grandparents provided the teachings. (Archibald 2008, 74–5)

Ann Lindley remembers Joe Lorentzo saying, 'Don't tell them everything, give them enough to keep them curious all the time' (Archibald 2008, 77).

These elders reinforce the importance of grandparents, the old people (elders), as cultural teachers to the grandchildren through the use of stories. They remember that stories were and are a vibrant part of everyday life. The Stó:lō have two genres of oral narratives: sxwōxwiyam and sqwelqwel. Sxwōxwiyam are traditional stories; sqwelqwel are historical narratives or personal life experiences (Galloway 1993, 613). Either genre makes children think, imagine, be curious, feel, and reflect about themselves, their relationships with others, and their relationship with their environment. Stories create a wholistic epistemology to address children's intellectual, spiritual, emotional, and physical natures. A close affinity, like a kinship, was established with the environment. Stories also taught aspects of environmental science, history, geography, and more. Children were expected to engage in a process of learning. They were not given a didactic lecture, and they were not expected to write answers to a list of comprehension questions about the stories. Stories or parts of stories were repeated at different occasions and heard many times over one's lifetime. The meanings that one drew from a story changed over time. As the elders spoke about their past experiences of living storied lives, I felt that we had lost much over the years. I also felt fortunate that I could learn from these loving and knowledgeable teachers.

The time spent with the Stó:lō elders helped me to appreciate the teaching, learning potential, and power of stories. For them, stories were, and are, an important means of learning about cultural values and knowledge, as well as a means of understanding ourselves and our relationships with others and the natural world. Aboriginal stories used responsibly will benefit any learner. We have Stó:lō stories that survived generations of colonization because the elders learned the cultural core of the stories and kept them alive in their memories and in their hearts. Most important, they resumed their storywork leadership role. In the *Stó:lō Sitel* curriculum the elders encourage us to tell and use these stories. In storytelling we may use tools of literacy and multimedia to complement the story's orality, especially for curriculum purposes. The important factor is that the framework used for telling the story is a cultural and oral one.

The next section tells a story of elders and Aboriginal educators who walked away from the cosy fire to take up the challenge of developing educational curricula with an Aboriginal story framework that benefits Aboriginal and non-Aboriginal learners.

Going to New Territory

The Law Courts Education Society of British Columbia is a non-profit organization that provides educational programs and services about the justice system in Canada and British Columbia 'to the general public, as well as to youth, First Nations people, ethnic and immigrant communities, deaf people, those with special learning abilities, and other groups as needed' (Law Courts Education Society 2009). From 1990 to 1997 I was a board member of the society and chaired its Native Advisory Committee (NAC). In order to address social justice issues and to introduce Aboriginal concepts and practices of justice through stories, we recommended the development of a sequential elementary-school First Nations justice curriculum for kindergarten to Grade 7. Once funding was secured, a Teachers' Advisory Committee (TAC) was formed and curriculum staff were hired. Both advisory committees included Aboriginal leaders, educators, and justice professionals. The curriculum was called *First Nations Journeys of Justice*, and with a vision of 'building bridges between the First Nations and Canadian systems of law, this education program honours orality – a traditional approach to education among First Nations of British Columbia – and teaches concepts and practices of justice from the perspectives of First Nations ways of knowing' (Law Courts Education Society 1994a).[10]

The *First Nations Journeys of Justice* curriculum was developed in collaboration with First Nations communities, educators in public and band schools, elder storytellers, and staff working in the justice system. The two advisory committees merged to form the NACTAC. I chaired the committee and worked closely with the curriculum staff. The NACTAC took the leadership role in creating the curriculum's philosophical framework and developmental learning outcomes. They also guided the curriculum development and implementation processes. Ellen White (Kwulasulwut), of the Snuneymuxw people, became the project elder. Kwulasulwut is a wonderful storyteller who has worked at all levels in the education field for many years.[11] She mentored the curriculum staff and taught us more about the characteristics of stories and the cultural ways to work with stories for teaching and learning. Her teachings form the foundation of the storywork approach used in the *First Nations Journeys of Justice* curriculum.

Beginning the Storywork Approach

The curriculum staff sought permission and support from tribal councils, elders' groups, First Nations cultural and friendship centres, and key individuals to work in their traditional territories with elders and storytellers. Once permission was granted, staff identified and contacted individuals who had story knowledge. Storytellers were often elders.[12] At least fifteen BC First Nations cultural groups are represented in the curriculum. For various reasons, not every tribal group is included. Some chose not to be included, and limited funding and time prevented full tribal representation.

NACTAC and the staff developed two principles regarding the use of First Nations stories (Law Courts Education Society 1994a, 36):

1 The individual storyteller maintains copyright to his or her story. (The story was 'loaned' to the Law Courts Education Society for this curriculum project.)

2 Individual storytellers verify the printed version of their stories. (In addition, they were consulted on how the stories were to be used in the curriculum.)

Each storyteller identified the story that she or he wanted to include in the curriculum and highlighted particular story 'teachings' that were applicable to the justice concept and could be developed for the age and grade levels. Sometimes the storytellers gave suggestions for the ways of teaching and learning with the story. The sessions were tape recorded and then transcribed. The printed version of the stories and the lesson activities were given back to the storytellers for their verification and approval for use in the curriculum.

Traditional cultural stories and life experience stories are the two predominant types of stories used. The teacher's guide contains suggestions on how to tell stories and includes detailed unit and lesson plans. The elders' storywork knowledge is very pivotal to developing the *First Nations Journeys of Justice* pedagogy. First, we listened to the elders' story teachings; second, we sought to understand the teachings in relation to story pedagogy; and, third, we developed teaching approaches for the stories. Imagine hearing Ellen White talk about considerations for teaching approaches: 'It's the first phase of training or going inside your own self ... If you don't go inside yourself, you will never learn what you want to be learning ... You [must] open yourself and go inside and communicate with yourself' (Archibald 2008, 135). 'Storytellers have to be very responsible. They are setting the pace of breathing. A story is, and has, breath. Storytellers learn to let that happen' (Law Courts Education Society 1994a, 50).

Elders Vincent Stogan, Ann Lindley, and Ellen White all spoke about giving story listeners just enough of a story to ensure understanding and to pique curiosity to learn more. Ellen says it this way: 'This is where we call it – *shallow* stories. We go to the shallow stories and the stories that we can understand today ... We were dealing with something that could never possibly happen in our time. But yet it still has a very good teaching that we can use for youth today. So we give them just enough of a block [of a story] to understand' (Archibald 2008, 136).

The curriculum staff developed introductory information in the teacher's guide and accompanying video, based on the elders' pedagogy. This information helped the teacher to become familiar with the cultural considerations for learning about the nature of First Nations stories and to appreciate the responsibility they had as teachers to facilitate and guide the students' story learning.

Storywork Teaching Approaches

There are various teaching and learning strategies for the *First Nations Journeys of Justice* curriculum. Some approaches are appropriate for any story, such as telling the story (or segments of it) and then letting the students think about the story for a while with no immediate discussion; using a talking circle for subsequent discussions; having fun with the story through the use of creative expression such as role playing, simulation activities, and art; and retelling the story in subsequent units. We hear the elders say that they listened to stories at night, just before going to sleep, and that they were expected to think about their behaviour. In response, we wrote in the teacher's guide:

> When you have finished the first part of the story, tell the children that they will hear the rest of it later. Also tell them that you will not be discussing the story right away. Explain that in First Nations cultures, long ago, storytellers often told stories and the listeners would not ask questions or talk about the story. They would think about the story and what it meant to them. Often stories were told at night, and children would listen while they fell asleep. Some Elders say that we would think about the story in our dreams. So, you will be discussing it later when they have had time to think about it, and 'sleep on it.' (Law Courts Education Society 1994b, 71)

Ellen White suggests that we use a blanket metaphor to symbolize time to think, talk, and make meaning from the story. In the teacher's guide a picture icon of a student holding a blanket and peeking under one part of it is a signal that the students are going to go within themselves to think, and then share their thoughts. We developed and used this icon after hearing Ellen say, 'They have to know that one day we're going to ... look at it [the story]. We're going to lift all the little corners of it ... To bring in their interest [say] ... we're going to talk about the story. We're going to lift this end, and lift it and peek under there to see what is going on in there' (Archibald 2008, 135).

The talking circle is used for a variety of purposes and has different ethics and protocols, depending upon the culture of the First Nations and the circumstances in which it is used. *First Nations Journeys of Justice* provides the following suggestion for the teachers:

> A talking circle may be used to discuss aspects or to share individual understandings of the story. Sitting in a circle is symbolic of the notion that all are equal and that what is said is respected. Some basic questions may be asked in relation to the concepts of the unit lesson, but the purpose of the questions is not to check comprehension. It is expected that children and adults may not understand all of a story. That is all right. With discussion and active engagement in the story's aspects, understandings may increase. (Law Courts Education Society 1994a, 38)

The talking circle used in the *First Nations Journeys of Justice* context is to allow students an opportunity to share their thoughts and reflections regarding the curriculum's stories. Sometimes this kind of sharing creates a synergy among the group so that ideas flow and expand. Students are allowed to 'pass' and forgo their turn to speak if they wish. If a student does not speak at that moment, it does not necessarily mean that she or he is not engaged in the story. There are many other opportunities for that student to participate in other story activities if the teacher is concerned about evaluating that student's learning. The lesson plans also contain guiding questions for the teacher to use during group discussion, which may be separate from the talking circle. Probing questions encourage the students to react to the story characters' situation by relating their own feelings and experiences to those of the characters in the story. The students then think more broadly by suggesting solutions to problems that particular characters face. At times, comprehension questions are asked to ensure basic understanding of aspects of the story.

Throughout the grade levels, role playing is recommended. Traditionally, some stories were theatrically presented at large gatherings, and often they were accompanied by song and dance. Empathy with the characters and their situations, and students' personally relating to the stories, is facilitated through various forms of role play. Sometimes the teacher directs the role play; at other times the students choose parts to act out. In later grades, they collectively write scripted role plays as a continuation of a story. Many of the stories are used in more than one grade level. The concepts for these stories are sequentially developed so that the students' understanding of a concept, such as responsibility, increases over a few grade levels. By Grade 7 the students progress to more sophisticated role play with mock trials about Aboriginal rights cases involving hunting and fishing, which are adaptations of actual legal cases.

The Law Courts Education Society launched the *First Nations Journeys of Justice* curriculum in 1994.[13] For a few years the society conducted in-service workshops with teachers throughout the province. In order to determine the impact of this curriculum on students' knowledge, attitude, and behaviour, a multi-year follow-up study was carried out in six BC schools that had used the curriculum from 1997 to 2000. The results indicate that there was an increase in student learning and that the Aboriginal stories had a positive impact on student attitude and behaviour. Over the years, the *First Nations Journeys of Justice* curriculum has been given a 'recommended for use' status by the BC Ministry of Education. This means that ministry officials have evaluated the curriculum, and it has met provincial curriculum and learning standards; teachers in the public school districts may therefore use *First Nations Journeys of Justice* in various subject areas. As this part of the curriculum story ends, one may wonder if the bone needle was found. Old Man Coyote comes back to taunt us once more.

Where Is the Bone Needle Now?

In British Columbia, since the mid-1970s, much work has been undertaken at both the local community and the provincial levels to develop Aboriginal curriculum resources. Some Aboriginal people have played key roles in improving educational curricula. These roles range from producing and publishing single books to developing comprehensive curriculum units, for both public and First Nations schools. The BC Ministry of Education prescribes learning outcomes and recommends instructional strategies and resources for all grade levels and subject areas in an integrated resource package. In 1998 the ministry released a comprehensive document, *Shared Learnings: Integrating BC Aboriginal Content K–10*, developed mainly by Aboriginal educators, including elders. It provides teachers with a substantial framework of learning outcomes, teaching strategies, student evaluation, cultural awareness information, and recommended resources for integrating Aboriginal content into all grade levels and all subjects. A senior Ministry of Education official noted in his letter of 17 September 1998 announcing the document, 'We hope the document will hasten the arrival of the day when all British Columbia educators will integrate Aboriginal content into their classrooms for the benefit of all students' (British Columbia Ministry of Education 2006a, letter attributed to Don Avison, former deputy minister). This resource was revised and redistributed in 2006. However, the fact remains that *Shared Learnings* is used at teachers' discretion, and Aboriginal curricula are still not part of the core curriculum, even though many more curricula have been developed since the presentation of *Stó:lō Sitel* and *First Nations Journeys of Justice*. In 1999, Aboriginal educators developed a new high-school course, First Nations Studies 12, which was revised in 2006. It is an elective course for social studies and may now be taken in lieu of the required Grade 11 social studies. However, it is still not a core part of the high-school curriculum. One important shift towards Aboriginal curricula becoming part of the high-school core curriculum is the development of the 2008 English 12 First Peoples course that can be taken in lieu of English 12.

If a curriculum evaluation, similar to the Werner et al. study cited earlier, were to be conducted today, would we find the quality of curriculum and textbooks significantly improved? Penney Clarke (2007) addresses the quality question through her examination 'Representations of Aboriginal People in English Canadian History Textbooks: Toward Reconciliation.' Clarke reviews the high-school textbooks used in the Yukon Territory, British Columbia, Manitoba, Ontario, and Nova Scotia from 1911 to recent years. She concludes that 'Aboriginal peoples are "othered" in this [Canadian history] narrative of progress' (111). One of her recommendations echoes what many Aboriginal educators have said over the years: 'The voices of Aboriginal people should be heard in the textbooks. In addition to greater use of examples of literature and art, as suggested by Dion, more use should be made of primary sources of various kinds' (112).

Old Man Coyote asks, though, 'Will more teachers use Aboriginal curriculum, and if they do, how will they teach it?' He muses, 'When will Canadian educators move away from the fire and find better ways to place Aboriginal knowledge and Aboriginal curriculum more centrally and more meaningfully into Canadian educational systems?' Unfortunately Aboriginal knowledge and curriculum are hidden in plain sight because they are often thought of as add-ons and not considered part of the academic core of education (Dion 2009; Royal Commission on Aboriginal Peoples 1996). At best, the curriculum is recommended for use in lieu of another subject or course. In response to cogent challenges, an important teaching that Indigenous elders show us is persistence and resilience.

The stories of *Stó:lō Sitel* and *First Nations Journeys of Justice* would not have been told if the elders had not shown us how to engage in storywork. Their leadership, persistence, and resilience have ensured that their Indigenous stories have been transmitted to many others in various forms and ways. Despite the usage issues raised above, Indigenous elders' teachings and epistemologies can become vibrant and strong threads for shaping the educational fabric of Canadian culture and identity, which is the story that I have told.

Expanding the Circle

The leadership of Aboriginal elders in improving educational curricula, and their persistence in sustaining Aboriginal knowledge (especially through stories), is exemplary. Their active participation in improving the curricula demonstrates that they still have important educational roles and contributions to make. The movement to develop a locally designed Aboriginal curriculum honours the cultural diversity that is an important facet of Canadian culture, and one of its identifying features. Even though my article focuses on British Columbia, the elders' teachings and leadership have made a significant difference to education across Canada (Royal Commission on Aboriginal Peoples 1996). Aboriginal communities in other provinces and territories could tell a (true) *sqwelqwel* of developing an Aboriginal curriculum and its positive impact upon Aboriginal and non-Aboriginal students. In order for Canadian educational systems to place

Aboriginal knowledge into core curriculum areas, Aboriginal people, especially elders, now need to be part of the curriculum policymakers and decision makers.

As Old Man Coyote joins us in the circle of learning and sharing, he holds out his palm and smiles, knowing that we and the future generations of educators will continue to look for the bone needle.

Notes

1 The term *Sne Nay Muxw* or *Coast Salish* is used to describe the First Nations along the southwest coast of British Columbia. Stó:lō is one of the Coast Salish Nations. *Stó:lō* means 'river' in the Halq'eméylem language. The lower Fraser River and its tributaries between Yale and the Strait of Georgia are the river boundaries of the Stó:lō cultural area.

2 Parts of this chapter were first written for my doctoral dissertation, 'Coyote learns to make a storybasket: The place of First Nations stories in education' (1997) and then revised for my book, *Indigenous Storywork: Educating the Heart, Mind, Body, and Spirit* (2008), published by UBC Press. This text is used with the permission of UBC Press. I also use the terms *Aboriginal*, *First Nations*, and *Indigenous* interchangeably, even though *First Nations* in some contexts is limited to mean status Indian people. For the purposes of this chapter, *Aboriginal*, *First Nations*, and *Indigenous* refer to a person of Aboriginal ancestry. The term *wholistic* is spelled with a *w* to denote an Indigenous concept of wholeness.

3 The elders' opening prayers help to establish a respectful interactive atmosphere. Of course, the prayers vary, but they often ask the Creator to guide the participants so that they have clarity of thought in order to make good decisions. The elders' prayer and opening words often contain cultural teachings. Their prayers link people to the spiritual, to each other, to Aboriginal knowledge, and to the past and future generations. Their prayers become a form of ontology and epistemology.

4 For a fuller discussion of these lessons see Archibald (1997). Principles of respect, responsibility, reverence, reciprocity, holism, interrelatedness, and synergy create a Stó:lō and Coast Salish theory for storywork as pedagogy and research methodology.

5 There are many complex issues concerning the appropriation of First Nations stories, the culturally appropriate times to tell particular stories, and the authority to tell stories. The solutions to the issues are diverse, which reflects the diverse nature of Aboriginal people in Canada. In this chapter, basic examples of ethical practices for storywork are introduced. Asking permission to tell

a story and stating the name and nation of the person from whom the story has been acquired are examples.

6 I share the 'Old Man Coyote and the Bone Needle' story because it is one of the stories that made me shift my thinking and challenged me to continue learning about the cultural and educational significance of Stó:lō stories.

7 The Aboriginal student population attending public schools in British Columbia in 2009–10 comprised approximately 11 per cent (61,828) of the total student population (British Columbia Ministry of Education 2010).

8 *Sitel* is a Halq'eméylem word for a type of basket used to store treasures. The guiding committee for the project felt that the curriculum based on Stó:lō knowledge was a treasure. For a complete description of the *Stó:lō Sitel* curriculum project see Archibald (1995). Since the development of the *Stó:lō Sitel*, the Stó:lō Heritage Trust has developed new curricula: *You Are Asked to Witness* (1997); *I Am Stó:lō: Katherine Explores Her Heritage* (1998); and *Stó:lō Atlas* (2001).

9 Wholism has been symbolized in different ways. The Plains cultures use the medicine wheel; others use a sacred circle. I use the term to mean that the spiritual, emotional, physical, and intellectual realms of our human nature are distinct entities, but they also interact and are interrelated. Wholism encompasses the interrelationships among self, family, community, nation, and environment.

10 Four major justice concepts were developed: being safe, being responsible, being fair, and getting along. Other principles that supported these concepts include sharing, reciprocity, cooperation, respect, rights, and importance of caregivers, harmony, interdependence, honour, and balance. *First Nations Journeys of Justice* also contained information about the contemporary Aboriginal justice initiatives and the Canadian court system.

11 *Kwulasulwut* means 'Many Stars.' Ellen's stories have been published by Theytus Books, an Aboriginal-owned publishing house. Her books include *Kwulasulwut: Stories from the Coast Salish*; *Kwulasulwut II: More Stories from the Coast Salish*; and *Legends and Teachings of Xeel's, the Creator*.

12 Thirty-one storytellers and consultants are listed in the *First Nations Journeys of Justice* acknowledgments (Law Courts Education Society 1994a, iii). Some storyteller consultants were not from British Columbia, but their expertise was invaluable to the staff, and some of their teachings are included in the curriculum.

13 In 1995, the U.S. National Association for Court Management gave the Law Courts Education Society a Justice Achievement Award for the *First Nations Journeys of Justice* curriculum. This association has over 2,000 member groups in the United States, Canada, Australia, and elsewhere.

Bibliography

Archibald, Jo-ann. 1995. Locally developed Native studies curriculum: An historical and philosophical rationale. In *First Nations Education in Canada: The Circle
Unfolds*, ed. Marie Battiste and Jean Barman. Vancouver: UBC Press.

– 1997. Coyote learns to make a storybasket: The place of First Nations stories in
education. PhD diss., Simon Fraser University, BC.

– 2008. *Indigenous Storywork: Educating the Heart, Mind, Body, and Spirit.* Vancouver:
UBC Press.

British Columbia Ministry of Education. 2006a [1998]. *Shared Learnings: Integrating BC Aboriginal Content K–10.* Victoria: Aboriginal Education Initiative, British
Columbia Ministry of Education.

– 2006b [1999]. *First Nations Studies 12: Integrated Resource Package 2006.* Victoria:
BC Ministry of Education.

– 2010. *How Are We Doing? An Overview of Aboriginal Education Results for Province
of BC 2009–10.* http://www.bced.gov.bc.ca/abed/perf2010.pdf. Accessed 13
March 2011.

British Columbia Ministry of Education and First Nations Education Steering
Committee. 2008. *English 12 First Peoples: Integrated Resource Package 2008.* Victoria: British Columbia Ministry of Education.

Carlson, Keith Thor, ed. 1997. *You Are Asked to Witness: The Stó:lō in Canada's Pacific
Coast History.* Chilliwack, BC: Stó:lō Heritage Trust.

– 2001. *A Stó:lō–Coast Salish Historical Atlas.* Vancouver: Douglas and McIntyre.

Carlson, Keith Thor, and Albert 'Sonny' McHalsie. 1998. *I Am Stó:lō! Katherine
Explores Her Heritage.* Chilliwack, BC: Stó:lō Heritage Trust.

Clarke, Penney. 2007. Representations of Aboriginal People in English Canadian
history textbooks: Toward reconciliation. In *Teaching the Violent Past: History
Education and Reconciliation*, ed. Elizabeth Cole. New York: Rowman and Little-
field.

Dion, Susan. 2009. *Braiding Histories: Learning from Aboriginal Peoples' Experiences
and Perspectives.* Vancouver: UBC Press.

Galloway, Brent. 1993. *A Grammar of Upriver Halkomelem.* Berkeley, CA: University
of California Press.

Law Courts Education Society. 1994a. *First Nations Journeys of Justice: A Curriculum
for Kindergarten to Grade Seven; Teachers' Guides for K–7.* Vancouver: Law Courts
Education Society.

– 1994b. *First Nations Journeys of Justice: A Curriculum for Kindergarten to Grade
Seven; Grade One Teacher's Guide.* Vancouver: Law Courts Education Society.

– 2009. Mission and objectives. http://www.lces.ca/mission_and_objectives/.

Royal Commission on Aboriginal Peoples. 1996. *Report of the Royal Commission on*

Aboriginal Peoples. Vol. 3, *Gathering Strength.* Ottawa: Canada Communications Group.

Werner, Walter, B. Connors, T. Aoki, and J. Dahlie. 1997. *Whose Culture? Whose Heritage? Ethnicity within Canadian Social Studies Curricula.* Vancouver: University of British Columbia, Centre for the Study of Curriculum and Instruction.

White, Ellen. 1981. *Kwulasulwut: Stories from the Coast Salish.* New ed. Penticton, BC: Theytus Books.

– 1995. *Kwulasulwut II: More Stories from the Coast Salish.* Penticton, BC: Theytus Books.

– 2006. *Legends and Teachings of Xeel's, the Creator.* Vancouver: Pacific Educational Press.

Profile of Verna Jane Kirkness (1935–)

Cree, Educator, and Curriculum Consultant

Among the most prominent of Aboriginal educators, Professor Emerita Verna Jane Kirkness has worked tirelessly in the field of Indian education for more than fifty years. She is recognized for her contributions to Indian education in Canada.[1] She believes that Indians must be educated about their ancestry while being supported culturally in order for them to achieve their full potential.[2]

Cree and a member of the Fisher River First Nation, Kirkness was born on 20 November 1935 on the Fisher River Indian Reserve near Koostatak, Manitoba.[3] She was born the daughter of Fredrick Tomas and Gladys Grace Williams.[4] Her interest in education began early. Although she tried to start school at a very young age, she was sent home because she was not old enough.[5] As an adult, Kirkness has served in various capacities in the Manitoba education system. After receiving a teacher's certificate in 1954, she began her teaching career in a one-room school in a Métis community.[6] She then returned to her home community of Fisher River, where she taught and later became principal.[7] She also worked as a teacher and an administrator at residential schools in the province.[8]

Kirkness's strong belief in the power of education resulted in her earning several university degrees, including a bachelor of arts, a bachelor of education, and a master of education. She joined the faculty at the University of British Colombia as an assistant professor of Native studies in 1980. The following year she became program supervisor for the Native Indian Teacher Education Program (NITEP).[9] In 1984 Kirkness was promoted to director of Native Indian education. While in this position she started the Ts'kel ('Golden Eagle,' in the Stó:lō language) Graduate Education Program.[10] In 1987 she worked to extend support services and cultural enrichment to all Native students at the university and served as the director of the First Nations House of Learning from 1987 to 1993.[11]

Kirkness's dedication to the development and improvement of Aborigi-

Verna Kirkness. Photo courtesy of Verna Kirkness.

nal education is conveyed in her books and published articles. She served as editor or co-editor of the *Canadian Journal of Native Education* from 1986 to 1992. Her books include *Indians of the Plains* (1984), *First Nations and Schools: Triumphs and Struggles* (1992), *Khot-La-Cha: The Autobiography of Chief Simon Baker* (1994), *Aboriginal Languages: A Collection of Talks and Papers* (1998), and *O Great Creator: A Collection of Works by Ruth Elizabeth (Bette) Spence* (1999).[12]

Verna Kirkness received an honorary doctorate in humane letters from Mount Vincent University in 1990 and an honorary doctorate of laws from the University of British Colombia in 1992.[13] In addition to her education degrees and many publications, she has received numerous awards and titles for her work furthering Aboriginal education. The Kirkness Adult Learning Centre was named in her honour in Winnipeg, Manitoba, in 1984.[14] She won the National Aboriginal Achievement Award for Education in 1994 and was elected Canadian Educator of the Year in 1990. Kirkness was made a member of the Order of Canada in 1999;[15] she was awarded the Order of Manitoba in 2007.[16]

Although retired, Verna Kirkness continues to maintain her vibrant presence in the Canadian Aboriginal community. She now lives in Arnprior, Ontario.[17]

NICOLE ROSE

Notes

1 Winona Stevenson, 'Verna Kirkness,' in *The Encyclopedia of Native American Biography: 600 Life Stories of Important People, from Powhatan to Wilma Mankiller*, ed. Bruce E. Johansen and Donald A. Grinde Jr (New York: Henry Holt, 1997), 141.
2 Ibid.
3 Elizabeth Lumley, ed., 'Verna Kirkness,' in *Canadian Who's Who*, vol. 35 (Toronto: University of Toronto Press, 2000), 697.
4 Ibid.
5 Barbara Hager, 'Verna Kirkness: Lady of the Longhouse,' in *Honour Song: A Tribute* (Vancouver: Raincoast Books, 1996), 69.
6 Ibid., 70.
7 Ibid., 71.
8 Ibid.
9 Ibid., 77.
10 Ibid.

11 Ibid.
12 Lumley, 'Verna Kirkness.'
13 Ibid.
14 Stevenson, 'Verna Kirkness,' 142.
15 Lumley, 'Verna Kirkness.'
16 http://www.lg.gov.mb.ca/awards/order/bios.html (accessed 14 January 2011).
17 Ibid.

Narrating Cultural Contact in Northern British Columbia: The Contributions of Gitksan and Tsimshian Oral Traditions to Canadian Historiography

ANDREW NURSE

Long regarded as mythology, folklore, or a fount of anthropological data, the oral traditions of First Nations are a rich source that contributes to our understanding of Canadian history. The ways in which they do so only recently have become the subject of scholarly attention (Wickwire 1994, 20). Increasingly, historians have come to realize that First Nations' traditions provide valuable historical information, affording an alternative window into Canada's past, compensating for the biases inherent in non-Native primary documents. However, relatively little attention is paid to the historiographical value of oral traditions. Historiography differs from history in that it is concerned not with the 'facts' of the past – the empirical details of what happened – but with the way the past is understood and recounted, and with the meanings it holds for people today.[1] In this chapter I will argue that First Nations' oral traditions provide a significant alternative way of understanding Canada's history and its meanings. The oral traditions of First Nations do not simply tell the 'Native side' of Canadian history or provide another source of data for historical researchers. They suggest a new way of reading the past and its meaning that merits the attention of all Canadians. In brief, First Nations' oral traditions provide an alternative model for understanding history that captures the complex human dynamics of Canada's past.

For Canadians today, these are important considerations. In recent years the significance of Canadian history and the value of Canadian heritage have become matters of controversy and debate. Highlighted by the high-profile CBC television series *Canada: A People's History*, the debates surrounding the documentary *The Valour and the Horror*, and the increased concerns over so-called historical illiteracy, a wide-ranging discussion has engaged Canadian historians and others regarding the meaning of the country's past and its legacy for the present. Noted historian Jack Granatstein has argued that misunderstandings of the past can only promote a misunderstanding of the present (Granatstein 1998). Yet it is also clear that there is no common agreement on the meaning of Canadian history and its implications.[2] In providing an alternative model of historical understanding, First Nations' oral traditions can contribute to a rethinking of Canadian history that is clearly needed.

No element of Canada's history is likely more deserving of this kind of rethinking than is the history of cultural interaction between First Nations and white Canadians. The contact and ongoing cultural interaction between Europeans (and Euro-Canadians) and First Nations is one of the essential themes of Canadian history. This interaction is a key factor affecting Canada's historical development and directly bears on a series of important contemporary issues, ranging from land claims to Aboriginal self-government. The character and nature of First Nations' and white Canadians' historical interaction are a matter of interpretive controversy that is all too often played out in the courtroom (Bell 1998, 36–72). Outside the courtroom, debates about First Nations' history proceed apace in books, newspaper articles, on the news, and in the conversations of ordinary Canadians.

The oral traditions of First Nations are particularly valuable in this regard. These traditions tell complicated but illuminating stories about the ways in which different peoples and cultures interacted with each other and how this affected the lives of those involved. Using the specific example of early-twentieth-century Gitksan and Tsimshian oral traditions, this chapter will illustrate how First Nations' oral traditions can enhance our understanding of these interactions and of Canadian history in general. The chapter begins by describing the oral traditions as a form of historical understanding. Next, it examines the ways in which these traditions present the history of Native-white interaction, noting particularly how their interpretations differ from those of written scholarship. Finally, it concludes by discussing the contributions that oral traditions make to historical understanding, focusing particularly on their relevance for Canadians today.

Oral Traditions as Historiography

Oral traditions are a fundamental element of First Nations culture. They record history, teach cultural norms,[3] and define rules of social conduct. However, there is still a great deal of misunderstanding surrounding oral traditions.[4] They are not simply stories, told and retold in varying ways according to the individual storyteller's inclination. Rather, they are major, complex narratives, respected precisely because of their complexity and importance. The Gitksan and Tsimshian peoples of northern British Columbia often heard oral traditions told by elders at solemn and ceremonial occasions. These narratives can be remarkable in terms of their length, depth, and scope, as well as for their range of specific details. Their significance has not diminished with time or with the development of written historical scholarship. Oral traditions continue to be a central mode of historical awareness for individuals, for families, and for nations as a whole (Culhane 1998). Among the First Nations of northern British Columbia the best-known oral traditions are extended family histories and what might be called legend cycles. Some of these have been published or used as primary evidence in Aboriginal-rights court cases (Barbeau and Beynon 1987).[5] However, with the beginning of interaction between northern British Columbia First Nations and Europeans in the nineteenth century the scope of oral tradition was expanded to narrate the impact and effects of this development.

For the Gitksan and Tsimshian peoples of northern British Columbia, contact and interaction with Europeans and Euro-Canadians occurred later than it did for other First Nations in Canada. Long settled along the northern coastal and interior regions of BC, the Gitksan and Tsimshian peoples are noted for their elaborate arts (such as carving and carpentry), rituals (such as the potlatch), and graded social structure. At the time of contact with Europeans their economy was based on the rich regional ecology and trade with other peoples, and their lives were rooted in large villages and defined family and national territories. Family ties reached beyond individual communities to extensive economic interaction with other peoples that linked the Gitksan and the Tsimshian to a wider world. The first Europeans who encountered these peoples found a settled, rich culture with its own world view, economy, and political system.

A significant European presence did not develop in northern BC until the last half of the nineteenth century, when missionaries, explorers, and traders began to enter the region in appreciable numbers (Galois 1997–8). For this very reason the Native peoples attracted the sustained attention of white anthropologists and historians. White scholars believed that the later development of colonialism on the northwestern coast had allowed the First Nations of this region to maintain their values and traditions better. Here, one could still find the 'authentic' or 'traditional' First Nations culture that had supposedly been destroyed in other parts of Canada through interaction with white society and culture. Beginning in the last decades of the nineteenth century, anthropologists scoured northern BC to collect and preserve 'authentic' traditions before they supposedly disappeared.[6] The terms *authentic* and *traditional* were used to indicate cultural traits predating the arrival of Europeans. Scholars of that era believed that interaction with Europeans corrupted Native traditions by altering them so as to produce a hybrid culture, which they felt could not properly be called Aboriginal (Darnell 2000, 45–6).

Among the key figures in this era studying First Nations culture was Marius Barbeau, perhaps the leading figure in pre–Second World War Canadian anthropology (Nowry 1995). Barbeau began fieldwork in northern British Columbia in 1914 and over the course of his career amassed the most extensive collection of northern BC oral traditions to that time. Like other white scholars of his period, Barbeau subscribed to the 'vanishing race' theory and believed that First Nations were rapidly disappearing. Unlike other scholars, however, he did not confine his work to material that he regarded as representative of the pre-colonial era. He became interested in the effect of cultural interaction on First Nations and, in the 1920s, began to collect material relating to more recent historical developments. Barbeau found no shortage of material. Although he was primarily interested in material culture (arts and crafts), he collected a large number of Gitksan and Tsimshian oral traditions relating to increased interaction between First Nations and Europeans in the colonial era. These traditions, now stored in the Barbeau Fonds at the Museum of Civilization, constitute an important historiographic school, narrating and interpreting the meanings of cultural contact for the Gitksan and Tsimshian peoples (Cove 1985).

Complexity and Humanism: Narrating Cultural Contact

The implications of cultural contact for First Nations have long been the subject of historical discussion. Older scholarly interpretations portrayed cultural contact as an encounter between primitive 'savages' and more advanced 'civilizations.' This interpretation contended that the encounter led inexorably to the dislocation of First Nations culture and the inevitable 'disappearance' of First Nations. The story that this scholarship told was one of First Nations decay and collapse; on account of their very 'primitiveness,' traditional First Nation societies could not adapt to the modern changes that were overtaking them. Their fate was sealed, and they were left with the unpleasant choice of either abandoning their values, traditions, and culture – all that made them separate and distinct peoples – or accepting increased marginalization in the modern age as they awaited their inevitable demise.[7]

In recent years, the First Nations' increased political and cultural activism, combined with extensive new research, has made it impossible to maintain this interpretation.[8] It is now self-evident that First Nations are not on the verge of disappearing. Accordingly, Canadian historians have developed a more detailed and nuanced interpretation of First Nations and European peoples' interaction, focusing on its diverse effects and the ways in which First Nations resisted the imposition of colonial rule (Coates 2000). The grave repercussions of colonialism included disease, warfare, residential schools, and a host of other factors that had markedly negative effects on First Nations. Yet First Nations people did not disappear. Newer interpretations of Native-white interaction focus on how Native people responded to European expansion, on the damage done to their societies, and on the ways they worked to maintain their cultures and autonomy in a dramatically changing historical situation. The picture of cultural interaction presented in Gitksan and Tsimshian oral traditions from the 1920s adds considerably to this interpretation. There are several matters on which we need to focus in this regard.

First, in terms of their content, Gitksan and Tsimshian oral traditions of the 1920s do not present a single, unified narrative of cultural contact. Rather, they describe a series of events that had diverse effects on First Nations, both individually and at a community level. The different ways in which Native-white cultural interaction was narrated in oral tradition suggest not only that this was how the event was remembered but also that its impact needs to be seen as a multifaceted process, affecting technology and spirituality, culture and interpersonal relations, politics and economics, as well as First Nations power and autonomy. The key point is that cultural interaction is seen as a diverse, many-sided process, the impact of which is felt on personal, community, and national levels.

A primary concern of the 1920s oral tradition was the response of First Nations people and communities to the introduction of new material goods and new technologies. For older scholarship, it was precisely the introduction of these goods and technologies that doomed First Nations. In contrast, more recent scholarship has focused on how Native people looked to adapt new technology to their own circumstances or to make use of the new material goods that they found to be convenient. The oral traditions in the 1920s also focused on how individuals dealt with this changing material culture, often highlighting the humorous ways in which different Native people responded to the introduction of new material goods. As historical narratives, these traditions tend to observe a broadly similar plot. Usually they begin by stating that the story to follow describes the first axe, accordion, kettle, gun, or some other material good in a particular village or region. They then move to the response of specific individuals to this development. Normally, the person involved – who becomes the central character – knows nothing of the particular item and makes a relatively amusing mistake in its application. This is, at first, accepted by other members of the community because they are just as unfamiliar with the new good. The person who owns it becomes quite proud and begins to show off the item in a self-aggrandizing manner. The narrative concludes when a Native person familiar with European culture arrives on the scene and demonstrates the item's correct use. The whole village then has a laugh at the lead character's expense.

One such example appears in a tradition that was recorded in 1920 by a man named John Brown, who had heard it an unspecified number of years earlier from his father. The lead character is a man named Gamagagex[9] from Kisgegas. Gamagagex is particularly proud of a new type of European axe head that has come into his possession. Neither he nor anyone else in his town has seen this type of axe head before. It is much admired, and Gamagagex begins to wear the axe head as an ornament to further impress the villagers. Soon people from surrounding communities are arriving to admire it, making Gamagagex even more proud. As Brown recounted, 'So he suspended the axe on a piece of string and wore it from his neck so that it hung over his breast. And he [would] go around to all the people with this. They were all astonished and pleased with the ornament. In order to make a bigger show of it, he hung it on his back. And everyone was envious of him' (Barbeau, Fieldnotes, 1920 B-F90.11).

However, Gamagagex's local celebrity suffers dramatically with the arrival of Tags, a man from the Nass valley who obviously knows more about European culture than do the people of Kisgegas. When Tags points out the mistake, Gamagagex is embarrassed and tries quietly to stop wearing the axe. However, the villagers, now aware of its true use, notice that it is no longer part of his apparel and begin to tease him. Barbeau reports: 'There was a [jester] among the Kisgagas named Kwaxt. He said to Gam: what became of the beautiful ornament you had?' (Fieldnotes, 1920, B-F-90.11).

This story, and others like it, illustrates several major interpretative themes of oral traditions relating to cultural contact. First, the story itself focuses on an object – a material good – that does not result in monumental change for Kisgegas. This highlights the fact that the first contact that First Nations often had with European culture was through goods moving into regions in trade (Harris 1997–8). It also suggests that the initial material impact of cultural contact was marginal or nil. Rather than causing significant changes in material life, the introduction of the new trade good produces humorous confusion, which results in little more than embarrassment. The narrative's plot climaxes when confusion gives way to understanding, brought about by another Native person. In this sense, the tradition is telling a story of both the confusing impact of cultural interaction and of the way in which Native people mastered that confusion, coming to understand the uses of new goods. While the introduction of new technologies or goods is confusing, this does not mean that Native people cannot master changing technologies or material cultures. A key theme of these traditions, then, is the way in which Native people ultimately learn to understand the new culture affecting their lives.

According to oral tradition, a similar type of misconception and confusion also affected the first Europeans who settled in northern British Columbia. One tradition describes the activities of a missionary attempting to promote Christian marriages in a First Nations community. The weddings he attempts to perform are plagued by mishaps. The Indian agent (the local federal official) cannot be found to issue the correct licences, the ceremony is delayed while the couples and guests are forced to wait in the cold, and the ceremony itself degenerates into farce as the bride and the groom do not understand the rites. The missionary, it seems, finds this disconcerting, but for the guests it is a comic event that provokes laughter (Barbeau, Fieldnotes 1929, B-F-89.14). Confusion and humour is a two-way street: if the Gitksan and Tsimshian could laugh at themselves, they also found humour in the absurdities of colonialist pretensions.

A second revealing theme of these traditions is their clarification that the northern BC First Nations were aware of Europeans long before they (or trade goods) first appeared in the region. According to these traditions, European culture caused little upset because word of it had already filtered into northern BC from other parts of the country. Traditions also confirm that the arrival of white people and goods into the region did not surprise Native peoples, because they had heard rumours for some time. 'Nothing,' one tradition noted, 'ever arrived without it being known before hand' (Barbeau, Fieldnotes, undated, B-F-89.12, 1). The arrival of firearms, the same tradition explained, was exactly like this. 'It was rumoured that they would have guns for many years. It was before guns arrived when it was rumoured they would have them. It was rumoured for about ten years' (Barbeau, Fieldnotes undated, B-F-89.12, 1). In this tradition, the second-hand acquaintance with European technology is long-standing. European culture may still be unusual, but it is not surprising or awe-inspiring. It is something with which Native people have a second-hand familiarity before cultural contact actually begins.

The exact reason that Native peoples came into contact with European culture is also the subject of different interpretations in these traditions. The cast of white people who appear in Gitksan and Tsimshian traditions is, perhaps, exactly what one would expect: missionaries, prospectors, traders, loggers, and explorers in various narratives. The impetus for Native-white interaction, however, is not solely the result of Europeans arriving in northern BC. In a number of stories, Native people initiate contact. Recent scholarship has argued that Native people actually sought out and maintained alliances with Europeans because they were interested in obtaining European material goods.[10] Northern BC traditions from the early twentieth century provide some evidence of this, but curiosity is the more standard reason that is given for Native people initiating contact with European culture. In one tradition, when a white man visits Kisgegas, he meets a Gitksan man named Waiget who invites him back to his place for dinner. Soon the entire village shows up at Waiget's house to watch the white man eat: 'The house was crowded for the people. It is the white man eating fish' (Barbeau, Fieldnotes, undated, B-F-90.15, 1). In other instances, kettles are purchased as curiosity items, and coffee as a potential health aid; one man buys a rifle because he finds it interesting.

These traditions point out the various factors that can occasion cultural contact, ranging from the arrival of Europeans in northern British Columbia to the possibility of material gain to the impetus of curiosity. Here, Native peoples are not simply 'discovered'; they themselves initiate a process of discovery. Their reason for doing so is not purely (or even significantly)[11] materialistic; it is triggered by curiosity, a desire to know more about new things and people.

A final key theme of these traditions is their interpretation of the long-term effects of Native-white cultural interaction. This interpretation is important because the traditions are related in a way that is different from the Western ideal of 'objective' historical understanding (Novick 1988). Nor were oral traditions 'subjective.' They related historical 'facts'; the stories they told were intended to be heard as truthful accounts of events that did happen. They neither elaborate on the past nor do they present the purely personal perspectives of the informant from whom they were collected. Instead, oral traditions retell history so that it is infused with meaning. They do not simply recount the past for its own sake; they retell history because it contains important lessons for the present. Both the teller and the listener are supposed to draw these lessons out of the traditions. Many traditions are accompanied by the narrator's own reflections, explaining the moral and political instruction that could be taken from the history of Native-white interaction. Thus, for the Native people of northern British Columbia, there were valuable lessons to be learned from their past.

One central lesson concerned the disruptive effects of colonization on Native communities. For example, the traditions describe Christianity as a culturally and morally disruptive force. One tradition presents conversion as part of a process that led to personal corruption. 'All those that were baptized,' this informant concluded, 'turned out to be the biggest thieves and the biggest drunkards. And [those who were not] baptized never stole or never drank' (Barbeau, Fieldnotes, undated, B-F-90.15, 13). The implication here is clear: Native spirituality guarded against personal corruption in a way that European religion could not. The adoption of European culture brought with it personal corruption.

In other instances, oral traditions clearly recognize the conflicts that have marred Native-white relations through long periods of Canadian history. In the first decades of the twentieth century, Native-white conflicts in British Columbia centred on misappropriation of Native land and Native resistance to the federal laws regulating their lives and their culture.[12] Isaac Tens, one of Barbeau's principal informants, commented on these matters at some length. Infusing his recounting of the past with moral and political messages for the present, Tens's narrative focused on two levels of antagonism between First Nations and white Canadians. The first was a personal level, in which he told of acts of theft and the misappropriation of Native lands. On the second level, Tens addressed the issue of the relations between the Canadian state and the Native peoples. In one tradition he described the arrival of missionaries as part of a more encompassing program designed to steal Native land. 'The government,' he recounted, 'first sent out the ministers, in order to pacify the natives so that they will not fight' (Barbeau, Fieldnotes, undated, B-F-658.8, 1). White people, he also noted, had the force of the law and the state behind them, a fact that made Native resistance to white incursion difficult. Exactly what the Gitksan could do to redress their grievances was not clear because, in Tens's view, historical processes had created a condition of manifest inequality between Native and white people. 'And the government has stolen that land from them and sold it all to these white people,' he explained. 'Now, we cannot help ourselves[;] we have to let it go' (Barbeau, Fieldnotes, undated, B-F-658.8, 1).

Tens did not suggest, however, that the Native peoples of northern British Columbia should passively accept their fate. He promised that protest would continue and ventured the possibility of forming alliances with other peoples as one potential tactic (Barbeau, Fieldnotes, undated, B-F-658.8, 4). For Tens, the history of Native-white interaction was not a story of confusion occasioned by new things (triggered by curiosity) or of Native people learning to master new material goods or technologies. It was a story of lies and betrayal, deception and antagonism, a story he felt on a deep, personal level. It was also a story that was not over. In his interpretation, history weighs heavily on the present. The very injustices of the past are at once the effect and cause of history, ensuring that the story of Native-white interaction is far from done. For Tens, the past is not simply a lesson to be learned but part of an unfolding present that will continue into the future. It is our ability to understand this past that allows us to make sense of the present. The history of cultural contact is a history that must continue to unfold.

Meaning, Interpretation, and Tradition

What can one learn from the oral traditions? The answer is necessarily complicated because the traditions themselves are complex, treating the history of Native-white interaction in various and, at times, seemingly contradictory ways. Within their own cultural context these stories were crucial and widely shared among the Native – and white – population of northern British Columbia. They retain their importance today because of their subject matter and what they can tell us generally about the meaning of Canadian history.

As we have seen, the oral traditions suggest an alternative way of thinking about the impact of Native-white interaction. Here the very diversity of the traditions and the different ways they present this history are central. Gitksan and Tsimshian oral traditions interpret the history of Native-white cultural contact as a varied process triggered by a range of factors. From these traditions we can see that cultural contact had many different effects at the same time. It was at once confusing (for both parties), amusing, a source of injustice, and a matter of curiosity. It was something new and at the same time something that was, in the words of one tradition, 'no novelty' (Barbeau, Fieldnotes, undated, NB-F-90.15, 8) because news of Europeans had circulated in the country for some time. In the past, white scholars found the variance in oral traditions frustrating, seeing it as the result of the different storytellers' personal preferences (Darnell 2000, 44–5). A key contribution that these traditions make to Canadian historiography, however, is precisely this diversity. In recognizing that cultural contact triggers a wide range of responses, these traditions capture the real complexity of the contact experience, and the fact that cultural contact was several things at once. Once we grasp that this was actually the case, our understanding of the complicated process of cultural interaction will be deeply enriched.

Furthermore, Gitksan and Tsimshian oral traditions interpret cultural contact and interaction on two levels simultaneously. One level is concerned with individuals and their responses to changing situations – a major consideration that is often neglected in written studies of Native-white interaction, where the focus is, almost always, on how different cultures interacted with each other. In featuring the history of individuals, oral traditions allow us to understand how they saw, responded to, and were part of that history. Their interpretations of history show us that it is a human process involving real people. On the second level, these are not the 'great men' who, it is often claimed, 'make history' but the ordinary people grappling with broad processes of change. By focusing on them, these traditions transform history into a human process marked by very real emotions, ideas, and ways of thinking. The lives of regular people – not the actions of the great and powerful – take the central place in this historiography.

Finally, these traditions help us understand both the significance of history and its relevance. They allow us to see the history of Native-white cultural contact from another perspective and also suggest a different outlook on understanding Canadian history more generally. For the Gitksan and Tsimshian people who retold these traditions, history was not a parade of names and dates to be memorized but a living and still unfolding process. This is perhaps the paramount contribution that First Nations oral traditions make to Canadian historiography.

Recent debates about the importance of Canadian history have focused on what Canadians should know about their past (Granatstein 1998). Oral traditions do not treat the past as something that should be known simply for the sake of knowledge. Instead, they treat historical understanding as a dialogue in which the teller and the listener draw out the meaning of a process that is ongoing. Rather than simply presenting history as facts to be learned, they challenge the teller and the listener to draw meaning from the past and see how it continues to be relevant today. In other words, they challenge us to see ourselves as part of an unfolding history that has yet to be recounted, whose future direction we ourselves can influence.

This is an important message for Canadians today. As we struggle to redefine our country and rebuild the relationship between Native and non-Native Canadians, we need to recognize the contributions that First Nations have made to the Canadian experience. We also need a model of historical understanding that animates action and keeps our gaze steadily focused on the very human implications of broader processes. Oral traditions allow us to do this by forcing us to see Canada as a work in progress. By challenging us to reach our own understanding of the past, its implications and its relevance, oral traditions provide an alternative model for historical understanding that makes a needed contribution to Canadian culture. As constructed by oral traditions, history is not over. It is still being made. Once we understand this, both our past and our present gain a new significance.

Notes

1 As examples, see Daniel Francis (1997) and Carl Berger (1986).
2 For a particularly informative discussion of this point see Ian McKay (1998).
3 Here the term *cultural norms* implies a wide range of philosophical, ecological, political, and social ideas.
4 For an important discussion of this point see Jo-Anne Fiske (1997–8).
5 On the use of oral traditions in court see Dara Culhane (1998).
6 For a fuller discussion see Douglas Cole (1985).
7 For examples of this historiography see Marius Barbeau (1931) and Diamond Jenness (1937). For a fuller discussion of the ideology of this perspective see Peter Kulchyski (1993).
8 For an example of a recent effort to reassert a modified variant of this interpretation see Tom Flanagan (2000).
9 In this chapter I have retained the spelling employed in the archival fonds.
10 See Trigger (1983), and Reid (1987, chapter 1).
11 Northern BC oral traditions tend to mock those people who have materialistic aims. This is, of course, in keeping with the cultural values of Tsimshian-speaking peoples, who tended to look on the accumulation of wealth for its own sake as a personal failing.
12 The most notorious of these was the law against the potlatch, which made it illegal for BC First Nations to practise their culture. See Cole and Chaikin (1990).

Bibliography

Barbeau, Marius. 1931. Our Indians – their disappearance. *Queen's Quarterly* 38 (4): 691–707.
– Fieldnotes. Marius Barbeau Northwest Coast files. Canadian Museum of Civilization.
Barbeau, Marius, and William Beynon. 1987. *Tsimshian Narratives*. Ed. John J. Cove and George F. MacDonald. Ottawa: Canadian Museum of Civilization.
Bell, Catherine. 1998. New directions in the law of Aboriginal rights. *Canadian Bar Review* 77 (1/2): 36–72.
Berger, Carl. 1986. *The Writing of Canadian History: Aspects of English-Canadian Historical Writing since 1900*. 2nd ed. Toronto: University of Toronto Press.
Coates, Ken. 2000. Writing First Nations into Canadian history: A review of recent scholarly work. *Canadian Historical Review* 81 (1): 99–114.
Cole, Douglas. 1985. *Captured Heritage: The Scramble for Northwest Coast Artifacts*. Seattle: University of Washington Press.

Cole, Douglas, and Ira Chaikin. 1990. *An Iron Hand upon the People: The Law against the Potlatch on the Northwest Coast.* Vancouver: Douglas and McIntyre.

Cove, John J., ed. 1985. *A Detailed Inventory of the Barbeau Northwest Coast Files.* Ottawa: National Museum.

Culhane, Dara. 1998. *The Pleasure of the Crown: Anthropology, Law and First Nations.* Burnaby, BC: Talonbooks.

Darnell, Regna. 2000. The pivotal role of the northwest coast in the history of Americanist Anthropology. *BC Studies* 125 (6): 33–52.

Fiske, Jo-Anne. 1997–8. From customary law to oral traditions: Discursive formation of plural legalism in northern British Columbia, 1857–1993. *BC Studies* 115 (6): 267–88.

Flanagan, Tom. 2000. *First Nations? Second Thoughts.* Montreal and Kingston: McGill-Queen's University Press.

Francis, Daniel. 1997. *National Dreams: Myth, Memory, and Canadian History.* Vancouver: Arsenal Pulp Press.

Galois, R.M. 1997–8. Colonial encounters: The worlds of Arthur Wellington Clah. *BC Studies* 115 (6): 105–48.

Granatstein, J.L. 1998. *Who Killed Canadian History?* Toronto: Harper Collins.

Harris, Cole. 1997–8. Social power and cultural change in pre-colonial British Columbia. *BC Studies* 115 (6): 56–7.

Jenness, Diamond. 1937. *The Indian Background of Canadian History.* Museum of Canada Bulletin, 86. Ottawa: King's Printer.

Kulchyski, Peter. 1993. Anthropology in the service of the state: Diamond Jenness and Canadian Indian policy. *Journal of Canadian Studies* 28 (2): 21–51.

McKay, Ian. 1998. After Canada: On amnesia and apocalypse in the contemporary crisis. *Acadiensis* 28 (1): 76–97.

Novick, Peter. 1988. *That Noble Dream: The 'Objectivity' Question and the American Historical Profession.* Cambridge: Cambridge University Press.

Nowry, Laurence. 1995. *Marius Barbeau: Man of Mana.* Toronto: NC Press.

Reid, John. 1987. *Six Crucial Decades.* Halifax, NS: Nimbus.

Trigger, Bruce. 1983. The deadly harvest. In *Economy and Society during the French Regime, to 1759,* ed. Michael S. Cross and Gregory S. Kealey, 154–82. Toronto: McClelland and Stewart.

Wickwire, Wendy. 1994. To see ourselves as the Other's other: Nlaka'pamux contact narratives. *Canadian Historical Review* 75 (1): 1–20.

Profile of Marlene Brant Castellano (1935–)

Mohawk, Educator, and Professor Emerita

Professor Marlene Brant Castellano has made significant contributions to the establishment of Native studies as a credible academic discipline in Canada[1] and spent years teaching in this field.

She was born in 1935 on the Tyendinaga Mohawk Territory on the Bay of Quinte in Ontario to Hubert Brant and Pearl Brant (née Hill). Her junior high school teachers recognized her outstanding academic abilities, and her Grade 8 teacher entered her into a competition for the 1947 Warden's Medal, which was awarded for the highest standing in high-school entrance examinations[2] – which she won. Brant Castellano nurtured her love of language and literature throughout high school and went on to attend university, earning a bachelor of arts from Queen's University in 1955, a bachelor of social work from the University of Toronto in 1956, and a master of social work from the University of Toronto in 1959.[3]

In 1960 she married Vincent Castellano, and they have four children, Vincent, Gregory, Daniel, and Steven.[4] Brant Castellano's focus for the next decade was raising her children and homemaking. She moved to Peterborough, Ontario, in 1969 and joined the faculty of Trent University's newly established Department of Native Studies in 1973. This department was the first to offer a Native studies diploma in Canada. It grew to include a bachelor's degree, a master's degree, and eventually a doctorate in Native studies.[5] Over the next two decades she was promoted to full professor and served three terms as chair of the department.[6] Professor Brant Castellano took leave from Trent University, and from 1992 to 1996 she served as co-director of research for the Royal Commission on Aboriginal Peoples. She retired from Trent University in 1996 and was subsequently named professor emerita. After retirement, Brant Castellano served as the research director for the Aboriginal Healing Foundation. She went on to serve on the federal government's Tri-Council Ethics Secretariat,[7] chairing the committee that developed the *Guide for Ethical Research with Aboriginal Peoples*.

Marlene Brant Castellano. Photo courtesy of Terry Bush.

Brant Castellano's literary and academic contributions include an article entitled 'Vocation of Identity? The Dilemma of Indian Youth' in the early and influential book *The Only Good Indian*.[8] She also contributed 'The Information Legacy of the Royal Commission on Aboriginal Peoples'[9] and co-authored the introduction and the conclusion for the book she co-edited, *Aboriginal Education: Fulfilling the Promise* (2000),[10] among other writing projects. In 2006 she co-authored with Linda Archibald the final report of the Aboriginal Healing Foundation.

Marlene Brant Castellano has been formally recognized for her outstanding contributions to the Aboriginal community and to Canadian society. She received honorary doctorates of law from Queen's University, St Thomas University, and Carleton University. She was inducted into the Order of Ontario in 1995 and received a National Aboriginal Achievement Award in 1996.[11] Brant Castellano was recently honoured as an elder by the Aboriginal Education Council during Trent University's celebration to commemorate the thirty-year anniversary of its Native studies program.[12] She serves on the advisory board of the Canadian Institutes of Health Research's Institute of Aboriginal Peoples' Health as well as the College of Reviewers for Canada Research Chairs. Most recently, Dr Marlene Brant Castellano has been named an Officer of the Order of Canada.[13] She now resides in Tyendinaga Mohawk Territory on the Bay of Quinte with her husband.

BRIAN CALLIOU

Notes

1 Elizabeth Lumley, ed., 'Marlene Brant Castellano,' in *Canadian Who's Who*, vol. 37 (Toronto: University of Toronto Press, 2002), 222.
2 Ibid.
3 Panel on Research Ethics, 'Panel members: Marlene Brant Castellano,' 2009. Cf. http://www.pre.ethics.gc.ca/eng/panel-group/about-apropos/members-membres/marlene/.
4 Ibid.
5 Allison Kydd, 'Indigenous knowledge a formula for success,' *Windspeaker* 17 (9): 29.
6 Lumley, 'Marlene Brant Castellano.'
7 The Tri-Councils include the Canadian Institutes of Health Research (CIHR), the Natural Sciences and Engineering Research Council (NSERC), and Social Sciences and Humanities Research Council (SSHRC). All are federally funded research granting agencies.

8   Marlene Brant Castellano. 'Vocation or identity? The dilemma of Indian youth,'
    in *The Only Good Indian: Essays by Canadian Indians*, ed. Waubageshig (Don
    Mills, ON: New Press, 1970), 52.

9   Marlene Brant Castellano, 'The information legacy of the Royal Commission on
    Aboriginal Peoples,' in *Aboriginal Education: Fulfilling the Promise*, ed. Marlene
    Brant Castellano, Lynne Davis, and Louise Lahache (Vancouver: University of
    British Columbia Press, 2000), 147.

10 Marlene Brant Castellano, Lynne Davis, and Louise Lahache, introduction and
    conclusion to *Aboriginal Education*.

11 Lumley, 'Marlene Brant Castellano.'

12 Kydd, 'Indigenous knowledge,' 29.

13 Panel on Research Ethics, 'Marlene Brant Castellano.'

The Master of Life and the Person of Evolution: Indigenous Influence on Canadian Philosophy

J. DOUGLAS RABB

The Iroquois concept *Rawen-Niyoh* has been variously translated as 'the Master of Life,' 'Great Spirit,' and even 'Creator' (Hatzan 1925, 40, 44, 46, 218). Of these, 'the Master of Life' seems the most literal, least Eurocentric rendering. At least, *The Master of Life* was the title that Canadian philosopher William Douw Lighthall (1857–1954) chose for his 1908 novel about the formation of the Iroquois Confederacy. Beginning with Lighthall, in this chapter I explore some of the major influences of Indigenous philosophy on the development of Canadian thought and identity.[1] It has been argued that the Iroquois Confederacy inspired the constitution of the United States (Johansen 1982; Barreiro 1992; Grinde and Johansen 1995). What is not so well known is that as early as 1925 similar claims were made in the Canadian context about the confederation of Canadian provinces. Anthropologist Leon Hatzan (adopted into the Bear clan of the Cayuga Nation as Tsa-da-ga-hes) makes the claim in his 1925 study of the Six Nation Indians: 'This – the Iroquois Confederacy – was a model upon which the British colonists based their provincial government, and it supplied the basic idea upon which rests the foundation of the present system of political government of the Great Southern Republic, also the constitution of the Canadian Provinces with the central power at Ottawa' (45).

I am more interested in the Indigenous influence on the underlying accommodationist principles of this kind of confederation than in joining the debate about how much these constitutions were actually developed on the model of the Iroquois Confederacy. I suspect, however, that the U.S. constitution is more closely modelled on the Iroquois Confederacy than is the Canadian. As anthropologist Jack Weatherford points out in his classic study, *Indian Givers: How the Indians of the Americas Transformed the World*, at least the United States followed the Iroquois in the civilized practice 'of allowing only one person to speak at a time in a political meeting.' This contrasts embarrassingly with the way Canada followed 'the British tradition of noisy interruptions of one another as the members of Parliament shout out agreement or disagreement with the speaker' (1988, 140).

I want to argue that the essential nature of Canadian philosophical thought itself was influenced – perhaps even inspired – by the Indigenous values and world views that were flourishing at first contact in what is now Canada. Certainly there is ample textual evidence that William D. Light-hall's major philosophical study, *The Person of Evolution* (1930), was inspired by what he calls 'the Red Man's mind, life and melancholy,' which is depict-ed in *The Master of Life* (1908, v). The same inspiration is also evident in sev-eral more scholarly studies he presented to the Royal Society of Canada, for example, 'Hochelagans and Mohawks: A Link in Iroquois History' (1899) and 'Hochelaga and "The Hill of Hochelaga"' (1924).

Lighthall's book *The Person of Evolution* is in many ways typical of Cana-dian philosophy published between 1850 and 1950. In it he attempts to rec-oncile the theory of evolution with a more spiritual world view. Although he is attempting to balance science and religion, his focus is on science, not theology. He argues against a purely mechanistic or material account of evolution, but he is no idealist. 'It is now a truism that not even at his highest can Man escape his place as part of Nature … Anatomically, he is a lump of jelly – but how wonderful is jelly, when so completely organ-ized!' (1930, 65, sc. 73). Even the 'directive power' of evolution itself, which Lighthall calls 'the Person of Evolution,' is conceived of as a vast, composite biological entity, not unlike the more recent Gaia hypothesis. 'It is a bio-logical entity – a vast composite, living, reasoning being, of which all lesser individuals are extensions' (1930, 37, sc. 29).

Lighthall is intentionally doing science, not theology, and he is avow-edly not an idealist. Nevertheless, he does attempt to accommodate both religion and metaphysical idealism. 'The contribution of this new thinking, inductively based on the new foundation of facts, may perhaps in the end be synthesized with the contributions to reason from other sources, such as Idealism; Instinct as such; the Traditional Wisdom of religious thought, in which instinct plays a part; and legitimate Mysticism, where instinct also plays a part' (1930, 62, sc. 67). He regards instinct itself as a form of knowl-edge 'directed to more and more perfect adjustment of the organism to the environment' (1930, 67, sc. 76).

Lighthall's attempt to reconcile religion and science, and to accommo-date both realism and idealism, is typical of English-Canadian philoso-phy published at the time. In their study of early Canadian philosophy, *The Faces of Reason: An Essay on Philosophy and Culture in English Canada, 1850–1950*, Leslie Armour and Elizabeth Trott argue that what they call an accommodationist use of reason is, or at least was at that time, characteristic of English-Canadian philosophers. It manifests itself as a willingness or tendency to try to take seriously, to learn from, and to accommodate those philosophical positions that are opposed to one's own. Armour and Trott introduce the term *philosophical federalism* to describe this tendency. They see this use of reason 'as a basic theme which constantly lies just below the surface.' It captures something of the distinctiveness of Canadian philosophy. In *The Faces of Reason* they argue that in early Canadian philosophy 'there is … a kind of philosophical federalism at work, a natural inclination to find out why one's neighbour thinks differently rather than to find out how to show him up as an idiot' (1981, 4).

What most of the early Canadian philosophers had in common was their commitment to some form of post-Kantian or post-Hegelian idealism. They argued that primordial reality was somehow more like mind than matter. Their thought can, nevertheless, be described in terms of philosophical federalism because they seem to have taken realist claims about the nature of the material world, and the nature of the 'not-self,' much more seriously than did their British and continental counterparts.[2] In *Religion and Science in Early Canada* (Rabb 1989a) I offered one possible explanation for this. (I must admit that my own thesis is not all that original. I have simply taken the thesis put forward by Northrop Frye and his student Margaret Atwood concerning Canadian imaginative literature and applied it to the philosophical literature of Canada.) The 'Nature' that the early settlers in Canada encountered was a more or less hostile, or at least indifferent, nature. It was a far cry from the Wordsworthian romanticized English Lake District in which, as Margaret Atwood puts it, 'Nature was a kind of Mother or Nurse who would guide man if he would only listen to her' (Atwood 1972, 50). The idealists writing in eighteenth- and nineteenth-century Britain and Germany had to account for a not-self that was either an English country garden or the completely urbanized setting of a large industrial city. In either case these philosophers were surrounded by the works of our own creation, the works of mind. In such a setting it is not too difficult to maintain a metaphysical idealism, which argues that nature is more like mind than matter and that only mind is ultimately real. However, when we move this view of nature to the 'bush-garden' that is Canada, an idealistic account of nature is far more difficult to establish. If Nature is ultimately good, then more nature ought to be better. And one thing Canada had, and still has, is lots of nature. But the nature that newcomers encountered in Canada was not like that at home in Britain or on the Continent. In her major study of Canadian literature, aptly titled *Survival*, Atwood argues, 'If Wordsworth was right, Canada ought to be the Great Good Place. At first complaining about bogs and mosquitoes must have seemed like criticising the authority of the Bible' (1972, 50). Atwood's thesis is, of course, that 'Nature seen as dead, or alive but indifferent, or alive and actively hostile towards man is a common image in Canadian literature' (1972, 52).

When the Frye-Atwood thesis is applied to the early Canadian idealists, we find that the early Canadian philosophers present an idealism that is much more sympathetic to the claims of the materialists. It is an idealism that has learned much from the opposing theory of realism. In short, we find an idealism that attempts to accommodate materialist claims about the nature of the real. The philosophy of Lighthall's former professor at McGill University, John Clark Murray, is a case in point. Murray accepts the real objective world with real objects in real space and time. 'But he thinks that the nature of this real world is that it is the objectification of rational intelligence and that one can no more think of the object without the subject – or as he puts it, the notself without the self – than one can think of colour without space or change without time. They are simply interrelated concepts' (Armour and Trott 1981, 168–9).

Now it can certainly be argued that the Frye-Atwood thesis about hostile nature would have little application to a McGill professor like Murray living in civilized Montreal from 1872 to 1917, much less to his young student Lighthall. In fact, Armour and Trott suggest that living in industrializing Montreal gave Murray insights into the problems of labour that had escaped the philosophers teaching in more idyllic rustic settings back in Britain. 'The intellectual life of Montreal was quite sufficient for a civilized and scholarly man and with its growth and industrialization ... he could observe ... firsthand the realities of moral issues which seem, all too often, disguised from philosophers whose fate it is to live out their lives in more traditional and bucolic academic surroundings' (Armour and Trott 1981, 106). Certainly, Murray strongly supported the rights of labour in his social and political philosophy (1982). There too, we can see an accommodationist sense of reason at work. I am now convinced that something more than the Frye-Atwood thesis is required in order to explain this accommodationist tendency in early Canadian philosophy. What their thesis ignores, at least in so far as the development of Canadian philosophical thought is concerned, is the influence of Indigenous values and world views.

Murray and Lighthall, to an even greater extent, spent much of their lives in the thriving, cosmopolitan city of Montreal. They were hardly contending with a hostile forest wilderness. Yet both adopted some form of the accommodationist use of reason. Although both were sympathetic to metaphysical idealism, they could not ignore the claims of materialism. Certainly, Murray strongly influenced Lighthall's thought. In fact, his name appears in the dedication of Lighthall's *The Person of Evolution*. However,

Lighthall's thought goes well beyond that of his former professor. Even his interest in the city of Montreal takes a different slant. As we have seen, Murray is interested in the social problems of a rapidly industrializing Montreal. Lighthall seems more interested in a pre-contact Montreal. He writes about the possible location, within the modern city, of the Indian village of Hochelaga. Explorer Jacques Cartier had visited it in 1535, but it had completely disappeared by the time Samuel de Champlain founded Quebec near the site of Stadacona in 1608 (Lighthall 1924). Lighthall's novel, *The Master of Life*, tells one possible story about Hochelaga's disappearance. It also presents a possible answer to the question with which Lighthall grapples elsewhere in a more academic fashion: Who were the Hochelagans? Were they Iroquois, Mohawk, Huron, Algonquin? (Lighthall 1899; 1932).

Lighthall's philosophical position – his metaphysics – also differs from Murray's. Armour and Trott characterize Murray's thought as 'a kind of critical objective idealism which goes beyond Kant but does not quite extend to the radical reconstruction envisaged by Hegel' (1981, 168). As we have seen, Lighthall was not an idealist, though he claimed that his position could be synthesized with idealism. This suggests that it is hardly inconsistent with idealism. Lighthall, unlike Murray, is not an idealist who takes realist claims seriously. Nor, as might be thought, is he a realist who takes idealist claims seriously. Lighthall represents a further development in Canadian philosophy, which still exhibits the accommodationist use of reason but in a slightly more sophisticated manner. Like a number of Canadian philosophers writing around the 1930s, Lighthall tends to adopt a kind of multi-perspectival approach. I have elsewhere called this *the polycentric perspective* (Rabb 1989b, 1992; McPherson and Rabb 1993, 10–11; 2001, 2003). This polycentrism recognizes that we finite human beings can never obtain a God's-eye view – a non-perspectival view – of reality. Every view is a view from somewhere. Hence it follows that no one philosophical perspective can ever provide an entirely adequate philosophy. However, this does not mean that such perspectives do not point towards truth; it merely follows that no one perspective can contain the whole truth.

Lighthall argues that understanding his concept of the Person of Evolution and directivity in evolution 'calls for a large revision of our homocentric and individual views of will and consciousness' (1930, 77, sc. 85). By this he does not mean adopting a God's-eye view. He is not looking for a grand Hegelian synthesis. Lighthall explains: 'In our pride of intellectual forms, we should keep in mind that there is deep knowledge in Instinct (including function); that warnings of "Common Sense" should never be lightly dismissed, that the trust of the infant and of all animals, in the order of things, is founded on a hidden reason, that the voice of conscience comes out of a larger world, and that "the wisdom of the body" and "the wisdom of the heart" – both products of ancient experience, have each a right to be put into relation with our latest learning' (1930, 85, sc. 97). I suggest that this kind of multi-perspectival or polycentric perspective is a natural outcome of the accommodationist use of reason common among earlier Canadian philosophers. It is not a very large step, for example, from being an idealist who takes realist claims seriously to accepting that there is truth in both idealism and realism without being committed to either. In fact, polycentrism is simply another example of the accommodationist use of reason, of what Armour and Trott call philosophical federalism.

It is fascinating that this multi-perspectival approach is also evident in the traditional thought of many Indigenous peoples of North America. Although the term *polycentrism* was first used to describe this phenomenon in a study by Ojibwa philosopher Dennis McPherson and myself (McPherson and Rabb 1993, 10–1), it has since been picked up by Cherokee philosopher Jace Weaver. Citing our study, *Indian from the Inside*, Weaver argues: 'Given the diversity of Indian cultures and worldviews, Native theology is what McPherson and Rabb call "polycentric"' (1997, 32). With the help of a story told by Osage scholar George Tinker, Weaver goes on to explain the significance of the polycentric perspective for what he calls Native theology:

> Ultimate reality, which we see through a glass darkly, is like a child's kaleidoscope. How it is perceived depends on how the cylinder is held, even though the bits of glass that form the picture are unchanging. The task must be to learn as much as one can not only about the given pattern but about the individual bits of glass, so that when the cylinder is shaken we can know something about the new image when it forms. In his essay 'An American Indian Theological Response to Ecojustice,' George Tinker alludes to a story that illustrates the polycentric approach. Imagine two Indian communities who live in close proximity to each other, separated by a mountain. A non-Native visitor arrives at the first community. In the course of the stay, she is informed that the tribe's council fire is the center of the universe and creation myths are told to demonstrate this concept. The following day, the outlander and representatives of the first tribe travel to the other community. The elders of the new tribe declare that their council fire is the center of the universe, and the members of the first tribe nod their assent. Confused, the visitor asks her host, 'I thought you said that your fire was the center.' The Indian replies, 'When we're there, that is the center of the universe. When we are here, this is the center.' Tinker concludes, 'Sometimes a single truth is not enough to explain the balance of the world around us …' We need to examine as many different

cultural codes as we can to re-create the structure of human life – self, community, spirit, and the world as we perceive it. (Weaver 1997, 33)

It is important not to interpret this kind of Indigenous pluralism as leading to any kind of relativism. Even Canadian historian Michael Ignatieff, in
defending his 'patchwork-quilt vision' of Canadian identity, makes it quite
clear that 'pluralism does not mean relativism. It means humility' (Ignatieff
2000, 104).

Although he does not discuss the early Canadian philosophers, John
Ralston Saul, in *A Fair Country: Telling Truths about Canada*, seems to be
struggling to get at this same Indigenous concept of polycentrism or multi-
perspectival pluralism as an integral part of his argument that Canada is
a Métis nation with Indigenous philosophical roots. This is evident in his
use of such concepts as the philosophy of interdependence and complexity
(2008, 106–7). Cree scholar Michael Hart, in the following account of a traditional sharing circle, explains more clearly what is involved in this kind of
multi-perspectival pluralism: 'Symbolically, the topic is placed at the centre
of the circle and everyone has a chance to share their views about the topic.
Since everyone is in a circle they will each have a different perspective of
the topic or part of the picture. Everyone expresses their views so that a
full picture of the topic is developed. Individual views are blended until
consensus on the topic is reached. A community view is developed and
knowledge is shared for the benefit of all members' (Hart 1996, 65).

Now, I am arguing that Indigenous intellectual practices of this kind
influenced Canadian philosophers like Lighthall in their acceptance of a
multi-perspectival approach. Of course, there is no evidence that Lighthall was aware of Cree sharing circles. However, he was well aware of the
accounts of the intense discussions surrounding the founding of the Iroquois (Haudenosaunee) Confederacy. These he attempts to depict in his
novel, *The Master of Life*. There we see the message of Peace debated from
all sides. Lighthall goes so far as to envisage a speaker with the unlikely
name Two-Equal-Statements. The following passage is representative:

But while the coming of Hiawatha and his general sentiments were approved,
the independent minds were not ready to give up the war on the Onondagas.
Shadeka spoke strongly in favour, but after he had finished the Chief named
Two-Equal-Statements went to the speaking mat and said: 'The arguments for
war are these: The young braves prove themselves men; the enemy are driven
off from the country; the hunting grounds are preserved; the people are made
proud by trophies; the wisdom won by warriors keeps the nation safe; and
foes are weakened by destructive blows. And the arguments for peace are the

following: The losses by death are diminished; the people rest and labor in confidence; the people grow numerous and rich; extended trade rejoices the hearts of all; travel is possible; friendship gladdens the hearts of those who roam.' (Lighthall 1908, 206–7)

Lighthall's novel, incidentally, should not be taken as another retelling of the founding of the Iroquois Confederacy. It is a piece of historical fiction which appropriates that story in a way that would, quite rightly, be frowned upon today. My only point is that the novel shows that Lighthall did have some understanding of Indigenous or Native philosophy early in his writing career. In fact, in the preface to the novel, Lighthall actually uses the term *philosophy* (as opposed to, say, *mythology* or *religion*) to characterize Native belief. Speaking about the North American Indian, he says, 'To understand his philosophy it is necessary to remember that he was a mystic; yet he believed one thing firmly, that the whole world of objects was living: nothing to him was inanimate: he himself was but part of a living world, and so were his dreams' (1908, v–vi). Now, I am not arguing that this represents a good understanding of an Indigenous philosophy – some Native languages do have the animate-inanimate distinction, for example – but for 1908 the novel itself does indicate some positive grasp of the Native perspective. Let us keep in mind that, for Lighthall, *mystic* is not a negative term. In fact, I see *The Person of Evolution* as Lighthall's attempt to present a more scientific confirmation of the Native world view that he depicts in *The Master of Life*. As we have seen, he is convinced that the conclusions of *The Person of Evolution*, 'inductively based on the new foundation of facts, may perhaps in the end be synthesized with … legitimate Mysticism' (1930, 62, sc. 67).

His multi-perspectivalism is not limited to the different branches of science or even to 'competing' metaphysical theories. Lighthall makes it quite clear at the conclusion of *The Person of Evolution* that he sees religion and science as approaching the same thing from different perspectives. 'Finally, I conclude, without prejudging the argument, that religion and science are not in two compartments, as nearly all the leading theologians and nearly all the leading present men of science say they are' (1930, 204–5). He argues that knowledge must be seen as a unity. This has important metaphysical implications.

To the Person of Evolution the individual is an organ, a member of its community body, a kind of cell of its multicellular whole. It sees all and feels for and in each, but with wider vision. To it there is, in a sense, no such thing as a subordinate individual: all are one creature: the whole process of subdivision has never obliterated that unity nor dissolved the connection between each part. The disconnection of individuals is an illusion. There is no such thing as a fully disconnected individual ... As the Outer Will, it guides the amoeba in its attraction to food, and in its reproduction by self division, the ant and the bee in all their cooperative community behaviour ... it directs the bear, the deer and the wolf in the wisdom of the wilds and the love of their young: it calls the buffalo bull to die for the herd, teaches the beaver how to fell trees and build dams and family dwellings, constructs their bodies as wonderfully as their minds, their communities as wonderfully as their bodies, and effecting these ends still more marvellously in men, urges them also to the complex endeavours of civilization and culture ... to the scientists' passion of truth, and to the apparent self-destruction of the martyr. None of these urges can be understood from the point of view of the individual: but they can be understood from that of one community being. (Lighthall 1930, 50–1, sc. 48)

This holistic account, in which everything is alive and interrelated, is certainly compatible with Lighthall's depiction of the Native world view in *The Master of Life*: 'the whole world of objects was living: nothing to him was inanimate: he himself was but part of a living world, and so were his dreams' (1908, v–vi). In *The Person of Evolution*, Lighthall even argues that dreams are a link between our individual consciousness and the 'Outer Consciousness' of the greater community of which we are a part – the Person of Evolution. 'Dreamlife is one of the spheres of the Outer Consciousness, apparently somewhat as it is one of the spheres of the inner – a borderland of both, and not fully expressing either' (1930, 29, sc. 16). In *The Master of Life*, dreams and visions obviously transport the individual to other realms where real knowledge is acquired. Lighthall describes in detail a vision quest undertaken by Hiawatha. 'He built himself a slight lodge of poles and bark, on the edge of a marsh, where he sat for several days, fasting and haunted by visions' (1908, 136). The dream or vision itself – including a talking elk suspended in mid-leap within a shadow forest, every part of which seemed to look at Hiawatha – was obviously a journey to another world:

> Hiawatha, whose soul had thus visited the other world, knew that his vision was a message from the gods. The passage back from one world to the other was not made instantaneously. The objects of the strange forest he had just left mingled in equal reality with the poles of his lodge, and the still reeds of the marsh, and even when the world of the living gradually attained dominance over that of the dead, the sight of the four scalped men and the cries of the

storm-gods pursued him as omens of utmost gloom. He sat motionless and light-headed for several hours, abandoning his consciousness to the super-natural. (Lighthall 1908, 139)

Hiawatha acquired real knowledge in this dream. We see this demonstrated some time later, when, in attempting to convince the Onondaga to cease their war with the Mohawk, he describes in great detail the scalped men of his dream. He had learned from his dream how many Mohawks had been killed on the last raid and the details of their deaths. This he relates to the Onondaga to prove that his words of peace are from the gods:

'Brothers of the Hill,' he said. 'The gods have spoken to me. Do you wish a sign? Then hear – In my vision I saw the number ye have slain was four. If this be right my words are from the gods.'

The exclamations of the assembly showed that he had spoken correctly. 'I see,' he continued, 'at the head of the four who are travelling an old chief. His forehead is painted and his left breast is pierced by a broken arrow. If this be right my words are from the gods.'

The chiefs ejaculated their astonishment and groans came from the aged matrons.

'The youngest,' Hiawatha went on, 'is a youth without a feather, but a hammer has crushed his skull and he carries a broken knife; if this be right my words are from the gods.'

Hiawatha continued and related his journey, his battle on the mountain, his dream, and his communion with the supernaturals during the past night. Even Atotarho was compelled to regard him as a prophet.

Finally the speaker declared that the Mohawk war should end, that the prisoners should be released, and that they be sent home with large presents to the relatives of their dead companions. (Lighthall 1908, 148–9)

In Lighthall's account, Hiawatha acquires his message of peace in a totally different kind of vision, a waking vision in which the Master of Life seems to be speaking through him. Lighthall also discussed this sort of waking dream in *The Person of Evolution*. 'Dreamlife we have suggested is one of the spheres of the Outer Consciousness; even when most awake we also dream; the dreamlife suggestions push themselves up' (1930, 36, sc. 28). In conversation about the war against the Mohawks with his adopted Onondaga father, the Arrowmaker, Hiawatha finds himself saying things about war that he himself had not thought, that no one had ever thought.

'Son,' said the Arrowmaker, at last. 'I have told them that this war is evil.'

'All war is evil,' returned Hiawatha bitterly; and as he said it he realized that the gods were speaking by his lips, for he had not thought so wide a thing.

The Arrowmaker spoke no more, he waited patiently for hours, for Hiawatha to break silence, and found no fault that he did not do so [a Native thing to do] ... Hiawatha placed some sticks on the fire and returned to his brooding. The Master was in him, the Fire was in him, the Sun was in him; and in his exalted spirit a thought was being born. This thought was – to abolish war.

All through the night, as he sat pondering, it surged before his sight in a crowd of forms ... By alliance forever might come the death of war forever ...

At the dead of night the spirit of the Sun appeared to him, among the embers, in the form of a red flame ... Then the Thunder passed over the mountain-top and the Echo God repeated his reverberating voice through the valley. 'War against war!' it sounded, and pondering the meaning of this, Hiawatha formed his revelation to completeness. (Lighthall 1908, 143)

I should note in passing that few scholars attribute the inspiration of the Great Peace to Hiawatha. In fact, since A.C. Parker's classic study, *The Constitution of the Five Nations*, it is generally agreed that the founder of the Confederacy is Dekanawida. As Parker, who is Seneca, put it, 'the Mohawk nation recognizes in Dekanawida its great culture hero and the founder of its civic system, giving Haiyentwatha (Hiawatha) a second place. Nearly all authorities among the other nations of the five agree in this and attribute to Dekanawida the establishment of the Great Peace' (Parker 1968, 8). Interestingly enough, Lighthall's *The Master of Life*, in describing the leadership of the Confederacy and their hereditary titles, does name Dekanawida the founder: 'The Council of the House are fifty chiefs – and their noble blood shall compose the Council forever – Atotarho shall follow Atotarho, Tekarihoken Tekarihoken, and Shadekaronyes shall succeed Shadekaronyes unto all generations. One alone shall not be succeeded – he is Dekanaweda [*sic*], for none can replace the Founder' (1908, 257). This speech, however, is attributed to Hiawatha. Lighthall seemed to want to accommodate both traditions.

This aside, there can be little doubt that Lighthall's major philosophical study, *The Person of Evolution*, presents an account of evolution that accommodates, among other things, the Indigenous perspective portrayed in *The Master of Life*. However, I am arguing much more than this. I contend that Lighthall's very concept of the Person of Evolution was actually inspired by that Indigenous perspective, by accounts of the founding of the Iroquois Confederacy. Although, as we have seen, *The Master of Life* is by no means an accurate retelling of that story, Lighthall had to be aware of such accounts in order to write the novel. In the traditional narrative of the founding of the Iroquois Confederacy, Dekanahwideh (Dekanawida) creates a symbol of the union by taking an arrow from each of the Five Nations, 'which we shall tie up together in a bundle which, when it is made and completely tied together, no one can bend or break' (Parker 1968, 101). The bundle of five arrows is probably the best-known symbol of the Iroquois Confederacy. Immediately after declaring, 'We shall tie this bundle of arrows together with deer sinew which is strong, durable and lasting and then also this institution shall be strong and unchangeable,' Dekanahwideh introduces a further symbol: the autonomous members of the Confederacy united as a single person. 'This bundle of arrows signifies that all the lords and all the warriors and all the women of the Confederacy have become united as one person' (Parker 1968, 101). This concept of person as one community being is exactly the concept of person used in Lighthall's *The Person of Evolution* (1930, 50–1, sc. 48). It is important to remember that this does not lessen the importance or uniqueness of the individual member of the Community Person, without whom the latter would not be what it is. Lighthall's concept of the Person of Evolution is a unity that includes difference, a unity that includes the diversity of the entire planet. In a strikingly parallel way, the individual members of the Iroquois Confederacy are all one person, yet maintain their individual identities. 'Before the real people united their nations, each nation had its council fires … The five Council Fires shall continue to burn as before and they are not quenched' (Parker 1968, 55–6).

The Iroquois Confederacy is a marvellous example of the accommodationist use of reason that, as we have seen, came to characterize philosophy in English Canada between 1850 and 1950. In Lighthall, we have evidence that at least one philosopher, whose work manifests this accommodationism, was obviously influenced by Indigenous thought. Not only was he well acquainted with the academic literature on the topic, as his own academic papers show, but there are also countless small details in his novel, including use of Iroquois and Algonquian terms, that show that his knowledge of Native people was more than a reading knowledge. To give but one example, the conversation between Hiawatha and the Arrowmaker, cited more fully above, is interrupted by a long silence. 'The Arrowmaker spoke no more, he waited patiently for hours, for Hiawatha to break silence, and found no fault that he did not do so' (Lighthall 1908, 143). This is a classic instance of the Native value of non-interference. This value has since been documented by Mohawk psychiatrist Clare Brant (1990), and, with more detail, in Cree and Ojibwa communities by Cree philosopher Lorraine Brundige (1997a, 1997b). But Lighthall picks this up back in 1908. He recognizes that Native conversations can be punctuated by long silences, and, more important, he recognizes that this is considered entirely appropriate. I suggest that he could only have known this kind of detail if he had been personally well acquainted with fairly traditional Native people. I fully realize that the appearance of such detail in his novel does not in and by itself prove that he actually was so acquainted. Fortunately, we do have additional textual evidence.

In 1889 Lighthall published a collection of Canadian poetry entitled *Songs of the Great Dominion: Voices from the Forests and the Waters, the Settlements and Cities of Canada*. In the section on 'The Indian,' Lighthall includes a song translated from the Mohawk especially for the book. As he explains in the introduction to his collection, 'a curious Indian song, representing a small but unique song-literature which has sprung up among the tribe at Caughnawaga Reservation, near Montreal, since barbaric times, "from the sheer necessity of singing when together," was translated specially for me by Mr. John Waniente Jocks, the son of a Six-nation chief of that Reservation. Mr. Jocks, who is a law student, is of pure Mohawk origin' (1889, xxxiv).

Lighthall seemed to have a particular interest in the Caughnawaga Reserve. He even wrote a poem entitled 'The Caughnawaga Beadwork Seller,' which he included in his anthology. In the notes at the back of the book he explains the term *Kanawaké*, which appears throughout the poem: 'Kanawaké ("By the rapid") is the present native form of the name of Caughnawaga Indian village, which is situated in its reservation, at the head of the Sault St Louis Rapid, and opposite Lachine, about twelve miles from Montreal' (1889, 455).

Lighthall also includes two poems by E. Pauline Johnson in his anthology, though neither appears in 'The Indian' section. One appears under 'Sports and Free Time,' the other under 'Places.' In his biographical note on Johnson, Lighthall says in part: 'Miss E. Pauline Johnson is interesting on account of her race as well as her strong and cultural verse. She is of the Mohawks of Brantford. This race, to-day thoroughly civilised, and occupying high positions all over Canada, have had a wonderfully faithful record of unswerving British alliance for over two hundred and twenty years, during which their devoted courage was the factor which decided the predominance of the Anglo-Saxon in North America' (1889, 453). This notion that the British succeeded in North America precisely because

– and perhaps only because – they linked themselves to the Covenant Chain of the Iroquois League comes out very strongly in Lighthall's novel *The Master of Life* as well. Speaking of Hiawatha, the novel concludes by asking:

> Now, who was this savage that he should go down in history among the great and glorious of the world, whose work endures and lives? It might be enough that his soul was heroic, it might be enough that his thought was broad … But also, the Master of Life decreed that his League should turn and guide the mighty currents of the World itself. When a generation later, the white men came, they came in two directions. The Frenchman, Champlain, came up the St. Lawrence; the Netherlander, Hudson, up the Hudson. The former rashly took up the unjust quarrel of the Huron and the Algonkin against the Mohawk; the League replied by crippling the colony of France until its doom was written before all eyes and its dominion passed away. The Netherlander linked his future with the Silver Chain; he held to it for himself and the Briton; and the League was the bulwark which protected them during years of weakness and prepared the way for the spread of British principles in North America.
>
> What vast issues then are due to the thought of a savage! Was he a savage? (Lighthall 1908, 260–1)

I think that if current members of the Iroquois Confederacy really thought that they had 'prepared the way for the spread of British principles in North America,' they might well say, with deep regret, that they had much to answer for. Still, Lighthall was correct in suggesting that the League believed its mission was to 'guide the mighty currents of the World itself.' As Native (Lumbee) legal scholar Robert A. Williams Jr has argued, 'In their American Indian vision of law and peace, the Iroquois saw themselves as constitutionally obligated by Deganawidah's divine command to bring all nations under the spreading branches of the Great Tree of Peace and to establish the law of the Great Peace' (1997, 119–20). Lighthall recognized this and was inspired by it. He notes that the doors of the Longhouse (the League) are open to all (1908, 257). In *The Master of Life*, Hiawatha proclaims the 'Laws of the Longhouse' as follows: 'If any tribe submit to the League, there shall be peace with it and it shall be added to the Chain. If any hurt not the League, the League shall hurt it not. But if the hindmost cub of the League be snapped at, the Wolf-pack shall be on the hunter's scent. Yet after the biter be bitten, he shall not be eaten; he shall be adopted: the Chain shall be a Chain of Peace. Thus your Tree shall grow great of girth and put forth spreading boughs, until wailing no more be heard in the houses nor blood of men be met with in the woods' (Lighthall 1908, 154).

I want to emphasize the point that the Iroquois originally conceived the ideal confederacy of all nations as one which, following the ethic of non-interference, clearly accommodates the diversity of those nations. The Dekanawida narrative states quite explicitly that 'whenever a foreign nation is conquered or has by their own free will accepted the Great Peace, their own system of internal government may continue so far as it is consistent but they must cease all strife with other nations' (Parker 1968, 10). Lighthall was clearly inspired by this sort of ideal. In the introduction to his anthology of Canadian poetry he writes of an ideal that will keep Canada, and indeed the British Empire, together, an ideal 'worthy of long and patient endeavour,' an 'IDEAL THAT MEN WILL SUFFER AND DIE FOR.' This ideal, it turns out, 'may be found in the broad-minded advance towards the voluntary Federation of Mankind' (1889, xxiii).

Several Canadian philosophers whose thought exhibits an accommodationist use of reason were inspired by this Indigenous ideal of world federalism. John Watson (1847–1939), who replaced Murray at Queen's University when Murray left for McGill, argued for a federation of independent nation states in his 1919 book, *The State in Peace and War*. W.A. Crawford-Frost (1863–1936), one of the many famous students of University of Toronto philosopher George Paxton Young (1818–89), wrote to U.S. President Wilson advocating, in his words, 'a plan for a Federation Of Free Nations, which resembled in a general way the one adopted when the League of Nations became a fact in 1920' (Rabb 1989c, 182). In 1931 Crawford-Frost suggested, 'The League of Nations should be changed to a world federation,' arguing that 'it seems suitable that a person who was one of the first to suggest a League of Nations should be the first to declare that having done its duty the League should now be honorably discharged, with the thanks of the world, and something more effective substituted for it' (Rabb 1989c, 171).

Lighthall's *Songs of the Great Dominion* is dedicated 'to that sublime cause, The Union of Mankind.' There can be no doubt that Lighthall and several other early Canadian philosophers were inspired by this ideal of a voluntary federation of mankind.

At the very foundation of the drive to such a federation are Indigenous values, such as respect for and accommodation of difference, as well as non-interference and what I have called a polycentric perspective. Thus far I have argued that these Native values can also be found in – and probably inspired – the thought of early Canadian philosophers writing between roughly 1850 and 1950. Does this mean that Native values and world views have made a significant contribution to Canadian culture today?

Does this distinctive form of Canadian philosophy, identified by Armour and Trott in *The Faces of Reason*, continue to exist and develop in Canada today? Apart from some very rare exceptions, courses in Canadian or Native philosophy are not taught in Canadian universities – certainly not in their philosophy departments (cf. McPherson and Rabb 2008). The early Canadian philosophers mentioned above, Watson, Lighthall, Murray, are seldom if ever discussed in philosophy courses offered at Canadian universities. One possible explanation for this is that, immediately after the 1850–1950 time period covered by Armour and Trott's study, there was an unprecedented increase in both the number of Canadian universities and the number of students enrolled in them. It has been well documented that, while universities were expanding in the early 1960s, 'Canada had to import the vast majority of its new social scientists, along with large numbers of professors in virtually every other arts discipline. It was estimated that in 1968 over 80 percent of new appointments went to non-Canadians ...' (Jasen 1989, 258). Of course, one teaches what one knows, and these imported professors knew nothing of early Canadian philosophy, not to mention Indigenous values and world views. In actual fact, most knew nothing at all about Canada. Nor did they confront the kind of Canada that had so influenced the earlier influx of professors from abroad – the Watsons, Murrays, et cetera. By the 1960s the majority of the universities at which these new academics arrived were in urban settings not unlike those they had left behind.

Even if the newly arriving academics of the 1960s had entered a unique environment that might have influenced their thought, they were not really interested in learning all that much about the new country in which they found teaching jobs. Most thought of themselves as just visiting, rather than emigrating. It has also been well documented that 'because a majority of American-born professors had at that time no intention of remaining in Canada or becoming Canadian Citizens, their choice of research topics was guided by the American academic market ... The content of their lectures was similarly foreign in emphasis, and the use of American text-books was taken for granted' (Jasen 1989, 258). This was even true of such disciplines as sociology, though one would think that sociology in Canada would surely take notice of Canadian society. In fact, Canadian content in sociology texts was exceedingly rare in the 1960s and even in the early 1970s. Actually, the first text in Canadian sociology was introduced as early as 1961, and its editors justified its publication by arguing: 'Students of sociology in Canadian universities have had to rely heavily on textbooks in which the greater part of the illustrative data concerns the United States. As teachers in Canadian universities we have felt for a long time that it would be a great advantage for students to have available a book that brings together representative material on Canadian sociology' (Blishen et al. 1961, ix).

In disciplines like philosophy, where universal truth seems to be on the agenda, there was no motivation at all to look at Canadian content. At that time the Anglo-American analytic tradition tended to dominate the English-language philosophy curriculum, regardless of the country in which a university was located. Many, and I dare say most, graduates of such programs would regard the loss of a distinctive Canadian or even Indigenous philosophy as no loss at all, or even as a good thing.

Despite the publication of a number of studies in Canadian philosophy, including Armour and Trott's *The Faces of Reason*, Brian McKillop's *A Disciplined Intelligence: Critical Inquiry and Canadian Thought in the Victorian Era*, Carl Berger's *Science, God and Nature in Victorian Canada*, and my own *Religion and Science in Early Canada*, I had begun to think that Canadian philosophy had been relegated to the status of an esoteric fact about Canada's history in the period between approximately 1850 and 1950. Then I read Michael Ignatieff's *The Rights Revolution*. There I found the distinctive characteristics of Canadian philosophy: the accommodationism, the respect for difference, the learning from opposing views in true philosophical humility, the pluralism that is not a relativism – all leading to what Ignatieff calls 'the essential distinctiveness of Canada itself [which] lies in the fact that we are a tri-national community trying to balance individual and collective rights without sacrificing the unity and equality of our citizens' (2000, 125). Ignatieff even goes so far as to say, 'If you ask me what I love about my country, this is it' (2000, 125). It is here, in 'the essential distinctiveness of Canada itself,' that Canadian philosophy is to be found today – not in the philosophy departments of Canadian universities. Given, as I have argued, that Indigenous values and world views influenced early Canadian philosophy, it follows that Indigenous values and world views are also at least partly responsible for what Ignatieff calls 'the essential distinctiveness of Canada itself.'

Ignatieff does not himself seem to be aware that he is discussing the unique features of Canadian philosophy, much less Indigenous values. He does not mention Armour and Trott or the early Canadian philosophers whom they examine. Ignatieff actually writes as if the necessity of balancing individual and collective rights in a tri-national community had somehow forced us to invent our unique rights culture. 'We are a community forged by the primal experience of negotiating terms of settlement among three peoples: the English, the French, and the aboriginal First Nations. This gives us a particular rights culture and it is this rights culture that makes us different' (2000, 14).

Ignatieff neglects to mention that those originally charged with responsibility for these negotiations, those engaged in this unique balancing act, actually had a strong foundation of accommodationist principles on which to draw. The connection with the philosophical federalism of the early Canadian philosophers, and thus Native values, is not difficult to find. The date of Confederation is 1867. Who were the people behind the scenes, the members of the developing public service, the budding constitutional lawyers, et cetera, attending to the details and thus setting the direction for the next hundred years or so? They were, for the most part, the graduates of Canada's new universities. They were students trained by the John Watsons at Queen's, the George Paxton Youngs at Toronto, and the John Clark Murrays at McGill. It should really come as no surprise then that what Ignatieff discovered that makes Canada's rights culture distinct should so closely resemble what Armour and Trott found to be characteristic of early Canadian philosophy.

I think it is significant that Ignatieff came to his conclusions quite independently, without discussing and seemingly without knowing the early Canadian philosophers. Yet much of what he says corroborates the link and brings to mind the Indigenous values that are so apparent in the thought of these early Canadian philosophers. It is important to note that, although Ignatieff acknowledges collective rights in the Canadian constitution, when collective and individual rights come into conflict he favours individual rights. This, he suggests, is because 'group rights – to language, culture, religious expression, and land – are valuable to the degree that they enhance the freedom of individuals' (2000, 24). However, his position is tempered somewhat by his view of the nature of the individual, arguing that 'our very individualism is social' (2000, 138). This puts his position much closer to a Native view of the self than he acknowledges. Cherokee philosopher Jace Weaver, for example, following Professor Donald Fixico (Shawnee-Sauk and Fox-Muscogee-Seminole), argues that 'Natives tend to see themselves in terms of "self in society" rather than "self and society"' (1997, 39). This notion is, of course, also close to Lighthall's claim that 'there is no such thing as a fully disconnected individual' (1930, 50–1, sc. 48).

Ignatieff also finds in the Canadian rights revolution the kind of pluralism and respect for difference that we have seen in both Lighthall and in Indigenous thought. Ignatieff argues that 'rights not only help to make disputes precise, and therefore manageable, but also help each party to appreciate that the other has some right on its side' (2000, 9). He notes, for example, that 'when one side realizes that the other has a rights claim too, compromise can become possible' (25). To acknowledge that those who oppose us may have some right on their side is to begin to acknowledge 'the other' and to respect difference. Ignatieff proclaims that the challenge of the rights revolution is 'to reconcile community with diversity in an age of entitlements' (137). He argues: 'The rights revolution has made us all aware how different we are, both as individuals and as peoples' (ibid.). These differences are of utmost importance. 'Our differences, small as they may seem, are the basis of our identity' (ibid.). Given the importance of this respect for difference, Ignatieff is compelled 'to acknowledge that it is the very essence of nation-states that they harbour within them incompatible visions of the national story' (136). However, 'holding a nation together does not require us to force these incompatible stories into one, but simply to keep them in dialogue with each other and, if possible, learning from each other' (136).

This is certainly reminiscent of George Tinker's story, which Jace Weaver cites in explaining the polycentric perspective. It is, indeed, possible to live with and respect incompatible stories. This is a form of multi-perspectival pluralism. Yet, as noted above, 'pluralism does not mean relativism. It means humility' (Ignatieff 2000, 104). To learn from those with whom we disagree presupposes 'the capacity to understand moral worlds different from our own' (138). Given this respect for difference, Ignatieff defends what he calls 'the patchwork-quilt vision of our land as a network of overlapping forms of self-government' (77–9).

As Armour and Trott point out, the development of a distinctive Canadian identity cannot be attributed to one person or even to an influential group. This, they suggest, points to one of the ways in which Canada differs from the United States. Observing that past 'attempts to paint our Fathers of Confederation and make them look like the signers of the Declaration of Independence … generally provoked laughter,' they go on to explain, 'We have not seen them as very important because we have not thought, for the most part, that anyone could have the kind of importance that Americans assign to their historic figures' (Armour and Trott 1981, 24).

Armour and Trott give the example of the formation of the United Church of Canada to illustrate that the thousands of students who studied under Watson, Murray, Paxton Young, and other early Canadian philosophers went on to influence Canadian society using various forms of accommodationist reason. Referring specifically to Watson, they argue: 'For more than fifty years, Watson was a dominant – sometimes the dominant influence – at Queen's. He played a significant role in the intellectual background and even in some of the practical negotiations, which led to the United Church of Canada' (Armour and Trott 1981, 216). They point out that graduates of Queen's University at the time not only went into the

civil service but also staffed the Presbyterian churches and the new universities in western Canada. Watson had had a strong influence on them
all. 'His pupils seemed to have carried with them an echo of that dry voice
and its persistent demand for reasonableness and it often stayed with them
for life' (216). In 1973 I had some personal confirmation of this as I inter-
viewed Dr Hugh McLeod, a former moderator of the United Church, about
his experience as a student of Watson at Queen's. Of course, no one person,
not even John Watson, is responsible for the creation of the United Church.
The clergy who negotiated union, as Armour and Trott acknowledge, 'had
been educated, over a span of time, by men like Paxton Young, John Clark
Murray … and of course, in large numbers, by Watson himself' (301). What
they all did have in common were the accommodationist principles that
are so characteristic of early Canadian philosophy and, I have argued, were
inspired and reinforced by Indigenous values and world views. If my thesis
is correct, then the United Church of Canada presents us with one of the
strangest ironies in Canadian history. In running Indian residential schools,
the United Church would have been trying to remove Native children from
the Indigenous cultures that inspired the very accommodationist principles
that facilitated the formation of their church in the first place (cf. Sinclair
2000; Wilson 2000). These same values – the respect for difference, the polycentrism, et cetera – I have argued were also the foundation of the rights
revolution, which Ignatieff contends constitutes 'the essential distinctiveness of Canada itself.' Of course, even Ignatieff is forced to admit that this
distinctive rights culture in Canada is at best only an ideal (Ignatieff 2000,
79–84; cf. McPherson, Nelson, and Rabb 2004, 8–10).

Within Canada today some provinces are asking why they should stay
in Confederation if they see no benefit to themselves from doing so. Does
this suggest that we may have forgotten the Indigenous teachings about
accommodating difference within community? Perhaps if we are reminded
from time to time how much and in what ways we have been influenced by
Indigenous peoples we will continue to learn from them.

We learn today, for example, from Blackfoot-Métis architect Douglas Cardinal, who designed the Canadian Museum of Civilization in Hull, Quebec.
The museum overlooks the Ottawa River and the back of the Parliament
Buildings across the river in Ontario. Cardinal is fond of pointing out that
the cities of Ottawa and Hull were built with their backs to the river and,
hence, to each other. This is a perfect representation of contemporary English and French Canada: their backs to nature and to each other. Cardinal
deliberately designed the Canadian Museum of Civilization facing the river
in order to encourage English and French Canada to notice nature and to
face one another. This is a typically Native, indirect, deeply symbolic way

of offering advice without violating the value of non-interference. We still have much to learn from our Native neighbours. Remembering how much they have already tried to teach us will, I hope, facilitate this learning in the future. We must never forget, for example, the ideals inherited from the Iroquois Confederacy. As Lumbee tribal member Robert Williams points out, 'the good news of Deganawidah's message envisioned a multicultural community of all peoples on earth, linked together in solidarity under the sheltering branches of the Tree of the Great Peace' (Williams 1997, 60).

> The five Council Fires shall continue to burn as before and they are not quenched. (Parker 1968, 55–6)

Notes

1 An earlier version of this chapter was first published in *Ayaangwaamizin: The International Journal of Indigenous Philosophy* 2 (2): 125–42. I thank the editors for permission to use it in this revised and expanded form. I also thank my colleague the Ojibwa philosopher Dennis McPherson and our many Native students, as well as the post-doctoral Visiting Humanities Research Fellows in our Native philosophy project, all of whom have taught me how much more I need to learn.

2 I have explored this with special reference to George Paxton Young, John Watson, William Albert Crawford-Frost, Herbert Leslie Stewart, and others. Compare my 'Canadian Idealism, Philosophical Federalism, and World Peace' (Rabb 1986a); 'Herbert L. Stewart, Thomas Carlyle, and Canadian Idealism' (Rabb 1986b); 'The Fusion Philosophy of Crawford-Frost' (Rabb 1986c); and 'Reason and Revelation Revisited: A Canadian Perspective' (Rabb 1983).

Bibliography

Armour, Leslie, and Elizabeth Trott. 1981. *The Faces of Reason: An Essay on Philosophy and Culture in English Canada, 1850–1950*. Waterloo, ON: Wilfrid Laurier University Press.

Atwood, Margaret. 1972. *Survival: A Thematic Guide to Canadian Literature*. Toronto: House of Anansi.

Barreiro, José. 1992. *Indian Roots of American Democracy*. Ithaca, NY: Akwe:kon Press.

Berger, Carl. 1983. *Science, God and Nature in Victorian Canada*. Toronto: University of Toronto Press.

Blishen, B.R., F.E. Jones, K.D. Naegele, and J. Porter, eds. 1961. *Canadian Society: Sociological Perspectives*. Toronto: Macmillan.

Brant, Clare. 1990. Native ethics and rules of behaviour. *Canadian Journal of Psychiatry* 35 (6): 535–9.

Brundige, Lorraine. 1997a. Continuity of native values: Cree and Ojibwa. Master's thesis, Lakehead University.

– 1997b. 'Ungrateful Indian': Continuity of Native values. *Ayaangwaamizin: The International Journal of Indigenous Philosophy* 1 (1): 45–54.

Grinde, Donald A., and Bruce Johansen. 1995. *Exemplar of Liberty: Native America and the Evolution of Democracy*. Los Angeles: University of California American Indian Studies Center.

Hart, Michael Anthony. 1996. Sharing circles: Utilizing traditional practice methods for teaching, helping, and supporting. In *From Our Eyes: Learning from Indigenous Peoples*, ed. Sylvia O'Meara et al., 59–72. Toronto: Garamond.

Hatzan, A. Leon. 1925. *The True Story of Hiawatha and History of the Six Nation Indians*. Toronto: McClelland and Stewart.

Ignatieff, Michael. 2000. *The Rights Revolution*. Toronto: House of Anansi Press.

Jasen, Patricia. 1989. In pursuit of human values (or laugh when you say that): The student critique of the Arts curriculum in the 1960s. In *Youth, University and Canadian Society*, ed. P. Axelrod and J.G. Reid. Kingston, ON: McGill-Queen's University Press.

Johansen, Bruce. 1982. *Forgotten Founders*. Boston: Harvard Common Press.

Lighthall, William Douw, ed. 1889. *Songs of the Great Dominion: Voices from the Forests and the Waters, the Settlements and Cities of Canada*. London: Walter Scott.

– 1899. Hochelagans and Mohawks: A link in Iroquois history. *Transactions of the Royal Society of Canada* 14 (2): 199–211.

– 1908. *The Master of Life: A Romance of the Five Nations and of Prehistoric Montreal*. Toronto: Musson Book.

– 1924. Hochelaga and 'The Hill of Hochelaga.' *Transactions of the Royal Society of Canada* 18 (2): 91–106.

– 1930. *The Person of Evolution*. Toronto: Macmillan.

– 1932. The false plan of Hochelaga. *Transactions of the Royal Society of Canada* 26 (2): 181–92.

McKillop, Brian. 1979. *A Disciplined Intelligence: Critical Inquiry and Canadian Thought in the Victorian Era*. Montreal: McGill-Queen's University Press.

McPherson, D.H., and J.D. Rabb. 1993. *Indian from the Inside: A Study in Ethno-metaphysics*. Thunder Bay, ON: Lakehead University Centre for Northern Studies.

– 2001. Indigeneity in Canada: Spirituality, the sacred and survival. *International Journal of Canadian Studies / Revue internationale d'études canadiennes* 23 (Spring/Printemps): 57–79.

– 2003. Restoring the interpretive circle: Community-based research and education. *International Journal of Canadian Studies / Revue internationale d'études cana-diennes* 28 (Fall/Automne): 137–65.

– 2008. The Native philosophy project: An update. *American Philosophical Association Newsletter on American Indians in Philosophy* 7 (2): 5–8.

McPherson, Dennis H., Connie H. Nelson, and J. Douglas Rabb. 2004. Applied research ethics with Aboriginal peoples: A Canadian dilemma. *National Centre for Ethics in Human Research NCEHR Communiqué CNÉRH* 12 (2): 6–12.

Murray, John Clark. 1982. *The Industrial Kingdom of God*. Ed. L. Armour and E. Trott. Ottawa: University of Ottawa Press.

Parker, Arthur C. 1968. The constitution of the Five Nations. In *Parker on the Iroquois*, ed. William N. Fenton. Syracuse, NY: Syracuse Univerity Press.

Rabb, J. Douglas. 1983. Reason and revelation revisited: A Canadian perspective. In *Religion and Reason*, ed. J. Douglas Rabb. Winnipeg, MB: Ronald P. Frye.

– 1986a. Canadian idealism, philosophical federalism, and world peace. *Dialogue* 25 (1): 92–103.

– 1986b. Herbert L. Stewart, Thomas Carlyle, and Canadian idealism. *Canadian Literature* 111:211–4.

– 1986c. The fusion philosophy of Crawford-Frost. *Idealist Studies* 16 (1): 77–92.

– ed. 1989a. *Religion and Science in Early Canada*. Kingston, ON: Ronald P. Frye.

– 1989b. The polycentric perspective: A Canadian alternative to Rorty. *Dialogue* 28:107–15.

– 1989c. *The Christian Cosmology of Crawford-Frost*. Kingston, ON: Ronald P. Frye.

– 1992. From triangles to tripods: Polycentrism in environmental ethics. *Environmental Ethics* 14:177–83.

Saul, John Ralston. 2008. *A Fair Country: Telling Truths about Canada*. Toronto: Viking.

Sinclair, Donna. 2000. Living out the apology. *The United Church Observer* N.S. 64 (4): 32–4.

Watson, John. 1919. *The State in Peace and War*. Glasgow: J. MacLehose and Sons.

Weatherford, Jack. 1988. *Indian Givers: How the Indians of the Americas Transformed the World*. New York: Fawcett/Ballantine.

Weaver, Jace. 1997. *That the People Might Live: Native American Literature and Native American Community*. New York: Oxford University Press.

Williams, Robert A., Jr. 1997. *Linking Arms Together: American Indian Treaty Visions of Law and Peace, 1600–1800*. New York: Oxford University Press.

Wilson, David. 2000. Residential schools: History on trial. *The United Church Observer* N.S 64 (4): 28–32.

Profile of Beverly (Buffy) Sainte-Marie (1941–)

Cree, Musician, Educator, and Activist

A globally recognized personality, Buffy Sainte-Marie is motivated by many interests. Through her involvements in music, theatre, film, and education she has influenced many people's lives. Buffy Sainte-Marie was born on 20 February 1941 on the Piapot Reserve near Craven, Saskatchewan.[1] Orphaned at five months old, she was adopted by Americans Albert and Winifred Kendrick Sainte-Marie and raised in Maine and Massachusetts.[2] She was drawn to music at a very young age. At age four she discovered the piano, and her world changed forever.[3]

Education has always been important to Sainte-Marie. She excelled academically in high school and attended the University of Massachusetts, where she earned a philosophy degree in 1963.[4] She later obtained a teaching degree as well as a doctorate in fine arts.[5] Sainte-Marie's love of music, however, put her teaching aspirations on hold. In the early 1960s she took a break from her studies to sing professionally. Penning protest songs such as 'Now That the Buffalo Are Gone' and 'Universal Soldier,' as well as love songs like 'Till It's Time for You to Go,' marked her as a legitimate folk-singing star.[6] She signed with Vanguard Records in 1964.[7] Her first album, *It's My Way*, won Billboard's Best New Artist Award.[8] Between the mid 1960s and the late 1970s she released fourteen albums and performed for audiences all over the world.[9]

The birth of Sainte-Marie's son, Dakota Wolfchild Starblanket, in 1976 caused her to retire from the music scene.[10] However, her acting career was launched through involvement with the children's television program *Sesame Street* between 1976 and 1980.[11] She appeared on the show to educate people about Native American culture. Sainte-Marie took her passion for education to a higher level in 1969 when she founded the Nihewan Foundation for American Indian Education.[12] The foundation's unique methods have been recognized as effective ways of teaching and of helping Indigenous students to learn, while aiding non-Indigenous people to learn about Native culture.

Buffy Sainte-Marie.

Buffy Sainte-Marie has received numerous awards and distinctions. In 1982 she won an Academy Award for composing 'Up Where We Belong,' the theme song for the movie *An Officer and a Gentleman*.[13] In 1993 she won the Charles de Gaulle Award for Best International Artist for her compact disc *Coincidence and Likely Stories*. In 1995 she was inducted into the Juno Hall of Fame by the Canadian music industry.[14] In 1997 Sainte-Marie received both a Juno and a Gemini Award for her album *Up Where We Belong*.[15]

Buffy Sainte-Marie has also been recognized for her dedication to children's education. For example, she was given the Louis T. Delgado Award as Native American Philanthropist of the Year for her work in the Nihewan Foundation in 1997.[16] She also received the American Indian College Fund's Lifetime Achievement Award in 1998 and served on the former First Lady's committee to save America's treasures. Her achievements were recognized in 1998 when she was invested as an Officer in the Order of Canada, the highest honour a civilian can receive in Canada.[17] Buffy Sainte-Marie currently lives with her family in Hawaii, where she continues to pursue her passion for music, art, and children's education.[18]

MICHAEL MUZECHA

Notes

1 Bruce Weir, '"Indians exist" is the message from lifetime achiever,' *Windspeaker* 16, no. 1.
2 Bruce E. Johansen and Donald A. Grinde Jr, eds., 'Buffy Sainte-Marie,' in *The Encyclopedia of Native American Biography: 600 Life Stories of Important People, from Powhatan to Wilma Mankiller* (New York: Henry Holt, 1997), 320.
3 Cynthia Kasee, 'Buffy Sainte-Marie,' in *Notable Native Americans*, ed. Sharon Malinowski (New York: Gale Research, 1995), 377.
4 Johansen and Grinde, 'Buffy Sainte-Marie,' 332.
5 'Buffy Sainte-Marie,' in *The Canadian Encyclopedia 2000 World Edition* (Toronto: McClelland and Stewart, 2000).
6 Ibid.
7 Kasee, 'Buffy Sainte-Marie,' 320.
8 Colette P. Simonot, 'Buffy Sainte-Marie,' in *Encyclopedia of Saskatchewan*, http://esask.uregina.ca/entry/sainte-marie_buffy_beverly_1941-.html (accessed 30 April 2009).
9 'Buffy Sainte-Marie,' http://www.creative-native.com/biograp.htm.
10 Ibid.
11 Kasee, 'Buffy Sainte-Marie,' 321.

12 Weir, '"Indians exist."'
13 Ibid.
14 Weir, '"Indians exist."'
15 'Buffy Sainte-Marie,' http://www.northernstars.ca/actorsstu/saintemariebio.html.
16 Ibid.
17 Ibid.
18 Ibid.

Canada – Its Cradle, Its Name, Its Spirit: The Stadaconan Contribution to Canadian Culture and Identity

GEORGES E. SIOUI

I am a Huron and a Canadian Indian. I am well aware that my nation originates essentially from the Wyandot, once proprietors of a small country located in present-day Ontario, and that the name *Huron* was given by the French to the Wyandot as a way to belittle, negate, and ultimately dispossess them. However, I am able to fully assume the history that made me and my people what we are today, that is, Huron. That name allows us to see the whole picture of where we have been, where we are, and where we want to go. To me, *Huron* means being Canadian in a uniquely profound way, a sacred way. Being a Huron means being directly related to the Stadaconans, the people who were there before Quebec City existed, just like the rocks, the trees, and the Saint-Charles and St Lawrence rivers. The Stadaconans were those of my ancestors who, in 1535, gave Jacques Cartier a cradle, a name, and a spirit for the country he fancied he had discovered: *Kanatha*.

I guess my dear reader already has a sense that if I am asked to talk or write about Aboriginal contributions to Canadian culture and identity, I can really get going. I will use this opportunity to share with my fellow Canadians some of my secret Huron knowledge about what the most ancient Canadians, the Stadaconans, did in order to help create a country that would, from then on, have to include Cartier's people and, as they already knew, so many other Europeans. I use the words *have to* because the French and others, such as the Basques, showed clear signs, by 1535, that they were going to keep coming here, many to stay. We knew this from at least two of our own Stadaconan youth who had been deceitfully captured by Cartier the year before and brought back home to Stadacona in 1535 on Cartier's second voyage.

At this point, some readers may object that the Huron, reputed to have come from what is now Ontario to what is now Quebec about 115 years later (1650), when their country was definitively destroyed 'by the Iroquois,' cannot claim to be ethnically related to the Stadaconans. I would answer that recent archaeological findings have confirmed our *returning* to Quebec in 1649–50. It was, indeed, a return home for many of our families who had their roots as Stadaconans but had had to flee from their ancestral 'Quebec' lands as a result of the first impact of the French and European invasion in Cartier's time. More than any other Amerindian group, the Huron of today, though few in number, carry the heritage of the Stadaconans, just as they are the principal carriers of the spiritual and intellectual heritage of many of the great Nadowek (Iroquoian) peoples and confederacies that have disappeared: the Tionontati or Tobacco, the Attawandaron or Neutral, the Erie or Cougars, the Wenro, the Susquehanna, the Hochelaga, and others.

Cartier first used the word *Canada* in his log book in 1535, on his second voyage, to designate both the town of Stadacona (now Quebec City) and the country whose centre it was, which extends approximately from Trois-Rivières to l'Île-aux-Coudres. The previous year, Cartier's three ships had entered the Gulf of the St Lawrence and had encountered two groups of Amerindians: Mi'kmaq and Stadacona. These people possibly journeyed far away from their homes with other people from 'Canada' in pre-contact times. The Stadaconans were camped at present-day Gaspé and were catching lots of fish and smoking them.

On Friday, 24 July 1534, Cartier planted a large cross that he had had made, bearing the inscription *Vive le Roi de France*, at the entrance to Gaspé Bay. Donnacona, whom Cartier would identify a year later (8 September 1535) as the 'Seigneur du Canada,' paddled up to Cartier's ship with three of his sons. This historically important moment was described in some detail by Cartier. First, we learn that the Stadaconan leader and his people did not come as close to the French as they had during the initial days of this one-week encounter. Rather, Donnacona's canoe remained at a distance while he addressed the French to explain to them that, as Cartier understood, 'all the land was his' and that his people opposed the making and the planting of that object that the French called a cross and collectively worshipped. (We know from many early sources that Aboriginal people were then able to and, in fact, did enforce their strict prohibition of the Europeans cutting even a twig or taking anything from their land without their permission. We also learn that even though they were very far away from their homes and immediate country, these first Canadians shared territorial rights and therefore land stewardship with the Mi'kmaq. Also important, we learn that the Frenchmen, far from being affected by this defensive act against their intrusion, had a subterfuge ready to use that was intended to make the Native people understand that the French did not believe they had to respect the political order already established by the First Peoples on their lands.) At the end of Donnacona's harangue, which Cartier found lengthy, he showed the Stadaconan leader an axe, feigning a wish to barter it for a bearskin that the chief wore. The latter, moved by this gesture, came closer to the French ship, 'believing he was going to get [the axe].' Upon this, one of the sailors grabbed the Stadaconans' canoe, which allowed two or three Frenchmen to get into it and force two of Donnacona's sons to climb into Cartier's boat. Fear of French arms, and the vulnerability of the women and children present, may have been a factor in the lack of Stadaconan resistance to the treacherous act of the French, to whom the Aboriginal people had given no motive whatsoever for them to conduct themselves in such an underhand manner.

The French, on board their ship, made 'a great show of love' for their two captives in the presence of the Stadaconans gathered in many canoes in the Gaspé Bay. Cartier then responded to Donnacona's speech about the cross and about Aboriginal ownership of the land by explaining (again deceitfully) that the cross was only meant to be a landmark for future visits, which they intended to make soon, and that, at any rate, they would then bring with them all sorts of gifts, of iron and otherwise, for Donnacona's people. This, of course, meant that the French, despite the strange way they had acted by seizing Donnacona's sons, still felt that they had to pay for using the land and, furthermore, had to account to the Aboriginal people for that use and for their presence. The Stadaconans considered all the components of this new necessary relationship: the love and solicitude the French showed for their two captured 'sauvages,' their promise to bring them back soon, and the strategic knowledge about the French these two young men would bring back. The Stadaconans then decided that they would, in time, be able to control and contain the newcomers. They showed themselves to be happy enough about everything. They even promised that they would not cut down the cross. Thus ended, on 24 July 1534, this prelude to France's Canadian adventure.

Over the next year spent in France, Cartier's two Stadaconan captives, Domagaya and Taignoagny, studied the French in order to understand their motives and their aims and devised their own Aboriginal strategy. Most certainly, the two young men, probably drawing maps, had spoken to Jacques Cartier and other Frenchmen about their Kanatha, that is, their chief town, which was Stadacona (present-day Quebec City). Little did they know that the French would use this descriptive word as the name of a country, an actual kingdom called Canada. Nor could the two Stadaconans imagine that their father, Donnacona, would be made a European-style monarch in this new land, which the French fancied and planned to conquer (steal). Certainly, these two sons of an important Aboriginal headman could not have foreseen that their father, too, would soon be deceitfully and forcefully captured by Cartier and his men, on 3 May 1636, and would die in France less than two years afterwards, sick and mortally sad for his lost people and country.

However, much happened before Donnacona's capture that is very significant as regards the Stadaconan contribution to Canada's culture and identity. As promised, Cartier did return on a second voyage, the following year. His three ships left Saint Malo on 19 May 1535. Taking advantage of their two Amerindian guides' knowledge of the geography of the two coasts from the entrance of the gulf right up to Montreal (Hochelaga) and beyond (Cartier is explicit about that knowledge and assistance), the French took their time to reconnoitre (they, of course, said *discover*) the country, where they saw human settlements and met inhabitants in every part.

The French were intent on visiting three countries, namely, Canada, Saguenay, and Hochelaga. Cartier's account and other evidence, including our own oral tradition, indicate that Donnacona's sons, already well trained in the region's geopolitics, had reasoned that such an exploratory plan, still to be approved by leading Stadaconan councils and their allies, could potentially develop into an eventual alliance between their people and the French. They first took the French to Canada's chief town, Stadacona, where Donnacona, their father and first headman, lived. Donnacona was a man whose authority, the French already knew, extended at least as far east as Gaspé.

Cartier and his people believed that Domagaya and Taignoagny, during their year spent in France, had become naturally imbued with a sense of French cultural and religious superiority in relation to their own people and would therefore, once they were back home in Canada, be perfectly prepared to help the French conquer their own land and peoples. To Cartier's dismay, the attitude of the two young men changed radically from the moment they set foot on their own soil once again. Understandably, that evening and night of 8 September 1535 was spent in intense discussion and long-awaited revelations about the French and the Stadacona's land. The Aboriginal people of the region had, by this time, been aware of and mystified by the Europeans for almost four decades.[1]

Fixated on the idea of finding a passage to the Orient, its gold, and its other riches, the French were determined to visit Hochelaga and, at a later date, Saguenay, another very rich kingdom, according to the two Stadaconan captives and guides. During the trip back to their land the Stadaconans had agreed that they would lead the French to Hochelaga. However, Donnacona and other council leaders did not think that the time was appropriate. Not only was the season too advanced to travel much more, but also there were strict protocols to be learned and observed regarding the laws of a particular territory, the respect to be paid to its leaders, the customs of different Aboriginal nations, the advance notice to be sent to another country that one wished to visit, and many, many other things of which to be aware.

The French had only been in Canada for six days when, on 14 September, they began pressing their two former captives to lead them to Hochelaga. On the next day Taignoagny, whom Cartier resented more than he did Domagaya, informed the French captain that Headman Donnacona was annoyed to see the French constantly bearing arms, to which Cartier replied that Taignoagny knew very well that this was the way in France and that he would therefore let his men bear arms. Still, the Stadaconans remained cheerful and optimistic that they would eventually find common ground and make the French see their real interests, which meant using the friendship that was being offered to them to create a larger, more affluent and powerful society from the uniting of the two peoples.

On 16 September Donnacona and five hundred of his people (roughly the population of the town of Stadacona) approached Cartier's two main boats anchored in the harbour of the Saint-Charles River. The leaders entered Cartier's boat to once again try to impress on the French that they should not navigate towards Hochelaga (today's Montreal) at this time; the Stadaconans, of course, thought of another time, likely the following spring. Taignoagny, once again acting as the spokesman for the Stadaconans, withdrew his offer to guide Cartier, stating that his father, Donnacona, did not wish him to go, because the headman had said, '*La rivière ne vaut rien*' (the river forebodes nothing good). The French explorer answered that his mind was set to go anyway, adding that should Taignoagny change his mind and agree to accompany them as he had promised, he would receive gifts and attention from the French that would make him happy. At any rate, Cartier explained, his aim was only to make a quick trip to see Hochelaga and then return to Canada.

Taignoagny remained firm in his refusal to go, and the visit ended.

The next day the Stadaconans staged a very sensitive and solemn effort to make the French reconsider their plan to go to Hochelaga and especially to appreciate the great solidarity that would result from uniting their two peoples. They attempted this by actually marrying Jacques Cartier to the highest-ranking of their marriageable young women. To this day, an account other than Cartier's own has never been presented to Canadians about this very meaningful event in their country's history.

I have personally witnessed wedding ceremonies and other similar ceremonies still practised by Canadian Aboriginal peoples whose spiritual ways are almost identical to those of our Wendat people. I will take the reader through Cartier's account of what happened to him, the young maiden, and the people of Canada that day. First, we are told that the people of Stadacona walked up to the French boats at low tide with large quantities of eels and other fish as gifts for the French. Then there was much chanting and dancing, which usually occurred at such visits, said Cartier. What Cartier did not see, at this point, was that these particular songs and dances were preparatory to a specific ceremony that was about to take place. As well, the abundant quantities of fish and the prevailing festive atmosphere that was described indicate that the whole town, very likely with many guests and visitors from neighbouring places, was present for a very important event – a ceremony ordained after much praying, chanting, council making, and quite likely fasting, under the highest spiritual leadership.

Then the Agouhanna (a title carried by Donnacona, which implies very high standing in society) had his people (likely the other leaders) stand to one side, and he drew a circle on the sand, inside of which he had Cartier and his own principals stand. Donnacona then made a long speech in front of the thus reunited French and Stadaconans. While he spoke, the headman 'held the hand of a girl of about ten to twelve years old'; after he had finished speaking, he presented her to the French captain. At this point, all of Donnacona's people began to 'scream and shout, as a sign of joy and alliance.' Now the fact that Cartier accepted the girl was affirmed by the loud, festive reaction of the throng. At any rate, were not Cartier and all these Frenchmen, in the eyes of the Amerindians, much too long deprived of normal social relations, including those of a man with his wife, or the companionship of a woman, as sadly seen in their disorderly behaviour and appearance? Could so many negative traits in the present state of their intercultural relations not be modified by beginning to create a normal human life, a society, around these angry, rude, rowdy strangers?

Following this ceremony two younger boys were given to Cartier in the same official way, upon which the Stadaconans made similar demonstrations of joy.[2] Cartier then officially thanked Donnacona for these presents. Finally, a crucial detail was given by Taignoagny: the 'girl' (in Aboriginal cultural terms, as well as in French social and cultural terms, she is a *young woman*) who was ceremonially given (again, in the Aboriginal social frame of reference, that gift was a wife) to Jacques Cartier was Lord Donnacona's sister's own daughter. This, in the matrilineal system of these Nadowek (Iroquoians), meant that the young woman was called 'my daughter' by Donnacona because she belonged to the same clan as he did, as opposed to his own children, who belonged to their mother's clan.

Thus, the young woman was the highest, as well as the purest, gift that could possibly have been offered to the first man among these Frenchmen.

The Stadaconans probably thought that, given these gifts and a chance to establish a normal life in this new land, the Frenchmen would not care about an oppressive monarch back in problem-ridden France and about the lifelong odious obedience that was owed him; this land was Donnacona's, this was a pure and abundant free country, this was *Canada*. Most surely and naturally, there was a burning desire in many of the French hearts present to make the Canadian way of thinking their own.[3] Unfortunately, of course, it was impossible for that time. It was almost entirely a matter of religious prejudice.[4]

Cartier had his human gifts 'put on board the ships.'[5] He gave no details about what occurred to the three young Stadaconans thereafter, except that the 'older girl' fled the ship three days later and a special guard was arranged so that the two boys would not do likewise. When finally found by Donnacona and her own family, the young woman explained that she had escaped because 'the pages had beaten her' and not, as the French contended, because her own people had tried to make her (and the two boys) leave the French. Cartier showed reluctance to take the young woman back until, he said, the Stadaconan leaders (her family) begged him to do so. (To them, at least, Jacques Cartier and she were husband and wife.) She was accompanied to the ship by her father and other relatives. Nothing further is said about her.

Cartier tells us that Taignoagny said to him after the bride-giving ceremony that these three human presents had been given in order to keep the French from going up to Hochelaga. I have already presented my reasoning based on the available evidence, which includes my own culturally informed perception, about the Stadaconans' motives for trying their hardest to create unifying bridges between themselves and the French. At any rate, I believe Cartier's blinding obsession about going to Hochelaga is self-evident. The last-ditch attempt of the Stadaconans the next day to make him stay and the strange but accurate warning that he received about having to prepare for wintering right away are further proof of Cartier's foolhardiness and spite towards his Aboriginal hosts, friends, and benefactors.

On 18 September 1535 the Stadaconans, again attempting to avert misfortune for the French, turned to supernatural forces. Cartier described how this was acted out before his eyes. First, three men clothed themselves in black and white fur (Cartier disparagingly says 'dog skins') and wore long horns on their heads. The three men hid in a canoe and, momentarily, rose up as their craft approached the boats. The spirit-being in the middle began to make a 'marvellous' speech directed at the French, even though the three 'devils' never even took notice of the French as they floated past the French boats. The canoe was steered back to shore. Upon arriving, the three beings dropped to the bottom of the canoe, as though they had died. They were then carried to the woods in the canoe by Donnacona and other men. Every single Stadaconan followed their leaders into the forest and disappeared from sight. Then began a half-hour 'predication' by the three spirit-beings. At the end of this, Taignoagny and Domagaya came out of the woods and, after the Catholic way they had observed over their seven-month stay in France, the previous year, walked towards the French, their hands joined as if in prayer. 'Showing great admiration,' they advanced with their eyes lifted towards the sky and pronounced the words *Jesus, Maria, Jacques Cartier* as though (my interpretation) asking for protection for Cartier and his men. At that moment the French captain, seeing their grave countenance and having witnessed their 'ceremonies,' enquired 'what the matter was, what new things had occurred.' The two young men answered that there was 'pitiful news,' that nothing foreboded well (*'il n'y a rien de bon'*). When pressed further by Cartier, his two usual interpreters told him that Cudouagny (likely the Great Spirit for the Stadaconans and possibly the Hochelagans) had spoken in Hochelaga and, through the three spirit impersonators mentioned above, had announced that there would be so much ice and snow that they (the French) would all die. (Actually, twenty-five sailors died of sickness and hardship over the winter. At one point Cartier became quite certain that all, including himself, would die. We will later see how they were saved by their hosts.)

To be sure, Cartier made light of the Stadaconans' way of trying to make him stay and to persuade his companions to start preparing for their first Canadian winter. 'Go tell your messengers that your god Cudouagny is a fool who does not know what he talks about,' retorted Cartier amid laughter from all the French who were there. 'If you just believe in Jesus, he will keep you from the cold,' added a sailor. As a way of restoring balance in the communication, the two youths then diplomatically asked Cartier whether he had had Jesus's word on the matter, to which the captain curtly replied that his priests had asked him (Jesus) about it and learned that the weather was going to be all right. Taignoagny and Domagaya gave many thanks to Cartier for this exchange and returned to fetch from the woods their own townsfolk who, as Cartier detected, could not conceal their disillusion even amidst their cheers, shouts, chants, dances, and other expressions of joy.

The next day, on 19 September, Cartier's smaller vessel left for Hochelaga. The round trip lasted twenty-four days, during which the rest of his men, back in Stadacona, mostly used their time bracing for imagined attacks from the Stadaconans. As for the Stadaconans, they continued to demonstrate goodwill and humanity towards their strange visitors, bringing them victuals and waiting for their visits, which were, in fact, quite infrequent. Because the French did not visit very often, they began suffering from a lack of fresh food, especially meat and fish.

The rest of the story of Cartier's second voyage to Canada is better known. In brief, things soon turned very badly for the French, as foreseen by the Stadaconans. From mid-November the cold was brutally felt by the ill-prepared Frenchmen. In December the whole crew was hit hard by scurvy. By mid-February eight sailors were dead. By mid-April twenty-five had succumbed to the scourge, and another forty were dying; of a hundred and ten 'there were not three healthy men,' wrote Cartier. 'We were so overtaken by the said disease,' confided the explorer in his chronicle, 'that we had almost lost all hope of ever returning to France.'[6]

Most readers will already know that people stopped dying in Cartier's fort thanks to a remedy (very likely the white cedar) that the Stadaconans gave the French and taught them how to prepare. The credit for this human solicitude and actual salvation from sure catastrophe, however, was entirely given to God, the Europeans' god. The surviving crewmen, further strengthened by the fresh meat and fish that the Amerindians brought them every day, got better so rapidly that in less than three weeks they were ready to set sail for France. However, as many readers must also know, they did not depart from Canada before realizing a very pressing dream, that of capturing Donnacona, Domagaya, and Taignoagny, along with two other prominent headmen and two other young Stadaconans, one of whom was another pubescent girl. To succeed in laying his hands on these people, especially the leaders, Cartier had to act in his wiliest way and also use force, as he proudly recounted in his journal. We know that ten Stadaconans, probably all belonging to Donnacona's immediate family, were in the possession of the French when they left for France on 6 May 1536. Among them were Donnacona, Taignoagny, Domagaya, two headmen, a girl 'of about ten,' almost certainly Cartier's Canadian wife and his two given sons, and two other persons of unknown gender or age.

One of the promises that Cartier made to appease the Stadaconans after so callously and treacherously stealing their leaders and people was that he would bring back all ten of them 'in ten or twelve moons' (as, in fact, he had done with his first two captives). When he finally came back five years later without his captives and was asked by the Stadaconans what had become of their Agouhanna and other people, Cartier, still his deceitful self, replied that Donnacona had died and been buried in France (which was factual) and that all the others had remained there, where they were now married and had become 'grands Seigneurs' (great Lords). We know from Cartier's own chronicle that eight more of his captives had died by then (French archival sources confirm that they all died within two years), except a girl of about ten (at the time of her capture).

This time, in August 1541, the French arrived in Canada to find an Aboriginal population in a state of virtual panic. Diplomacy was still present but was mostly dictated by fear. The French had brought heavy weaponry and were ready for any eventuality. They were here to create a French colony. The Canadians' country would be theirs, for civilized Europeans were not bound to the virtues practised by 'savages.'

However, for now, the task proved too great, support from France was not quite sufficient, and the enmity of the First Peoples was too overwhelming. Cartier's third and last voyage ended in failure. However, the French (and Basque) presence in the Laurentian region increased year by year because of the wealth of fur and fish. Hochelaga and Saguenay endured, but Canada's peoples, directly and forcibly affected by the European invasion (not just by the sheer human pressure but even more by the ever-present, devastating new epidemic diseases), had to seek refuge. Archaeology in the last few decades has revealed, again confirming our own traditional belief, that they mostly found refuge among the Wyandot of present-day Ontario (in the Lake Simcoe–Georgian Bay area). According to leading archaeologists,[7] the original Canadians joined the Wyandot Confederacy in the last decades of the sixteenth century, becoming its Nation of the Rock – maybe in remembrance of Stadacona, the place of the Big Standing Rock.[8]

Conclusion

No foundation can forever rest on lies, especially lies rooted in racial prejudice. While it is necessary to find the reasons and to understand why the French, like many Europeans at the time, perceived reality and other peoples as they did and acted with corresponding spite and inhumanity, it is equally necessary to help today's heirs to that ancient society – which means most of us in greater or smaller measure – shed any lingering thinking and behavioural patterns related to that inheritance. We are long past the time when Europeans came here needing new places and new conditions for a renewed lease on life. However, after having provided the same 'Canadian' generosity and contributed the very best of themselves and what they have, our Aboriginal peoples are still being deceived, mistreated, and visibly destroyed as peoples in this great, rich, and powerful country. One can take the Stadaconans' history of contact with Europe and, thereafter, non-Aboriginal Canada and apply it exactly to the historical and present-day experience of any other Canadian Aboriginal group or nation. After all the political, social, academic, and religious rhetoric the very real fact remains that Canada, born with an Aboriginal spirit in 1534, given an Aboriginal name in 1535, and tenderly cared for in an Amerindian cradleboard by the people of Stadacona, has seen and caused its Aboriginal peoples to waste away ever since its birth while everyone else who has come here has been, as Jacques Cartier and his men were, cared for, healed, and helped to find a new life. Can we now stop saying that this was, and will continue to be, the price to pay for a true civilization until Canada's 'Indian problem' has been settled?

In this chapter I have mainly wanted to suggest to my readers and fellow Canadians that a better understanding of what happened in our country at the beginning of the contact between Aboriginals (the first Canadians) and Europeans is necessary if one is to also understand why all Canadians are still collectively afflicted by an immense incapacity to empathize, communicate, and construct as we should the kind of secure, happy future that we all desire for our children and their descendants. As an Aboriginal historian I believe that an ignorance of history is the major cause of the glacial indifference of mainstream society that is still felt by most of my Aboriginal fellow citizens and is known and denounced by many non-Aboriginal Canadians and others. I believe that it is primarily this ignorance that so impedes us collectively from tackling and conducting our many common affairs in normal, empathetic, and intelligent ways.

Finally, I am grateful for this opportunity to write about our peoples – their very many important past, present, and, maybe especially, future contributions to our great and dear country's culture and identity. I also wish to greet and thank my readers for their time.

Long live my country, Canada!

Notes

1 Two centuries or so after the Vikings had ceased coming to the region, vivid memories of them were certainly still present. This time, however, the newcomers behaved in very different, much more aggressive ways than had their Norse predecessors.

2 With a high-ranking young wife given to him by the first headman of the land, and two young boys, one of whom was Donnacona's own son, did Cartier not have prime human material with which to start a very good life in Canada? The Stadaconans certainly thought he did.

3 The *ensauvagement* (the irresistible attraction of the free life of the *sauvages*), mostly a view held by the French coureurs de bois, probably was the most marked trait (and simultaneously the one most damned by the religious

authorities) in French-Indian relations throughout the next two centuries. It produced Canada's Métis nation.

4 Cartier exhibited his deep European religious conditioning, and unfeelingly uttered a very dark sentence regarding the original Canadians, when, pondering what little he knew about their spiritual beliefs, he simply wrote, 'One must be baptized or go to hell.'

5 See Jacques Cartier, *Voyages en Nouvelle France*, ed. Robert Lahaise and Marie Couturier, Collection Documents d'Histoire, Cahiers du Québec, Hurtubise/HMH, 1977, p. 93.

6 Since mid-November the Stadaconans also had lost about fifty people. Cartier, reflecting the knowledge of his epoch, could and did blame the Canadians for his crew's sickness. Today's science, however, informs us that, rather, the Stadaconans' disease was caused by the Europeans' presence, because they were beginning to be struck down by contact epidemics.

7 For sources, readers may consult my book *Huron-Wendat: The Heritage of the Circle* (Vancouver: University of British Columbia Press and Michigan State University Press, 1999).

8 Owing to the imposing rocky promontory it presents, Quebec has historically been called Canada's Gibraltar. I encourage readers to consult a remarkable book on the city of Quebec, edited by Serge Courville and Robert Garon, *Québec, ville et capitale*, in the series Atlas historique du Québec (Ste-Foy: Les Presses de l'Université Laval, 2001).

Profile of Malcolm King (1947–)

Ojibwa, Professor, and Medical Researcher

From humble beginnings on a reserve just southeast of Brantford, Ontario, Dr Malcolm King has risen to become not only a professor of medicine and a prolific researcher but also an acclaimed champion of Aboriginal health. His leadership has helped inspire a new generation of Aboriginal medical students.

King is a member of the Mississauga of New Credit First Nation. He was born to a Swiss mother and an Ojibwa father in 1947 on the Six Nations reserve at Ohsweken, Ontario.[1] He follows the footsteps of his ancestors: his grandfather was a traditional healer; his father was a teacher and the first from his reserve to graduate from university. Furthermore, his brother is an educator and a school principal.[2]

Always an excellent student, King attended high school in Hagersville, Ontario, where he first became interested in chemistry. After graduation he attended McMaster University in Hamilton, where he completed a bachelor of science (honours) in chemistry in 1968.[3] He then went on to study at McGill University in Montreal, where he obtained a doctorate in polymer chemistry in 1973. Dr King took a position at the Weizmann Institute of Science in Israel.[4] By 1980 he held appointments as both assistant professor of medicine at McGill University and medical scientist at Montreal's Royal Victoria Hospital. However, in 1985 he moved to Edmonton to take up a position as co-director of the Pulmonary Research Group at the University of Alberta.[5] King continues to work at the University of Alberta but has also been a visiting professor at Berne University in Switzerland, São Paulo University in Brazil, and the University of Freiburg in Germany. He reads German and is bilingual in English and French. In 1990 he was appointed a full professor of medicine at the University of Alberta, the first Aboriginal to hold such a position in Canada.[6]

King is an important contributor to medical research in Canada, specializing in the area of mucus secretion and clearance, an important area for

Malcolm King. Photo courtesy of Laura Commanda.

the treatment of lung diseases. His research is also oriented towards cystic fibrosis. He is the author of more than 128 scholarly publications and is the co-holder of two patents for medical procedures used in the treatment of the disease.[7]

From 2000 to 2004 Dr King was a member of the governing council of Canadian Institutes of Health Research (CIHR), the Canadian federal granting council that funds Canadian health research through its $970 million annual budget.[8] He is the president of the Canadian Thoracic Society and chair of the Special Interest Group on Aboriginal Health Education of the Association of Canadian Medical Colleges. In 1999 Dr King was awarded the Aboriginal Achievement Award in Medicine.[9] Alongside Dr Nancy Gibson and nine other health researchers, he co-founded the Alberta ACADRE research institute, which examines issues of importance to Aboriginal health.[10] In October 2008 he was appointed the scientific director of the Institute of Aboriginal Peoples' Health at Canadian Institutes of Health Research, a role he took up in January 2009.[11]

Dr Malcolm King has risen to the top of Canada's health research field but has not forgotten his Aboriginal roots. His leadership has helped the University of Alberta to become well known for the training of Aboriginal students, and his research involves using evidence-based science to demonstrate the effectiveness of traditional Native healing methods. He brings traditional Aboriginal medicine and Western science together, to the benefit of both.[12]

PAUL MILLAR

Notes

1 J. Black, 'Champion of Aboriginal health looks to traditional remedies: Malcolm King,' *Windspeaker* 16 (1999):17.

2 N. Lees, 'Celebrated MD promotes native herbal treatments,' *Edmonton Journal*, 28 March 1999, A2.

3 Lees, 'Celebrated MD.'

4 Biospace, 'Dr. Malcolm King: Cough, Cough Clearance,' http://biospace.intota.com/viewbio.asp?bioFile=/xml/biofull/615555data.xml&bioID=615555&strQuery=malcolm+king (accessed 4 July 2003).

5 Biospace, 'Dr. Malcolm King.'

6 Lees, 'Celebrated MD.'

7 *First Nations Drum*, '1999 Aboriginal Achievement Awards.'

8 Canadian Institutes of Health Research, 'Biography of the Scientific Director,

Malcolm King,' http://www.cihr-irsc.gc.ca/e/9111.html (accessed 18 January 2011).

9 *First Nations Drum*, '1999 Aboriginal Achievement Awards.'
10 Canadian Institutes of Health Research, 'Biography of the Scientific Director, Malcolm King.'
11 http://www.cihr-irsc.gc.ca/e/9130.html (accessed 17 January 2011).
12 H. Kent, 'U of A proving popular with Native students,' *Canadian Medical Association Journal*, 2000:162.

Transformations:
A Stó:lō–Coast Salish Historical Atlas

DAVID A. SMITH

A Stó:lō–Coast Salish Historical Atlas (2001), winner of the Roderick Haig-Brown Regional Prize and the City of Vancouver Book Award, was also a number-one bestseller in British Columbia and has been described as a 'unique' and 'landmark' publication. In the opinion of historical-geographer Cole Harris, 'there is nothing like it elsewhere in Canada, perhaps on the continent' (Harris 2002).[1]

The atlas spans fifteen thousand years of natural, cultural, and spiritual history, from the last great glaciation period to the twenty-first century. It places *Stó:lō* traditional territory in historical perspective by, in a sense, reclaiming the landscape itself with the area's original place names and with the maps to locate them. Using maps as a means to reach across cultures, the atlas examines a broad range of subjects, including language expansion, collective identity, changing technology, labour, architecture, military campaigns, prophecy, justice systems, and environmental change. Throughout all the plates the *Stó:lō* are alerting people to the fact that they still claim their territory and that they possess an inherent right to self-government.[2] But the *Stó:lō* are saying something else too: they bring a vast range of knowledge to these lands, a distinct way of looking at the world, and their own contributions can enrich the larger Canadian society. As this chapter will attempt to demonstrate, the atlas documents some of these world views and contributions by conveying the *Stó:lō* experience prior to contact and the more familiar story of Native-newcomer relations from an Indigenous perspective. In what is essentially a reversal of the dominant culture's portrayal of the past, it is a story of newcomers in *Stó:lō* history rather than the other way around.

While the atlas is told from a Native perspective, it is also an inclusive story. All who played a role in creating this book – and there were many (including members of the *Stó:lō* community, elders, *Stó:lō* Nation's Aboriginal Rights and Title department staff, and university academics) – hoped that the book would help the general public to understand the *Stó:lō* and themselves better, to understand the people in this corner of Canada in space and time. Through oral histories, ethnographies, maps, charts, photographs, original artwork, and other resources the atlas demonstrates the complex relationships that developed between Aboriginal people and newcomers in southwestern British Columbia and northwestern Washington State. The atlas itself is dedicated, in part, to all those *Stó:lō* and non-*Stó:lō* 'who saw fit to preserve and share their knowledge for future generations' (Carlson 2001). The fact that such a broad range of individuals and printed and oral resources were consulted to produce this publication is a reflection of the ways in which the histories of the Coast Salish and the newcomers to the territory have become so closely intertwined.

In the atlas's foreword, Judge Steven L. Point (former *Stó:lō* Nation *Yewal Siyá:m* and the current lieutenant governor of British Columbia) describes the purpose and philosophy behind the atlas:

> I love this country, Canada ... My uncle died for this country in the Second World War. Our people fought for this country. This country has a tremendous history. But it did not start in 1871 and nor did it start in 1867. It started thousands and thousands of years ago when the Creator put us in our own homeland. The governments know we are still here. We have changed a little bit – we eat pizza on Friday night, we rent videos, we play country music, and I go to church on Sunday and to the longhouse on Saturday – but we are still here. We are not invisible.
>
> We have a wealth of knowledge passed down to us that we would love to share with non-Natives ... Our values and our systems are not European. However, the more I study Europeans and the more I learn about my own history, the more I find that in fact we are the same. You love your Elders, you love your God, you cherish your young people, and you have a strong sense of justice, just as we do. In fact, if you look long and hard enough, you will find that there are probably more similarities than there are differences. This historical atlas represents a significant attempt to bridge those differences, to build cross-cultural understanding, and to establish respect. We have both paid too much attention to the differences between us, and I want to see that change. I hope that you do, too. (Carlson 2001, xiv)

The Making of the *Stó:lō* Atlas

Over the past decade or two some dramatic changes have taken place in the field of Aboriginal scholarship. As the atlas's editor, Keith T. Carlson, points out, the fact that Aboriginal leaders and community members are

Stó:lō Second World War veterans Benny Joe, Wes Sam, Joe Alex, and Harold Wells were among those who received the recognition that they had so long desired, at the first *Stó:lō* Remembrance Day ceremony on 11 November 1993. Photo courtesy of *Stó:lō* Tribal Council.

now encouraging popular and academic works about their cultural history is indicative of a growing sense of confidence within Aboriginal communities. For decades a legacy of fear that outsiders might use or misuse information has been a major factor in preventing significant reports by and about First Nations communities from leaving band office shelves and tribal council archives. Today, however, a shift towards a more balanced power relationship between Native and non-Native society has encouraged publications that discuss not only Aboriginal-newcomer relations but also the relationships and tensions between and within Aboriginal communities themselves. Carlson explains that these latter accounts, which contain no clear consensus of a 'good guy–bad guy' relationship, reflect a kind of 'decolonization of thought processes' and that this new openness is, in fact, a reassertion of older Coast Salish cultural values. These traditional values called for the expression of many opinions on a wide range of topics to be shared in public and openly debated or discussed. 'Such is the spirit,' Carlson writes, 'in which this historical atlas was produced' (2001, xv).

The *Stó:lō–Coast Salish Historical Atlas* was put together by a community of joined individuals, members of *Stó:lō* Nation's Aboriginal Rights and Title department, and a few of our *siyá:ye* (friends). The editorial board consisted of both Aboriginal and non-Aboriginal members, including a cultural advisor, a historian, an archaeologist, an environmental planner, a geographic information systems specialist, and myself, an archivist. *Stó:lō* Nation historian Keith T. Carlson, who is now in the history faculty at the University of Saskatchewan, was the atlas editor. Jan Perrier, with whom we had the good fortune of working on two previous publications, was our team's graphic artist and illustrator. She worked tirelessly on the project, and her creative talents were clearly a major factor in the positive response that the book received from critics and the public.

There were, in all, fifteen Aboriginal and non-Aboriginal authors with a wide range of expertise who were asked to contribute to the atlas. Early on, it was decided that a large format would be most appropriate for the book and that its arrangement would be roughly chronological within a series of thematic groupings. The visual nature of a historical atlas was seen as being the most effective way of crossing cultural barriers and communicating cultural information in a way that could be understood and appreciated by the broadest spectrum of people. The project was not intended to be exhaustive or definitive. As Carlson (2001) pointed out, 'there has never been a single definitive voice in either Aboriginal or non-Native discourse' (xv). Rather, the *Stó:lō* hoped that the atlas would encourage others to research and publish new information that challenged or built upon the materials presented in the atlas.

The final arrangement of the specific plates varied little from the original outline, though almost one-third of the plates were identified *after* the project was well underway. The atlas begins with *Stó:lō* creation stories and the populating of the *Stó:lō* world – juxtaposed with maps and descriptions of Wisconsin and Holocene deglaciation periods. A look at the rich *Stó:lō* cultural life prior to contact is explored next, with topics such as settlement patterns, populations and house types, language and dialect regions, geopolitics and warfare, traditional resource procurement strategies, and trading and kinship networks. Then follows the largest section of the book, which explores the arrival and impact of European settlement in southwestern BC from both a *Stó:lō* and a *Xwelítem* (non-Aboriginal) perspective. The rapid changes to the *Stó:lō* world are revealed in plates on topics that look at the introduction of exotic diseases, the gold rush, the new experience of Catholic and Methodist residential schools, the establishment of the reserve system, labour in the commercial salmon canneries and hop yards, and the introduced and traditional systems of law and justice. There is also a series of plates tracing the transformations of the environment since the arrival of the newcomers, as well as the *Stó:lō* place names, both of which will be explored later in this chapter. The atlas's appendices include a historical timeline, with dates describing important events in the *Stó:lō* past, and the reproduction of forty-seven petitions and letters (dating from 1864 to 1976) related to the 'land question' – testament to the *Stó:lō* struggle to maintain their identity and have some of their lands returned to them.

The Aboriginal Rights and Title department's executive director, Clarence (Kat) Pennier (now the elected *Stó:lō Yewal Siyá:m*), saw the atlas as being a powerful educational tool for both the general and the *Stó:lō* public that could be directly applied to *Stó:lō* treaty negotiations. He wanted to ensure that the atlas would serve that purpose and so suggested an eighteen-month publication deadline. The chief who carried the portfolio for our department, Lester Ned, stated our mandate succinctly: 'Tell us what we need to know, not what we want to hear' (Carlson 2001, xv). Although consultation with *Stó:lō* politicians was ongoing, there were no politicians on the editorial board or among the authors, and these leaders made a conscious effort to avoid interfering with any of the work's content or appearance. Some of the most profound insights and recommendations came from the late Elizabeth Herrling and the late Rosaleen George, a duo of fluent *Halq'emeylem*-speaking elders who over a period of many months met with *Stó:lō* cultural advisor Sonny McHalsie (now co-manager and cultural advisor of the *Stó:lō* Research and Management Centre). McHalsie also arranged for a number of meetings between the *Lalems ye Selyolexwe* (the *Stó:lō* Nation House of Elders) and individual authors and with the editorial board as a whole.

The Foundations of *Stó:lō* Culture and History

As readers work their way through the *Stó:lō* atlas, it will become clear that in order to understand *Stó:lō* culture and history, they must appreciate the relationships that built them. Carlson writes as follows:

> The *Stō:ló* have developed relationships with the land, water and air, and these relationships have changed over time. The *Stō:ló* have special family relationships with the animals and plants and certain physical landforms that make up the non-human living component of their territory. They live in a world where transformations are not only accepted, but are essential to their understanding of how the world came into being and how it will unfold in the future. Their world has never been static. The relationship with the spirit world of transformers and ancestor spirits informs all aspects of *Stō:ló* identity. Increasingly, relationships with non-Aboriginals, *Xwelítem*, have helped to shape *Stō:ló* views of themselves and their place in the world. (2001, 1)

Some aspects of these relationships are described in the opening plate of the atlas, 'Making the World Right Through Transformations.' In these pages McHalsie writes about oral histories describing a time 'when the world was not quite right.' The *Stó:lō* believe that the Creator, *Chíchelh Siyá:m*, put them here, but that the world was chaotic. So according to *Stó:lō sxwōxwiyam* (stories of the distant past), *XeXá:ls* (the Transformers) came to make the world right and transform it into its present form. In their travels throughout *Stó:lō* traditional territory, *XeXá:ls* (the Transformer bear brother and sister) are believed to have punished many of the hurtful and inconsiderate people responsible for the chaos affecting the world. The people were turned into stone and remain, to this day, in this form. To complete their work, the Transformers rewarded some *Stó:lō* ancestors for their generosity by changing them into valuable and useful resources like the cedar tree, salmon, sturgeon, beaver, and black bear. Some, like *Lhílheqey* (Mt Cheam), were transformed into mountains. These transformations are said to have fixed the world and established the present landscape. McHalsie notes that information about the journey of *XeXá:ls* is also known among other Coast and Interior Salish peoples, suggesting that the travels of *XeXá:ls*, which centred in *S'olh Téméxw*, ranged beyond this area. He also points out that in some recent tellings of these oral histories, the plural *XeXá:ls* is replaced by the singular term *Xá:ls*, perhaps as a result of the introduction of Christian influence. 'This influence,' writes McHalsie, 'is apparent in English translations, which variously describe *Xá:ls* as "Jesus," "the little Christ," "the Magician," "the Transformer" or "The Miracle Worker"' (Carlson 2001, 6).

McHalsie's plate lists and describes different types of transformations and includes a map depicting some of the surviving knowledge of transformation sites within *Stó:lō* territory. Many of these sites appear in photographs in the atlas and remain visible throughout the present landscape; several sites have been destroyed through various developments, and some more 'portable' transformations have even been relocated. According to *Stó:lō sxwōxwiyam*, long ago there was a man, *T'íxwelátsa*, who challenged *XeXá:ls* and was turned to stone. For more than a century, the transformed man was held in the Burke Museum collection in Seattle, Washington; *T'íxwelátsa* was returned to *Stó:lō* territory in 2006. The carriers of the name can be traced to Herb Joe, now living in Chilliwack, British Columbia, who bears the same honoured name and can be seen in the following figure, visiting the original *T'íxwelátsa* with his grandson.

The *Halq'eméylem* Language and *Stó:lō* Culture

In one of the plates that I authored on language and dialects, near the beginning of the atlas, I repeated the widely acknowledged observation that language can be used as a window for understanding a culture. Language can help us to comprehend expressions of continuity and change

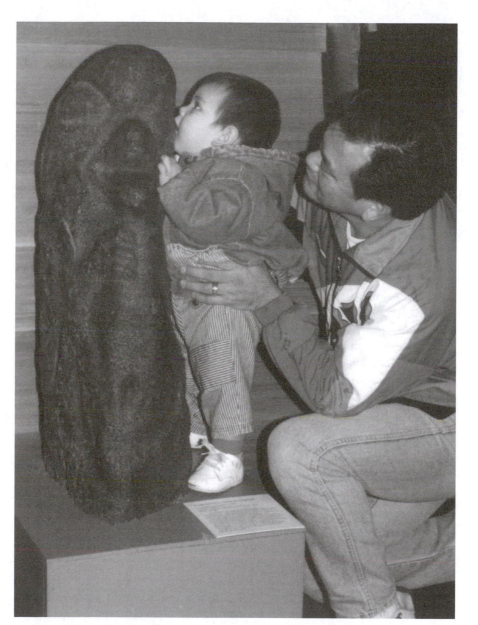

Herb Joe and his grandson visiting the original *T'íxwelátsa*. Photo courtesy of the Joe family.

within a culture, as well as a people's traditions and values, its relationship with the environment, and its connections with the land.[3] *Halq'eméylem*
is the traditional language spoken by the *Stó:lō* people and their relatives
and neighbours from southeastern Vancouver Island. It is a member of the
Coast Salish language family.[4] Linguist Brent Galloway explains that there
are words in *Halq'eméylem* that 'encapsulate the whole knowledge of the
culture … *Halq'eméylem* has a rich literature, which was translated orally.
The language itself incorporates a whole way of looking at the universe,
which is different from the world view conveyed by English or French'
(Grescoe 1996, 19).

While reflecting a *Stó:lō* world view, many *Halq'eméylem* words also found
their way into European vocabularies. Among the English words that have
been derived from the *Halq'eméylem* language are *coho* (from *kwōxweth*),
sockeye (from *sthéqi*), and the name for the giant animal of the Chehalis area,
sasquatch (from *sásq'ets*).

Today the *Halq'eméylem* language is in danger of extinction. In 1993 there
were between fifty and seventy-five fluent *Halq'eméylem* speakers; by the
year 2000 the number of fluent speakers had declined to less than twelve.
The *Stó:lō Shxweli Halq'eméylem* program at *Stó:lō* Nation, the Seabird Island
Language Program, and the *Hul'q'umín'um* Language program at Cow-
ichan First Nation are three efforts underway to save and revitalize the language for present and future generations (Carlson 2001, 21–2).

Stó:lō Identity

Language and identity have a close correlation. In a series of plates
authored by Keith Carlson, entitled 'Expressions of Collective Identity,' the
atlas examines *Stó:lō* identity on a host of levels. *Xwélmexw* (human beings
who speak the same language) is the term that *Halq'emeylem* speakers used
to identify themselves, while *lats'umexw* is the expression used for different
people. Within the *Xwélmexw* society there are numerous, sometimes even
competing expressions of collective identity. *Xwélmexw* ideas of collective
identity derive from common language and beliefs, shared communication
systems, the 'tribal' proximity of villages along the Fraser River watershed,
the belief in a common descent from transformed immortal ancestors, kinship ties, and spiritual connections among and between diverse groups of
people and animals, both living and deceased. Carlson (2001, 24) argues
that 'depending on the circumstances, *Xwélmexw* emphasize certain relationships over others to ensure that their various economic, diplomatic,
spiritual and sustenance needs are accounted for.'

Many of the most important indicators of *Xwélmexw* identity transcend time and space. The *Xwélmexw* are described in the atlas as sharing a common cosmology and world view that takes into account a belief in a supreme being responsible for creating the universe and all life within it. This creative energy is usually referred to today as *Chíchelh Siyá:m* ('Lord Above' or 'Most High Respected Leader'). There would appear to be some obvious parallels here with Christian and other religious beliefs in God. Interestingly though, Carlson states that the evidence, in both the form of oral histories and early Hudson's Bay Company records, indicates that this belief in a supreme spiritual force pre-dates the arrival of Christian missionaries (Carlson 2001, 28).

According to *Stó:lō* beliefs, *Xwélmexw* are said to live in a world where humans are subordinate to the metaphysical world of spirits. Within each individual person's body, a number of spiritual forces are believed to coexist, and these create ties to the collective group that are much more significant than the existence of the individual on his or her own. Each person and all living things have a *shxwelí*, or life force, that connects them together through the Creator. Individuals are not islands but are all connected to one another. Within each person there also exists a delicate, separate spirit force called *smestíyexw*, sometimes referred to as both thought and vitality, which is needed for day-to-day living and survival. Sometimes, through participation in the winter dance ceremony or other means, people may also acquire the assistance of spirit helpers over the course of their lives. After a person dies, their 'ghost' or ancestor spirit, their *spoleqwíth'a*, lives on and continues to interact with the living.

These relationships can reveal a great deal about the rationale behind past and current *Stó:lō* decision making. For example, before *Stó:lō* people can change or alter the environment, many believe that they must first consider the way that their actions will affect the living spirits of their ancestors. The way that the landscape is used should be consistent with their beliefs, relations, and general world view. Today the *Stó:lō* people state frequently that they must reassert their responsibility as caretakers of the land for the benefit of their current and future generations. To understand much of the context of these statements, it is necessary to gain some appreciation of the nature of *Stó:lō* spirituality.

The *Stó:lō* spiritual world includes a special link that exists between the past, the present, and the future. This connection is expressed in a number of ways. In the *Halq'eyméylem* language, for example, the word *tómiyeqw* translates into English as both 'great-great-great-great-grandparent' and 'great-great-great-great-grandchild,' and as 'great-great-great-great-grand-uncle or -aunt' and 'great-great-great-great-grand-niece or -nephew.' The relationship expressed in this word connects people seven generations past

The Connection between Past, Present and Future Generations

The *Halq'eméylem* language reveals the connection between past, present and future generations.
Bolded figures represent the living, and faded ones stand for people who are deceased or yet unborn.

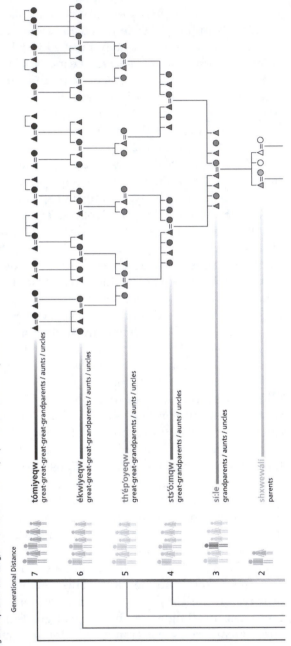

tómiyeqw
great-great-great-great-grandparents / aunts / uncles

ékwiyeqw
great-great-great-grandparents / aunts / uncles

th'ép'oyeqw
great-great-great-grandparents / aunts / uncles

sts'ó:mqw
great-great-grandparents / aunts / uncles

si:le
grandparents / aunts / uncles

shxwewáli
parents

Generational Distance

7

6

5

4

3

2

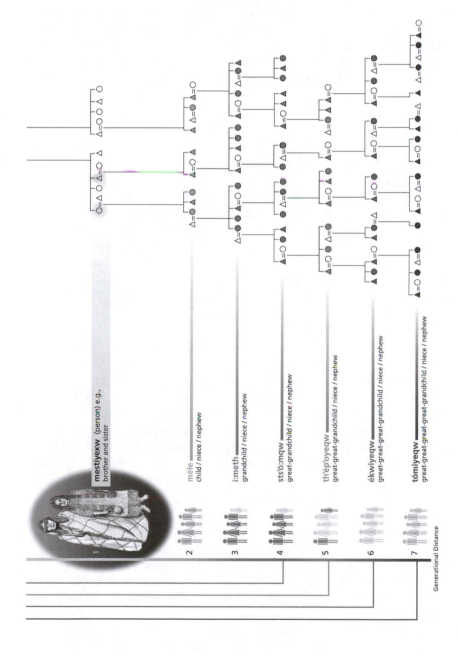

mestíyexw (person) e.g.,
brother and sister

1

méle
child / niece / nephew

2

í:meth
grandchild / niece / nephew

3

sts'ó:mqw
great-grandchild / niece / nephew

4

th'ép'oyeqw
great-great-grandchild / niece / nephew

5

ékwiyeqw
great-great-great-grandchild / niece / nephew

6

tómiyeqw
great-great-great-great-grandchild / niece / nephew

7

Generational Distance

The connection between past, present, and future generations. Chart courtesy of Jan Perrier.

with seven generations in the future (see the accompanying figure). The connection between the past and the future rests with those *Stó:lō* living today, in the present. *Xwélmexw* people, the *Stó:lō* believe, can learn from lessons of the past and have an understanding of the needs for the future when making contemporary decisions. Here too, the *Stó:lō* commitment to the past and future of the land, environment, and other issues emphasized in the atlas is a reflection of this relationship and their sense of long-term responsibility.

First Encounters

One of the most fascinating series of plates in the *Stó:lō* atlas, 'Perceptions and Perspectives of "Other,"' focuses on some of the first, cross-cultural memories of contact between Europeans (*Xwelítem*) and *Stó:lō* people. For the *Stó:lō* these stories have been passed down in oral form, while European accounts have usually taken the form of journal entries. These varying accounts from *Stó:lō* chiefs and from informants and explorers such as George Vancouver, Simon Fraser, and Hudson's Bay Company botanist Dr John Scouler can often tell us more about the people who made the observations and about their values, culture, and traditions than they do about the 'reality' of the people they were observing. Carlson (2001, 84) takes an even-handed approach to the subject: 'Just as we would not assume that the ethnographic observations of Europeans provided in Aboriginal oral traditions necessarily depict "realities" of European experience, the same applies in reverse: European accounts of Aboriginal people are not necessarily "true" depictions that coincide with Indigenous people's understanding of themselves.' Still, as Carlson explains, when placed in the proper context, some of these records have great historical value and have been used as evidence in court cases supporting claims for Aboriginal rights and title; as valuable resources for Aboriginal artists and others wanting to revive certain designs, technologies, and architectural styles; and as important insights for ethnographers, historians, and geographers into understanding the dates and regions of the first smallpox epidemics.

A few of the stories and journal entries, which span a full eight pages, are unintentionally comical, such as the explanation that a *Nlaka'pamux* (or Thompson) man made to Simon Fraser about his journey to the sea: 'Ship's captains are "well dressed and very proud. This is the way they go," he noted, clapping his hands upon his hips, then strutting about with an air of consequence.' Others are tragic, such as Captain George Vancouver's June 1792 account of the numerous deserted villages, scattered human bones, and maimed survivors (often left blind in one eye) of the previous decades' smallpox epidemic. This first epidemic reached the Coast Salish area from the south a full decade before Vancouver, Galiano, Valdes, and the like had even arrived on the scene. Vancouver described 'this deplorable disease' as 'not only common, but ... greatly to be apprehended as very fatal amongst them.' There are other accounts of rare or now extinct species of plants or animals in *S'ólh Téméxw* and the surrounding region. The Woolly dog, now extinct, was highly valued among the Coast Salish for its hair, which was used in making blankets and clothing. Members of the Vancouver, Galiano, and Valdes expeditions of June 1792 were the first newcomers to report of these animals. In an account from Valdes, the dogs were described as being 'of moderate size, apparently similar to English-bred sheep dogs, very long-haired and generally white.' Not unlike some of the visitors' descriptions of Aboriginal people themselves, though, their comparisons of these Coast Salish area dogs to the European versions were typically unfavourable, for 'among other characteristics which distinguish them from those of Europe is their manner of barking, which is no more than a miserable yelping.'[5] This account is just one example of both the evidential value and the evidential limitations on these journals as reliable historical sources. While the European newcomers provide us with some excellent description of the Woolly dog's appearance, their account also contains biases that better reflect their own preconceptions about the inherent inferiority of the 'new world' type than any kind of historical 'reality.' This lack of objectivity, it would seem, found its way not only into descriptions of human beings and their life ways but into accounts relating to domesticated animals as well.

Stó:lō Technologies and Seasonal Rounds

As mentioned in the introduction to this chapter, much of the *Stó:lō–Coast Salish Historical Atlas* focuses on the interaction of the Coast Salish and European settlers in the area. In '*Stó:lō* Communications and Transportation Routes, c.1850,' archaeologist Dave Schaepe looks at the extensive network of waterways and mountain ridges throughout *S'ólh Téméxw*, along with the variety of skilfully designed craft including canoes, sailboats, and catamaran-like rafts, and the trails that were used by the *Stó:lō* to navigate them. On the land much of the physical evidence for pre-settler *Stó:lō* transportation routes is no longer visible; a good portion of the communication infrastructure, however, remains intact. This original network of trails, depicted in detail in the atlas, has simply been appropriated as part of the modern grid of highways and roads that have been built overtop of them throughout the territory.

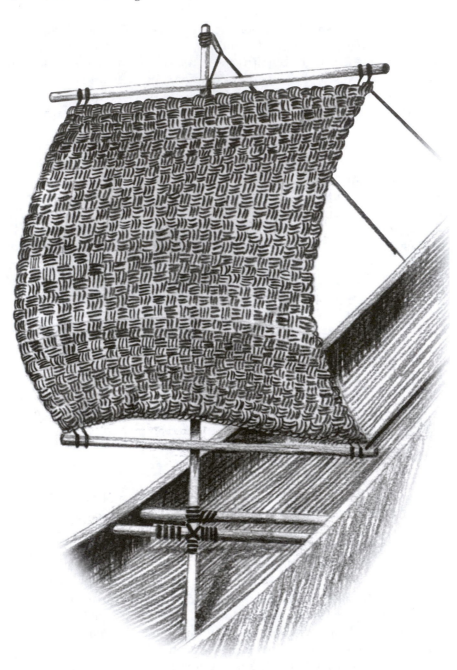

Stó:lō canoes with woven reed sails were used for fishing and for transporting people, goods, and messages across waterways. Illustration courtesy of Jan Perrier.

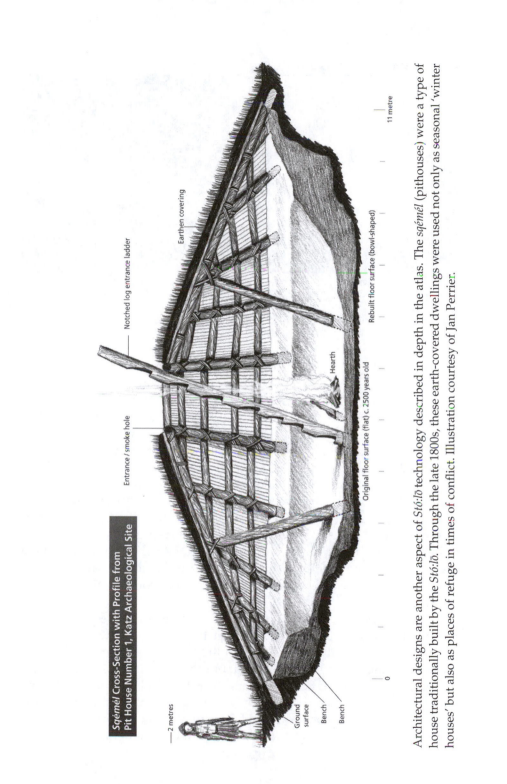

Sqémél Cross-Section with Profile from Pit House Number 1, Katz Archaeological Site

2 metres

Entrance / smoke hole

Notched log entrance ladder

Earthen covering

Hearth

Original floor surface (flat) c. 2500 years old

Rebuilt floor surface (bowl-shaped)

Ground surface

Bench

Bench

0

11 metre

Architectural designs are another aspect of *Stó:lō* technology described in depth in the atlas. The *sqémél* (pithouses) were a type of house traditionally built by the *Stó:lō*. Through the late 1800s, these earth-covered dwellings were used not only as seasonal 'winter houses' but also as places of refuge in times of conflict. Illustration courtesy of Jan Perrier.

Humidity and wind in the Lower Fraser Canyon. Illustration courtesy of Jan Perrier.

One of the most common uses for both pre- and post-contact transportation routes has been to facilitate seasonal rounds. University of Victoria historian John Lutz explains that in pre-contact times the *Stó:lō* efficiently adapted their seasonal rounds to the timing and availability of diverse natural resources in *S'ólh Téméxw*. A variety of effective technologies were employed for storing food during the winter months – allowing time for cultural and spiritual events, along with the opportunity to trade. One of the most important of these technologies was the wind-drying of salmon, especially during the main fish population's arrival in the Fraser Canyon in July and August. Before the invention of artificial refrigeration and canning technology, only in the Fraser Canyon did just the right climatic conditions make wind-drying possible. This Aboriginal technology allowed salmon to be consistently and reliably processed for later consumption, trade, or exchange.

In the post-contact, industrial world Lutz describes how seasonal rounds remained a 'defining feature' of *Stó:lō* society well into the twentieth century. The places to which they went, what they did there, and their decisions about these things may have changed, but the role that seasonal activities played in *Stó:lō* culture had not. Trade with the Hudson's Bay Company, participation in the gold rush economy and the railway construction, work in the canneries and hop yards, and farming provided *Stó:lō* people with continuing opportunities to socialize, to share information, and to pursue

Wind-drying of salmon in the Fraser Canyon. Photo courtesy of Gary Fiegehen, *Stó:lō* Nation Archives, no. 98-P3-466.

spiritual and social activities at other times of the year. Some were very successful in these pursuits; others were left destitute.

In Lutz's chart depicting seasonal rounds in the early twentieth century, one observes that seasons still determined what most *Stó:lō* people were doing. During the summer fish harvest (which continues today) and the fall hop harvest, families spent extended periods of time away from home. Many children were in residential school from October to June. In the winter and spring, shorter hunting and trapping trips were made. For a few men, wage work in the logging camps, in the sawmills, or on farms typically took them away from home for a good part of the year. The impact of these long excursions on family and social life was often profound.

'Reclaiming' the Environment: From Sumas Lake to Sumas Energy 2

As in many other urbanized areas of Canada, the environment and wildlife of southwestern British Columbia has undergone dramatic and ever-quickening physical change since the late nineteenth century. The atlas provides numerous examples of this through its examination and mapping of the impacts of clear-cuts, of sloughs diked and diminished, and of streams channelled and reapportioned among different users. The rapid growth

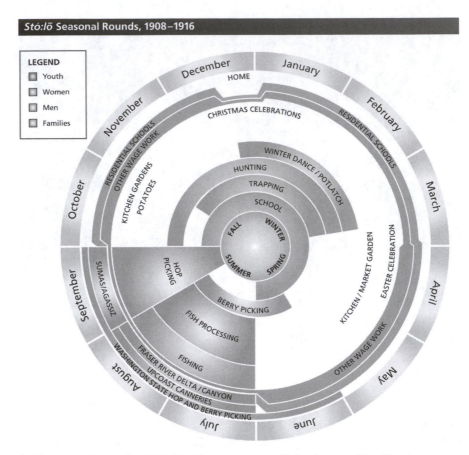

Stó:lō seasonal rounds, 1908–16. Chart courtesy of John Lutz and Jan Perrier.

of third-party resource extraction is also a point of great concern. Most of these activities, carried to excess, are viewed by the *Stó:lō* as being destructive and as an infringement upon their Aboriginal rights. Sometimes they have proved harmful to *Xwelítems* as well.

One of the most striking examples of change occurred at Sumas Lake in the central Fraser Valley. A number of stories (*sxwōxwiyam*) allude to this body of water (which at times grew to as many as 12,000 hectares or 30,000 acres in size) as having always been a *Stó:lō* place of transformations. However, as Jody Woods explains in the atlas, during the mid-1920s Sumas Lake 'underwent transformations of a different nature' (Carlson 2001, 104). Through the use of enormous pumps, dykes, and canals all of the water was drained from the lake so that fertile farmland could, in the language of the day, be 'reclaimed' from its bottom. The end result, Sumas Prairie, was intended to help facilitate *Xwelítem* settlement and the desire for agricultural land. With the draining of Sumas Lake, what had served as an important spawning route and rearing habitat for salmon, a stopover place for migrating birds, and a body of water that supported a wide variety of fish, birds, plants, and animals was eliminated. The event took place without any consultation with those whose past was so closely intertwined with the lake; even today it is only by a complex nature of pumps and dikes that the former lake bottom, what is now known as Sumas Prairie, is prevented from transforming back into its previous state.

The atlas demonstrates that the work of protecting *S'ólh Téméxw* for future generations has been extremely challenging in southwestern British Columbia – the most heavily developed area in western Canada. However, some recent successes are indicative of the gradual change in the relationship between the *Stó:lō* and non-Aboriginal Canadians. At no time has this been reflected more dramatically than in the recent outcome of another environmental controversy centred on the area of Sumas. In direct contrast to the events surrounding Sumas Lake in the mid-1920s, in 2002–4 the *Stó:lō* became active and welcome participants in a cooperative effort to protect the air quality over their traditional lands. The environment staff of the Aboriginal Rights and Title department worked in combination with local city councils and other groups to oppose a plan by Sumas Energy 2, a U.S. company, to build a controversial power plant just south of Abbotsford, BC, in the Fraser Valley. In the end, the National Energy Board of Canada denied an application by the American company to construct the Canadian portion of an 8.5-kilometre international power line – thereby preventing the project from going ahead. In their final decision the federal board sided with the *Stó:lō* and other groups, who had argued that Sumas Energy 2 would send immense amounts of air pollution into the Fraser Valley and create the potential for serious health problems (National Energy Board 2002).

Significantly, the *Stó:lō*, both historically and today, have never taken the position of 'no environmental change.' Indeed, as the atlas demonstrates through many of its plates – especially those describing the pre-contact period – *Stó:lō* cultural occupation has involved a wide variety of activities that modify the environment. These activities include the construction of permanent dwellings (including pithouses, plank houses, and longhouses); establishment of both small, permanently occupied settlements (villages) and large ones (towns); creation of cemeteries; construction of rock-wall defensive sites; carving out of trail networks; use of a wide variety of resources such as fish, animals, and berries for subsistence, trade, exchange, and spiritual practices; and the use of controlled burnings, a practice that occurred throughout many areas of the pre-contact northwest coast.

Sumas reclamation map, 1919. Courtesy of Library and Archives Canada, RG-89, vol. 269, file 3594, C147370, Ottawa.

The contemporary Sumas Prairie, a place of transformation. Photo courtesy of
Gary Fiegehen, *Stó:lō* Nation Archives, no. 98-P3-984.

However, several plates towards the end of the atlas illustrate the dramatic impact of the influx of as many as thirty thousand immigrants per year
on the environment and natural resources of the *Stó:lō's* traditional lands.
The atlas demonstrates that over the last century and a half the actions of
the newcomer society have resulted in a clear and accelerating deteriora-
tion of *S'ólh Téméxw's* environmental integrity – due in part, it is argued, to
the non-Aboriginal society's failure to understand and respect the natural
system on which the *Stó:lō* have relied. The *Stó:lō* hope, by demonstrating
these impacts over a series of atlas plates, that all who live in the territory
and care about the future of *S'ólh Téméxw* will understand and respect the
Stó:lō's environmental concerns, along with some of the *Stó:lō* methods of
environmental management. Many *Stó:lō* are strongly motivated to promote
the environmental integrity and well-being of the land and all its people,
both *Stó:lō* and non-*Stó:lō*. They see this as a commitment and a responsibility that requires the effort of all people to maintain a healthy environment.
The phrase *Xólhmet te mekw'stám ít Kwelát* (we must take care of everything
that belongs to us) is among the most important principles of life.[6]

Halq'eyméylem Place Names in *Stó:lō* Territory

The heart of the atlas lies in its descriptors of *Halq'eyméylem* place names.

The activity of naming and renaming locations on a map is something that has happened around the globe for thousands of years (it has occurred at least eight times in Britain alone) and is typically an act that the dominant culture imposes on the conquered. The Aboriginal people living in British Columbia were never militarily conquered; they did not have their lands taken away from them 'legally' through treaties. Yet the *Stó:lō* and other Aboriginal groups have been overwhelmed by the sheer numbers of people who have moved into British Columbia from elsewhere; currently more than two million non-Natives live in the small area of *S'ólh Téméxw* alone. As a result, the current names for much of the landscape reflect this ultimate expression of power and control. *Vancouver, Victoria, Port Moody, Abbotsford, Mission* – these are all names that newcomers have imposed on the landscape. With the atlas the *Stó:lō* are, in a sense, reclaiming the landscape, using the area's original place names and the maps to locate them. The *Stó:lō* will use them, and the non-*Stó:lō* will acknowledge their existence – perhaps even use some alongside the later names – and, in so doing, affirm the *Stó:lō* themselves, the fact that Aboriginal people were here first, and that their culture continues to live and enrich the larger Canadian society.

Sonny McHalsie has had a deep and abiding interest in place names since 1985. In twenty pages of atlas text, maps, and images, he includes 727 *Halq'eméylem* place names, extending from north of Yale in the Fraser Canyon to the mouth of the Fraser River. The place-name plates provide the translation of each name and its significance. Photographs of many sites as they appear today also accompany the text. McHalsie attempts to present the results of all the documented place-name research in existence from both documentary sources and collections of oral traditions. Much of this work was conducted under the careful guidance of contemporary elders such as the late Elizabeth Herrling and the late Rosaleen George.

McHalsie identifies *Stó:lō* place names as falling into three broad categories: historical happenings, or *sqwelqwel*; geography; and 'names associated with miraculous events from the *sxwōxwiyám*, the distant past when the world was transformed into its present recognizable form.' The first category would include names such as *Yeqwyeqwi:ws* (burned out many times), a name that speaks to a series of repeated, tragic historical events that, as such, are associated with a particular place and the people who lived there. *Staán*, which in English means 'head of bay,' and *Chowéthel*, the name of a village near Hope (derived from the word pertaining to a prominent gravel bar), are two examples of the second category – geographical place names. *Sxwóymelh*, the name given for the location of New Westminster, means 'place where people died' and refers to a warrior who was transformed to

The *Qoqolaxel* (watery eaves) place name derived from an inverted gable long-house that was once situated near modern-day Vedder Crossing in Sardis, BC. Elder Bob Joe built this model in the 1960s. Photo of *Qoqolaxel* in the Chilliwack Museum and Archives courtesy of Jan Perrier.

stone there by *XeXá:ls* (the Transformers). For *Sxwóymelh* and the numerous other sites belonging to the third category, the *Stó:lō* consider these names sacred and unchanging. Here there is considered a sacred significance to the stories, the essence of which must be preserved intact and in an unaltered form. It is in this category that the knowledge of the elders, or Old People, is most important as they come to share their perspectives with others (Carlson 2001, 134).

Sonny McHalsie argues that the naming of places within *S'ólh Téméxw* began thousands of years ago and continues to this day and that such activity has been altered from its Indigenous course only by the forces of colonialism. He adds that the stories and lessons associated with these place names give the sites meaning, making them an important aspect of *Stó:lō* cultural revival. Furthermore, he regards this work as an obligation to past and future generations to ensure that the *Stó:lō* identity and connections to the land are maintained. McHalsie presents his findings 'in the hope that others may share my experience. Our history and our own personal connections to the land are out there waiting for us' (Carlson 2001, 135).

In an interview with the *Chilliwack Times* in May 2002, McHalsie discussed place names and the purpose of the atlas in general. He told reporter Jennifer Feinberg that 'it's important for people to get a sense of the diversity of all the different First Nations. Even the title of the atlas makes it clear that we are part of the larger Coast Salish group.' McHalsie believes that the book itself 'will make it easier for the general public to accept and respect the perspectives that we have on cultural issues. It's not something we're imposing; it's a way of sharing our culture so that they can better understand how we view the land around us' (Feinberg 2002, 16). In the same article archaeologist Dave Schaepe added that the atlas was aimed at raising cross-cultural awareness and 'filling the divide' between Aboriginal and non-Aboriginal communities. The atlas 'contributes to a better understanding and enjoyment of the landscape that's here ... and the long-term relationship between the *Stó:lō* and the land and parts of the Lower Fraser River ... It's the cultural history that many are not familiar with. As well ... the maps are something people can enjoy traveling through the area, looking at the mountains, and getting an understanding of the cultural significance of those places that would otherwise go unknown' (Feinberg 2002, 3). Schaepe affirmed the sentiments of all involved in the project when he stated that he hoped the work would help bring British Columbians together.

While the team of contributors made every effort to present information in *A Stó:lō–Coast Salish Historical Atlas* in an accurate and respectful manner, its readers were invited in the preface to publish new information or interpretations that would challenge the material presented in its pages. Since 2001, reviewers of the atlas have made some excellent criticisms and recommendations for improving the publication. In his review for the *Oregon Historical Quarterly*, William Wyckoff (2002) argues, correctly in my view, that 'more might have been said about the increasingly urban experience of many *Stó:lō* who have left their home settlements.' The late Wayne Suttles (2002, 483) wrote in the *Pacific Northwest Review* that the atlas lacked a key to pronunciation, something that had been included in its predecessor publication, *You Are Asked to Witness: The Stó:lō in Canada's Pacific Coast History* (1997). There are also a few errors or omissions that have been discovered in the book as well, either by the atlas participants themselves or the reviewers. For example, in one of my plates on the *Halq'eméylem* language, Suttles (2002) points out that it appears I have mislabelled one photograph as showing a 'bracken' fern (an important food plant) when it is in more likelihood a wood fern. Suttles is correct. In addition, not all readers will agree with the interpretation and methodologies applied in this publication. Such criticism and diversity of opinion is to be expected and welcomed as a healthy exchange of opinions and viewpoints on issues that deserve much more attention than they have typically received in the past.

Conclusion

A Stó:lō–Coast Salish Historical Atlas helps to reveal many of the unique contributions that the *Stó:lō* and the Coast Salish have made to Canadian identity and culture, by describing the *Stó:lō* experience and some familiar encounters from an Indigenous, rather than a European, perspective. As we have seen, whether the atlas explores issues of identity, spirituality, environment, first contact, technology, labour, or place names, it places consistent emphasis on the *Stó:lō* point of view. Through the format of this historical atlas, the *Stó:lō* make use of their own oral traditions along with the research tools of the broader Canadian society to tell a story of newcomers in *Stó:lō* history, rather than the other way around. The atlas, then, is a direct challenge to the generalized assumptions that history begins with the newcomers' 'pioneer' history and that the Aboriginals' own history prior to contact (so-called prehistory) is just some sort of vague and uncertain past.

There are many ideas in the atlas that the *Stó:lō* believe might be analogous to other situations as well. As the broad range of Aboriginal accomplishments explored in *Hidden in Plain Sight* attests, the *Stó:lō* people's own experience both before and after contact, their ongoing relationship with the landscape, their spirituality and rich world of stories and beliefs, their changing and evolving social and cultural institutions, and their ongoing efforts to work with non-Aboriginal Canadians to build a better world for all of us contain some notable similarities to what has transpired in other parts of the country. There are lessons for all of us if we all make the effort to understand and appreciate them. Steven Point stated in the first pages of *A Stó:lō–Coast Salish Historical Atlas* that the publication was an effort to contribute to bridging those differences between Aboriginal and non-Native society, helping to build cross-cultural understanding, and establishing mutual respect between two (increasingly intertwined) societies. If the book has helped forward any of these goals or even encouraged others to work harder towards achieving them, then the atlas has succeeded.

Acknowledgments

The author would like to thank Dr Keith T. Carlson of the University of Saskatchewan's history department (and the atlas's editor) for his constructive comments and suggestions on earlier drafts of this chapter.

Glossary

Chíchelh Siyá:m – 'Lord Above' or 'Most High Respected Leader'
Halq'eméylem – The language spoken by the *Stó:lō* people
si:yá:m – Respected leaders, the highest mark of esteem in *Stó:lō* society
S'ólh Téméxw – Literally 'our land,' but also used to mean '*Stó:lō* territory'
sqwelqwel – Narratives of more recent history often pertaining to personal experience
Stó:lō (pronounced 'stah-low') – 'River' and the name of the people who live along the lower Fraser River in southwestern British Columbia and the adjoining watersheds
sxwōxwiyam – Stories about the distant past, when the world was chaotic and in the process of being 'made right'
XeXá:ls – The Transformers (*Xá:ls* – the singular form)
Xwelítem – Literally 'hungry ones' or 'starving ones'; a term still in common use that refers to non-Aboriginal people and non-Aboriginal society
Xwélmexw – Human beings who speak the same language

Notes

1 In another critique of the atlas, ethnographer Barry Gough (2002, 949) wrote that it provided 'an excellent model for other multi-century books on aboriginal experiences' and described it as being 'in a league of its own.' The atlas was also named a *Choice* Outstanding Academic Title (Gough 2002).
2 A plate is a full-size colour map including accompanying text, graphs, and illustrations. Unless otherwise noted, plates in this chapter have been reproduced, by permission, from *A Stó:lō–Coast Salish Historical Atlas*, ed. Keith T. Carlson (Vancouver, Seattle, Chilliwack: Douglas and McIntyre, University of Washington Press, *Stó:lō* Heritage Trust, 2001).
3 In the plate 'History Revealed through Salishan Languages' I describe how linguists are now applying data from all Salishan languages to determine the origin of the speakers of these languages.
4 Throughout this chapter and most of the atlas itself, the Upriver pronunciation

and orthography – termed *Halq'eméylem* – was used. On the map that appears in the atlas depicting Halkomelem dialects, the generic term for the language, *Halkomelem*, has been applied so as not to bias the map in favour of one of the three orthographies (Upriver, Downriver, and Island). This map is based primarily on Galloway's 'Halkomelem Language Area' map in *A Grammar of Upriver Halkomelem* (1993). The atlas's inset map of language families is based on Wayne Suttles (1985).

5 Excerpts from Lamb (1960), quoted in Carlson, *A Stó:lō-Coast Salish Historical Atlas* (2001, 84); excerpts from Vancouver (1801), quoted in Carlson (2001, 86); Cecil (1971[1930]) quoted in Carlson (2001, 86).

6 Sections of the previous three paragraphs have been paraphrased from the *Stó:lō* Environmental Conservation and Land Use Policy (n.d.).

Bibliography

Carlson, Keith T., ed. 2001. *A Stó:lō–Coast Salish Historical Atlas.* Vancouver, Seattle, Chilliwack: Douglas and McIntyre, University of Washington Press, *Stó:lō* Heritage Trust.

Cecil, Jane, ed. 1971 [1930]. *A Spanish Voyage to Vancouver and the Northwest Coast of America: Being the Narrative of the Voyage Made in the Year 1792 by the Schooners 'Sutil' and 'Mexicana' to Explore the Strait of Fuca.* Trans. Jose Espinosa y Tello. New York: AMS Press.

Feinberg, Jennifer. 2002. Stó:lō atlas brings home the prize. *Chilliwack Times*, 7 May, pp. 3, 16.

Galloway, Brent D. 1993. *A Grammar of Upriver Halkomelem.* Berkeley: University of California Press.

Gough, Barry M. 2002. Review of *A Stó:lō–Coast Salish Historical* Atlas. *Choice* (January): 949.

Grescoe, Taras. 1996. Native tongues. *Georgia Straight*, 21–28 November: 19.

Harris, Cole. 2002. A Stó:lō–Coast Salish Historical Atlas. *BC Historical News* 35 (3): 25–6.

Lamb, W.K., ed. 1960. *The Letters and Journals of Simon Fraser, 1806–1808.* Toronto: Macmillan.

National Energy Board of Canada. 2002. NEB denies an application from Sumas Energy 2, Inc. to construct an international power line in Abbotsford, BC. News release, 4 March.

Stó:lō Environmental Conservation and Land Use Policy. n.d. *Stó:lō* Nation Archives, Chilliwack, BC.

Suttles, Wayne. 1985. *Native Languages of the Northwest Coast Map.* Portland: Oregon Historical Society.

– 2002. Review of *A Stó:lō–Coast Salish Historical Atlas*. *Pacific Historical Review* 71 (3): 482–3.

Vancouver, George, ed. 1801. *A Voyage of Discovery to the North Pacific Ocean, and Round the World: In Which the Coast of North-West America Has Been Carefully Examined and Accurately Surveyed*. 6 vols. London: Printed for John Stockdale.

Wyckoff, William. 2002. A Stō:ló–Coast Salish Historical Atlas. *Oregon Historical Quarterly* 103 (Spring): 136.

Profile of Marie Ann Battiste (1949–)

Mi'kmaq and Educator

Professor Marie Battiste has worked in the field of Indian education for over thirty years. She has made significant contributions to its development in Canada and to Indigenous knowledge theory on the international stage. She is also renowned for her work in revitalizing the Mi'kmaq language in her home community of Chapel Island, Nova Scotia.[1]

Marie Battiste is a Mi'kmaq of the Potlotek First Nation. She was one of four children born to John and Annie Battiste. As a child she was strongly influenced by her mother's strength, drive, and dedication and by her father's honesty, integrity, and encouragement.[2] She was also influenced by the 1960s civil rights movement and its leader, Dr Martin Luther King Jr.

Battiste became aware of the struggles of the poor, the powerless, and the marginalized and that the educational curriculum did not reflect her identity or culture. Her belief that education could assist her and others to overcome the obstacles to leading satisfying lives brought her to earn a bachelor of science in elementary and junior high education from the University of Maine in 1971, a master of education in administration and social policy from Harvard University in 1974, and a doctor of education in curriculum and teacher education from Stanford University in 1984.[3]

Marie Battiste taught at various Nova Scotia schools and received a TC8 teaching licence from the Nova Scotia Department of Education. She served as education director and principal at the Chapel Island reserve from 1984 to 1988. She also was a Mi'kmaq cultural curriculum coordinator from 1988 to 1989 and a classroom consultant to the Eskasoni School from 1989 to 1993.[4] She has served as a board member in many educational organizations; she was an expert to and the co-chair of an Indigenous heritage workshop, and a delegate to the United Nations' Workshop on Indigenous Peoples and Higher Education.[5]

Dr Marie Battiste's research focuses on the decolonization of Aboriginal

Marie Battiste. Photo courtesy of Bill Hamilton, Hamilton Photo Graphics.

education, the post-colonial study of education, the renewal and reconstruction of Aboriginal languages and cultures, the protection of Aboriginal heritage and culture, qualitative research on Aboriginal teachers' experiences in Saskatchewan public schools, and ethnographic and historical studies of the Mi'kmaq.[6] She serves as a mentor and supervisor to many graduate and undergraduate students at the University of Saskatchewan.

Battiste's academic and literary contributions include journal articles, book chapters, and books. She has co-authored a book with Jean Barman, *First Nations Education in Canada: The Circle Unfolds* (1995), and with Sakej Youngblood Henderson, *Protecting Indigenous Knowledge* (2000). The latter work won that year's Saskatchewan Book Award.[7] Battiste also edited *Reclaiming Indigenous Voice and Vision* (2000).

Battiste was recognized with eagle feathers in 1993 and 1995 for her work with the Mi'kmaq community. She received the Queen's 125th Award for Community Service in 1992. That same year, she was awarded the Nova Scotia Social Studies Curriculum Development Award. Marie Battiste has received two honorary doctorates: an honorary doctorate of laws from St Mary's University in 1987 and an honorary doctorate of humane letters from the University of Maine in 1997.[8] She won a National Aboriginal Achievement Award in 2008.

Marie Battiste lives in Saskatoon, Saskatchewan, with her husband, Sakej Henderson, and their children. She continues to teach and conduct research at the University of Saskatchewan.

BRIAN CALLIOU

Notes

1 http://www.usask.ca/education/people/battistem.htm.
2 Tracy Robinson, 'Like eagles,' *Saskatchewan Indian* 23, no. 6 (July/August).
3 http://www.usask.ca/education/people/battistem.htm.
4 Ibid.
5 Ibid.
6 Ibid.
7 Marie Battiste and Sakej Youngblood Henderson, *Protecting Aboriginal Knowledge* (Saskatoon: Purich Press, 2000).
8 http://www.usask.ca/education/people/battistem.htm.

PART 4

POLITICS AND NORTHERN POWER

Profile of Thelma Chalifoux (1929–)

Métis and Senator

Thelma Chalifoux was a young single mother struggling to put food on the table for her seven small children, but she worked hard to 'make it' and became one of Canada's most ardent advocates of Métis culture and identity. She was born the second of five children to a Métis father, Paul Michel Villeneuve, and an American mother, Helene Ingerson, in Calgary, Alberta, during the Great Depression. At eighteen years old she married a man in the military and then found herself raising a young family on her own while her husband was dispatched to different assignments.

At the age of twenty-five Chalifoux was abandoned by her abusive husband. She had a Grade 9 education and seven young children to care for. Living by her belief that 'the good Lord will look after us,' she completed her education and raised her family. Chalifoux studied at the Chicago School of Interior Design, the Southern Alberta Institute of Technology (construction estimating), and Lethbridge Community College (sociology).[1]

Thelma Chalifoux's professional experience as a consultant, entrepreneur, and negotiator is extensive and impressive. She served as a land-claims negotiator (1979–82 and 1996–8), a consultant and senator for the Métis Nation of Alberta Association (1990–5), and a consultant for Chalifoux and Associates (1996–8), a company that provides workshops on development training to community and volunteer organizations. She also served as a panel member for Alberta Provincial Appeals/Alberta Family and Social Service (1989–98), and has been an active member of the Métis Nation of Alberta since 1961. Her career includes a foray into journalism, where she was a newscaster, producer, host of a weekly show, and freelance writer.[2]

After receiving a National Aboriginal Achievement Award in 1995, Chalifoux was appointed to the Senate of Canada by Prime Minister Jean Chrétien on 26 November 1997. She was the first Aboriginal woman, and the first Métis, to be appointed to the Senate, and she served until her mandatory

Thelma Chalifoux.

retirement at age seventy-five in 2004.[3] Complementing her efforts as a senator, Chalifoux has worked to strengthen cross-cultural understandings by accepting positions in various sectors of civil society: community development, wellness, justice, education, and economic initiatives. As a senator she has addressed the issues of Métis housing, genetically modified foods, drug company relations with the federal government, and environmental legislation.[4] Chalifoux gained notoriety for championing the Louis Riel Act in 2001. The purpose of the act is to honour Riel and the Métis people by commemorating the leader's unique and historic role in the advancement and development of the Canadian confederation.[5]

Thelma Chalifoux served as chairperson of the Senate Standing Committee on Aboriginal People and appointed a task force to discuss with Edmonton Aboriginal groups, leaders, elders, and youth the issues of urban Aboriginal youth gangs and to seek solutions to the problems facing the youth.[6] According to Senator Chalifoux, 'we don't need another study ... we need an action plan for change. The communities need to be empowered to take positive action in what is happening within their own communities.'[7]

In discussing her role as a senator, Chalifoux noted, 'My role there was partly education and partly bringing the issues forward, especially for the Métis because we are truly the forgotten people.'[8] Thus she endeavoured to give Métis people a voice in government. Thelma Chalifoux is over eighty years old and has a great number of grandchildren and great-grandchildren.[9]

MYLES WIESELMAN

Notes

1 Terry Lusty, 'Thelma Chalifoux: Senator,' Alberta Community Heritage Foundation, http://www.abheritage.ca/albertans/profile/thelma_chalifoux.html (accessed 27 January 2011).
2 Ibid.
3 Ibid.
4 University of Alberta, 'Senator Thelma Chalifoux,' in *Leadership Pages*, http://www.ualberta.ca/~walld/chalifoux.htm.
5 *The Windsor Star*, 10 December 2001.
6 *Edmonton Journal*, 11 April 2003.
7 *Calgary Herald*, 9 January 2003.
8 University of Alberta, 'Senator Thelma Chalifoux,' http://www.ualberta.ca/~walld/chalifoux.htm.
9 Thelma Chalifoux, 'Liberal Party profile,' Liberal Party of Canada in Alberta, 2003, online.

Profile of Elijah Harper (1949–)

Cree, Rights Activist, and Politician

The name Elijah Harper is synonymous with Canadian Aboriginal issues, politics, and especially the failure of the Meech Lake Accord. Elijah Harper's influence spanned local, provincial, and national scenes during his political career. He was born on 3 March 1949 in the community of Red Sucker Lake, Manitoba, the second of thirteen children born to Allan and Ethel Harper.[1] When he was five years old, a doctor who was visiting the reserve noticed a lump under his chin. The lump was diagnosed as tuberculosis, and Harper spent the next six months in a sanatorium at The Pas, Manitoba.[2] He was placed in a residential school at Norway House, Manitoba, in 1957, where he spent ten months of each year for the next decade.[3]

Harper had his first brush with politics when he ran for Grade 9 class president, a contest that he won convincingly. After completing high school in Winnipeg, he attended the University of Manitoba. While there he made contact with political representative groups including the Manitoba Association for Native Youth and the Manitoba Indian Brotherhood.[4] He also helped form the university's Native student association with fellow students and future national chiefs of the Assembly of First Nations Ovide Mercredi and Phil Fontaine.[5] Elijah eventually became the 'behind the scenes' man for Mercredi.[6]

In 1973 the newly married Elijah Harper returned to Red Sucker Lake and worked for several years as a community development worker.[7] From 1978 to 1981 Harper was chief of the Red Sucker Lake reserve.[8] During his term he brought television, a permanent nursing station, and an expanded infrastructure to the community.[9] In 1981 Harper was elected to represent the Rupertsland riding in Manitoba's provincial legislature.[10] He was re-elected in 1986, 1988, and 1990.[11] He joined the provincial cabinet as minister without portfolio in 1986 and became minister for northern affairs in 1987.[12]

It was Harper's resolve that catapulted him into 'infamy.' The summer of

Elijah Harper. Photo courtesy of Terry Lusty.

1990 was one of unrest in Canada's Aboriginal community. At Oka, Quebec,[13] the Mohawks of Kanesatake occupied disputed land as a result of the Town of Oka's plans to use it to expand its golf course. During a violent clash between the provincial police force and the Mohawks, policeman Marcel Lemay was shot and killed. Meanwhile, the vote to adopt the Meech Lake Accord (which had been negotiated three years earlier) was on the federal government's political agenda. The Meech Lake Accord proposed an amendment to the Canadian constitution that would have given Quebec 'special status' designation in the constitution,[14] while not recognizing Aboriginal peoples' role in the creation of Canada.[15] Aboriginal leaders had suffered many indignities at the hands of provincial premiers and the prime minister during the drafting of the Meech Lake Accord; for example, they had been virtually shut out of participating in, or even observing, the highly charged talks.

On 22 June 1990, backed by other Manitoba First Nations leaders, Harper refused to ratify the Meech Lake Accord. While holding an eagle feather, he scuttled the process. This action captured media and public attention. Harper, the First Nations legislator from Manitoba, became a folk hero for his principled stand.[16] A movie about that fateful month in 1990, *Elijah*, was produced by Brian Unwin in 2007. First Nations actor Billy Merasty played the role of Elijah Harper.[17]

Harper has received several accolades over the years; he was named a lifetime honorary Red Sucker Lake chief in 1990 and received an Aboriginal Achievement Award in 1996.[18] Moreover, there currently is a movement to place Elijah Harper into Manitoba's vacant Senate seat in Ottawa. Today he can be found delivering speeches at universities and other venues. Elijah Harper's greatest accomplishment is that he helped bring Aboriginal issues and rights to the forefront of the federal government's agenda.

BYRON BROWNE

Notes

1 Barbara Hager, 'Elijah Harper,' in *Honour Song: A Tribute* (Vancouver: Raincoast Books, 1996), 119.
2 Ibid.
3 'Elijah Harper,' in *Native North American Biography*, ed. Sharon Malinowski and Simon Glickman (Toronto: UXL, 1996), 175.
4 Ibid.
5 Ibid.
6 Ibid.
7 'Elijah Harper,' in *Native North American Biography*.
8 'Elijah Harper,' in *Who's Who in Canada*, vol. 35, ed. Elizabeth Lumley (Toronto: University of Toronto Press, 2000), 547.
9 Pauline Comeau, *Elijah, No Ordinary Hero* (Vancouver: Douglas and McIntyre, 1993), 70.
10 Bruce E. Johansen and Donald A. Grinde Jr, eds., 'Elijah Harper,' in *The Encyclopedia of Native American Biography: 600 Life Stories of Important People, from Powhatan to Wilma Mankiller* (New York: Henry Holt, 1997), 702.

11 Comeau, *Elijah*, 87.
12 'Elijah Harper,' in *Canadian Encyclopedia 2000 World Edition* (Toronto: McClelland and Stewart, 2000).
13 The standoff lasted seventy-eight days.
14 Johansen and Grinde, 'Elijah Harper.'
15 Hager, 'Elijah Harper,' 124.
16 'Elijah Harper,' in *Native North American Biography*.
17 'Elijah Harper,' http://en.wikipedia.org/wiki/Elijah_Harper (accessed 30 April 2009).
18 'Harper, Elijah,' *Historica: The Canadian Encyclopedia*, http://www.thecanadianencyclopedia.com/index.cfm?PgNm=TCE&Params=A1ARTA0010844.

White Paper / Red Paper: Aboriginal Contributions to Canadian Politics and Government

LAURIE MEIJER DREES

> Everyone should recognize that Indians have contributed much to the Canadian community.
> – Indian Chiefs of Alberta (1970)

> Within my own lifetime I have seen my people ... make the beginning of the long, hard struggle back to the plateau that is our proper place in the world ... What little change there has been has occurred in the decade of the 1960s.
> – George Manuel, in Manuel and Posluns (1974)

In the early 1970s the Canadian public began to hear the voices of First Nations leaders in Parliament, on the radio and television, and through books readily available on local newsstands and in libraries. Although Indian communities had long been sending their leaders into the Canadian political system in hopes of improving conditions for their peoples, it was not until the 1970s that their struggles and accomplishments became more visible to other Canadians across the country. Men like George Manuel, James Gosnell, Harold Cardinal, Dave Courchene, Walter Deiter, John Tootoosis, Paul Okalik, Howard Adams, Georges Erasmus, and Ovide Mercredi, women like Marlene Brant Castellano, Sandra Lovelace Sappier, and Louise Mandell, and many others worked to advocate for positive change in Canadian society and politics. Their legacy – legal recognition that Canada is a diverse society – affects all Canadians today. In the words of the Indian chiefs of Alberta, 'There is room in Canada for diversity. Our leaders say that Canada should preserve her "pluralism" and encourage the culture of all her peoples' (1970, 5).

What, specifically, have Aboriginal peoples (defined constitutionally as Indian, Inuit, and Métis) contributed to the Canadian state? First and perhaps foremost, Aboriginal leaders facilitated the securing of the recognition of Aboriginal rights in Canada, thereby reinforcing the idea that 'special' rights can exist and be held by Canadians, as expressed in Canada's constitution. Second, they continue to contribute new ideas about government within Canada's political system by pioneering new governing bodies through the emergent land-claims process. Third, they have consistently exerted considerable pressure on Canada's political system to support new ideas and change.

Although Indian peoples, as defined by the Indian Act, did not receive the universal federal vote until 1960, Aboriginal participation in, and sometimes against, Canadian politics has done much to shape the character of Canada's political institutions and the ideals they serve. Indian, Inuit, and Métis leaders have used the flexibility of the Canadian state system to forge new pathways towards support for diversity in Canada. The work of Aboriginal leaders is far from finished, yet Canada has already accommodated many of the changes introduced as a result of their work. As a direct consequence of the contributions from its Aboriginal citizens, Canada and its politics continue their evolution, featuring new forms of governance and rights never envisioned before 1970. This chapter earmarks the significance of the 1969 White Paper and the 1970 Red Paper in launching the formidable changes in Canadian politics that developed in subsequent decades. In fact, the 1970 presentation of the Red Paper to Parliament by the Indian chiefs of Alberta should be viewed as a noteworthy milepost in Canada's political history.[1]

Until recently the work of Aboriginal leaders was poorly described and, therefore, received little recognition in existing literature dealing with Canada's political history. Although Aboriginal leaders may be well known within their home communities, they are not regularly acknowledged as meaningful contributors to Canada's political development outside that setting. A handful of biographies and autobiographies of these Aboriginal leaders exist, but many have now been forgotten or are out of print. To further obscure matters, few scholarly analyses related to Aboriginal political philosophies, their cultural context, or the leaders advocating them have been published.[2] In contrast, far more attention has been given to the history and development of Canadian Indian policy and law, primarily from a governmental perspective rather than from an Aboriginal perspective.[3] Historical and contemporary Aboriginal perspectives on that same history are still few and far between. Underscoring this notion is the fact that a great deal of attention has been given to the White Paper on Indian Affairs of 1969, but little has been devoted to the Red Paper.[4]

Despite this gap in the literature, Aboriginal scholars and leaders are making the point that Canada has long ignored their collective impact on Canadian governance. In the words of John Borrows, Anishinabe legal scholar, 'Canadian law concerning Aboriginal peoples partially originates in, and is extracted from, the diverse institutions contained in Canada's Aboriginal cultures ... [M]ost accounts of Canada's jurisgenesis do not recognize the importance of its Indigenous sources' (2002, 4). David Newhouse, professor of Native studies at Trent University, adds to this position the significance of Aboriginal contributions to governance, stating, 'Aboriginal governments now go far beyond any limited idea of "municipal governments" envisioned before 1982 ... [T]hey now encompass federal, provincial and municipal authorities as well as some unique Aboriginal authorities ... This is a history of the last thirty years that needs to be told in a comprehensive way' (2004, 11). Both scholars draw attention to the idea that law and the political-legal system in Canada owe a great deal to Aboriginal influences.

Clearly, awareness of Aboriginal political action in the past and present is critical in order to understand Canada's recognition of 'special rights' properly, the development of the Canadian constitution, or the evolution of the various governance structures in the nation.

The White Paper and the Red Paper, 1969–70

The struggle of Aboriginal leaders to access the Canadian state system and to gain a voice within it has deep roots. Since Confederation, individual leaders have fought hard, both quietly and loudly, to gain recognition of their concerns. Only inconsistently, if at all, did Canadian governments listen to their messages. Until the second half of the twentieth century, changes to the Indian Act or policies affecting Aboriginal peoples were rarely made in consultation with Aboriginal communities. Few opportunities existed for Aboriginal leaders to voice their concerns to government representatives, except through messages delivered to Ottawa via their fledgling political organizations. Even then, leaders often found their perspectives discredited, ignored, or only minimally acknowledged. It is recognized by scholars that early political activists from Aboriginal communities had a difficult time delivering their messages to bureaucrats and politicians in Ottawa before the 1960s, despite their ongoing efforts to do so. Consultation with Aboriginal peoples by Ottawa was rare. On a mere handful of occasions before 1960 did the Canadian federal government solicit input from its registered Indian population on issues affecting Indian peoples. An early example of such consultation was the meetings of the Special Joint Parliamentary Committee on Indian Affairs in the late 1940s. This committee was concerned only with registered Indian issues; Métis and Inuit communities were ignored, for the most part.

This lack of consultation of Aboriginal peoples by the federal government began to change in the 1960s, when ideas of civil rights and the significance of social democracy began to filter through the Canadian political system and political ideologies, in part influenced by developments in the United States and the experience of minorities in the Second World War.

A turning point in this situation came in 1970. In that year Indian leaders gained the needed foothold within the political system that allowed them to initiate discussions; these discussions led directly to the new ideals and institutions that are still operational within Canada today. Indian peoples from across Canada presented to the government of Prime Minister Pierre Elliot Trudeau a position paper that reflected the vision of Canada's Indian chiefs regarding their place in the Canadian state. Entitled *Citizens Plus*, but more popularly known as the Red Paper, it stood as a written response to a very contentious federal policy proposal, a White Paper entitled *Statement of the Government of Canada on Indian Policy*, which had been made public in 1969. The events surrounding this specific White Paper and its antithesis, the Red Paper, served as the starting point for significant change in Canadian governance.

The history of the government's *Statement of the Government of Canada on Indian Policy* is perhaps best described by Sally Weaver in her renowned book, *The Making of Canadian Indian Policy* (1981). In that work Weaver outlines the development of this particular White Paper, which proposed the termination of all special treatment of Indian peoples in Canada as well as the elimination of the federal statute governing registered Indian people – the Indian Act (Weaver 1981, 4–5). The stated goal of this dramatic change in federal dealing with Indian peoples was that, through the elimination of 'special status,' Indian peoples would gain 'equal' status with all other Canadians. In the eyes of the federal policymakers, the Indian Act (and the special rights of Indian peoples as configured by the British North America Act), various federal-provincial agreements and statutes, and even the treaties were the major cause of the problems faced by Indian communities. Furthermore, the 1969 White Paper proposed that the administration of services to Indian peoples be transferred from the federal government to the provincial governments. Despite section 91(24) of the British North America Act, 1867, outlining 'Indians, and Lands reserved for the Indians' as a federal responsibility, the Trudeau government stood poised to do away with its obligations on this front in the name of creating a more 'just society.' In terms of treaty rights, the policy suggested directly: 'The significance of the treaties in meeting the economic, educational, health and welfare needs of the Indian people has always been limited and will continue to decline … [T]he anomaly of treaties between groups within society and the government of that society will require that these treaties be reviewed to see how they can be equitably ended' (Canada 1969, 11). Treaty rights, therefore, would also be dissolved. Developed in semi-secrecy in 1968–9, the policy proposal was presented to the Canadian public in June 1969.

The release of the White Paper that year was not surprising. In fact, its publication was a direct response to pressure emanating from Indian communities and their leadership. Indeed, Indian spokesmen had been calling for revision in the federal approaches to its administration of Indian communities in earnest since the mid-1960s. One organization at the forefront of the calls for change in that period was the Indian Association of Alberta. At that time, the association had just elected a new and vibrant young president, Harold Cardinal, to revitalize their organization, and in 1968 they accepted federal funding from the Department of Indian Affairs to strengthen and advance their calls for political change on behalf of the Indian people of Alberta and Canada. Cardinal and his supporters represented a new generation of leaders: formally educated men and women who were savvy about the politics in Ottawa and who, for the first time, worked as professional politicians. Backing the Indian Association of Alberta as a regional association was a new national organization: in that same year of 1968 a new union, the National Indian Brotherhood, was formed with the goal of uniting Indian people across Canada in their efforts to gain more direct influence over the government's decision making regarding registered Indian peoples. Together, these two political associations and their leaders represented the pressure from which Prime Minister Pierre Trudeau and his Minister of Indian Affairs sought relief.

Although the Trudeau government claimed that it had consulted Indian representatives on the matter, many First Nations leaders were outraged at what they considered the lack of Indian participation in the development of the policy. They also resented the secretive manner in which bureaucrats developed the policy. Most significant, they were alarmed at the suggestion that Ottawa planned to eliminate their special status. In their view, the place of Indian peoples in Canadian society was solidly based upon their unique treaty agreements with the Crown and on the special rights those agreements conferred. Indian leaders were adamant that their historic rights could not be unilaterally swept away by the federal government. As Weaver notes, 'Indians responded to the policy with a resounding nationalism unparalleled in Canadian history' (1981, 5).

At the time of the White Paper's release, Indian organizations in Canada lacked significant resources. Although several noteworthy formal political associations existed, including the newly formed National Indian Brotherhood, these organizations were not well poised to take on the tremendous task of responding quickly to the unexpected federal initiative. Their organizations were relatively new, even if their perspectives on treaty rights, Aboriginal rights, and Ottawa's responsibilities to Indian and Aboriginal peoples were not. Historically, factors including lack of funds, the diversity of First Nations communities, the poor socio-economic state of reserves, and long-standing distrust of the federal government had worked against unifying the voices of Indian peoples in their attempts to have their concerns made known to government. However, the National Indian Brotherhood made a great effort to do so. When the White Paper was released, for example, the union had only been operational for one year. Despite their seemingly diverse and under-resourced position, Indian spokesmen across Canada did manage to offer a firm rejection of the policy within days of its release. By the fall of 1969, Indian organizations had secured permission and funding from the Trudeau government to study the White Paper and offer a formal response. The official response from the National Indian Brotherhood came exactly one year after the release of the White Paper. Entitled *Citizens Plus*, it offered the nation a new political perspective on the place of Indian peoples in Canada and opened up significant new discussions and developments on that question.

Fondly and sarcastically dubbed the 'Red Paper,' *Citizens Plus* represented a blistering attack by Indian leaders on Ottawa's lack of respect for, and interest in, Indian peoples in Canada. Significantly, the document was originally drafted by the Indian Association of Alberta and represented that provincial group's historic grievances and ideals in the area of treaty rights and economic development. The association and its president, Harold Cardinal, spent the winter of 1969–70 writing this response paper with the assistance of M and M Systems Research (a firm established by the former Social Credit premier of Alberta, Ernest Manning, and his son Preston Manning) for a reputed fee of $25,000 (Wuttunee 1971, 58; Dobbin 1991, 39; Maria Campbell, personal communication, 3 June 2001). The resulting *Citizens Plus* document was ready for public distribution in spring 1970. In early June 1970 Aboriginal leaders from across Canada gathered at Carleton University to plan their strategy for presenting their response to the Trudeau government. After revising the Indian Association of Alberta's document by adding additional comments on treaties and Aboriginal rights, the National Indian Brotherhood adopted *Citizens Plus* as its own and as the Indian peoples' official national response to the White Paper. On 4 June 1969, the Red Paper was presented to the Liberal cabinet in the Railway Committee Room on Parliament Hill by Indian

Association of Alberta members John Snow and Adam Soloway, with Harold Cardinal speaking to the significance of treaty and Aboriginal rights (Weaver 1981, 183–4).

The Red Paper promoted two main initiatives: economic development and education. It also took the significance of Aboriginal and treaty rights as its central theme and borrowed the term *citizens plus* from *A Survey of the Contemporary Indians of Canada: Economic, Political, Educational Needs and Policies* (Hawthorn 1966–7), also known as the Hawthorn Report. Not surprisingly, the red-covered booklet opened with a quote from the Hawthorn Report: 'Indians should be regarded as "Citizens Plus"; in addition to the normal rights and duties of citizenship, Indians possess certain additional rights as charter members of the Canadian community' (Indian Chiefs of Alberta 1970, 1). Very significantly, *Citizens Plus* opened by emphasizing Indian peoples' treaty rights. In doing so, it positioned treaty rights as foundational to Indian peoples' participation in Canadian society.

Following discussions of treaty rights and a critique of Indian policy in Canada, the Red Paper moved into concrete proposals for on-reserve educational programs and strategies for economic development. A little noted but noteworthy aspect of the document was that its rather lengthy economic development section promoted a corporate model based on profit and non-profit organizations that would serve reserve communities. The Red Paper described how the development of an Indian corporate structure could emphasize the development of both industrial and human resources on Indian reserves. Such a suggestion, basing Indian community development on a corporate model, was not a new one for that time. In this same period, Native peoples of Alaska were in the process of negotiating a remarkably similar corporation-based land-claim settlement. The Red Paper section on economic development had many similarities to Alaskan Natives' final settlement, the Alaska Native Claims Settlement Act (1971).

The Red Paper marked a turning point in Indian-government relations in Canada. Harold Cardinal likened the success of the Red Paper to Custer's Last Stand: 'Politically, this was our high point; our greatest success, our political equivalent to Little Big Horn' (1977, 184). Indeed, with the Red Paper the Indian Association of Alberta and the National Indian Brotherhood made a significant mark on the landscape of Native political action in Canada in several ways. First and foremost, it led to the open retraction of the White Paper and the Prime Minister suggesting that his government's approach may have been 'misguided' (Weaver 1981, 185). For the first time in their discussions with the federal government, First Nations leaders successfully and directly quashed a government initiative. Furthermore, the Red Paper opened up discussion on Aboriginal and treaty rights apart from their relation to specific social and economic conditions in reserve communities. By presenting the paper directly to Cabinet, the National Indian Brotherhood circumvented the traditional channels for voicing grievances to government. As Richard Price, a scholar and a former director of treaty and Aboriginal rights research at the Indian Association of Alberta, writes: 'The White Paper–Red Paper exchange created a new situation for Indian policy making in Canada. Unilateral policy-making by government had been found to be unworkable' (1977, 50). Following release of the Red Paper, the federal government moved towards a joint-policymaking model, approving a special 'Indian Rights Process' in 1977 whereby Indian leaders would have direct input on Indian policy creation.

Perhaps even more significant, the Red Paper caught the Canadian public's attention. In its efforts to have Indian peoples' voices heard, the National Indian Brotherhood successfully used the media to broadcast its message to all of Canada. By this action alone, the leaders involved represented a new approach to Canadian politics: one led by professional politicians, who used the media to their advantage, and one that more systematically embraced the Canadian political system.

After the Red Paper, federal funds played a major role in financing Aboriginal political organizations. Previously Aboriginal organizations had run on shoestring budgets directed by volunteer efforts, but then they transformed themselves into professional organizations with a recognized lobbying role. Finally, an important legacy of the Red Paper was that it sharpened Indian commitment to special rights discussions (Weaver 1981, 189). Discussion on the nature of those rights continues to this day.

Contributions to Constitutional Change

Following the presentation of the Red Paper to the Trudeau government in 1970, the political landscape in Canada was altered to the point where denial and neglect of Aboriginal issues and perspectives was less possible. Although various subsequent federal governments undertook only a few initiatives to address Aboriginal issues, two developments in 1979 influenced further change in Canada's political structure and the role of Aboriginal peoples in Canada's political process. First, in May 1979, the National Indian Brotherhood secured participatory status in the first-ministers' conferences during the planned repatriation of Canada's constitution. This represented a momentous occasion because, as sociologist J. Rick Ponting and political scientist Roger Gibbins point out, 'in marked contrast to but five years earlier when NIB had difficulty procuring a meeting with even the DIAND (Indian Affairs) Minister, NIB had been accepted as a participant in constitutional negotiations at the First Ministers level' (1980, 215). Second, in June 1979, the National Indian Brotherhood created a stir in London, England, when it sought to challenge the return of Canada's constitution. The presence of the brotherhood in England established an overseas foothold for Canadian First Nations. When the brotherhood allowed and encouraged Métis and Inuit to join them in presenting a unified case to the British government against patriation, they further solidified their position as lobbyists in the international arena.[5]

Achieving participatory status in the constitutional repatriation process represented an enormous accomplishment on the part of Aboriginal leaders. Throughout the 1970s the National Indian Brotherhood and the First Nations leaders began emphasizing their sovereignty and demanding control over certain aspects of community life, rather than continuing to negotiate for greater powers from the federal government (Ponting and Gibbins 1980, 213). Aboriginal associations produced many reports and documents restating their commitment to self-determination within Canada.[6] In 1978 they asserted their right to participate in ministerial meetings related to the repatriation of the Constitution and announced to the Prime Minister their intention to attend the proceedings. Although First Nations leaders initially had not been invited to the meetings, their pronouncements on that front resulted in them gaining observer status and, soon after, participant status.

By January 1981 their influence in constitutional renewal in Canada could be measured by the inclusion of a tremendously significant section into the patriation resolution: 'the aboriginal and treaty rights of the aboriginal peoples of Canada are hereby recognized and affirmed' (Woodward and George 1983, 125). A slightly revised form of this section became section 35(1) of the Constitution Act, 1982. The significance of this section cannot be underestimated. As expressed in the 1993 Royal Commission on Aboriginal Peoples:

> In effect, section 35 serves to confirm and entrench the status of Aboriginal peoples as original partners in Confederation ... [S]ection 35 not only entrenches the particular rights of these communities, it also reaffirms and guarantees their status as distinct constitutional entities ... [And that i]n the Peacemaker's vision the Tree of Peace extended beyond the Five Nations and potentially included the whole of humanity. In a way, Canada can be seen as a partial and imperfect realization of this ideal, as a multinational Confederation of peoples and communities united in peace and fellowship. (Canada 1993, 29–31)

As a result of these constitutional changes, Aboriginal peoples are part of a process by which Canada forges a new notion of statehood out of its constituent nations, allowing different peoples to coexist within a single state using sui generis solutions.

The pursuit of international lobbying activities by Aboriginal peoples both in Britain and at the United Nations was given support by the events of 1979. Although the Westminster lobby of that year was unsuccessful in stopping the repatriation of Canada's constitution, it did remind the Canadian federal government and Aboriginal leaders that international pressure could be brought to bear on Canada to effect political change. As with the Red Paper, the constitutional repatriation process and Aboriginal participation in overseas lobby activities served to redirect the way in which the federal government gained access to Aboriginal perspectives on its policies and laws.[7]

Before the 1970s Aboriginal peoples were rarely successful in using international pressure to effect change in Canada. Since the mid-1970s their role as a lobbying force at the United Nations has increased, and various successful protests have been launched by Canadian Aboriginal groups in the international setting. In 1990, for example, the James Bay Cree successfully fought for the cancellation of further hydro development in their territory by lobbying for acknowledgment of their rights in New York State. Rather than working through established governmental communication channels, Aboriginal leaders have pioneered new pathways through the state bureaucracies to ensure that their voices are heard.

Aboriginal Governments

In addition to broadening the rights discourse in Canada and opening new communication channels in Canada's political process, Aboriginal leaders have successfully expanded and diversified the Canadian conceptions of *government*. The White Paper/Red Paper dialogue of 1969–70 emphasized the significance of Aboriginal and treaty rights and initiated a broader movement towards changing relations between the Canadian state and its Indigenous peoples.

As the Royal Commission on Aboriginal Peoples has shown, the federal government has been preoccupied with discussions about Aboriginal governments since 1969, which expanded greatly to include 'more participants, processes, and ideas' in the 1990s (Graham, Dittburner, and Abele 1996, 156). As a result of that reaffirmation of Aboriginal rights through the constitutional process, Canadian governments began the slow task of accommodating those rights into existing governmental structures. Today this process is ongoing and by no means complete; however, power-sharing with Aboriginal communities is now a reality for all divisions of Canadian government.

The first step in the expansion of the Canadian definitions of governments began with the Nisga'a Nation's claim to its ancestral territories in British Columbia. The Supreme Court of Canada's decision in the *Calder* case (1973) found that Aboriginal rights to land (Aboriginal title) did exist in law. This significant case openly challenged the notion that Aboriginal land rights had been extinguished. A momentous decision in Canadian history, the ruling spurred the federal government to reformulate its land-claims policy and establish an Office of Native Claims in 1974 to deal with outstanding Aboriginal land-claim issues in Canada and begin to consider the nature of Aboriginal governance. The land-claims process marked the start of Aboriginal negotiations with Canadian governments regarding new land bases and governance powers for Aboriginal communities in many areas of Canada. Although Aboriginal leaders emphasize that the right to self-govern has always existed, it was not until after the White Paper–Red Paper exchange that the federal government began to engage in this discussion, if only minimally at first.

Today there exist many examples of Aboriginal governments emerging out of land-claims agreements. The James Bay Cree of northern Quebec, for example, completed the first comprehensive-land-claim agreement in 1975 and established a new form of government for themselves through the James Bay and Northern Quebec Agreement and the Cree-Naskapi (of Quebec) Act, legislation dealing with their community governance. In subsequent comprehensive-land-claim settlements throughout Canada the federal and provincial governments have gradually devolved many powers to Aboriginal communities. To date, agreements relating to land and self-governance have been concluded with Aboriginal communities as follows: Northeastern Quebec Agreement (1978), Inuvialuit Agreement (1984), Gwich'in Agreement (1992), Nunavut Land Claims Agreement (1993), Sahtu Dene and Metis Agreement (1994), Nisga'a Agreement (2000), Tlicho Agreement (2005), and Labrador Inuit Agreement (2005). Some agreements have also been negotiated by groups of Aboriginal communities sharing common interests in land and governance, such as the Yukon First Nation Final Agreements based on the Umbrella Final Agreement concluded with eleven Yukon First Nations in 1993. Although these agreements represent the efforts of many Aboriginal communities to regain varying degrees of control over governance, many communities – especially in British Columbia – continue to negotiate within, or challenge, the self-government negotiations process. The governments resulting from these land-claims and self-governance agreements have been supported by subsequent legislation and then set to work within the existing Canadian system. A closer look at the agreements, however, reveals the varying forms that new Aboriginal-controlled governments can take. Each negotiated self-government agreement changes the face of power-sharing in the Canadian state.

Since the creation of the Office of Native Claims, negotiations between various federal and provincial governments and Aboriginal peoples have expanded the definition of self-government to include more powers and to define this as an Aboriginal right. Significant steps along this path have included not only the conclusion of self-government agreements through land claims but also the recognition of self-government rights for Aboriginal peoples, which have stemmed from special committee investigations launched by the federal government, public affirmation of Aboriginal self-government in a national referendum in 1992, and the recognition of self-government as an Aboriginal right by the Supreme Court in 1997.

Internally, the Canadian federal government has also initiated investigations to broaden the understanding of Aboriginal governance issues. Two significant investigations were carried out in the 1980s and 1990s. The first, a Special Committee on Indian Self-Government was launched in 1982 and reported in 1983, followed by the larger Royal Commission on Aboriginal Peoples, which reported in 1996. Both investigations brought forward new understandings of Aboriginal governance and the place of Aboriginal governments within the Canadian nation state. Although neither of these initiatives represented a distinct Aboriginal perspective on the question of self-government, each contributed to new understandings of self-government, and both benefited from significant Aboriginal input. The ideas promoted by these two investigations also became codified in the (then Liberal) federal government policy on Aboriginal self-government in 1995 and 1999 respectively.

The work of the Special Committee on Indian Self-Government, headed by Mr Keith Penner, was launched in 1982, and its findings were published in 1983. Limited to investigating self-government for registered Indian people only (not general Aboriginal self-government), the committee received assistance from Aboriginal organizations including the Assembly of First Nations, the Native Women's Association of Canada, and the Native Council of Canada. It also canvassed testimony at public hearings with Indian governments. The Penner report served, in the eyes of some scholars, as constituting a fundamental 'paradigm shift' for Parliament. In its conclusion it recommended the 'recognition of Indian self-government' and 'that the right of Indian peoples to self-government be explicitly stated and entrenched in the Constitution of Canada ... Indian governments would form a distinct order of government in Canada, with their jurisdiction defined' (Canada 1983, 141).[8] With these words, the conclusion of the Penner report hints that Canadians were beginning to assimilate the idea of Aboriginal governments.

The Royal Commission on Aboriginal Peoples offers similar examples of self-government ideals being expressed in federal reports. The commission represents one of the most extensive investigations into the position of Aboriginal peoples in Canada ever undertaken by a federal government. Co-chaired by the well-respected Dene leader Georges Erasmus, it produced voluminous reports containing many significant insights into Aboriginal issues and perspectives. The final report in 1996 included many recommendations, and among those were a number relating to Aboriginal governance. The final report of the Royal Commission on Aboriginal Peoples recommended the passage of an 'Aboriginal Parliament Act, to establish a body to represent Aboriginal peoples within federal governing institutions and advise Parliament on matters affecting Aboriginal people,' as well as other changes to other governing bodies in Canada, in support of increasing Aboriginal presence within those bodies (Canada 1996, under 'How to Begin'). As with the Penner report, the federal government found itself confronted with its own members seeking recognition for Aboriginal governments.

Although neither of these reports has been explicitly acted upon, they have served to entrench the validity of new styles of government into Canada's political discussions as well as to normalize the notion of Aboriginal governance. Proof of that entrenchment lies in the fact that when Canadians were asked to vote on the acceptance of a new package of constitutional amendments known as the Charlottetown Accord in the 1992 national referendum – including amendments that would allow for the creation of a third order of government in Canada, Aboriginal government – Canadians rejected such ideas only by a narrow margin of approximately 54 per cent. Despite the rejection of the Charlottetown Accord, negotiations and conversations within governments about Aboriginal government continue.

The entrenchment of the notion that Aboriginal governments work within the Canadian political system is further evidenced in the Liberal policy evolution of the late 1990s. In 1995 and 1999 the Liberals adopted key policy principles including 'recognizing the inherent right of self-government' and their commitment to 'implement it without reopening constitutional discussions' (Wherrett 1999, 7). As the governing party of the 1990s the Liberals reflected an important aspect of Canadian political development with this policy position.

Finally, another recent contribution to the rethinking of Canada and its governments came through the Supreme Court of Canada ruling on the *Delgamuukw* case in 1997. A case resulting from the Gitksan and Wet'suwet'en

First Nations claims to land in northeastern British Columbia, the *Delga-muukw* ruling opened the door for further discussion and definition of Aboriginal self-government as an Aboriginal right. Although the justices involved in the ruling did not comment directly on the scope or the content of Aboriginal self-government, they did acknowledge the existence of those rights. Ongoing and future cases continue to refine and redefine the nature of Aboriginal self-government as an Aboriginal right.

Today, the carefully and intensely negotiated land-claim and self-government agreements with Aboriginal peoples represent the interface where significant change is occurring with regard to the implementation of ideas related to Aboriginal governance, the recognition of diversity in Canada, and the contribution of Aboriginal peoples to the changing nature of Canadian politics. Court rulings and federal reports play a more supportive role.

Conclusion

The process of consultation and negotiation that was initiated by the White Paper/Red Paper exchange remains with Canada up to the present day. Aboriginal peoples' drive to have their unique histories and rights recognized has contributed directly to the understanding and recognition of diversity in Canada. The process of recognition initiated by the White Paper/ Red Paper is now expressed through the renegotiation of powers and the recognition of the power of Aboriginal peoples in land-claims negotiations, in policy formation, and in the courts. The White Paper/Red Paper history also lives on in the new pathways forged by Aboriginal leaders in Canada's political system and by the now-accepted notion of 'special' rights that is entrenched in Canada's constitution and embodied by Aboriginal governments. The idea of governance is now conceptualized in Canada based on ideas of heritage and community, rather than geographic location. Finally, as a result of the changes initiated by the participation of Aboriginal peoples in the late-twentieth-century Canadian political conversation, current Canadian governments also regularly deal with collective rights, as opposed to individual rights, when working with all their constituents. This change is directly related to the recognition of Aboriginal rights in Canada as collective or community rights.[9]

Of course, the journey is far from complete. Aboriginal leaders are quick to point out that Aboriginal governments are still not recognized as sovereign and that Canada still has a long way to go when it comes to recognizing Aboriginal and treaty rights. In the words of Harold Cardinal in 1999, 'much has changed, but much more remains the same' (xvii). Yet he concedes that 'there has been a time of transition ... Unheard of in the Canadian/First Nation dialogue of 1969, the dialogue of today is about how First Nation governments can be accommodated as a constitutional third order of government in Canada. This shift is in large part a result of the efforts put forth by the Aboriginal leadership of Canada and is reflective of the institutional and organizational changes which have occurred in Indian country' (Cardinal 1999, xx). New types of governments are emerging in Canada, and these governments are representing specific minority populations, their languages, their cultures, and their histories. Change is occurring slowly; much like at the end of a long Canadian winter, the snow is melting even if it is sometimes difficult to see.

Notes

1 In his work *Citizens Plus: Aboriginal Peoples and the Canadian State*, Alan Cairns notes from the Royal Commission on Aboriginal Peoples that 'since the White Paper, constitutional thought has progressively departed from the assumptions of past governments. The premise is now that there will be a permanent Aboriginal presence in Canada' (2000, 70). This supports the notion that 1969–70 represented a turning point in Canadian political history. Yet, the philosophical foundations of the Red Paper, and its impact, are only cursorily addressed.

2 Works dealing with Aboriginal political leaders, their political philosophies, and their biographies are disparate. Many are memoirs or popular biographies. More recently academic analyses of Aboriginal epistemologies and how these relate to political culture are emerging. Related works include Jean Goodwill and Norma Sluman, *John Tootoosis* (1984); Alan Morley, *Roar of the Breakers: A Biography of Peter Kelly* (1967); Herbert Francis Dunlop, *Andy Paull: As I Knew and Understood His Times* (1989); James Spradley, ed., *Guests Never Leave Hungry: The Autobiography of James Sewid, a Kwakiutl Indian* (1972); Waubageshig, ed., *The Only Good Indian: Essays by Canadian Indians* (1970); Joseph F. Dion, *My Tribe the Crees* (1979); George Manuel and Michael Posluns, *The Fourth World: An Indian Reality* (1974); and Gary Botting, *Chief Smallboy: In Pursuit of Freedom* (2005). These works represent a small selection of writing on or by Aboriginal leaders. Examples of works related to political philosophy, or understandings of law and culture, include Antonia Mills, *Eagle Down Is Our Law: Witsuwit'en Law, Feasts, and Land Claims* (1996); Diane Knight, *The Seven Fires: Teachings of the Bear Clan as Told by Dr. Danny Musqua* (2001); E. Richard Atleo, *Tsawalk: A Nuu-chah-nulth Worldview* (2005); George Blondin, *Trail of the Spirit: The Mysteries of Medicine Power Revealed* (2006).

3 For example, established works relating to the history of Indian policy and law include J. Rick Ponting and Roger Gibbins, *Out of Irrelevance* (1980); J. Rick

Ponting, *Arduous Journey: Canadian Indians and Decolonization* (1986); James Roger Miller, *Skyscrapers Hide the Heavens* (1989); Bruce Clark, *Native Liberty Crown Sovereignty* (1990); James Roger Miller, *Sweet Promises: A Reader on Indian-White Relations in Canada* (1991); Katherine Graham, Carolyn Dittburner, and Frances Abele, *Soliloquy and Dialogue: Overview of Major Trends in Public Policy Relating to Aboriginal Peoples, 1965–1992, Volume 1* (1996). More recent works dealing with Indian policy and related law, including Aboriginal perspectives in the subject area, comprise John Borrows, *Recovering Canada: The Resurgence of Indigenous Law* (2002); Patrick Macklem, *Indigenous Difference and the Constitution of Canada* (2001); Taiaiake Alfred, *Peace, Power, Righteousness: An Indigenous Manifesto* (1999); Alan Cairns, *Citizens Plus: Aboriginal Peoples and the Canadian State* (2000).

4 The most comprehensive analysis of the White Paper comes from Sally Weaver, *The Making of Canadian Indian Policy* (1981). Harold Cardinal provides an Aboriginal perspective on the White Paper in his book *The Unjust Society* (1999), as does William Wuttunee, *Ruffled Feathers* (1971). The Red Paper and White Paper are discussed superficially in most introductory texts dealing with First Nations in Canada.

5 As Woodward and George point out regarding the 1979 Aboriginal lobby in London, 'the emergence of Indians as political actors of the highest caliber, on a national and international level, illustrated by the London campaign, will have repercussions … [T]he overall results of the Indian lobby in Westminster remain a tremendously enhanced political role for Indians and a remarkable effect on political consciousness' (1983, 140).

6 See Graham, Dittburner, and Abele (1996, 82–4). Graham, Dittburner, and Abele give the example that the Union of British Columbia Indian Chiefs, the Native Council of Canada (representing Métis and non-status peoples), and Métis Association of the Northwest Territories had all issued documents that bore relevance to the discussion of Aboriginal rights and the constitutional repatriation.

7 Ponting writes, 'Through intensive political lobbying on constitutional matters native organizations have made significant progress in educating provincial and federal bureaucrats and political leaders as to the present need for that self-determination, the historical precedents for it, and the prospective benefits it offers for the future' (1986, 406).

8 Ponting refers to the Penner report as marking a 'paradigm shift,' in *Arduous Journey* (1986, 402).

9 The value versus the danger of entertaining notions of separate rights for Aboriginal peoples is debated in Alan Cairns' *Citizens Plus* (2000), Patrick Macklem's *Indigenous Difference and the Constitution of Canada* (2001), and Michael Ignatieff's *The Rights Revolution* (2000).

Bibliography

Alaska Native Claims Settlement Act, Public Law 92-203, *U.S. Statutes at Large* 85 (1971): 689, codified as U.S. Code 43, 1601 et seq. as amended.

Alfred, Taiaiake. 1999. *Peace, Power, Righteousness: An Indigenous Manifesto*. Toronto: Oxford University Press.

Atleo, Richard. 2005. *Tsawalk: A Nuu-chah-nulth Worldview*. Vancouver: UBC Press.

Blondin, George. 2006. *Trail of the Spirit: The Mysteries of Medicine Power Revealed*. Edmonton, AB: NeWest Press.

Borrows, John. 2002. *Recovering Canada: The Resurgence of Indigenous Law*. Toronto: University of Toronto Press.

Botting, Gary. 2005. *Chief Smallboy: In Pursuit of Freedom*. Calgary, AB: Fifth House.

Cairns, Alan. 2000. *Citizens Plus: Aboriginal Peoples and the Canadian State*. Vancouver: UBC Press.

Calder v. Attorney-General of British Columbia (1973), 34 D.L.R. (3d) 145.

Canada. 1969. Department of Indian Affairs and Northern Development. *Statement of the Government of Canada on Indian policy*. Ottawa: Queen's Printer.

– 1983. Parliament. House of Commons. *Special Committee on Indian Self-Government: Second Report*. Ottawa: Queen's Printer.

– 1993. Royal Commission on Aboriginal Peoples. *Partners in Confederation: Aboriginal Peoples, Self-Government and the Constitution*. Ottawa: Minister of Supply and Services Canada.

– 1996. Royal Commission on Aboriginal Peoples. *People to People, Nation to Nation: Highlights from the Report of the Royal Commission on Aboriginal Peoples*. Ottawa: Minister of Supply and Services. http://www.ainc-inac.gc.ca/ap/pubs/rpt/rpt-eng.asp#chp4/.

Cardinal, Harold. 1977. *The Rebirth of Canada's Indians*. Edmonton, AB: Hurtig.

– 1999. *The Unjust Society*. Vancouver: Douglas and McIntyre.

Clark, Bruce. 1990. *Native Liberty, Crown Sovereignty*. Montreal: McGill-Queen's University Press.

Dion, Joseph F. 1979. *My Tribe the Crees*. Calgary, AB: Glenbow Alberta Institute.

Dobbin, Murray. 1991. *Preston Manning and the Reform Party*. Toronto: James Lorimer.

Dunlop, Herbert Francis. 1989. *Andy Paull: As I Knew Him and Understood His Times*. Vancouver: Order of the OMI of St Paul's Province.

Goodwill, Jean, and Norma Sluman. 1984. *John Tootoosis*. Winnipeg: Pemmican Publications.

Graham, Katherine, Carolyn Dittburner, and Frances Abele. 1996. *Soliloquy and Dialogue: Overview of Major Trends in Public Policy Relating to Aboriginal Peoples, 1965–1992, Volume 1*. Ottawa: Minister of Public Works and Government Services Canada.

Hawthorn, Harry Betram. 1966–7. *A Survey of the Contemporary Indians of Canada: Economic, Political, Educational Needs and Policies*. 2 vols. Ottawa: Queen's Printer.

Ignatieff, Michael. 2000. *The Rights Revolution*. Toronto: House of Anansi Press.

Indian Chiefs of Alberta. 1970. *Citizens Plus*. Edmonton, AB: Indian Association of Alberta.

Knight, Diane. 2001. *The Seven Fires: Teachings of the Bear Clan as Told by Dr. Danny Musqua*. Prince Albert, SK: Many Worlds Publishing.

Macklem, Patrick. 2001. *Indigenous Difference and the Constitution of Canada*. Toronto: University of Toronto Press, 2001.

Manuel, George, and Michael Posluns. 1974. *The Fourth World: An Indian Reality*. New York: Free Press.

Miller, James Rodger. 1989. *Skyscrapers Hide the Heavens*. Toronto: University of Toronto Press.

– 1991. *Sweet Promises: A Reader on Indian-White Relations in Canada*. Toronto: University of Toronto Press.

Mills, Antonia. 1996. *Eagle Down Is Our Law: Witsuwit'en Law, Feasts, and Land Claims*. Vancouver: UBC Press.

Morley, Alan. 1967. *Roar of the Breakers: A Biography of Peter Kelly*. Toronto: Ryerson Press.

Newhouse, David. 2004. Emerging from the shadows: The idea of Aboriginal government, 1969 to 2002. Draft of unpublished paper.

Ponting, J. Rick. 1986. *Arduous Journey: Canadian Indians and Decolonization*. Toronto: McClelland and Stewart.

Ponting, J. Rick, and Roger Gibbins. 1980. *Out of Irrelevance*. Toronto: Butterworths.

Price, Richard T. 1977. Indian land claims in Alberta: Politics and policy making, 1968–1977. Master's thesis, University of Alberta, Political Science Department.

Spradley, James, ed. 1972. *Guests Never Leave Hungry: The Autobiography of James Sewid, a Kwakiutl Indian*. Montreal: McGill-Queen's University Press.

Waubageshig, ed. 1970. *The Only Good Indian: Essays by Canadian Indians*. Toronto: New Press.

Weaver, Sally. 1981. *The Making of Canadian Indian Policy*. Toronto: University of Toronto Press.

Wherrett, Jill. 1999. Aboriginal self-government. *Current Issue Review*, 96-2E. Ottawa: Parliamentary Research Branch. http://www2.parl.gc.ca/content/lop/researchpublications/962-e.htm.

Woodward, Michael, and Bruce George. 1983. The Canadian Indian lobby of Westminster, 1979–1982. *Journal of Canadian Studies* 18 (3): 119–43.

Wuttunee, William. 1971. *Ruffled Feathers*. Calgary, AB: Bell Books.

Profile of Paul Okalik (1964–)

Inuit and Former Premier of Nunavut

Paul Okalik was the first premier of Nunavut. Not only was he the political leader of Canada's newest territory, but he played a powerful role in its creation. His focus over the years has been to find a balance whereby the issues that are central to Inuit concern can figure more prominently in the Canadian government's interests and issues.[1]

Okalik was the youngest of ten children born to Auyaluk Okalik and his wife on 26 May 1964 in Pangnirtung, Northwest Territories (now Nunavut).[2] He is part of the first wave of Inuit leaders who were not born to the traditional, nomadic way of life.[3] Despite a promising childhood setting, Okalik's teen years were fraught with struggle and tragedy. In Grade 10, after his older brother had committed suicide, Okalik was expelled from school for drinking.[4] Subsequently he was sentenced to a three-month prison term for a breaking-and-entering conviction.[5] Despite these difficulties he was able to turn his life around.

After high school Okalik enrolled in a welding course in Fort Smith, NWT, and secured employment at the Nanisivik Mine on Baffin Island. Soon, however, he became bored with the job.[6] It was not until the early 1980s, when he was offered a position as a researcher and negotiator with the Tunngavik Federation of Nunavut (an organization representing the Inuit in land-claim negotiations with the federal government), that his political aspirations took flight. He earned the respect of his colleagues as an effective negotiator,[7] and, as deputy chief negotiator, Okalik played a key role in the formation of Nunavut.[8]

His love of politics resulted in a decision to further his education. In 1995 he graduated from Carleton University with a bachelor of arts in political science. He continued his education at the University of Ottawa, where he obtained a bachelor of law in 1997.[9] Okalik returned to Iqaluit in the hopes of assisting his people with an educated political voice. He worked in the Iqaluit legal aid office from 1997 to 1999.[10] With his call to the bar in 1999

Paul Okalik.

he became the first Inuk lawyer in the Northwest Territories. Okalik later ran for political office. On 5 March 1999, after being elected as a member of the Nunavut legislative assembly, he was chosen by his colleagues to act as Nunavut's first premier. He fulfilled this role, viewing himself as a bridge between Inuit and non-Inuit citizens.[11] As premier, Okalik faced such daunting challenges as organizing and staffing the new government of Nunavut, promoting Nunavut's economy, and dealing with a variety of social problems.[12] Despite overwhelming odds, Okalik helped the new territory to thrive. While he was premier he established the Nunavut Heritage Trust, the Nunavut Implementation Training Committee, the Nunavut Social Development Council, and the Nunavut Wildlife Management Board.[13]

Paul Okalik served two terms as the premier of Nunavut until October 2008 when he was defeated in his bid for the premiership by the member of the legislative assembly for Iqaluit East, Eva Aariak. He continues to represent his riding of Iqaluit West as a member of the legislative assembly of Nunavut.

MONIQUE DESLAURIERS

Notes

1 Gurston Dacks, 'Okalik, Paul,' in *The Canadian Encyclopedia*, junior edition, http://www.thecanadianencyclopedia.com/index.cfm?PgNm=TCE&Params=A1ARTA0009636.
2 Wikipedia, 'Paul Okalik,' http://en.wikipedia.org/wiki/Paul_Okalik (accessed 27 January 2011).
3 John Geddes, 'Northern son: Paul Okalik has wrestled personal demons to the ground. Now, two years into his job as Premier of Nunavut, he is struggling with the troubles of Canada's newest territory,' *Maclean's,* 23 April 2003, 16.
4 Wikipedia, 'Paul Okalik.'
5 Ibid.
6 Geddes, 'Northern son,' 16.
7 Wikipedia, 'Paul Okalik.'
8 Dacks, 'Okalik, Paul.'
9 Wikipedia, 'Paul Okalik.'
10 Dacks, 'Okalik, Paul.'
11 Geddes, 'Northern son,' 16.
12 Dacks, 'Okalik, Paul.'
13 Ibid.

Profile of Susan Aglukark (1967–)

Inuk, Singer, and Songwriter

Susan Aglukark has been called a Northern Star, the Arctic Rose, and an Aboriginal artist. She is adamant that she not be referred to as '"Susan, the aboriginal artist" but as "Susan, the artist."'[1] Aglukark was born to David and Dorothy Aglukark in Churchill, Manitoba, on 27 January 1967. She was born the fourth of seven children.[2] Her parents moved frequently to accommodate their work as Pentecostal ministers.[3] Aglukark's entire family was musically inclined, with five of the children playing musical instruments.[4] Her parents and all of her siblings sang. Her involvement with music began with the church and youth groups,[5] and she began writing songs at the age of eleven.[6]

After completing high school, Aglukark moved to Ottawa, where she worked first as a linguist in the Department of Indian and Northern Affairs and later for the Inuit Tapirisat of Canada.[7] Her musical career took off shortly after she began working at the latter, but, at this point in her life, singing was not her primary life goal.[8]

Aglukark's clear warm voice touches listeners with sensitive message-laden songs, sung in English and in her native tongue, Inuktitut. Aglukark's unique music intertwines traditional Inuit chants with contemporary pop melodies. She embraces the time-honoured rituals and values of her Inuit forefathers, but does not shy away from the tough social realities of life in today's Far North.[9] She has recorded several albums, including *The Dreams of You Sessions* (1990), *Arctic Rose* (1992), *Christmas Album* (1993), *This Child* (1995), and *Unsung Heroes* (2000).[10] Aglukark's audiences have included such luminaries as Queen Elizabeth II and Canadian prime ministers Brian Mulroney and Jean Chrétien.[11]

Susan Aglukark has received many awards over the years for her music and her contributions to Canada. Her video for the song 'Searching' (1991) won her a MuchMusic award for outstanding cinematography.[12] In 1993 *Maclean's* magazine named Aglukark as one of 'Canada's 100 Leaders to

Susan Aglukark.

Watch For.' In the same year, *Up Here Magazine* named her Northerner of the Year.[13] In 1994 Aglukark won the first ever National Aboriginal Achievement Award for Arts and Entertainment.[14] She received the Canadian Country Music Association's Vista Rising Star Award in 1994. Her talent was recognized by the entire Canadian music industry when she received two Juno awards: one for New Solo Artist and the other for her recording *Arctic Rose*, which won in the Music of Aboriginal Canada Recording category.[15] Her recent albums include *Big Feeling* (2004) and *Blood Earth Red* (2006).[16] In 2004 she was awarded an honorary doctorate of fine arts from the University of Lethbridge, and in 2005 she was given an honorary doctorate from the University of Alberta. She was also named an Officer of the Order of Canada in 2005.[17]

Susan Aglukark believes that Aboriginal people do not have to force themselves or prove Native identity to the world. She believes that it happens naturally when individuals are given the choice. 'That's when our identity gives us that sense of pride. I personally feel that this is how young people want to be represented.'[18]

TABAN BEHIN

Notes

1 D. Howell, 'Inuk singer Susan Aglukark is honest, open and warm,' *Southam News*, 30 May 1995.
2 Jeff Bateman, 'Aglukark, Susan,' in *The Canadian Encyclopedia 2000 World Edition* (Toronto: McClelland and Stewart, 2000).
3 Brian Bergman, 'Susan Aglukark,' *Maclean's*, 13 February 1995.
4 Ibid.
5 Bateman, 'Aglukark, Susan.'
6 Howell, 'Inuk singer.'
7 Elizabeth Lumley, ed., 'Susan Aglukark,' in *Canadian Who's Who*, vol. 35 (Toronto: University of Toronto Press, 2000), 9.
8 R. Overall, 'Inuk singer Susan Aglukark shines like a … Northern Star,' *Ottawa Sun*, 27 February 1998.
9 'Aglukark, Susan,' in *The Canadian Encyclopedia* (Toronto: Historica Foundation of Canada, 2002).
10 Lumley, 'Susan Aglukark,' 9.
11 'Aglukark, Susan: Biography,' in *The Canadian Pop Encyclopedia*, http://jam. canoe.ca/Music/Pop_Encyclopedia/A/Aglukark_Susan.html.
12 'Aglukark, Susan,' in *The Canadian Encyclopedia*, http://www.thecanadianency-clopedia.com/index.cfm?PgNm=TCE&Params=u1ARTU0003989.
13 'Aglukark, Susan,' in *Canadian Pop Encyclopedia*.
14 Lumley, 'Susan Aglukark,' 9.
15 'Aglukark, Susan,' in *Canadian Encyclopedia* online.
16 http://www.susanaglukark.com/home.html (accessed April 2009).
17 Ibid.
18 Anika van Wyk, 'Close up and personal with Susan Aglukark,' *Sun Country Editor*, 5 July 1998.

Canada's Eyes and Ears in Northern Communities: Aboriginal Peoples in the Canadian Rangers

P. WHITNEY LACKENBAUER

> Mr. Speaker, for the past 50 years the Canadian Rangers have acted as guides and advisors to the Canadian Forces as well as performing search and rescue duties in northern remote and isolated communities often in harsh weather conditions. The majority of Canadian Rangers are aboriginal, often unilingual, who have served Canada for more than 50 years ... I congratulate all Canadian Rangers for their outstanding dedication, and on behalf of all Canadians, thank them for their work and contribution to our great country. *Mutna*. Thank you.
> – Nancy Karetak-Lindell, MP [Nunavut],
> to the House of Commons, 14 February 2000

The Canadian Rangers remain one of the least known elements in the Canadian Forces, despite their unique contribution to Canadian defence. Officially established as a component of the military reserves in 1947, the Rangers continue to serve as the military's 'eyes and ears' in isolated, remote, and coastal regions of this vast country. Aboriginal peoples make up more than half of the force's strength, and their service is an important, visible contribution to Canadian sovereignty and security. This overview introduces the history of Aboriginal peoples' participation in the Rangers since the Second World War and provides a brief analysis of recent activities and contributions. The partnership that underlies the Canadian Rangers allows this force to fulfil operational requirements that are vital to the Canadian Forces, and contributes to capacity building in Northern communities.

The Pacific Coast Militia Rangers

Little attention was devoted to domestic defence in the first four decades of the twentieth century. 'Canada is a fireproof house, far from inflammable materials,' Senator Raoul Dandurand proclaimed in the 1920s (Lackenbauer

2007, 34). Most shared his view until the Second World War. Following the Japanese surprise attack on Pearl Harbor in December 1941, the Canadian government faced increasing pressures from worried residents on the west coast, who cried out for protection from possible attack. Although a full-scale Japanese invasion was unlikely, the federal government had to find a way to create a military presence in remote and sparsely populated areas where it would be too expensive to station full-time soldiers. As a result, the Pacific Coast Militia Rangers (PCMR) was formed in August 1942. The Rangers would be voluntary 'citizen-soldiers' who would help to defend Canada while pursuing their ordinary jobs and lifestyles. Their explicit duties were to patrol their local area, to report any findings of a suspicious nature, and to fight using guerrilla tactics in the case of enemy invasion. At its peak the Pacific Coast Militia Rangers comprised 14,849 British Columbians – many of them trappers, loggers, and fishermen – in 126 companies located in isolated communities from the Queen Charlotte Islands to the American border.[1]

Given the demographic and geographical realities of British Columbia, Aboriginal peoples made 'natural' Rangers in the eyes of journalists. 'Indians, with knowledge of trails that are charted imperfectly,' the *Vancouver Sun* noted on 6 March 1942, were 'given a chance to do heroic work in defence of a province … impregnable against the yellow menace through intelligent, understanding manning of its contours and natural barriers.' During the war, journalists readily embraced opportunities to highlight Indian patriotism, holding this up as a model for all Canadians to emulate (Sheffield 2004). The Native Rangers were depicted accordingly. 'Indicative of the way the Indians are backing the war effort,' one journalist highlighted, 'was the 102-year-old Dog Creek Indian who offered his services as a guide or marksman and pointed back to a long, successful career as suitable qualifications.' He was made an Honorary Ranger for his sincere offer (Angus 1943). In general terms, the PCMR gave Aboriginal peoples a chance to serve in the defence of their communities, while continuing their daily employment and traditional activities.

The community-based nature of this wartime force makes it difficult to generalize on a province-wide level. Perhaps the best way to give a sense of what the Rangers meant to Aboriginal communities is by looking closely at one region in particular. The Nisga'a have lived in the Nass Valley on the northwest coast since time immemorial. Volunteers rallied to defend their villages against Japanese attack; after all, 'the Nass Valley is the closest part of the Canadian mainland to Japan and a long way from the cities to the south' (Boston 1996, 240). In this light, Nisga'a representatives approached the Indian agent at Prince Rupert in mid-1942 and told him that they wanted to be organized into a PCMR company. The agent began to organize the Rangers in several Nass Valley communities and found a great deal of enthusiasm (Kardex Collection 1942–3). In late February 1943, Ranger instructor Brendan Kennelly arrived by boat at Kincolith Bay. He was greeted by eighty Kitkatla Rangers from the local community, who were flying the Union Jack, as well as by a twenty-five-piece brass band and forty members of the Indian Women's Red Cross Society. The officer commanding the 'all-Indian' Ranger company, fisherman Arthur Nelson, marched the procession through 'the village to the sounds of martial music and the beating of drums.' The Nisga'a community was evidently patriotic and involved, with 'Indian chiefs of their respective districts' serving as Ranger officers. At the same time, these leaders were strongly against the government conscripting their young men (forcing them to join the military) for overseas service, claiming that 'they have shown their loyalty and that Queen Victoria told them they would never have to fight unless they wanted to.' This stated, the Aboriginal communities fully supported the defence of their homeland. 'All the Indians of these parts are strongly and enthusiastically … for the Ranger organization,' Kennelly reported. 'They see in it their opportunity to do their bit & to be prepared to help in home defence in country … and in terrain & surroundings with which they were familiar and in which they would be most useful.' Over thirty more Rangers joined up during his visit, bringing the strength of the Kincolith unit to more than two hundred people (Kardex Collection 1943a).

On 26 March 1943 the *Globe and Mail* reported to its national audience that BC coast Indians had formed two complete PCMR units. 'At Port Simpson and Kincolith … the members of two companies meet regularly to drill and study the tactics of modern war,' it explained. 'Fully aware of the role they will play if the Japanese attack the west coast and imbued with the spirit of their warrior forefathers, they take their training seriously.' Captain Kennelly reported that on one occasion 'several of the Indians travelled 52 miles on foot over the frozen surface of the Nass River to tidewater, then rowed eight miles to meet him.' The leaders of the Aiyansh, Greenville (Laxgalts'ap), and Canyon City (Gitwinksihlkw) Rangers were anxious to discuss guerilla tactics with the instructor, who 'pleased them by saying we advocated the Rangers train to fight like "Indians" and not like soldiers and they began to recall their forefathers' days of fighting with the Alaskan and outer island tribes (Kardex Collection 1943a; *Globe and Mail* 1943; Boston 1996, 63, 65). In due course the Rangers in the communities along the Nass River elected their own officers and non-commissioned officers by secret ballot, and the respective Indian councils and Indian agent approved these recommendations (Kardex Collection 1942, 1943b).

On the whole, Aboriginal peoples represented a minority of the enlistments in the entire PCMR, but they did make a vital contribution in several areas, particularly along the extensive – and vulnerable – Pacific coastline. They served as guides and scouts for soldiers on active service and shared their homeland expertise. When six Nisga'a Rangers attended the training school at Sardis, reports of their exceptional performance so impressed the commander of the army's mountain and jungle warfare school that he requested they serve as instructors for soldiers who came through to train (Kardex Collection 1944; Steeves 1990, 57). More typically, PCMR members from Aboriginal communities provided important operational intelligence to the military, reporting unusual activities and phenomena (such as Japanese bomb-carrying balloons) until the war's end in September 1945 (Kardex Collection 1945).

Thankfully there was no large-scale invasion of British Columbia during the Second World War. Nevertheless, the Rangers played an important role in reassuring their communities that they would be safe in case of attack and in providing other military units with intelligence on local areas and unusual occurrences. In the words of official historian C.P. Stacey, 'had there been any active operations on the coast, this force would certainly have played a useful part' (1955, 174). As the war in the Pacific drew to a close, the government decided to disband the PCMR. In peacetime they would reassess whether the need existed for a voluntary home defence force along similar lines.

The Canadian Rangers

Canadians hoped that the end of the war would bring a period of peace and international stability, but instead, the superpowers of the atomic age – the United States and the Soviet Union – became locked in a cold war. The federal government in Ottawa had hoped to avoid the costs and complications of maintaining a large military force in peacetime, but in the Cold War the Arctic took on greater importance than ever before. The Canadian North[2] was the likely front in a future war between the superpowers, and the Americans lobbied Ottawa to have access for defensive purposes. The Canadian government faced a dilemma: the country had to be defended from potential enemies, and if Canadians were not prepared to do so themselves, the Americans would do it anyway, thereby threatening Canadian sovereignty. Furthermore, the government did not want to pay large numbers of combat forces in the North, so they sought an inexpensive solution. As Kenneth Eyre explains, 'neither the United States nor Canada looked on the North as a *place* to be protected because of some intrinsic value. Rather it was a seen as a *direction*, an exposed flank' (Eyre 1987, 294).

The Canadian Rangers, a new force created in 1947, provided a feasible solution. It drew upon the tradition of the PCMR but was extended nationally rather than being limited to the Pacific coast. Like its predecessor, the Canadian Rangers comprised part-time, unpaid volunteers who carried out military duties on a daily basis alongside their civilian lives. Each armed with only a .303 rifle, one hundred rounds of ammunition each year, and an armband, they had – and have – as their official purpose the provision of a military presence in the northern, coastal, and isolated areas of Canada that are sparsely settled and cannot be covered conveniently or economically by other elements of the Canadian Armed Forces.

In peacetime the Rangers had several roles. They acted as guides for southern troops on exercises in their region, drawing upon their intimate knowledge of the local area. This was important, given that the regular airborne troops, who would be dropped into the North in case of invasion, would require guidance from people who actually knew the lay of the land. Furthermore, the Rangers prepared local defence schemes with police authorities to discover and apprehend enemy agents or saboteurs and to report other suspicious activities. As the Rangers, in their civilian jobs, were out on the land in their local areas on a daily basis, this detection role seemed logical. Furthermore, the Rangers could provide rescue parties for civilian and military purposes when required. In wartime their roles also included watching the coast and providing local defences against small enemy detachments or saboteurs (Hitsman 1960, 4–5).

Given the demographics of isolated and remote areas – particularly in the North – military officials contemplated the role for Aboriginal Canadians in the force. Opinions were mixed. Major-General Chris Vokes dismissed the Aboriginal population of northern Ontario as worthwhile contributors to Canadian defence. 'The population is for the most part Cree Indian, some with Scottish names and blue eyes who exist by trapping and guiding for goose and duck hunters in the Autumn.' His derogatory assessment drew upon prevailing stereotypes: 'They are most indolent and unreliable and born lazy. Hunger is the only motivating force, plus the propagation of their race, at which they are very adept … I doubt the value of these Indians in a paramilitary organization.' The tenor of the general officer commanding at Quebec headquarters was much more positive regarding potential Aboriginal contributions. He recognized that 'the Eskimos and Indians living in isolated communities were excellent marksmen and probably would use the annual 100-round allotment of ammunition (the only remuneration they received) for hunting seal and reindeer' (LAC 1948a). This would be perfectly acceptable, in his eyes, as these hunters would be out on the land honing their rifle skills while at the same time providing food for their communities. The integration of Aboriginal peoples into the Rangers, with their intimate knowledge of the land and northern survival skills, was a perceived benefit. This latter, more encouraging view prevailed over the long term.

To turn the Rangers from a concept into a functioning organization, with only a shoestring budget, took time and dedication. The military, with little presence in northern and isolated regions of the country – particularly north of the tree line – had to draw upon regional and local expertise to establish Ranger units across this vast area. Members of Royal Canadian Mounted Police (RCMP) detachments, Hudson's Bay Company factors, and missionaries helped to organize local platoons and often served as platoon and company commanders. These were the rare non-Native individuals who stayed in northern communities long enough to maintain stability in the organization, and the federal government still believed that only 'White' men made suitable Ranger commanders (Hitsman 1960, 6–7, 10, 13, 14, 16).

Ranger units, their ranks filled with northern Aboriginal peoples, began to spread across the Arctic in the late 1940s and 1950s.[3] In 1949, for example, an intelligence officer with the army's Western Command tagged along with a medical doctor from Indian Health Services and established Ranger platoons in the western Arctic at Coppermine (Kugluktuk), Bathurst Inlet, Cambridge Bay, King William Land, Read Island, Holman Island, Aklavik, and Norman Wells (LAC 1949–50). Similarly, the military authorized the formation of companies on Baffin Island in 1951 – senior officials in Ottawa responsible for Eskimo Affairs believed that Ranger service would also be good for the Inuit. One official stressed that the Inuit were 'reliable, honest and intelligent and would make good Rangers,' but he also wanted to make sure that rifles issued to them were not 'free handouts.' After all, a rifle was 'a major asset to an Eskimo and something he had to earn by hard work,' and bullets for hunting cost significant money (LAC 1951). To others, the weapon and ammunition provided to the Rangers was seen as a quid pro quo – the Rangers served their country, and this was the remuneration they received. 'Nobody has ever attempted to calculate, or could if one wanted to, the number of caribou, moose, and seal that fell to Ranger marksmen,' Kenneth Eyre noted (1981, 178). Undoubtedly, the number would be substantial.

By the early 1950s the Canadian Rangers organization had taken its basic shape, and several Ranger units began to participate in annual training exercises with full-time, professional soldiers. The Rangers 'easily outdistanced and outpaced the enemy' – a product of their knowledge of both the land

and the movement in their home environment – even if they had difficulty passing along accurate information (Hitsman 1960, 19–21; LAC 1948b). In February 1954, Exercise Loup Garou was held near Sept-Îles, Quebec, to test the military's airborne capabilities in winter. However, it was not the professional soldiers that captured the attention of journalists. The 'local Canadian Rangers outfit made up of Indians, woodsmen and trappers … are emerging as the heroes of this fast-paced Arctic exercise,' the *Ottawa Citizen* reported. The Rangers served as the local defence force against the Royal Canadian Regiment and used cover and concealment in the surrounding woods, which they knew intimately, to take out their 'enemy's' positions. 'During the night Col. Trudeau sent out probing patrols aided by Indian Rangers who played a key role – even if these night operations were somewhat "restricted" by the Indians' inability to read maps' (*Ottawa Citizen* 1954; Kardex Collection 1945–54). In numerous exercises the Rangers earned praise from army officers for their roles as guides and scouts (Taylor 1956). The cooperation was intimate, and mock exercises allowed both the regular force and the Ranger units to learn from one another.

There was no discussion of dismantling the Ranger program in the 1950s and 1960s. For very minimal cost the military had a permanent presence in the North, and the popular articles that appeared on the Rangers were laudable. In 1959 Larry Dignum told readers of the *Beaver* magazine that this 'Shadow Army of the North' quietly performed its valuable duties to defend Canada and maintain law and order in isolated areas. The Rangers' mystique was clear: 'When on duty they wear a scarlet armband with the three maple leaves of the Canadian Army superimposed on a crossed rifle and axe. They have no uniforms, receive no pay, seek no glory, but these men of known loyalty, Indian, Eskimo and white, take pride in standing on guard in the empty and remote parts of Canada with vigilance and integrity, and in silence' (Dignum 1959).

In contrast to Vokes's earlier pessimistic appraisal of potential Aboriginal contributions to the Rangers, the *Beaver* article and others highlighted the vital Indian and Inuit cooperation. 'Some of [the Rangers] can't read their own names but they are the real scholars of this country when it comes to reading signs on the trails of the north,' *Star Weekly Magazine* reported in 1956. 'Eskimos, Indians, whites and all the mixtures of these races, they are united in one task: Guarding a country that doesn't even know of their existence.' They were not only 'the least expensive military force any nation has today' but also a useful source of reports on suspicious activities, and critical guides for regular forces on exercises in the north (Taylor 1956, 2).

By the 1960s, however, the Rangers were left to 'wither on the vine' (Eyre 1987, 296). In an era of thermonuclear weapons, citizen-soldiers seemed obsolescent. How could an Inuk or Cree hunter, armed with a rifle and an armband, defend against a long-range Soviet bomber or intercontinental ballistic missile? Technological solutions, like the mid-Canada and the distant early warning (DEW) radar lines across the Canadian North and strategies of 'mutually assured destruction,' placed a higher priority on electronic detection and vast arsenals of nuclear warheads than on part-time ground forces. As a result, annual visits to resupply the Rangers and to provide minimal training became increasingly scarce, lost and damaged rifles were not replaced, individuals who left communities were not replaced on the nominal rolls, and most units became moribund (Eyre 1981, 180). Nevertheless, the Rangers did survive, simply because they cost little if anything to retain on paper, and they were largely self-administered on a local level. In Ottawa it was easier to ignore their continued existence than to bear the political burden of dismantling the force.

A New Focus on Sovereignty

At the onset of the 1970s the federal government under Pierre Trudeau found renewed interest in the Canadian North. In 1969 and 1971 an American supertanker, the *Manhattan*, transited the Northwest Passage to study the possibility of using this route to transport oil from Alaska to the eastern seaboard. Canada considered the Northwest Passage to be internal waters, but the United States did not agree and considered the passage an international strait. Understandably, officials in Ottawa became concerned about Canadian sovereignty and took symbolic steps to assert Canadian control and effective occupancy of the Arctic. The government gave primary importance in its defence policy to the surveillance of Canada's territory and coastlines and to the protection of sovereignty. Thus it created a northern region headquarters in Yellowknife. This headquarters was responsible for the largest military region in the world but had almost no operational units under its direct command – except the Rangers, who had been badly neglected and needed revitalization. Politicians and military officials in the North recommended upgrades to the Rangers 'so as to use [better] the talents and knowledge of northerners for surveillance purposes and to assist the military' (Kirton and Munton 1987; Canada 1971). Limited progress was made in getting several northern units back on their feet. The Rangers still seemed appropriate: its members lived in the North (and thus demonstrated Canadian occupation), could provide surveillance in their homeland at little cost, and protected sovereignty without being overly 'militaristic.' The United States – our closest friend and ally – posed the most immediate threat to Canadian sovereignty, yet it was absurd to envision a war with them.

Revitalizing the Rangers in the Far North also fit with a broader fed-eral government agenda to increase northern Aboriginal participation in Canadian society. Beginning in the 1970s the military launched initiatives to increase Aboriginal peoples' representation in the armed forces. 'He has his own culture but is the sort of man who could become Western very eas-ily, become one of us,' one officer wrote of the northern Aboriginal peoples whom the military sought to recruit. 'The ones we're looking for are mobile and have a self-navigating capability and roam a lot,' another added. 'They can take a trip of 800 or 1,000 miles and know exactly where they are … with no gear, maps, or charts' (Balfour 1971; Kardex Collection, n.d.). By official standards these efforts to recruit northerners for the regular military failed. Few had the required education, and even fewer completed basic training. Perhaps this was a good thing. As Kenneth Eyre aptly observed, to take the best educated young people out of their communities to serve in the armed forces ran against 'the developing set of Inuit priorities of that period.' They needed lawyers to pursue their land claims, politicians and businessmen to run their communities and cooperatives, and teachers to educate their chil-dren. 'Surely, in terms of the federal government's northern goal of meeting native peoples' aspirations these latter professions should have taken pre-cedence over military service that would have taken Eskimo soldiers out of the mainstream of Inuit life' (Eyre 1981, 289). Canadian Ranger service avoided this predicament. A northern Aboriginal person could remain in and serve his or her community, while at the same time serving as a Ranger.

When the Americans abandoned their oil transportation plans, the threat to Canadian sovereignty subsided, and Ottawa again lost interest in the Rangers. During the 1970s the promised commitment to expand the force proved more rhetorical than tangible (Canada 1973, 15–16). Neverthe-less, the Rangers visibly asserted sovereignty at minimal cost – important considerations at a time when the government was cutting back military spending and personnel. Patrols already spanned the breadth of the Arctic, from the most easterly patrol at Broughton Island to the most westerly at Aklavik, and represented every Aboriginal group in the North (though the majority of members were Inuit). The Northern Region briefing book trum-peted the Rangers' involvement, although it too appeared to be shrouded in ambiguity and platitudes:

> The role that Rangers have as a component of the Armed Forces is not well understood even within the Armed Forces [and] far less by the populace as a whole. Nevertheless, their contribution to the defence of Canada and mainte-nance of sovereignty should not be underestimated. Given the circumstances and environment, it is a role that could only be filled by other components of

A regular force instructor and Canadian Rangers in traditional dress read a map near Grise Fjord, 1988. Photo courtesy of Department of National Defence.

the Forces with very much difficulty and more expense. It is significant also that the Ranger concept capitalizes on those attributes of native northerners that they themselves espouse as their traditional way of life – their knowl- edge of their environment, their ability to live and survive on the land, their hunting instinct. In sharing an important defence commitment, the Canadian Rangers fulfill a role no less important than any other component of the Cana- dian Armed Forces, and have a justifiable pride in doing so. (Canada n.d. c, 16–18; n.d. b)

The Rangers' interactions with the military contributed to greater cross-cultural awareness and the sharing of skills. Training programs in remote communities generated additional Inuit interest in the Ranger program during the early 1970s. Yearly or biannual Nanook Ranger exer- cises trained individuals to basic Ranger standards, and annual ammuni- tion resupply visits provided more sustained contact between the military establishment and the Rangers than had existed for decades (Canada n.d.

b; 1971–2). Regular force units resumed training with the Rangers in the North, learned about Indigenous cultures and survival techniques, and stressed that the Rangers had taught them invaluable skills – even if they did have 'a non-military way of doing things. We must remember that the Rangers have a different culture [and] have worked under arctic conditions for many generations,' one infantry officer wrote, 'and in order to survive, we must be prepared to accept their advice and assistance.' He continued:

> The Ranger's sense of loyalty is very high and we found that they watched over our well-being. We also learned a great deal from the Rangers by watching them do maintenance on stoves, lanterns, and skidoos. Their methods are quite unorthodox; however, no one blew themselves up and the end result was that the piece of equipment was normally fixed in half the time it would have taken us.
>
> The [Inuit] were willing to share their food while on the trail. Several members of the course tried eating pieces of raw frozen caribou covered with hair. It was different, filling and not unlike beef jerky. Eating raw char however, did not sit well with any of the personnel. The [Inuit] version of bread (banik) was excellent. We ate over 50 pounds of it in five days. Several people even took some loaves home along with the recipe. The purpose of existing on the native diet was to prove to everyone that we could survive on what was available in the North. (Reumiller 1985)

The message was clear: Aboriginal Rangers had much to teach members of southern units, and the soldiers were there to learn.

In 1985 the voyage of another American vessel, the *Polar Sea*, through the Northwest Passage renewed concerns about Canadian sovereignty in the Arctic. External Affairs Minister Joe Clark's statement on sovereignty encapsulated the growing concern and linked it to the Northern peoples: 'Canada is an Arctic nation … Canada's sovereignty in the Arctic is indivisible. It embraces land, sea and ice … From time immemorial Canada's Inuit people have used and occupied the ice as they have used and occupied the land … Full sovereignty is vital to Canada's security. It is vital to the Inuit people. And it is vital to Canada's national identity' (Canada 1985a). Low-level-flying controversies, environmental concerns, and public appeals by Aboriginal leaders to 'demilitarize' the North in the 1980s ensured that discussions of security and sovereignty had to acknowledge their particular interests in their homelands. Georges Erasmus, the national chief of the Assembly of First Nations, saw 'no *military* threat' to the Canadian North but worried that a military build-up would jeopardize the cultural survival of Indigenous peoples. Mary Simon, president of the Inuit Circumpolar Conference, explained that traditional military activities 'often serve to promote our [Inuit] *insecurity*' and pushed the idea that they should cease in the Arctic (Erasmus 1986; Simon 1989).

It is important that the Canadian Rangers were never included in the arguments put forward about demilitarizing the Arctic. After all, most of the Rangers in that region were Inuit, and their activities were not a threat to the environment or to Aboriginal cultures. Instead, the Rangers represented inherent cooperation. Mark Gordon of Inuit Tapirisat of Canada stressed that the Inuit had 'a valuable contribution to give' to northern security, and praised the Canadian Rangers for acting as 'the eyes for the Armed Forces' and for providing 'valuable services to our communities, such as search and rescue,' as well as 'help[ing] our communities a great deal in providing us with food.' The Rangers, 'who in most instances are the most experienced and the best hunters of the communities and the most knowledgeable of the area surrounding their communities,' already represented a 'vehicle' for constructive dialogue and partnership (Canada 1985b, 48–9, 56–7). Rhoda Innuksuk of the Inuit Tapirisat also saw the Inuit and the military as joint partners who had much to contribute for mutual advantage through this 'innovative' program (Canada 1985b, 28, 50–1).

With strong backing from the Aboriginal community, the government indicated in 1987 that the Ranger program would be continued and enhanced. The minister of national defence deemed them 'an important expression of sovereignty,' and the Standing Committee on National Defence expected that by 1995 the strength of the Rangers in the North would rise to about one thousand (Canada 1987, 29–30; 1988). In fact, the expansion was even more rapid and profound. By 1992 they had already reached 1,362 in the region. In contrast to most of the other military projects promised by the federal government in 1987, which were subsequently cancelled when the Cold War ended in 1989, the Rangers continued to grow and flourish in this new context. Almost every community that could sustain a patrol in the Far North had one by the end of the century. Moreover, units were again formed in Labrador and Nunavik (northern Quebec), along Hudson and James Bays, and along the BC coast. The Rangers had re-emerged from the shadows to play an increasingly prominent and symbolic role in promoting sovereignty and security.

Current Status, Roles, and Activities

In 2009 there were more than 4,100 Rangers in 163 patrols across Canada, organized in five Canadian Ranger patrol groups (CRPGs). The largest

Location of Canadian Ranger patrols across Canada, 2001. Map by Jennifer Arthur.

patrol group, 1 CRPG, encompasses fifty-eight patrols in the Northwest Territories, Yukon, and Nunavut, with 1,575 Rangers. The 2 CRPG includes the
twenty-three Quebec patrols, totalling 696 Rangers. 3 CRPG covers the fifteen patrols in Ontario, numbering 422 Rangers. 4 CRPG encompasses thirty-eight patrols in British Columbia, Alberta, Saskatchewan, and Manitoba,
with 695 Rangers. Lastly, 5 CRPG includes the twenty-nine Ranger patrols
in Newfoundland and Labrador, with 743 Rangers. While official statistics
do not break down the membership along ethnic lines, more than 50 per
cent of all Rangers are of Aboriginal descent, and patrols are representative of northern Canada's ethno-cultural and linguistic diversity. North of
the tree line, for example, the vast majority of Rangers are Inuit, and many
speak Inuktitut as their first (and sometimes only) language. South of the
tree line, Rangers speak Dene, Cree, or Oji-Cree, and Montagnais, as well as
English and French (Canada 2009a).[4]

    The only formal entry criteria for men and women wishing to join the
Rangers stipulate that they be over eighteen years of age, Canadian citizens
or landed immigrants, in sufficiently good health to carry out their duties,
and willing to be members of the Canadian Forces. In 2002 the average age
of the 1,430 Rangers in 1 CPRG was thirty-nine – the youngest was eighteen and the oldest seventy-eight. Nearly 16 per cent of the Rangers in this
region were women, varying from 60 per cent in Tsiigehtchic, NWT, to less

Ranger Millie Hatogina inspects her .303 Lee Enfield rifle during weapons practice on Lake Aptalok, 70 km east of Kugluktuk, Nunavut. Photo courtesy of Department of National Defence.

than 10 per cent in several patrols. One Ranger had served since 1952, and several since the 1970s, but the median date of enrolment was 1996.[5]

The Rangers remain a unique component of the Canadian Forces. Their role is, first and foremost, to provide a military presence in northern, coastal, and isolated areas of Canada. Each Ranger patrol remains rooted in the local community and operates on a group basis. Patrol leaders are elected by the other members – they are the only military units in Canada that get to choose their commanders – and operate according to local customs and norms. In Inuit communities, for example, patrol sergeants defer to elders' advice and direction rather than following a rigid command hierarchy. The accommodation of Indigenous practices and leadership styles is one of the key reasons that this military force proves to be so successful and popular in northern communities.

The commander of Land Forces Central Area remarked in 1999 that the Rangers 'are a truly multi-purpose component of the military that handles a myriad of tasks and acts in a variety of capacities for the people of the North' (Canada 1999). In what is perhaps their primordial purpose, they make several important contributions to support Canadian sovereignty. As the 'eyes and ears' of the Canadian military in isolated areas, they report unusual activities and suspicious persons in their communities and areas. For example, they have frequently reported submarines operating off the Arctic coast – and even taken the occasional potshot at them (Pugliese 2002, A1)! As local experts, they also provide the military with important information to support military operations, such as advice on weather conditions. In the North, individual patrols conduct surveillance and sovereignty patrols (SOVPATs) designed to 'show the flag' around patrol communities. About thirty of these patrols are conducted each year and provide a cost-effective, visible assertion of Canadian sovereignty in the North. Most important, they are run by a Ranger patrol without any outside Canadian Forces presence. More recently, the 1 CRPG Rangers have undertaken an annual enhanced SOVPAT, a long-range patrol in the Far North to a remote part of their area of responsibility to show the flag. For example, thirty-four Rangers ventured to the north magnetic pole in April 2002, and twenty Rangers and regular force soldiers set out on a gruelling 1,300-kilometre trek to the remote northern tip of Ellesmere Island two years later. These long-range patrols have become increasingly ambitious, demonstrating that the Rangers have gone from providing a quiet presence in the North to a bold, symbolic one. Operation Nunalivut 2008 also demonstrated the ways in which the Rangers provide practical support to national activities. In this case, they guided, sheltered, and assisted scientists who were conducting research on Ellesmere Island ice shelves. These enhanced SOVPATs allow Rangers to operate in unfamiliar environments, share skills, develop relationships with other Rangers from across the North, and build confidence (Humphreys 2004, A1, A9; Canada 2003b, 21; 2008b).

The Rangers also continue to provide vital assistance to Canadian Forces activities. For example, their local expertise and advice is crucial to regular and reserve force units that come to train in the north. On sovereignty operations (SOVOPS) Rangers frequently act as guides and teach southern-based units practical survival skills, such as how to hunt and skin animals or build a snow house, that are necessary to maintain a fighting capability in the region (Canada n.d. a; Couch 2000). 'It is an outstanding cultural exchange when that happens,' former 1 CRPG commanding officer Major Yves Laroche explained. 'We end up with better soldiers and better Rangers as a result of shared skills and knowledge' (Costen 2002). Ranger patrols near unmanned North Warning System sites and airfields also monitor the condition of these installations on a regular basis.

Over the last decade the Rangers' local assistance to search and rescue activities has attracted significant media attention and support. As a part of their training, Rangers learn warning procedures, wilderness first aid, crash-site security, communications, and navigation. In practice 'Canadian Rangers provide a range of specialized services to the peoples in their area,' the commander of the Northern Ontario Rangers explains, 'including humanitarian assistance, local search and rescue, rapid response for disaster situations, such as aircraft crashes, and support for evacuation in natural emergencies, such as forest fires and floods' (Canada 2008a). They act first and foremost as members of northern communities, seldom waiting for an official tasking before heading out to look for lost hunters, or helping communities cope with major disasters. On 1 January 1999, for example, members from eleven of the Ranger patrols in Nunavik responded immediately to news of a massive avalanche in Kangiqsualujjuaq. For days they made vital contributions by supporting local authorities in rescue efforts, securing the area, and assisting with funeral preparations. Additional support was provided by patrols that were as far away as Coral Harbour (nearly one thousand kilometres to the west), where Rangers harvested and shipped fresh caribou to the disaster site. The head of the Canadian Forces testified: 'Without their dedication, the toll in human suffering would surely have been higher … The leadership and moral support the Rangers provided in the face of this crisis was invaluable' (George 1999). For this extraordinary effort, 2 CRPG was awarded a Canadian Forces unit commendation – the highest honour accorded to a military unit (Canada 2000b).

In these roles the Rangers provide an important outlet for Aboriginal peoples wishing to serve in the defence of their country without leaving their communities. Ranger activities also allow members of Aboriginal communities to practise and share traditional skills, such as living off the land, not only with people from outside their cultures but also across generations within them. These skills are central to Aboriginal identities, and there is a persistent worry that these will be lost. 'Often traditions are no longer passed on to the next generation in the North,' a thirty-one-year-old Ranger sergeant, Levi Barnabas, in northern Baffin Island explained. 'Until I joined the Rangers five years ago, I could barely build an igloo' (*Ranger Report* 1997). It is the unique nature of the Rangers that facilitates the transfer of Indigenous knowledge among members of a patrol and thus aids the overall retention of traditional knowledge within communities and cultures. In turn, the unique knowledge of northern peoples is integral to military operations. It is this partnership, rooted in mutual learning and sharing, that has made the Rangers a long-term success on the local and national levels.

This partnership was extended to future generations when the Junior Canadian Rangers were established in 1996. The cadets had enjoyed a long

The Junior Canadian Rangers Program, a partnership between the federal government, northern communities, and Canadian Rangers, facilitates the transgenerational transfer of traditional skill and knowledge. Photo courtesy of Department of National Defence.

history in the North, but many Aboriginal communities could not meet the formal requirements of the cadet program. As a result, the Junior Canadian Rangers was conceived to provide a structured, community-based program for youth in remote and isolated communities. It was planned that the federal government would provide financial resources and instructors, but the local community – represented through the Ranger patrol and an adult committee – would determine more than half of what the Junior Rangers would be taught. The community would select the traditional and life skills to be taught to their youth, allowing the curriculum of the Junior Canadian Rangers to 'incorporate the diverse cultural and natural attributes of the North, cultural norms, local language, and particular social needs.' Traditional skills would include activities such as 'making shelters, hunting, fishing, living off the land, using sleds, Native spirituality, singing, dancing, and talk circles with elders.' Through life skills, youth would learn about healthy living, sexual and substance abuse, community responsibilities, and public speaking. Another component dealt with Ranger skills such as first aid, navigation, and weapon safety (Canada 1998a). The program proved extremely popular and has expanded rapidly throughout northern

Canadian Rangers at the magnetic North Pole, Operation Kigliqaqvik Ranger I, 2002. Photo courtesy of Julian Tomlinson.

Canada, particularly in Aboriginal communities. There are now 119 Junior Canadian Ranger patrols across the country, with more than 3,400 youth participating (Canada 2009b).[6]

Conclusion

The Canadian Rangers program represents a practical solution to Canada's rich cultural diversity. By accommodating multiple identities, it allows Aboriginal peoples to represent both their peoples and Canada simultaneously; they serve their country and their communities. For example, when Inuit members of the Rangers in Nunavut set out on exercises, they do so as Nunavummiut, as members of their local community, and as representatives of the Canadian Forces. Communities and people who would strongly oppose other forms of military operations readily accept the Rangers and their activities. This is very important, as the Department of Foreign Affairs has succinctly explained:

> Demilitarization of the Arctic would make it more difficult, and perhaps even impossible, for our military personnel to provide defence services available

to Canadians in other parts of the country. The Canadian Forces, for example, would be unable to conduct operations to protect our sovereign territory … or to provide humanitarian assistance … Additionally, the cultural inter-play of service people serving in our North has an intangible benefit in promoting a sense of national awareness among the military and those northern residents who come in contact with the military. A military presence in the North also provides Canada's Aboriginal peoples with an opportunity to serve their country and community through participation in the Canadian Rangers. (Canada 1998b)

By virtue of their disparate locations, Canadian Ranger patrols are representative of Canada's geographical and cultural diversity, and their presence is an important contribution to the assertion of Canada's national interests in northern, isolated, and coastal communities.

Acknowledgments

The author would like to thank Jim Miller (Canada Research Chair in Native-Newcomer Relations, University of Saskatchewan), the Social Sciences and Humanities Research Council of Canada, and the Department of National Defence for financial support, which made this research possible.

Notes

1 For an overview of the Pacific Coast Militia Rangers see Steeves (1990) and Lackenbauer (2007).
2 The Canadian North can be defined in several ways. For the purposes of this chapter, it will refer to the Yukon, Northwest Territories, Nunavut, Nunavik (northern Quebec), and communities along Hudson and James Bays.
3 Ranger units along the west and east coasts, which were formed in this same era, tended to be non-Aboriginal in their composition and, therefore, will not be described in this chapter. My forthcoming book on the history of the Rangers will provide a fuller picture of the Canadian Rangers' development in these regions.
4 Statistics as of October 2008.
5 Statistics provided by 1 CRPG, April 2002 (Canada 2002b). The percentage of women in the Rangers in 2002 slightly exceeded that in the Canadian Forces as a whole, in which 11.9 per cent of Canadian Forces' serving members were female (Asmar 2002). One out of every three Rangers in 3 CRPG (Northern Ontario) is a woman (Canada 2003a, 2).

6 Statistics as of February 2009. Of the 734 Junior Rangers in 1 CRPG in 2002, 440 were young men (60 per cent) and 294 young women (40 per cent). Statistics provided by Major Claudia Ferland (Canada 2002a).

Bibliography

Angus, Marion J. 1943. The Rangers. *National Home Monthly* 30 (July): 6–7.

Asmar, Najwa. 2002. Women Rangers: A perfect fit. *The Maple Leaf* 5, no. 25.

Balfour, Clair. 1971. Armed Forces recruiting Indians and Eskimos to help establish sovereignty in the Arctic. *Globe and Mail*, 23 September, p. 3.

Boston, Thomas. 1996. *From Time Before Memory*. New Aiyansh, BC: School District No. 92 (Nisga'a).

Canada. 1971. Parliament. House of Commons. *Debates*. 21 May, p. 6065 (R.J. Orange).

– 1971–2. Department of National Defence. Untitled historical booklet, entries 31 July 1971, 17 November 1971, and 13 January 1972.

– 1973. Parliament. House of Commons. Standing Committee on External Affairs and National Defence. *Proceedings and Evidence*. 29 May (Cloutier and Admiral John A. Charles). Ottawa: The Committee.

– 1985a. Parliament. House of Commons. *Debates*, 10 September, p. 6462–4.

– 1985b. Parliament. House of Commons. Standing Committee on External Affairs and National Defence. *Proceedings and Evidence*. 17 September. Ottawa: The Committee.

– 1987. Parliament. House of Commons. Standing Committee on National Defence. *Proceedings and Evidence*, 26 November.

– 1988. Parliament. House of Commons. Standing Committee on National Defence. *The Reserves*. Report, June.

– 1998a. Department of National Defence. Backgrounder: The Junior Canadian Ranger programme. BG-98.034, 16 July. Also available online at http://www.forces.gc.ca/site/news-nouvelles/view-news-afficher-nouvelles-eng.asp?id=845.

– 1998b. Parliament. House of Commons. Government response to Standing Committee on Foreign Affairs and International Trade Report 'Canada and the circumpolar world: Meeting the challenges of cooperation into the twenty-first century.' Ottawa: Government of Canada. Also available online at http://www.international.gc.ca/polar-polaire/response-reponse.aspx?lang=en.

– 1999. Department of National Defence. Land Forces Central Area. Review of limitations on Reserve service by Canadian Forces annuitants – Canadian Rangers, 28 September, file 1110-7 (G1 Pers).

– 2000a. Department of National Defence. Backgrounder: The Canadian Rangers.

18 February. http://www.forces.gc.ca/site/news-nouvelles/view-news-afficher-nouvelles-eng.asp?id=49.

– 2000b. Hansard. Remarks by Nancy Karetak-Lindell to the House of Commons. 36th edited Hansard, no. 48. http://www2.parl.gc.ca/HousePublications/Publication.aspx?Pub=Hansard&Doc=48&Language=E&Mode=1&Parl=36&Ses=2 (accessed July 2009).

– 2002a. Department of National Defence. Statistics provided by Major Claudia Ferland, 24 January.

– 2002b. Department of National Defence. Army. Canadian Rangers Patrol Group. Statistics provided by 1 CRPG, April.

– 2003a. Department of National Defence. 3rd Canadian Ranger Patrol Group: Canada's soldiers in Ontario's Far North. Pamphlet.

– 2003b. Department of National Defence. Canadian Forces Northern Area Headquarters. Level 1 business plan: Fiscal year 2004/05, 27 October, 21.

– 2008a. Department of National Defence. Army. Joint Task Force Central. 3rd Canadian Ranger Patrol Group: The Canadian Ranger mission. http://www.army.forces.gc.ca/3crpg/eng/mission-eng.html.

– 2008b. Department of National Defence. Canadian Forces Northern Area Headquarters. Joint Task Force North. Operation Nunalivut 2008, news backgrounder, BG-08.002, 20 March (accessed online, April 2008).

– 2009a. Department of National Defence. Army. Canadian Rangers. Canadian Rangers Patrol Group (CPRG). http://www.army.forces.gc.ca/land-terre/cr-rc/crpg-gprc-eng.asp.

– 2009b. Department of National Defence. Canadian Forces. Junior Canadian Rangers: Overview. http://www.jcr-rjc.ca/ove-ape/index-eng.asp.

– n.d. a. Department of National Defence. Canadian Forces Northern Area Headquarters. Briefing, Gough.

– n.d. b. Department of National Defence. Canadian Forces Northern Area Headquarters. Public Affairs Office, file NA 1325-1.

– n.d. c. Department of National Defence. Canadian Forces Northern Region. Northern Region Information.

Costen, S. 2002. 1 Canadian Ranger Patrol Group. *The Maple Leaf* 5 (10): 14.

Couch, G.L. 2000. Northern exposure for southern soldiers. *The Maple Leaf* 3 (13): 6.

Dignum, Larry. 1959. Shadow army of the North. *The Beaver*, Autumn: 22–4.

Erasmus, Georges. 1986. Militarization of the North: Cultural survival threatened. *Information North*, Fall: 1.

Eyre, K. 1981. Custos borealis: The military in the Canadian North. PhD diss., King's College, University of London.

– 1987. Forty years of military activity in the Canadian North, 1947–87. *Arctic* 40 (4): 292–9.

George, Jane. 1999. Nunavik Rangers honoured in Montreal. *Nunatsiaq News* (Iqaluit), 30 November.

Globe and Mail. 1943. [?] 26 March.

Hitsman, J.M. 1960. The Canadian Rangers. DND Army Headquarters, Historical Section, report no. 92 (1 December). Ottawa: National Defence Headquarters, Director of History and Heritage.

Humphreys, Adrian. 2004. 'Brutal' North hits patrol hard. *National Post*, 14 April.

Kardex Collection. 1942. O'Grady to SO Rangers, 1 Nov. 1942, DHH, file 169.009 (D94). Ottawa: Department of National Defence, Directorate of History and Heritage.

– 1942–3. O'Grady to SO PCMR, 19 July 1942, and Gillett to Taylor, 8 Apr. 1943, file 169.009 (D77). Ottawa: Department of National Defence, Directorate of History and Heritage.

– 1943a. Kennelly to SO Rangers, 28 Feb. [1943], DHH, file 169.009 (D94). Ottawa: Department of National Defence, Directorate of History and Heritage.

– 1943b. D'Arcy to S.O.i/c, PCMR, 30 June 1943, DHH, file 169.009 (D77). Ottawa: Department of National Defence, Directorate of History and Heritage.

– 1944. Hendrie to HQ 6 Canadian Division, 30 Oct. 44, DHH, file 169.009 (D94). Ottawa: Department of National Defence, Directorate of History and Heritage.

– 1945. Levelton to S.O.i/c PCMR, 18 Jan. 1945, DHH, file 169.009 (D87). Ottawa: Department of National Defence, Directorate of History and Heritage.

– 1945–54. Lessons Learned: Winter Exercises, 1945–54, DHH, file 81/675. Ottawa: Department of National Defence, Directorate of History and Heritage.

– n.d. Recruiting of Eskimos and Indians, DHH, file 71/386. Ottawa: Department of National Defence, Directorate of History and Heritage.

Kirton, John, and Don Munton. Manhattan voyages. In *Politics of the Northwest Passage*, ed. F. Griffiths, 73–5. Kingston and Montreal: McGill-Queen's University Press.

Lackenbauer, P. Whitney. 2007. Guerrillas in our midst: The Pacific Coast Militia Rangers, 1942–45. *BC Studies*, no.155:31–67.

Library and Archives Canada Collection (LAC). 1948a. Communications from Dec, Record Group (RG) 24, accession 83-84/215, box 321, file 2001-1999/0 v.2. Ottawa: Library and Archives Canada.

– 1948b. Canadian Rangers Liaison Letter No 2 and other documents. RG 24, accession 83-84/215, vol. 321, file 2001-1999/0, pts.4–6. Ottawa: Library and Archives Canada.

– 1949–50. Major C.R.R. Douthwaite, Survey of Western Arctic by SGO II (Int), Western Command, 14 Apr.–1 May 1949, 25 Oct. 1950. RG 24, accession 83-84/215, box 399, file 9105-25/0. Ottawa: Library and Archives Canada.

– 1951. Major F.B. Perrott to DMO&P, 11 July 1951. RG 24, acc. 83-84/215, box 321, file 2001-1999/0 v.2. Ottawa: Library and Archives Canada.

Ottawa Citizen. 1954. Arctic exercise: Indians point the way. 22 February.

Pugliese, David. 2002. The X-Files come North: A mystery in Arctic waters; Inuit hunters, rangers say foreign submarines are scouting the North. *Ottawa Citizen,* 18 August.

Ranger Report. 1997. Vol. 3 (October 30): 13.

Reumiller, Captain E.F. 1985. Winter warfare instruction course 8401. *Infantry Journal* 13 (Spring).

Sheffield, R. Scott. 2004. *The red man's on the warpath: The image of the 'Indian' and the Second World War.* Vancouver: UBC Press.

Simon, Mary. 1989. Security, peace and the Native Peoples of the Arctic. In *The Arctic: Choices for Peace and Security,* ed. Thomas Berger, 31–6. West Vancouver, BC: Gordon Soules Book Publishers.

Stacey, C.P. 1955. *Six Years of War.* Ottawa: Queen's Printer.

Steeves, Kerry. 1990. The Pacific Coast Militia Rangers, 1942–1945. Master's thesis, University of British Columbia.

Taylor, Robert. 1956. Eyes and ears of the North. *Star Weekly Magazine.* 22 December, 2–3.

Profile of Rosemarie Esther Kuptana (1954–)

Inuk, Politician, Broadcaster, and Writer

Rosemarie Kuptana is admired by many people in political, telecommunications, and environmental organizations. Her parents, grandmother, and extended family instilled values that guide her as she seeks to promote and preserve Inuit culture. Kuptana's negotiation skills and perseverance serve her well in the fight to achieve Inuit self-determination and self-governance.

Rosemarie Kuptana was born to William Seymour and Sarah (née Keogotuk) Kuptana on 24 March 1954 in Sachs Harbour, a small community of about 120 people on the Beaufort Sea in the Northwest Territories.[1] She was raised in the traditional Inuit hunting culture and spoke only Inuvialuktun.[2] At eight years old she attended a government residential school in Inuvik, a community located four hundred miles from her home. Here Kuptana was urged to speak English and adopt a foreign way of life.[3] These early experiences set off her resistance to white Euro-Canadian culture and her involvement with Inuit community organizations.

In 1979 Kuptana joined the Northern branch of the Canadian Broadcasting Corporation. Her radio programs discussed relevant social, cultural, and political issues, including the Inuvialuit land claim and Aboriginal self-governance.[4] Oil and gas explorations situated in Alaska and the Northwest Territories were also a topic of concern because of the environmental impact on the Inuit way of life.[5] Kuptana's career expanded when she accepted a position with the Inuit Broadcasting Corporation (IBC). She soon became network production coordinator and, in 1983, was elected the IBC president.

Kuptana's passions are not confined to broadcasting. After leaving the IBC she became the vice-president of the Inuit Circumpolar Conference, which represents the Inuit people and their collective interests, and works to preserve their identity. Kuptana also participated in the negotiations that led to the establishment of the Arctic Council.[6]

From 1991 to 1997 Kuptana served as the president of the Inuit Tapirisat of Canada. Representing forty thousand Inuit, she participated in political

Rosemary Kuptana. Photo courtesy of Inuit Tapiriit Kanatami Archives.

and constitutional negotiations involving Aboriginal leaders and Canada's various federal and provincial first ministers.[7] She was a leader in initiating negotiations regarding Aboriginal self-government.[8] Kuptana, with the Canadian government team, negotiated amendments to the Migratory Bird Treaty with the U.S. government. One amendment led to constitutional recognition of Inuit hunting rights. She also helped develop an environmental research department that deals with issues ranging from global warming and climate change to contaminants in the Arctic.[9]

Rosemarie Kuptana has received numerous awards for her service in the protection of Inuit culture and rights, including the 1992 Inuit Circumpolar Conference Award for Human Rights, nomination to *Maclean's* 1994 Honour Roll, and a National Aboriginal Achievement Award.[10]

Kuptana continues to be active in the public sphere. For instance, she coordinated a study on self-governance for the Senate Standing Committee on Aboriginal Affairs. She has written a book about child abuse called *No More Secrets*.[11] Kuptana is engaged by the Canadian Museum of Nature as the executive assistant for traditional knowledge.[12] She continues to speak publicly on environmental, social, constitutional, and human rights issues[13] and is an inspiration to her three children and to the Inuit people.

JULIA ARNDT

Notes

1 Barry Pritzer, *Native America Today: A Guide to Community Politics and Culture* (California: ABC-CLIO, 1999).
2 Ibid.
3 Ibid.
4 Duane Champagne, 'Rosemarie Kuptana,' in *Reference Library of Native North America*, vol. 5 (Farmington Hills, MI: Gale Group. 2001).
5 Ibid.
6 Pritzer, *Native America Today*.
7 Champagne, 'Rosemarie Kuptana.'
8 Ibid.
9 Pritzer, *Native America Today*.
10 Champagne, 'Rosemarie Kuptana.'
11 Rosemarie Kuptana, *No More Secrets* (Ottawa: Pauktuutit, Inuit Women's Association, 1991).
12 International Institute for Sustainable Development, 'IISD Board of Directors,' http://www.iisd.org/about/board_bio.asp?bno=364 (accessed 15 July 2003).
13 Pritzer, *Native America Today*.

PART 5

ARTS AND CULTURE

Profile of Jaime (Robbie) Robertson (1943–)

Mohawk, Singer, and Songwriter

The world has benefited from and enjoyed the musical talent of Aboriginal Canadian Jaime (Robbie) Robertson for more than forty years. Through his work in rock and roll, soundtrack composition, and, most recently, Native American music, Robertson is recognized as one of the most respected contemporary musical figures in the world.

Robertson was born in 1943 in Toronto, Ontario, to a Jewish father and a Mohawk mother.[1] While growing up, Robertson would spend his summers with his mother's people at the Six Nations Reserve, where he developed his interest in music. At ten years old he was taught to play guitar by his cousin and other relatives.[2] As a teenager Robertson played in several bands in the Toronto area, including Robbie and the Robots, Thumper and the Trombones, and Little Caesar and the Consuls.[3] By the age of sixteen he had dropped out of school and begun to pursue a musical career.[4] Robertson signed on to play bass with transplanted Arkansas rocker Ronnie Hawkins and his band, the Hawks. Hawkins recorded two songs written by Robertson, 'Hey Boba Lu' and 'Someone Like You,' on his *Mr. Dynamo* album.[5]

After the demise of this incarnation of the Hawks, some members, including Robertson, formed The Band. While in The Band, Robertson continued songwriting, producing such classics as 'The Night They Drove Old Dixie Down,' 'Up on Cripple Creek,' 'Acadian Driftwood,' and 'The Weight.'[6] The Band's farewell concert in 1976 featured guest performances by an impressive group of performers, including Neil Young, Eric Clapton, Bob Dylan, Ringo Starr, Joni Mitchell, and Van Morrison. The concert was filmed by a young Martin Scorsese, who later released the documentary as *The Last Waltz*. The music from the concert formed the basis of a three-record set.[7] The Band was inducted into the Canadian Music Hall of Fame in 1989 and the Rock and Roll Hall of Fame in 1994.[8] Following his stint with The Band, Robertson focused his attention on film scores,

Robbie Robertson. Photo courtesy Fred Chartrand/Canadian Press.

becoming one of the first rock and roll artists to work on film sound-
tracks.[9] He wrote source and background music for several movies including *Carny* (1979), *Raging Bull* (1980), *King of Comedy* (1983), and *The Color of
Money* (1986).[10]

Up to this point in his career Robertson had not used his music to share
his Native heritage. But in 1994 Robertson composed the music for the
television documentary *Music for the Native Americans*. He embraced the
opportunity. By collaborating with the Red Road Ensemble, Robertson was
able to create a soundtrack described as 'gorgeous, unsettling and provocative.'[11] Robertson's 1998 album, *Contact from the Underworld of Red Boy*, dealt
exclusively with the Native North American experience and helped bring
about greater awareness of many Native issues. In making this album,
Robertson drew on the traditional drumming and singing of his Aboriginal ancestry, while incorporating European techno sounds, which resulted
in haunting and powerful songs.[12] In 2008 the *Winnipeg Sun* reported that
Robertson was working on a new album with Eric Clapton, and in a May
2010 *Mojo* magazine interview Robertson claimed that he was working on
an autobiography. In 1998 Robertson was awarded the Lifetime Achievement Award at the Native American Music Awards for making the music
industry accessible to Native Americans.[13] In his current role as creative
executive with DreamWorks Records, Robertson signs new musicians and
is able to seek out new Indigenous artists.[14] He continues to use his musical abilities, and performed at the opening ceremonies of the 2002 Winter
Olympics in Salt Lake City. In 2003 Robertson received an honorary doctorate from Queen's University in Kingston, Ontario, and a second from York
University in Toronto in 2005.

JENNIFER GRAINGER

Notes

1 Bruce E. Johansen and Donald A. Grinde Jr, eds., 'Robbie Robertson,' in *The
   Encyclopedia of Native American Biography: 600 Life Stories of Important People,
   from Powhatan to Wilma Mankiller* (New York: Henry Holt, 1997), 308.
2 Sharon Malinowski and Simon Glickman, eds., 'Robbie Robertson,' in *Native
   North American Biography* (New York: UXL, 1996), 308–10.
3 'Robbie Robertson,' in *Biographical Dictionary of Indians of the Americas* (Newport
   Beach, CA: American Indian Publishers, 1991), 618–19.
4 Ibid.
5 Ibid, 618.

6 Jeff Bateman, 'Jaime Robbie Robertson,' in *The Canadian Encyclopedia 2000 World Edition* (Toronto: McClelland and Stewart, 2000).
7 Johansen and Grinde, 'Robbie Robertson.'
8 Ibid.
9 Ibid.
10 Ibid.
11 Paul Evans, 'The year in recordings,' *Rolling Stone*, December 1994: 169.
12 David Fricke, 'Native son,' *Rolling Stone*, April 1998: 46.
13 'Robbie Robertson,' *Rock on the Net*, http://www.rockonthenet.com/artists-r/robbierobertson_main.htm.
14 Ibid.

Yesterday's Dream and Today's Reality: Aboriginal Centre of Winnipeg – Adapting to Urban Life in Canada

WILLIAM (BILL) SHEAD

Since the early 1900s, Canadians in ever-growing numbers have been abandoning the countryside to seek their fortune and create a future for themselves in southern urban centres. Canada's Aboriginal peoples, too, are playing an increasingly important and more obvious role in the urbanization of Canada. This is particularly true for major western urban centres such as Calgary, Edmonton, Regina, Saskatoon, Vancouver, and Winnipeg. Aboriginal people make up a significant proportion of the populations of these cities. They are generally among the fastest-growing population segments in Canada and in urban centres.

For more than four decades, governments have funded several initiatives to help Aboriginal people to adapt to urban life. In doing so, they have worked closely with those Aboriginal people who have taken the lead role in turning their own dreams for a new future in cities into realities. The 1993–6 conversion of Winnipeg's historic Canadian Pacific Railway station and office building into the Aboriginal Centre of Winnipeg is one of the best examples of a successful initiative undertaken by Aboriginal people to help their community members adapt to modern urban life. It stands out because of its size, the impact it has had on Winnipeg's development, the example it establishes, and the hope its success may offer to Aboriginal people in other urban centres. This chapter discusses the evolution of urban Aboriginal issues underlying the development of the Aboriginal Centre of Winnipeg and the centre's role in helping Aboriginal people to adapt to urban life.

What Is the Aboriginal Centre?

Before discussing these urban issues, it would be helpful to have a basic understanding of the concept of the Aboriginal Centre of Winnipeg, which grew from the nature of government-funded programs for Aboriginal people. Governments have funded a variety of programs and numerous Aboriginal organizations focusing on helping Aboriginal people to adapt to life in cities. However, one basic shortcoming of these initiatives was that the funding to rent program space was often arbitrary and usually inadequate. As a result, funded organizations were only able to rent 'as is' space that had less than suitable working environments and was often located in areas inappropriate for delivering their services. To obtain more suitable space, several Aboriginal organizations in Winnipeg began exploring ways in which they could cooperate and coordinate their efforts. They formed the Aboriginal Centre of Winnipeg, Inc. (ACWI) in October 1990 and purchased Winnipeg's historic Canadian Pacific Railway station on 15 December 1992.

The station is a structure of some 3,085 square metres (140,000 square feet) that, in the Canadian Pacific Railway's prime, accommodated about 1,500 CPR employees. It was developed into the Aboriginal Centre, as a one-stop client service centre. Here, a number of Aboriginal non-governmental organizations and government agencies now provide health, employment, literacy, education, training, and other business and social support services to Winnipeg's Aboriginal community. In the centre, their work and services focus on, and are coordinated to meet, the needs of Aboriginal people as they adapt to the challenges of life in the more complex society of a modern urban setting.

Genesis of Urban Aboriginal Issues

Canada may be described as containing vast, sparsely populated rural and remote areas and a few very large, densely populated and geographically compact urban communities concentrated in the south. Manitoba's unique demography evolved from the system of rivers and lakes that stemmed from the gigantic prehistoric Lake Agassiz formed by the retreating Laurentide Ice Sheet around 9,200 years ago. Geography has worked to concentrate the bulk of Manitoba's population to the south, although Aboriginal people initially established their homes along the province's waterways.

The Aboriginal Centre's story, and the origins of Aboriginal urbanization in Winnipeg, began millennia ago when natural phenomena shaped the site around the junction of the Red and Assiniboine rivers (the Forks) in the heart of Winnipeg. The confluence of two or more rivers is often thought to represent a natural meeting place for people. Economists and historians call the phenomena a transportation node, an economically propitious place to build a village, then a city – a place where people naturally congregate.

For thousands of years Aboriginal peoples such as the Anishinabe, Assini- boine, Cree, and Dakota have been meeting at the Forks in Winnipeg. Now peoples of all races from around the globe have joined them to live and make Winnipeg a vibrant city. Two of every three Manitobans live within the perimeter of Winnipeg. In much smaller and shrinking numbers, the remaining third occupy a huge land area characterized by vast distances between communities. This move to urban living is almost universal and brings many advantages to all urban dwellers.

The concentration of urban populations eases communications and per- mits people to support one another more easily. Urban dwellers are likely to be younger than rural residents. Cities are able to draw strength from a constant immigration of other peoples. Winnipeg offers its citizens ready access to a wide range of community agencies to help them build a life that can be rich, varied, and fulfilling. Rural life, in contrast, is likely to be simpler.

Rural populations are likely to be older, with only a few young active people. Many rural communities – especially the most remote – are losing opportunities for economic and population growth. Their young people are moving to larger urban centres to pursue their education, to seek employ- ment, and eventually to become city dwellers. The shrinking populations and contracting economies severely limit the options available to these rural communities to take effective steps to improve their lot. Residents of rural or remote areas are likely to have a more traditional view of life, with a nostalgic attachment to the past rather than an optimistic view of a very different and richer future.

How then does this apply to Aboriginal people? During the eighteenth and nineteenth centuries and the first part of the twentieth century the fur trade created a reasonable working relationship between Aboriginal and non-Aboriginal peoples. Economic issues had an equal impact on them – if trade was prosperous, all parties could be prosperous. The environment affected all residents equally, and there was little difference between the states of their health. As well, because all were equally isolated from civi- lized society, there was only a very modest difference in their formal edu- cation and social life. However, the advent of modern systems of resource exploitation led to the demise of the fur trading partnership. As Canadian society modernized, there was a change from primary industries (for exam- ple, hunting, fishing, and gathering) to secondary and tertiary industries (for example, mining, and hydro development). These new activities called for workers with more skills, education, and training. The old partner- ships of the fur trade and other primary activities broke down, and the differences between the peoples who formed the old partnerships accelerated. Aboriginal people did not receive education or training. They were not given immediate and real opportunities to participate fully in the new economies. This led to a dramatic decrease in the economic and social conditions of Aboriginal peoples. At the same time, their old non-Aboriginal partners gained new opportunities to improve their economic and social conditions – particularly in the towns and cities where they concentrated in large numbers and became the dominant social group in the country. As circumstances changed, Aboriginal leadership began to focus on these new and evolving issues, and a new activism emerged.

Urban Aboriginal Leadership and Activism

The dramatic development of urban centres stimulated the rapid improvement of transportation and communications systems. While these systems played a pivotal role in the exploitation of resources in the remote areas of the north and west, they also helped to unite Aboriginal peoples across the country. Before the Second World War there was little contact between the different Aboriginal peoples across Canada. Their communities were isolated from one another by geography, language, and the restrictions inherent in the Indian Act. As well, the Canadian public was generally uninformed about the impoverishment of Aboriginal people and the deteriorating social conditions they were facing. As direct communication between Aboriginal peoples across the country accelerated, understanding and a common sense of purpose between them developed and improved dramatically. They were also able to communicate to Canadians the conditions that affected all Aboriginal peoples.

Both the First and Second World Wars brought Aboriginal people into the armed forces and into contact with modern urban life. Aboriginal people began to migrate in increasing numbers to urban centres. This led to the creation of many federal initiatives, such as friendship centres, to help Aboriginal people ease into urban life. In the span of a few short decades national Aboriginal organizations were funded, and their leadership developed to bring the issues affecting Aboriginal people to the attention of the Canadian public.

When an issue is spread thin, however, it is diluted and becomes invisible. At first, the issues facing Aboriginal people in Winnipeg in the late 1940s were scarcely noticed at all. Aboriginal people who had volunteered for active duty in the armed forces had experienced life beyond the boundaries of the reserve or their remote communities. They had learned trades; however, there were only very limited opportunities to use them on the reserves or in remote communities. Many opted to pursue employment opportunities in the cities and to establish their homes in urban communities. Some met hardship and were not successful in adapting to urban life. Those who were successful tried to help other Aboriginal people improve their lives.

After the Second World War, public discussion about the difficult social conditions of Aboriginal people found voice in provincial and national conferences sponsored by organizations such as the Indian-Eskimo Association of Canada (later known as the Canadian Association in Support of Native Peoples). These conferences and organizations offered a platform for emerging Aboriginal leaders. At the same time they brought the influence of these organizations and their non-Aboriginal sponsors to bear on governments. This led to government support for more studies, conferences, pilot projects, and programs directed at Aboriginal peoples and the conditions under which they were living. Several studies done between 1965 and 1972 noted that Aboriginal people themselves should be involved in developing solutions to these social and economic problems.

In the late 1940s, however, Aboriginal peoples comprised a very small part of Winnipeg's population, but by 1970 their numbers had grown to between 15,000 and 25,000. This set off alarm bells in various levels of government. In the 1970s and 1980s more initiatives were established to improve and expand the cadre of Aboriginal leaders. Of particular note were the core funding agreements for Aboriginal organizations and friendship centres (the first one was in Winnipeg). The government of Canada inaugurated the Native Law Students Program so that more Aboriginal people could play a role in the justice system. In 1975 the Public Service Commission's Office of Native Employment initiated a Native recruitment policy for the Public Service of Canada. At about the same time, Aboriginal leadership and government recognized the need to invest heavily in educating and training Canada's Aboriginal peoples. Only a very few Aboriginals had completed secondary school; fewer still attended post-secondary institutions. More money was invested to build schools on reserves, and more students were given funding for their post-secondary education. Today thousands of Aboriginal students attend university and community colleges and pursue other post-secondary and specialized skills training. Aboriginal graduates are working throughout the private, public, and volunteer sectors – both in Aboriginal and non-Aboriginal communities (see the National Aboriginal Achievement Foundation's website at www.naaf. ca for more information).

Revitalizing Winnipeg's Core Area

In the 1980s a wide variety of projects were funded under the umbrella of the Core Area Initiative Program to rejuvenate Winnipeg's deteriorating core area. Many of these had a direct impact on Winnipeg's Aboriginal people. For example, Aboriginal volunteer organizations multiplied and played vital roles in developing and delivering services to Winnipeg's Aboriginal people in need. The Core Area Initiatives Program demonstrated the success of cooperation and coordination, the basic tenet of the Aboriginal Centre.

To address some of the social issues facing urban Aboriginal people, the Aboriginal Centre of Winnipeg Inc. adapted the 1975 Project Neeginan (Cree for 'our place'), the ultimate dream being to establish an Aboriginal community within the city, similar to those created by other peoples immigrating to our cities. ACWI's premise was that all its member organizations needed proper space to deliver their services effectively and efficiently. It made economic and operational sense to cooperate. ACWI believed that the centre needed to be viable as a business if it were to survive over the long term. It built a competent team to manage the corporation, to operate the building, and to complete and implement a comprehensive business plan for the corporation's and the centre's development. With this core leadership and professional advisory team in place, the Aboriginal Centre of Winnipeg Inc. was able to establish real credibility with its stakeholders and transform the dream into reality.

Developing the Centre: Managing Risk and Expectations

The former CPR station occupies approximately half of the nearly two-hectare (4.7 acres) site at Higgins Avenue and Main Street, which ACWI purchased from the CPR for $1.1 million in December 1992. The historic designation of the station required ACWI, as owner, to protect and maintain certain architectural elements of the building. The whole project included restoring the facade and the rotunda (the former passengers' waiting hall), as well as retrofitting approximately 7,480 square metres (80,000 square feet) of the building's office space. An audit of the building and grounds revealed that there were no substantive environmental issues. A structural study showed that the building was suitable for renovation. The initial historic restoration was funded, in part, by grants from Canadian Heritage ($300,000) and Heritage Manitoba ($75,000), which ACWI matched with capital and labour.

The Aboriginal Centre of Winnipeg Inc. received about $2.65 million from December 1992 to fall 1995, from twenty-four different agreements with sixteen different agencies, to undertake planning and other work to prepare the building for a more complex renovation of the office space. Rental revenue from ACWI's member organizations, which moved into the centre before the renovations, funded the centre's operation and these early stages of development. During this period Aboriginal people contributed more than 70,000 hours of their labour, completing 70 per cent of the agreed historical restoration and 85 per cent of the demolition and preparation for the office retrofit. All asbestos was also removed from the centre through a special training program. The construction and business plan, setting out restoration and renovation details, was completed.

The key to the success of ACWI's initial business plan would be the leasing of all available space (about 7,480 square metres or 80,000 square feet). Fulfilment of this requirement would provide the necessary cash flow to cover the operating and financing costs of the complete retrofit of the centre. There were doubts that the leasing objectives could be achieved within the financial planning time frame. Not renovated and nearly vacant, the centre represented little value as a real estate investment. ACWI members received funding through contribution agreements from public programs that were subject to annual renewal, which effectively reduced the collateral value of their leases. The covenant for any loan was deemed to be weak because of these factors and the not-for-profit nature of ACWI and tenants. The complete retrofit program would have required an immediate lease of about 5,610 square metres (60,000 square feet) of office space just to meet operating costs and debt-servicing needs.

A limited retrofit program was conceived, which provided a much more flexible option – offering more easily achievable leasing objectives (about 3,270 square metres or 35,000 square feet) from the outset, as well as a better mix of leasing opportunities for prospective tenants. Western Economic Diversification Canada commissioned a viability study of ACWI's revised business plan. Subsequently, ACWI received $2.5 million through the Winnipeg Development Agreement (WDA) to implement the limited retrofit project. While waiting for these funds, ACWI received interim funding of over $300,000 from Western Economic Diversification Canada (WED).

The limited retrofit began on 25 October 1995, with the signing of the WDA Contribution Agreement, which outlines the 'contribution' to be made to the project proponent (ACWI) by WDA/WED under the general terms and conditions stemming from the WDA. It was completed in 1996. The centre officially opened on 21 June 1996, National Aboriginal Day. Completion of the renovation was accomplished in this short time because immediate objectives were modified to a manageable size, thereby reducing the risk of failure and ensuring success.

The objectives of all restoration and retrofit construction programs were met on schedule and within budget. The entablature of the rotunda (that is, its upper section that is supported by columns) was structurally stabilized, the vaulted ceiling was rebuilt, and other historic architectural features were restored to their original splendour. (ACWI received Heritage Winnipeg's 1997 Architecture Conservation Award for its historic renovation work.) All fire safety items, building code, and occupancy issues were completed. The top two floors of the west wing (2,800 square metres or 30,000 square feet) were refitted to a new building standard. The second floor upgrade was initiated, and disability access to the rotunda floor was finished.

Contributions and Benefits of Development

Aboriginal students have been employed during the summers since 1994 under the Manitoba Urban Green Team Program to assist in the restoration. Several Aboriginal trades people, labourers, and firms were hired to carry out specialized restoration work and painting. Fourteen Aboriginal workers were trained to handle hazardous materials, and received nationally recognized certification in asbestos removal; they removed all the asbestos from the centre. Hundreds of other Aboriginal people gave more than 150,000 hours of their labour to the centre through Human Resources Development Canada programs. ACWI developed effective commercial relations with scores of suppliers for millions of dollars worth of goods and services. Of the $2.65 million invested in the centre before October 1995, the Aboriginal community provided $1.03 million (38 per cent of the total). About $1.25 million of the $2.5 million received through the Winnipeg Development Agreement directly benefited Aboriginal enterprises. About 85 per cent of all the trades people and construction workers involved in the renovation and retrofit of the office spaces were Aboriginal.

Aboriginal people and firms are directly involved in the general operation of the centre. They provide building management, cleaning, security and food services, as well as communication, administrative, and financial services. ACWI established a restaurant and catering services for the occupants of the centre and users of the rotunda. A woodworking shop has been established to train people and to support construction and restoration activities in the centre. Personnel have been trained to provide security services for the property and the events at the centre. These activities give employment and business opportunities that otherwise might not have been available to Aboriginal people. Facilities include common conference rooms and breakout space for tenants and conference users of the centre's rotunda. In the end, the Aboriginal Centre exists for its tenants and the services they provide. All their activities directly support initiatives to address the urgent issues facing Aboriginal people living in Winnipeg. A brief discussion of these follows.

Centre for Aboriginal Human Resource Development

The Centre for Aboriginal Human Resource Development (CAHRD) is one of the centre's major tenants, providing quality education, training, and employment opportunities through partnerships with community, educational institutions, business, industry, and government. In addition to a variety of education and employment-related programs, CAHRD has initiated five programs that have their own institutional identities but operate legally as programs of CAHRD: Aboriginal Community Campus, which provides educational upgrading in math, English, chemistry, physics, biology, political science, and Native languages; Neeginan Institute of Applied Technology, which provides training in technical courses such as early childhood education, carpentry, and accounting, and positions such as building systems technician, medical laboratory technician, licensed practical nurse, educational assistant, and glassworker technician; Kookum's Place Daycare, a non-profit centre, which is licensed for forty-nine children of ages three months to six years; Neeginan Village, a thirty-two-unit students' housing complex; and Aboriginal Aerospace Initiative, an innovative program for training up to two hundred Aboriginal people in skilled jobs in the aerospace industry.

Aboriginal Health and Wellness Centre

The Aboriginal Health and Wellness Centre (AHWC) is a community-based health and wellness resource centre serving the Aboriginal community of Winnipeg. It provides a continuum of services and programs that uses both traditional and western resources to identify and support the aspirations, needs, and goals of individuals and families. Programs and services offered include a primary care clinic; community outreach and education; health promotion and prevention with the services of physicians, nurses, community health workers, and traditional healers; Abinotci Mino-Awawin (Children's Health) Head Start Program; and a fetal alcohol syndrome and effects prevention program.

Developments Stimulated by the Aboriginal Centre

The mid-1996 completion of the limited retrofit of the centre on schedule and on budget stimulated a series of other major developments at the centre and in the surrounding properties. Even as the limited retrofit was being finished, the provincial government funded a major program, which led to the complete development of another 1,400 square metres (15,000 square feet) in the west wing of the building. Almost simultaneously, Human Resources Development Canada agreed to the development of the Single Window Initiative to complete the refit of the centre's west wing. This initiative provided, for the first time, a coordinated pied-à-terre for most federal, provincial, and municipal agencies providing services to Aboriginal people. ACWI's annual revenues from renting office space progressed from $73,400 in 1993–4 to $440,000 in 1997–8. By the end of 2001 the last space in the centre, located in the east wing, had been renovated, resulting in total renovated and available rental space of 7,480 square metres (80,000 square feet). This space now generates $900,000 in rental revenue from the tenant organizations that offer a wide range of services to Aboriginal clients of all ages. In addition, the restaurant in the centre generates annual revenues of $200,000.

Across the street from the centre the city began developing the Circle of Life Thunderbird House. This is a magnificent building designed by the renowned Aboriginal architect Douglas Cardinal. The city also undertook a major street-scaping project for Main Street immediately west and south of the centre. The Manitoba Metis Federation purchased Canadian Pacific's office complex on Henry Avenue immediately south of the centre. The Centre for Aboriginal Human Resource Development expanded its program activities, leading to the development of four properties in the immediate vicinity of the centre. A former body shop just east of the centre was acquired and converted into a technical training facility for CAHRD's Neeginan Institute. This was followed by the purchase of a small property for a day-care facility. A third, larger property was purchased to build Neeginan Village, the students' housing complex. The most recent project is the development of a large training facility for the Aboriginal Aerospace Initiative, located between the centre and Neeginan Village. The area around the centre at Higgins and Main streets, one of Winnipeg's major intersections, has been transformed from a decrepit and scorned area, where fewer than one hundred people worked, into a vibrant area where thousands of Aboriginal people give new life to the neighbourhood.

Benefit to the Community

The railway station was the place where people from the old worlds of Europe and Asia began new lives and helped to create a great country. The building's restored architectural features are not Aboriginal; however, Aboriginal people accepted a stewardship responsibility to preserve this important part of a shared history for all Canadians. In return, Aboriginal people use the centre's office space to assist others in beginning new and better lives in the city. The rotunda has been the venue for powwows, conferences, trade shows, exhibitions, dramatic performances, fund-raising events, dinners, meetings, movie sets, special ceremonies, receptions, Christmas parties, and commemorations of historic events, to name but a few. ACWI incorporated ACWI Heritage Corporation, a registered charity, to raise funds for the restoration, operations, and provision of an interpretative centre for this historic site. Under the auspices of ACWI Heritage Corporation, prominent members of Winnipeg's private sector formed the Citizens and the Friends of the Centre committees to raise money for restoration and to expand public interest in the centre. Especially treasured by ACWI were the new friendships developed through the understanding and respect that all parties earned from each other.

Within a few short years Aboriginal people will make up 25 per cent of Winnipeg's workforce. Many young Aboriginal students are completing post-secondary education. There are expanding opportunities for them in non-Aboriginal and emerging Aboriginal enterprises and service sectors. Yet many Aboriginal people continue to experience serious economic, employment, social, and health problems. To improve life for less fortunate Aboriginal people, Canadians and their governments recognize that Aboriginal non-governmental organizations are effective service deliverers and agents for change. With the cooperation of governments, these organizations have evolved as surrogate government agents, delivering public services to Aboriginal people in need. With the expanding initiatives to address urban Aboriginal conditions, many Aboriginal people have begun taking an active role in the wider issues affecting all people in the communities in which they live. Hence, we see the rise of Aboriginal people who serve on local councils, provincial legislatures, and the Parliament of Canada.

To have hope, the citizens of any community must believe in or have a dream for its future. They must have effective leadership. Community leadership must be able to mobilize citizens to plan and organize in order to achieve agreed objectives. Finally, the community and its leadership must be accountable for the results of the work undertaken in the name of the community. Underlying these principles is the question, is there a will to do something? For Winnipeg's Aboriginal community the answer was and is *yes*, and the development of the Aboriginal Centre underscores it – *yes*!

Economic Impact of the Centre

The combination of salaries and the demand for goods and services by the centre and its tenants stimulates local businesses and generates significant tax revenues for federal, provincial, and municipal treasuries. With the concentration of organizations as tenants, the centre is a one-stop service centre that offers opportunities for inter-agency cooperation and coordination. The centre's tenants are able to cooperate in the purchase and delivery of goods and services, as well as in the more efficient use of space and common administrative support. Winnipeg's Aboriginal communities are receiving needed services in a more coordinated and efficient fashion from ACWI's member organizations and tenants.

The Aboriginal Centre is a successful social enterprise. The centre and its major tenants – specifically, the Centre for Aboriginal Human Resource Development and the Aboriginal Health and Wellness Centre – are instrumental participants in the social economy. They are part of a grassroots entrepreneurial movement whose objective is to improve the social and economic conditions of the Aboriginal people who are adapting to life in Winnipeg. The proponents of ACWI conceived of and implemented the development of the Aboriginal Centre by mobilizing public and private partners to allocate resources to achieve this objective. Together, the centre, its tenants, their public and private partners, stakeholders, and the Aboriginal community of Winnipeg have all benefited from this joint cooperation. Their work has included the following achievements: $15 million in property assets have been created for Winnipeg's Aboriginal community; the centre generates an annual income of $1 million from rents and restaurant and catering operations; about 200 people are employed in the centre, earning $5 million annually; over 4,000 Aboriginal people participate in education, training, and employment programs at the centre annually; over 2,000 Aboriginal people gain employment through their participation in programs at the centre, earning a potential $35 million annually; over the past ten years some 16,000 Aboriginal people have earned a potential $300 million; about $45 million in provincial and federal personal income taxes are generated annually; some $100,000 in GST and PST may be generated annually; and over $1 million in property taxes have been paid to the City of Winnipeg.

Achievements of the Aboriginal Centre

ACWI took the vacant, unused station, restored its major architectural features, and retrofitted its 7,480 square metres (80,000 square feet) of dilapidated office space to meet modern building standards. New partnerships were created between Aboriginal and non-Aboriginal enterprises. Aboriginal people were trained in new skills such as building operations, power engineering, building security, cleaning and maintenance, restoration work, proper handling and removal of hazardous materials, fund-raising, and public communications. ACWI created a fully functional service centre offering a wide range of services for people in need. In the process, ACWI made believers out of doubters and gained new friends throughout the city.

From Dream to Reality

Winnipeg's Aboriginal Centre is not the sole example of successful development of urban property in Canada by Aboriginal people. Nor will it be the last. It is part of a series of institutions that have been put in place across Canada to help address the needs of urban Aboriginals. Friendship centres were among the first efforts to provide needed services to Aboriginal people migrating into urban centres. Many First Nations, tribal groups, and other Aboriginal groups, organizations, companies, and individuals have done, and are undertaking, a wide range of property development in Canadian cities. In the more successful cases they do so, as did the Aboriginal Centre, with the willing and enthusiastic cooperation of other investors and stakeholders. These developments are providing investment and economic opportunities and influence for Aboriginal and non-Aboriginal citizens in our cities. In western Canada many towns and cities will reap great economic and social benefits from these Aboriginal development initiatives – in the same way that other urban centres have benefited from the vision and hard work of other citizens who have made these centres their home.

The realization of the dream of the Aboriginal Centre demonstrated what can be achieved through determination, hard work, and good management by a team of experienced and competent professionals complemented by generous support from stakeholders. The Aboriginal Centre has evolved as a partnership between the people of the inner city, their service providers, and governments. All the activities that are undertaken in the centre benefit Aboriginal youth, single parents, job-displaced people, and the Aboriginal community at large. With a large number of people working in the centre, other business opportunities in the immediate neighbourhood are being created and stimulated. A major intersection in Winnipeg's core area has been re-established.

The dream of the centre became a reality because a number of people went beyond dreaming, and acted. It is difficult to describe the drama, excitement, satisfaction, and pride associated with the development of the Aboriginal Centre. What was true thousands of years ago is still true today. The confluence of the Red and the Assiniboine rivers still constitutes a meeting place. Cree, Assiniboine, Dakota, Scot, English, French, and many other nationalities have left their mark here. In coming full circle, a part of this meeting place has changed its value and has changed its name to the Aboriginal Centre; in doing so, it has become a symbol for all those who participated in its transformation. It will always represent the power of dreams, determination, heroism, hard work, and hope.

Bibliography

Aboriginal Centre of Winnipeg. 1993. *Catching a Dream: 1993 Annual Report*. Winnipeg: Aboriginal Centre of Winnipeg Inc.
– 1994–2008. Annual reports. Winnipeg: Aboriginal Centre of Winnipeg Inc.
– 1996. *Centre Piece*. Winnipeg: Aboriginal Centre of Winnipeg Inc.
– 1998. *General Guide '98 '99*. Winnipeg: Aboriginal Centre of Winnipeg Inc.
– 2009. http://www.abcentre.org (accessed March 2009).
Canada. 2009. Indian and Northern Affairs Canada. http://www.ainc-inac.gc.ca/index-eng.asp (accessed January 2011).
Centre for Aboriginal Human Resource Development. 2008. *Annual Report*. Winnipeg: Centre for Aboriginal Human Resource Development.
– 2009. http:/www.cahrd.org (accessed March 2009).
City of Winnipeg. 2009. http://www.winnipeg.ca/interhom/ (accessed January 2011).
City of Winnipeg Committee on Environment. 1974. *Main Street 1980*. Winnipeg: City of Winnipeg.
Dumas and Smith Limited. 1975. *Neeginan: A Feasibility Report*. Winnipeg: Neeginan (Manitoba) Inc.
Levin, E.A. 1972. *A Proposal for the Urban Indian and Métis*. Winnipeg: City of Winnipeg.
Manitoba. 1998. Round Table on Environment and Economy. *Priorities for Action: Towards a Strategy for Aboriginal People Living in Winnipeg*. Winnipeg: Province of Manitoba.
Me-Dian Credit Union. 2000. *Annual Report 1999*. Winnipeg: Me-Dian Credit Union.
National Aboriginal Achievement Foundation. 2009. http://www.naaf.ca (accessed March 2009).
Peterson, Murray. 1996. *The Former Canadian Pacific Railway Station, 181 Higgins Avenue, Winnipeg: A Historical and Architectural Survey*. Winnipeg: Canadian Heritage.

Profile of Tantoo Cardinal (1950–)

Métis, Actor, and Activist

Historically, various art forms have served as vehicles for personal and political expression. Tantoo Cardinal is an example of an actor who approaches her roles and uses her experiences to bring about change in the ways that the Aboriginal community is viewed. Cardinal's artistic activities, as well as her career, span radio, theatre, television, film, and politics. With a long list of awards to her credit, she is one of North America's most widely recognized Native actresses.[1]

Cardinal was born in 1950 in Anzac, Alberta, about four hundred kilometres northeast of Edmonton. She was the youngest child born to a Cree mother and a Caucasian father. Her parents separated shortly after her birth, and she went to live with her maternal grandmother when she was six months old. She was nicknamed Tantoo[2] by her Cree grandmother.

Cardinal's political activism grew steadily when she was faced with negative attitudes towards Aboriginal people in Edmonton during the mid 1960s. While attending Bonnie Doon High School in Edmonton, she joined the United Native Youth, which helped her to forge links with other young Aboriginals.[3] At this time she was searching for her gift, her identity, and her community.[4] She had no status card, no reserve, and no Métis community.[5] Cardinal married Fred Martin in 1968.[6] In 1971 she won a small role in a CBC documentary on Father Lacombe, which started her acting career.[7]

Cardinal's approach to acting is strongly influenced by her interest in the Native movement. As a representative of the Canadian Indigenous arts community, she uses her craft to communicate who she is as an individual and who her people are. Her life experiences have become a natural part of her performances. She states, 'There is a well of emotional pain[;] although that feeds me as an actress it can also be horrible.'[8] Tantoo Cardinal has been recognized internationally as a result of her film roles. Her impressive filmography includes *Loyalties* (1987), *Dances with Wolves* (1990), *Where the Rivers Flow North* (1993), *Legends of the Fall* (1994), *The Education of Little Tree*

Tantoo Cardinal. Photo courtesy of Indiana University.

(1997), *Smoke Signals* (1998), *Memory* (2004), *Unnatural and Accidental* (2006), and *Older than America* (2008).[9] Her stage roles include performances in *Jessica*, an adaptation of Maria Campbell's autobiographical account *Halfbreed*; and in Floyd Favel's *All My Relations,* for which she won the 1990 Elizabeth Sterling Hayes Award for Best Actress.[10] In 2009 she acted in Tomson Highway's play *Ernestine Shuswap Gets Her Trout* at the Firehall Arts Centre in Vancouver, British Columbia.[11] She has taken a number of television roles in recent years including a recurring role on *Moccasin Flats* (2006) and *The Guard* (2008).[12]

Cardinal has received many nominations and awards for her acting from both the Aboriginal and the mainstream artistic communities. In 1998 she received the National Aboriginal Achievement Award for her contributions to the political and artistic communities.[13] She viewed this award not only as an acknowledgment of her work but as a celebration of her Aboriginal community.[14] She was given an honorary doctorate in fine arts from the University of Rochester in 1995. She won the Women in Film Award at the Vancouver Film Festival in 2008.[15]

Tantoo Cardinal feels that through acting she can tell her people's stories and tell them correctly. Her success is due to a mix of raw talent, smart choices, and the respect she has earned from her peers.

VALERIE KYNASTON

Notes

1 T.P. Kunesh, 'Tantoo Cardinal,' in *Notable Native Americans*, ed. Sharon Malinowski (New York: Gale Research, 1995), 70.
2 Tantoo is a brand of insect repellant.
3 'Tantoo Cardinal,' in *Who's Who of American Women* (New Jersey: Reed Publishing, 1993), 80.
4 Bernelda Wheeler, 'Tantoo Cardinal,' *Eagle Feather News*, February 2000:11, http://www.sicc.sk.ca/faces/wcardta.htm.
5 Ibid.
6 'Tantoo Cardinal,' in *Who's Who of American Women*, 80.
7 Elizabeth Lumley, ed., 'Tantoo Cardinal,' in *Canadian Who's Who, 2000* (Toronto: University of Toronto Press, 2000), 205.
8 Brian D. Johnson, 'Masks of a Métis star,' *Maclean's*, 20 October 1986, 63.
9 James Defelice, 'Tantoo Cardinal,' in *Canadian Encyclopedia, 2000 World Edition* (Toronto: McClelland and Stewart, 2000).
10 Lumley, 'Tantoo Cardinal.'
11 http://www.imakenews.com/spiritlink/e_article001422234.cfm. (accessed 20 April 2009).
12 Ibid.
13 Bruce Weir, 'Actress wants to tell stories that make people feel good,' *Windspeaker*, April 1998: 5 (Edmonton: Aboriginal Multi Media Society of Alberta).
14 Ibid.
15 Ibid.

An Emerging Narrative:
Aboriginal Contributions to Canadian Architecture

WANDA DALLA COSTA

Architecture is one of the most salient expressions of a culture. It draws from the past, defines the present, and envisions a future, all the while adapting to reflect the current values and aspirations of a society. The cathedral, for example, a space of stained glass and soaring heights, expressed the passions and ambitions of a faith. The tepee, ephemeral, harmonious with nature and meaningful in its layout, reflected the belief system and way of life of a group. These markers (or non-markers) in the landscape become a narrative, or a 'living' history, of the people.

The built history in our Canadian landscape is largely borrowed, primarily from a European heritage. The international style, a 1920s movement that still resonates today, translated the ideal of 'progress' into a functional layout and a 'modern' palette of material – glass, concrete, and steel – and in its path disregarded regional or cultural variations. As disillusion with an ill-fitting homogeneity set in, alternatives were sought.

This chapter highlights four projects that over the last thirty years have challenged architectural principles, in the search for a truly Canadian expression. These projects have become some of Canada's most celebrated and successful buildings, and all have drawn from Aboriginal culture. As Canadian architecture continues to define itself into the twenty-first century, these buildings allude to the depth and variety of inspiration in this country and stand as testament to Aboriginal peoples' contribution to Canadian identity and culture.

The buildings chosen are works that complement each other. Two are by Aboriginal architects and two by non-Aboriginal architects. All four buildings are sensitive and respectful of Aboriginal culture and highlight an emerging culturally inspired body of architectural work. These buildings have been recognized and awarded for their contribution to the body of architecture in Canada. Among the distinctions they hold are three Governor General's Awards, a Lieutenant Governor's Award, an American Institute of Architects Gold Medal, and one Quebec Order of Architects Award of Distinction. The level of work is outstanding and inspirational for future generations of both Aboriginal and non-Aboriginal architects.

The select buildings are documented in chronological order. The first is the Museum of Anthropology (1972–5) at the University of British Columbia in Vancouver, British Columbia, designed by one of Canada's leading architects, Arthur Erickson. The second is the Museum of Civilization (1984–9) in Hull, Quebec, designed by Douglas Cardinal, an Alberta-born Métis architect, and Tetreault Parent Languedoc et Associates Inc. The next is the Seabird Island School (1988–91) in Agassiz, British Columbia, a project by Patkau Architects, a firm that began in the Prairies and is now based in Vancouver. The final building is the Nicola Valley Institute of Technology (1999–2001) in Merritt, British Columbia, by Busby, Perkins + Will (formerly Busby + Associates Architects), led by Alfred Waugh, a member of the Fond du Lac Band in Saskatchewan.

Museum of Anthropology, University of British Columbia

Arthur Erickson (1925–2009) practised in his hometown of Vancouver, British Columbia, as Arthur Erickson Architectural Corporation. His large portfolio of work across Canada includes the University of Lethbridge in southern Alberta and Robson Square in Vancouver. He received numerous awards, notably the top honour in his field, the 1986 Gold Medal from the American Institute of Architects.

> Global architect, passionate advocate of cultural awareness, and fervent explorer of human and natural environments, whose buildings, though remarkably diverse, share deep respect for context, incomparable freshness and grace, and the dramatic use of space and light. (American Institute of Architects citation for 1986 Gold Medal to Arthur Erickson)

The Museum of Anthropology (70,000 square feet or 6,500 square metres) is one of the earliest major commissions that drew inspiration from Aboriginal culture, setting a precedent for the contemporary expression of traditional forms in Canada. Arthur Erickson took inspiration from a traditional longhouse to provide the visitor with a uniquely Canadian perspective, specifically that of the west coast culture. Being a member of the third or fourth generation of the modern movement in architecture, Erickson was not compelled to adhere to strict doctrines of the original modernist movement. Instead, he chose to combine the forms, materials, and spaces inherent in modern architecture with more social, cultural, and contextual responses.

The site is located on Point Grey cliffs on the University of British Columbia campus overlooking Vancouver's harbour. Erickson was asked to create a low-profile building to preserve the views for passing drivers on the adjacent scenic drive. His solution was to create a large earth berm, partially sink the building into the ground, and cover the roof in plantings and ponds of water.

As visitors approach the building, it barely seems large enough to house one of the world's most outstanding collections of Northwest Coast art and artefacts. Once inside, the visitor descends the main corridor towards the ocean, with animated artefacts coming to life against the bare concrete walls. The procession culminates with the Grand Hall, an expansive room made of glass and oversized post-and-beam gates with views to the surrounding glaciated parks and the wide straits of the harbour. The tension between the natural and the man-made illuminates the presence of the totem poles. It is a powerful sequence that Erickson has gifted the visitor: 'As you walk through ... you feel that the architect has revealed to you a new way of experiencing your world, that he had you in mind when he created this space or that view' (Erickson 1988, 11).

Arthur Erickson utilized the traditional structure of a longhouse to create the formal theme of the building. He imbued the horizontal beams and vertical posts with a largeness that captures the 'ponderous weight and disregard for structural reality' of the cedar split logs of traditional construction techniques (Erickson 1988, 88). He placed a series of gates at both the entrance to the museum and in the Great Hall, referencing the customary gate within a longhouse.

The inclusion of water on the site recalls the traditional positioning of longhouses next to bodies of water. Erickson states, 'When I was designing the museum, I remembered a photograph of an early Indian village between the edge of the forest and the edge of the sea' (Cawker and Bernstein 1988, 148). While Erickson was forced to pull the building back from the edge of the harbour, owing to erosion concerns, he chose to connect the visitor visually to the water by creating a pond that appears as a narrow inlet on the site.

At a time in Canadian history when Aboriginal culture in Canada was being marginalized, Erickson's solution for the Museum of Anthropology was innovative, thought provoking, and unabashed. He welcomed the people, their history, and their culture so vigorously and convincingly that the place of Aboriginal people within Canadian culture and identity could not be denied.

Museum of Anthropology, Arthur Erickson Architectural Corporation. Photo courtesy of Chris Erickson.

Museum of Anthropology, Arthur Erickson Architectural Corporation. Photo courtesy of Simon Scott.

Canadian Museum of Civilization

Douglas Cardinal moved his practice, Douglas J. Cardinal Architect, to Ottawa, Ontario, from his home province of Alberta. Among his many achievements, he was awarded the Gold Medal of the Royal Architectural Institute of Canada in 2001, the highest architectural honour bestowed upon an architect in Canada. He has been granted fourteen honorary doctorates in recognition of his significant contribution to excellence in architecture.

> Buildings are designed to fit into their environment, to appear as if they have always been there. The materials interact with each other, and their surroundings, the curves flow well with the natural curves of the land. (Government of Canada, *Celebrate Cardinal*)

Designed to house over 3.5 million artefacts and positioned prominently overlooking the Canadian Parliament Buildings, the Museum of Civiliza-

Grand Hall, Museum of Anthropology, Arthur Erickson Architectural Corporation. Photo courtesy of Simon Scott.

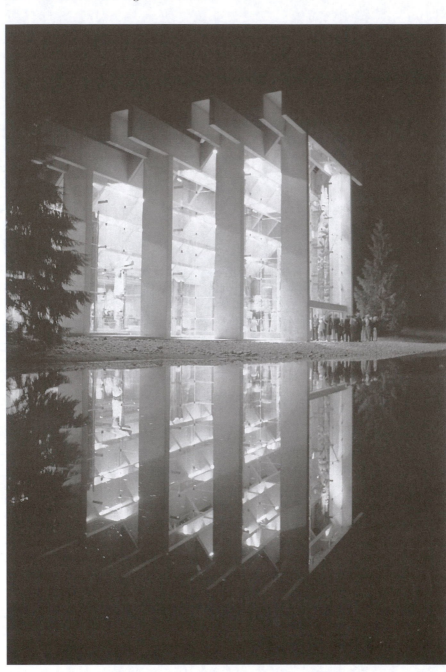

Museum of Anthropology, Arthur Erickson Architectural Corporation. Photo
courtesy of Simon Scott.

tion (420,000 square feet or 39,000 square metres) is one of the most distinguished commissions in Canadian history. It is also one of the most discussed. While current architecture at the time of its construction was doing little to capture the public's imagination, the popularity and sentiment evoked by Douglas Cardinal's sinuous form could not be ignored. Constructed with Manitoba's fossil-rich limestone, the building not only evokes the fertility of our land but also speaks to the evolution of this country. Douglas Cardinal captured Canadians' instinctive connection to the landscape, and in doing so, he resurrected a sensualism that has not been seen in architecture since the early part of the twentieth century.

In 1981, when Cardinal was put on the selection list for design of the museum, there was opposition on both the professional and the bureaucratic fronts. He was viewed as a risk for two reasons. First, his reputation among architectural circles of eastern Canada was that of a non-conformist who ignored the doctrines of both modernism and post-modernism, views which began early in his career.[1] Second, when compared to the firms vying for the commission, he lacked experience in a project of this scope and size. Despite Cardinal's unpopularity in architectural circles, Trevor Boddy, a contemporary architectural critic and writer, reminds us that not since the 1920s and 1930s when John Lyne covered a series of buildings with symbols of flora, fauna, and history has a Canadian architect 'so openly appealed to our national connection with the natural order, [and] addressed himself squarely to the ghost of wilderness that haunts our collective psyche' (Boddy 1989, 94–5).

The ineffable Canadian quality of his work is what captured the attention of the jurors, but it was the originality of the poetic text in his proposal for the museum that set him apart. While architects of the day were quoting 'the season's latest phrases from architectural salons of the northeast' (Boddy 1989, 87), Cardinal chose to capture the *spirit* of the building. He spoke of the emergence of our earth and its relation to the formation of our Canadian identity: 'From the ocean emerged land and the spines of mountain ranges to form the backbone of our continent. In time the sun, wind, and water moulded the jagged rock forms into the smooth, curved, sinuous form of the foothills and plains' (Boddy 1989, 87).

By daring to stand against convention, Cardinal came forward as the unlikely choice from the list of well-known firms competing for the commission. He emerged despite, but perhaps due to, the fact that his buildings defy classification. They are neither truly post-modern nor of the international style, the two dominating philosophies of the time. Rather they echo elements of expressionism and even earlier to the baroque period. Cardinal merges these architectural precedents with cultural elements and envi-

Canadian Museum of Civilization, Douglas J. Cardinal Architect. Photo property of Douglas J. Cardinal Architect.

ronmental influences in developing his original style. While one historian may see Antonio Gaudí in Cardinal's work, another references Frank Lloyd Wright. What matters is that it is a unique manifestation that resonates with the Canadian public.

Douglas Cardinal has reframed museum architecture, moving beyond the architectural tradition of museum as *container* to appeal to the cultural context of the artefacts within. While the museum's Grand Hall, a 300-foot-long, boat-shaped gallery with a 50-foot glass wall overlooking the river and the Parliament Buildings, offers visitors an inescapable sense of monumentality, it is the exterior form that sets this building apart, nudging Canadian architecture out of its borrowed fashions. It is earthly and spiritual, visceral and emotive. It is Canadian. As the copper roof vaults slowly turn from brown to green patina, Cardinal – a radical, an innovator, and an evoker – will be remembered for awakening the architectural landscape.

Seabird Island School

Patkau Architects was founded by John and Patricia Patkau in Edmonton, Alberta, in 1978. In 1984 the firm relocated to Vancouver, British Columbia. The firm has

Canadian Museum of Civilization, Douglas J. Cardinal Architect. Photo property of Douglas J. Cardinal Architect.

Canadian Museum of Civilization, Douglas J. Cardinal Architect. Photo property of Douglas J. Cardinal Architect.

Canadian Museum of Civilization, Douglas J. Cardinal Architect. Photo property of Douglas J. Cardinal Architect.

received numerous awards including three Governor General's Medals for Architecture and five Governor General's Awards for Architecture.

> We begin each project with a search for what we call the 'found potential' of the project. Found potential can exist in any aspect of a project. Program, building, context, local culture, the nature of a client – all of these are sources we use to develop an architectural order which is specific to circumstances. (Gili 1997, 13)

The Patkaus' work is innovative, provocative, and the result of a demanding process in search for the particular. In the case of the Seabird Island School (23,570 square feet or 2,190 square metres), their attentiveness to the site and to the First Nations client inspired a design that undoubtedly belongs to this region, this culture, and the primary users of the building, the children. The values of the community are everywhere, from its zoomorphic shape to the inclusion of local trades and industries in the construction process. The Patkau buildings are contextually and culturally relevant, and their bold and imaginative forms reflect the Canadian consciousness.

Many factors played a role in shaping this building: the site, the climate, the history, and the values of the Salish Nation. Seabird Island is a large island in the Fraser River surrounded by steep rugged mountains with a flat delta in the centre. The Patkaus described it as a great room: 'we felt that the building which was to inhabit this room should have an animated personality, something that could be perceived as a being of some kind' (Gili 1997, 14). The form, although not conceived with any one animal in mind, is definitely biomorphic and pays respect to the Nation's affinity with nature. Band members have responded positively, finding meaningful images such as the salmon in the final shape of the building. The choice of cedar shingles for the exterior, with its scale-like skin, elicits further salmon references while also representing the local building techniques of cedar-shingled log houses.

While the lines of the school emulate the mountain contours in the distance, climatic forces also played a role in generating the building's form. The cool winter winds coming down from the mountains are diverted from the southern public areas by the large mass of the closed northern facade. The southern edge, by contrast, changes scale and opens up to the village, becoming a welcoming and protected area for the teaching gardens and a children's playground. This zone, acting as an interface between the school and the village, begins to create an emerging village square. The porch is reminiscent of the coastal tradition of a boardwalk while the structure of heavy timber post-and-beam construction reflects the coastal communities of the northwest.

South porch of Seabird Island School, Patkau Architects. Photo courtesy of James Dow.

The building honours community values by providing amenities that tie into the daily lives of the members of the Salish Nation. The class-rooms are organized along the public southern face, each one opening onto the collective porch and play area, inviting the active participation of the community in the school's daily operation. The concept for internal organization honours the educational philosophy of the band, incorporat-ing spaces for staff and students to interact in a non-hierarchical arrange-ment, a contrast to the layout typically found in western educational facilities.

It is the responsiveness to human activities and experience that sets the Patkaus' works apart, but it is their physical geometries and materiality that articulate a uniquely First Nations and Canadian perspective. Animate and symbolic, these forms communicate without having to reproduce, inviting interpretation and imagination. As Dault states, 'Seabird Island School reaches a new level of romantic expressionism. It lands like a bird, suddenly transforming the subject of the painting, of the sculpture and of the Native habitat, and avoids any inanimate and trivial representation of this culture' (Dault 1992, 18–19).

With a single building, the Patkaus modified a microclimate, created a

Seabird Island School, Patkau Architects. Photo courtesy of James Dow.

Seabird Island School, Patkau Architects. Photo courtesy of James Dow.

Seabird Island School, Patkau Architects. Photo courtesy of James Dow.

village square, evoked the landscape, and illuminated elements of the Salish culture. In addition to its stunning form and contextual responsiveness, Seabird Island School is a rare example of a nationally and internationally recognized building that is located in an Aboriginal community. Its process and product stand as an example of what building *for*, and *with*, First Nations can be.

Nicola Valley Institute of Technology at the University College of the Caribou

The Nicola Valley Institute of Technology received the 2002 International Green Building Challenge, the 2004 Governor General's Medal of Excellence in Architecture, and the Lieutenant Governor of BC Medal for Excellence 2002. The achievements of Busby, Perkins + Will (formerly Busby + Associates Architects) include four Governor General's Medals and nine Lieutenant Governor's Medals in Architecture. Alfred Waugh, the project architect, practised with Busby, Perkins + Will for six years. In 2007 he established his own practice in Vancouver as Alfred Waugh Architect.

> It [Native architecture] embraces what happens whenever we take action to give order or meaning to the space around us. Naming space, designating

Seabird Island School, Patkau Architects. Photo courtesy of James Dow.

sacred parts of the wilderness, clearing village areas, garden plots, claiming food-gathering areas, planning and constructing buildings and arranging the spaces that surround and connect them are all components of Native architecture. Encoded into these buildings and social domains are the social and religious meanings particular to each Nation. (Waugh 2001)

The Nicola Valley Institute of Technology (NVIT), led by Alfred Waugh of Busby, Perkins + Will, presents a contemporary and refreshing perspective on First Nations' architecture by embodying intrinsic cultural values. The principles of environmental stewardship are captured by using innovative technologies that emulate the functional systems inherent in traditional structures. This eco-tech approach integrates the 'timeless lessons of the vernacular tradition with the aesthetic refinement and technical virtuosity of modernism' (Taggart 2002, 16). NVIT is a lesson for the future, not only for First Nations design but for the architectural profession.

The new post-secondary institute (48,400 square feet or 4,500 square metres) is tucked into a forested south-facing slope on the outskirts of Merritt, British Columbia. It is the first phase of a forty-three-acre campus. The semicircular plan emerges from the hillside and encloses classrooms, offices, laboratories, a bookstore, a cafeteria, a library, and an interior street complete with a fireplace to mark the centre of the building. Its layout is based on the non-hierarchical arrangement of functional spaces. A ceremonial arbour is planned for the centre of the site, which will become the focus of the future campus.

This building reinterprets traditional architectural archetypes, not as *formal* systems such as Erickson did with his reinterpretation of the traditional longhouse structure, but as *functional* systems. NVIT, designed as a cold-climate green building, uses principles drawn from both the tepee and the pit house. The simple and efficient ventilation system of the tepee promoted cooling by convection in the summer months, while the pit house, a south-facing earth-sheltered structure, minimized heat loss in the winter months. In NVIT, the two-storey atrium rises up to operable windows to naturally ventilate the space, a function similar to the role played by the flaps of a tepee. The roof is covered with earth and planted with the indigenous shrub kinnikinnick providing a layer of insulation and minimizing rainfall runoff. Without replicating the conical form of the tepee or pit house, the new building makes the most of their environmental principles (Taggart 2002, 19).

The structure and materials were selected based on their durability, efficiency, and regional availability. The exterior is clad in a horizontal wood frame rain-screen wall, made of resilient Alaskan yellow cedar. The win-

Nicola Valley Institute of Technology, Busby, Perkins + Will. Photo by Nic Lehoux.

Nicola Valley Institute of Technology. Busby, Perkins + Will. Photo by Nic Lehoux.

Nicola Valley Institute of Technology. Busby, Perkins + Will. Photo by Nic Lehoux.

dows are shaded with adjustable cedar louvres that are angled according to solar orientation. The spacing and slight tilt of the Douglas fir columns inside give a strong rhythm and character to the interior street and allude to the surrounding forest.

In giving the 2004 Governor General's Award for Architecture, the jury stated, 'This project pays homage to the cultural roots and philosophical principles of the First Nations community without resorting to icono-graphic quotations. It seeks sustainability with an imaginative palette of high- and low-tech green motifs. In its technology and composition, this "modern vernacular" expresses modesty and confidence as it incorpo-rates local materials and responds to its local micro-climate' (Baniassad 2004, 8).

The indigenous roof plantings and natural aging of the cedar cladding over time ensures that this building maintains strong ties to its landscape. Its response to the geography, topography, microclimate, and cultural con-text will ensure its place in the development of a modern vernacular style of architecture in Canada. By recognizing the underlying cultural principles and values that are meaningful to Aboriginal culture – values that will out-last the iconographic tepee poles that all too often frame this culture – the result is a timelessness that can invite and explore the depth and richness of Aboriginal culture in the search for Canadian identity and culture.

Conclusion

Although this chapter is far from an exhaustive study of Aboriginal con-tributions to Canadian architecture, these four buildings are landmarks, each one making significant contributions to an architecture of *this* place, and each one taking us one step closer to defining a regional Canadian architecture.

> We [Canadians] are in the process of developing our own distinct culture, a hybrid built on the variety of our constituent cultures. In this context, it is important to construct an architecture specific to place, developing local ways of working to resist being engulfed and recolonized by global culture. (Guft 1997, 14)

In Erickson's high-profile Museum of Anthropology we find one of Cana-da's earliest examples of an Aboriginal precedent in a contemporary form. Cardinal's Canadian Museum of Civilization seemingly borrows its form from nowhere but exposes a quintessentially Aboriginal and Canadian sen-timent, our connection to the land. The Patkaus' Seabird Island School, with its playful form that invites interpretation and inspiration, is testament to the process of working with Aboriginal communities to create place. And finally, the Nicola Valley Institute of Technology by Busby, Perkins + Will reminds us that one of the most powerful statements that Aboriginal architecture can make today is not about form and representation; rather it is about promoting an ecologically based value system.

As Canadian culture and identity continues to evolve, so will the list of contributors to our built environment. That list is becoming increasingly multicultural and finally includes a handful of emerging Aboriginal architects from First Nations across Canada. Patrick R. Stewart of the Nisga'a Nation was the first licensed architect in British Columbia and is the principal of his own practice, Patrick R. Stewart Architect, located in Chilliwack, British Columbia. Brian Porter is the principal of Two Row Architect located on the Six Nations Reserve in southern Ontario. Russell Everett, an Alberta-based architect, recently established his own practice, Russell Everett Architect Ltd., in Calgary, Alberta.

These talented architects, along with Alfred Waugh and Douglas Cardinal, are forming a body of work across Canada that is abundant with regional variations in history, precedents, and values and, in doing so, have begun to rework Canada's visual narrative or living history.

Notes

1 Cardinal's educational history is interesting and perhaps foreshadows his professional career. He entered the University of British Columbia's architecture program in 1952. He left three years later without a degree, having had difficulty conforming to the rectilinear geometry of mainstream modernism that was encouraged by the school. Cardinal eventually graduated with honours from the University of Texas, a school that espoused an eclectic variety of approaches to design and a liberal educational philosophy, allowing him the autonomy to develop his ideas.

Bibliography

Ballantyne, Andrew, ed. 2004. *Architectures: Modernism and After.* Oxford: Blackwell.

Baniassad, Essy. 1999. *Architecture Canada 1999: The Governor General's Awards for Architecture.* Halifax, NS: Tuns Press and the Royal Architectural Institute of Canada.

– 2002. *Architecture Canada 2002: The Governor General's Awards for Architecture.* Halifax, NS: Tuns Press and the Royal Architectural Institute of Canada.

– 2004. *Architecture Canada 2004: The Governor General's Awards for Architecture.* Halifax, NS: Tuns Press and the Royal Architectural Institute of Canada.

Boddy, Trevor. 1987. *Modern Architecture in Alberta.* Edmonton: Alberta Culture and Multiculturalism and the Canadian Plains Research Centre.

– 1989. *The Architecture of Douglas Cardinal.* Edmonton, AB: NeWest Press.

Canada. 2003. *Canada's Digital Collections Celebrate Cardinal.* Ottawa: Government of Canada and Summer Group Inc. http://epe.lac-bac.gc.ca/100/205/301/ic/cdc/E/Alphabet.asp.

Carter, Brian. 1994. *Documents in Canadian Architecture: Patkau Architects Selected Projects, 1983–1993.* Halifax, NS: Tuns Press.

Cawker, Ruth, and William Bernstein. 1988. *Contemporary Canadian Architecture.* Markham, ON: Fitzhenry and Whiteside.

Curtis, William J. 1986. *Modern Architecture since 1900.* 3rd ed. London: Phaidon Press.

Dault, Gary Michael, ed. 1992. *Architecture Canada 1992: The Governor General's Awards for Architecture.* Halifax, NS: Tuns Press and the Royal Architectural Institute of Canada.

– ed. 1994. *Architecture Canada 1994: The Governor General's Awards for Architecture.* Halifax, NS: Tuns Press and the Royal Architectural Institute of Canada.

– ed. 1997. *Architecture Canada 1997: The Governor General's Awards for Architecture.* Halifax, NS: Tuns Press and the Royal Architectural Institute of Canada.

Erickson, Arthur. 1988. *The Architecture of Arthur Erickson.* Vancouver: Douglas and McIntyre.

Gili, Gustavo, ed. 1997. *Patkau Architects: Selected Projects, 1983–1993.* Barcelona: Current Architectural Catalogues.

Guft, Andrew. 1997. *Prologue in Patkau Architects.* Barcelona: Current Architectural Catalogues.

Kapelos, George T. 1994. *Interpretations of Nature: Contemporary Canadian Architecture, Landscape and Urbanism.* Toronto: Herzig Somerville.

Sachner, Paul M. 1990. Collective Memory. *Architectural Record* 178:88–93.

Stewart, Patrick R. 1991. Designing for Canada's Native Population. *The Canadian Architect* 36:18.

Taggart, Jim. 2002. Modern Vernacular. *Canadian Architect* 8:16–19.

Waugh, Alfred. 2001. *Developing Sustainable Architecture for Aboriginal Communities.* Firm information, page 2. Vancouver: Waugh + Busby Architects.

Profile of Alexandre (Alex) Simeon Janvier (1935–)

Dene, Artist, and Educator

Alex Janvier is considered to be one of Canada's greatest artists and one of the first Native artists to paint in a style that blends 'traditional Native styles with abstract modernism.'[1] Painting since the early 1960s, Janvier broke into the mainstream art scene and paved the way for future Aboriginal artists.

Alexandre Simeon Janvier was born to hereditary chief Harry Janvier and his wife, Mary, on 28 February 1935 on the Cold Lake Reserve in northeastern Alberta. Cold Lake is unique in that the current reserve residents, numbering approximately one thousand, follow a traditional lifestyle of hunting, trapping, and fishing. Janvier describes Cold Lake as 'where the Plains ended and the North began.'[2]

At the age of eight Alex Janvier attended Blue Quills Indian Boarding School in St Paul, Alberta, where he felt the cultural shock of this new environment. Having spoken only the Chipewyan language previously, Janvier quickly learned English, and people at the school were calling him an artist by the time he was twelve years old.[3] Janvier recalls himself as a child on the reserve using a stick to draw on the ground, and he comments that others had as much artistic talent as he had.[4] It was at Blue Quills that he was provided the opportunity to develop his artistic abilities, and he learned how to paint. An art teacher from the University of Alberta, Karl Altenberg, was a regular visitor to St Paul. Altenberg encouraged young Janvier to expand his 'artistic horizons.'[5] Janvier says, 'They [the teachers and Altenberg] conspired to rush art on me' at age fourteen.[6]

Janvier attended the Alberta College of Art in Calgary, completing a bachelor of fine arts in 1960. He held a number of jobs after graduating from art school, and he became an activist in the Indian rights movement. Janvier taught for the Faculty of Extension at the University of Alberta from 1960 to 1962.[7] In 1964 his work was showcased at the Jacox Gallery in Edmonton.[8] By 1966 Janvier was working as an arts and crafts consult-

Alex Janvier.

ant, travelling across Alberta searching for new talent, encouraging young Aboriginals with artistic ability, and setting up exhibitions of their works for the Department of Indian Affairs. During Expo '67 in Montreal, Janvier helped to organize the Indian pavilion, for which he also provided a large circular mural.[9]

In 1968 Janvier met his wife-to-be, Jacqueline Wolowski, while teaching adult classes at Saddle Lake Indian School near St Paul. Wolowski was also a teacher, and together they taught an adult life-skills class until 1970 at Alberta Newstart Inc. in Fort Chipewyan.[10] Throughout Janvier's many years of teaching, he still found time to paint. However, in 1971 he decided to turn painting into his full-time job.

Alex Janvier achieved notoriety when he began using his band treaty number, 287, and his name to sign his paintings. However, for a period in the 1960s he used his treaty number alone as his signature. By using this number, Janvier mocked the system in which Aboriginal people were numbers controlled by a distant bureaucracy. This was a reflection of his attitude towards the paternalistic and depersonalizing government.[11]

Among Janvier's work, *Morning Star*, painted in the early 1990s, is considered a masterpiece. It can be seen in the domed ceiling of the Grand Hall of the Canadian Museum of Civilization in Hull, Quebec. Janvier has had many exhibitions: *Land Spirit Power* at the National Art Gallery (1992); *Alex Janvier: First Thirty Years' Retrospective* at the Thunder Bay Art Gallery (1993); and *Alex Janvier: New Works* at the Edmonton Art Gallery (2002). In 2003 he opened an art gallery in his home town of Cold Lake, Alberta.

Janvier has been recognized for his numerous contributions as an artist, educator, and political activist. In 1993 he was inducted into the Royal Canadian Academy of Artists, and the following year into the Northeastern Indian Hall of Fame.[12] On 10 March 2002 at the Ninth Annual National Aboriginal Achievement Awards in Winnipeg, he received the Lifetime Achievement Award. In 2008 Alex Janvier won a number of awards including the Governor General's Award.[13] He received honorary doctorates from the University of Calgary and the University of Alberta. He also won the Marion Nicoll Visual Arts Awards from the Alberta Foundation for the Arts in the fall of 2008.[14]

PHYLLIS CHAU

Notes

1 Cheryl Petten, 'Gala salutes achievement,' *Windspeaker* 20 (2002): 8.

2 Royal Ontario Museum, *Contemporary Native Art in Canada: Alex Janvier* (Toronto: Royal Ontario Museum, 1978), 2.

3 Canadian Press Newswire, 'Alberta artist recognized with Lifetime Aboriginal Achievement Award,' January 2002: 23.

4 Royal Ontario Museum, *Contemporary Native Art in Canada*, 3.

5 Ibid.

6 Ibid.

7 Ibid., 4.

8 Ibid.

9 Ibid.

10 Ibid.

11 Ibid., 6.

12 Elizabeth Lumley, ed., 'Alex Janvier,' in *Canadian Who's Who 2003*, vol. 38 (Toronto: University of Toronto Press, 2003), 671–2.

13 http://www.alexjanvier.com (accessed 28 March 2009).

14 Ibid.

Heartbeats:
Native Music in Aboriginal and Canadian Life

BRIAN WRIGHT-MCLEOD

Canadian Native music is both art form and identity. It is a living process of learning, evolution, and change that is rooted in tradition but transformed through time and through outside influences. From first contact to the present, outside influences, such as new instruments and musical forms, have stimulated a symbiotic interaction, integration, experimentation, and development of a new musicality, new ideas, and genres. We live in a time when musicians can easily access music from around the world and integrate it into their own compositions.

Native music encompasses the traditional music of all Native peoples across Canada as well as modern Native musical expressions of non-Native musical genres. The beat of the powwow drum now accompanies the heavy-metal onslaught of Native bands, and the plaintive notes of the cedar flute are accompanied by a symphony orchestra. In the twenty-first century, Native music is as difficult to compartmentalize as is non-Native music.

Traditional Music

Traditional Indigenous music is unique and distinctive, reflecting the diversity of Canada's Native cultures. The sound of the music resonates with history. In a very real sense, music is geography. One can identify the origin of the traditional music of a particular Aboriginal group by its sound, rhythms, language, structure, and instruments. Iroquois singing stands apart from a Plains First Nations song; equally, the haunting flute melodies of the Anishinabe and Inuit throat singing represent the tremendous variety of Native music.

Native flute player R. Carlos Nakai described traditional music as 'derived from the rhythms of the earth and the universe to express and confirm our existence in harmony and balance with all living things. It represents the foundation of our way of life. The making or "capturing" of a song also recognizes the life that each song possesses' (2003).

Music has maintained a constant presence in everyday experience and has continued to be a part of the ceremonies that underline Native peoples' connection to nature and everyday life. There is a song for everything. Music can function 'as a hunting "tool," an affirmation of one's clan identity, a means of lulling a child, or a "medicine" within a ceremony to heal both body and spirit' (Diamond et al. 2009). Songs are owned or kept by individuals, families, clans, and nations.

As traditional forms of Native music are so diverse, it is difficult to generalize. However, many agree that the drum is a common instrument played in almost all Native cultures (Keillor, Cle-alls, and Von Rosen n.d.). Drums differ in the materials used to make them, how they are played, and what role they play in rituals and ceremonies. Rattles, of all types and materials, are also present in many Native music traditions. Singing covers a wide range of styles from narrative songs to vocables (when a song is sung using syllables that do not have specific meaning) with distinct melodies and little harmonization. Often songs are integrated into dance and ceremony (Diamond et al. 2009).

Persistence and Adaptability of Native Music

Native musical traditions have been recorded by outsiders from the earliest contact between Native peoples and Europeans. However, most scholarship on this topic dates from the 1800s. This scholarship, primarily from a non-Native point of view, reflects a history of survival despite the colonization and the eventual absorption of new musical influences, which led to the creation of new forms and ways of expression.

Missionaries and government agents tried to extinguish traditional musical expression through cultural repression and the assimilation of Native people into mainstream society. Indeed, the Canadian government's oppressive policy of restricting Aboriginal cultural practices and language began in the 1880s and persisted for decades well into the twentieth century. As a result, playing Native music became a conscious act of resistance, preservation, and continuity of Native cultures and peoples. In the early part of the twentieth century an amendment was made to the Indian Act, giving Indian agents the power to approve any Native participation in dances, rodeos, and public exhibitions off reserve in the Canadian west and in the territories (Diamond et al. 2009). As late as 1920, Duncan Campbell Scott, deputy superintendent of the Department of Indian Affairs, sent the following to a government agent in Alberta:

> It is observed with alarm that the holding of dances by the Indians on their reserves is on the increase, and that these practices tend to disorganize the

efforts which the Department is putting forth to make them self-supporting. I have therefore, to direct you to use your utmost endeavours to dissuade the Indians from excessive indulgence in the practice of dancing ... [I]t is realized that reasonable amusement and recreation should be enjoyed by the Indians, but they should not be allowed to dissipate their energies and abandon themselves to demoralizing amusements. (Canada 1920)

Ceremonies were banned, sacred objects including musical instruments were destroyed, and practitioners punished. Until the Indian Act was revised in 1951, Native musicians could not perform in restaurants or bars licensed to sell liquor (Diamond et al. 2009). However, communities often secretly kept their musical traditions alive.

Fiddle Music

Native music proved to be resilient as new genres and instruments, such as the fiddle and the squeezebox accordion, were adopted through trade. One of the most documented examples is the introduction of the fiddle, probably by fur traders, in the late 1600s. This absorption marked the first musical transformation of the two cultures. In some cases, the fiddle replaced the drum after the latter was outlawed and practitioners of the old ways were arrested. James Cheechoo, a Cree from James Bay, Ontario, is part of a long line of fiddle players from his community. A living history is found in his music. For example, Cheechoo explained in a radio interview that the title of his 1999 album, *Shay Che Man*, was about the tall ships that came into James Bay, about seeing sails on the water. Cheechoo maintains that the only traditional music that has survived was carried down through the fiddle, not the drum.

Ironically, the Native communities that absorbed some of the old Scottish and Irish fiddle songs into their own music traditions became important sources of these compositions. So many British songs remain unchanged from the time they were first introduced to those communities. This strong connection was celebrated in the National Film Board's *The Fiddlers of James Bay* (1980), which followed two Cree fiddlers as they visited Scotland's Orkney Islands, the origin of the music they had learned from their fathers and grandfathers.

There are legions of Native fiddle players worthy of mention who play entirely different styles, from folk to country. Some of these musicians include Charlie Tumik, the Harrappasires, Esau Sinclair, Reg Bouvette, and Ryan Keplin. There are also classical violinists such as Heidi Aklaseaq Senungetuk (Inuit) and Tara-Louise Montour (Mohawk).

Perhaps the most legendary Native fiddle player was Lee Cremo, a Mi'kmaq from Eskasoni, Nova Scotia. A dynamic performer, he was the only artist outside Ireland to be recognized by the Irish recording industry as someone who embodied the essence of the Maritime fiddle music originally exported from the British Isles. His perseverance in practising his art enabled him to surmount the ill-treatment by his first record company, which had basically prohibited him from performing or releasing recordings until the late 1980s. His talent has inspired generations of fiddle players. This legend of east coast fiddle music, who won international acclaim, passed his knowledge on to students who have included Natalie McMaster and Ashley MacIsaac.

Church Music

Sacred music has always been significant in many Native communities, as, for example, prayer songs. Understandably, this connection to the spiritual was transferred to the Christian hymns and music that many Native communities began experiencing as missionary activity grew and churches were established. As traditional music was forced underground through government policy, new songs emerged. Many communities began singing hymns in their mother tongues and adapting Christian music to Native traditional models. For example, in the Naskapi and Montagnais communities, fiddle music and Christian hymns were adapted to 'create distinctive styles and newly created pieces between the late 16th and early 17th centuries on ... [Those] repertoires are regarded as "traditional" music in many communities' (Diamond et al. 2009).

Radio

In some areas the radio was a significant agent of musical change in Native communities. Radio began gaining listeners, including Native peoples, by the late 1930s, even though in the early years most radio stations were only on the air for a few hours in the evening. However, programs often featured local musicians, choral groups, concerts, and recordings (Canadian Communications Foundation 2006). Radio certainly was a major factor in popularizing country and western music in Inuit cultures and many Plains First Nations. Country and western music continues to be a dominant genre in these communities today. Native radio continues to be an important influence on musical expression. For example, CFWE, based in Edmonton, broadcasts to Native communities across Canada. Established in 1987,

CFWE programming continues to emphasize Native 'culture and interests through music and the spoken word.'[1]

Powwow Music

The greatest and most recognizable form of Native music is powwow music. The powwow is a social event born of various traditions of many nations, which can be private or public. Powwow music is the roots, folk, and classical music of Canada's Native peoples. This distinct music form embodies the philosophy, history, and contemporary influences that continue to affect and represent Native identity. Not only has the music adapted to the present day, but it has also translated new influences into a musical code that has been passed on from generation to generation as a living document of history. Over the years, powwows have become more intertribal, but music and dance continue to be the central unifying theme. However, every time a powwow is conducted, the event, the music, the dances, and other elements evolve into a stylized dynamic.

Often, two or more men sit around the large drum and accompany themselves as they sing. One man is a designated leader (accompanied by a second lead singer) 'usually because of his good song memory and vocal endurance. He begins the powwow song and is soon joined by the others … [T]he voice and drum rhythm, though often sounding independently, are actually coordinated. Vocal style varies, but can be generally described as high-pitched in vocal pulsations. Texts may be in Native languages, … in vocables, and occasionally in English' (Whidden 2009).

For some, powwow music, with its distinctive singing and drumming styles, personifies Native music and life. However, the symbolization is not always positive. For example, in 2002, *Toronto Star* columnist Rosie DiManno reflected, with a somewhat scathing view, on powwow music during Queen Elizabeth II's visit to Canada: '… no matter how urban or Anglo-centric the community, [it has] been subjected to an endless force-feeding of aboriginal content and multi-cultural schlock. Inuit teenagers may be sucking solvent fumes in Rankin Inlet – and if I had to listen to all that ceremonial drum-beating I might grab a hose myself – and Indian males disproportionately represented among mendicant street people in our cities, but the storybook versions of indigenous peoples represented to the Queen has them all the time dancing and singing and preening their feathers' (DiManno 2002). Perhaps DiManno was trying to say that Native culture is paraded out for the Queen while disturbing realities are hidden away. Whatever the intention, the perspective is issued from an untrained and unsympathetic voice.

Songs of Protest

In the mid-twentieth century, especially in the 1960s, political action and protest was prominent in all areas of society including that of Native peoples, who expressed their resistance to brutal legislation and policies such as the White Paper of 1969. This was the beginning of a cultural resurgence that instilled powerful feelings of 'Indian Pride' in many Native peoples. Protests against assimilation policies and extinguishment became rallying points for resistance alongside anti–Vietnam War protests, especially in the United States.[2] The American Indian Movement's 'Red Power' campaigns began to spread into Canada by the late 1960s (Dickason 2002). Native music was an active and a major element in the cultural revolution in which many Native people were participating. The music is a document of those times.

Combined with the political upheavals of the day, the Native voice rose in protest along with many other voices demanding justice. Many Native artists grabbed public attention with their music and words and brought Native issues into focus. Their songs gave voice, personality, and sometimes a name and a face to the message. In Canada, Buffy Sainte-Marie, Willie Dunn, Shingoose (Curtis Jonnie), Chief Dan George, and Willie Thrasher articulated their views on historical and contemporary issues. Many artists, who later became icons, spoke out, making their music a voice of the oppressed.

Mi'kmaq singer-songwriter Willie Dunn, through his insightful music and groundbreaking film work, delivered an outspoken view of Canada-Native relations. Beginning in the 1960s, Dunn wrote poignant songs that focused on historical and social topics. The ten-minute film he produced for the National Film Board of Canada in 1968, entitled *Crowfoot*, profiled the nineteenth-century Blackfoot chief to illustrate the sometimes brutal treatment of Native peoples by the government. Against the backdrop of historic photographs of the Canadian west in the late 1800s, the epic song told the story of the coming of colonialism and the ensuing tragedies. The film was remarkable for its day and is seen as a forerunner of the music video. It received regular airplay after its release and also helped keep the Native presence in the public mind. Dunn drew his material from the reality of oppression, residential schools, and individual tragedies. He made regular national appearances at folk festivals across Canada but became a star in Europe, predominantly in Germany, where his albums continue to be popular.

A contemporary of Dunn's, Abenaki singer and film-maker Alanis Obomsawin integrated poetic style into traditionally influenced music. Her spoken-word and drum-song performances were steeped in stories of survival. Both as a film-maker and as a performer, she opened many doors for other Native artists in Canada while creating an impact through her social and political statements. Through her early Canadian Broadcasting Corporation recordings she challenged the status quo and further educated mainstream Canada about the situation that Native people have to deal with daily. Obomsawin recorded several albums for the CBC during the early years of her recording career.

In the late 1970s and early 1980s Morley Loon, a young Cree performer from James Bay, Ontario, toured North America and recorded in his own language, which was unheard of at the time. Popular in folk music circles, Loon's music received national airplay. Not only was Loon influential in his time, but he also became an inspirational figure after his passing in 1986 at the age of thirty-eight. The Innu duo Kashtin cited Loon as a key motivator.

Protest songs continued into the 1980s and 1990s, delivered by other artists such as Ottawa-based Seventh Fire. The group's material was eclectic; it fused powwow music with Motown, rap, reggae, rock, and spoken-word compositions. Some of Seventh Fire's songs were satirical, dealing with the history of injustice and the Oka crisis of 1990.

Commercial Success of Native Musicians

One of the early Native singers who achieved some commercial success was Shingoose. His work in film and television, beginning in the late 1970s, brought national attention, not only to Native music but to other Native art forms as well. His title song for the National Film Board of Canada film *The Paradox of Norval* [Morrisseau] connected audiences directly to the fact that Native people are found in every art form in contemporary society. He went on to produce television shows showcasing Native talent.

As singers and songwriters, few Native artists can compare to the talent and popularity of Buffy Sainte-Marie, a Plains Cree. She has not only recorded some memorable work but also contributed significantly to the development and use of new music-related technologies throughout her career. For example, her album *Illuminations* was perhaps the first completely electronic album to be recorded. Her 1992 *Coincidences and Likely Stories* project was the first commercial recording to be developed solely on a computer hard drive. In 1993 mainstream Canada was introduced to the commercial potential of Native culture during Sainte-Marie's induction into the Juno Hall of Fame. The Alberta-based powwow group Stony Park and numerous powwow dancers performed on stage during the televised tribute. Both Stony Park and the Red Bull singers appeared on her 1994 EMI recording, 'Up Where We Belong.' She also uses her training as an educator to reach her audiences in ways that celebrate Native culture, while creating an appreciation for it and providing insight into Native life. Since 1964, Buffy Sainte-Marie has released over twenty-five albums, written musical scores, and appeared on film, video, and television.

The members of Kashtin, an Innu duo, sang in their own language in the early 1980s, citing Morley Loon as a direct influence alongside Cyrille Fontaine and Philippe McKenzie. Their albums earned platinum status and many awards in Canada and abroad. The duo's innocent manner and straight-forward rhythmic pop sound earned it a wide audience. Kashtin helped bring the Innu into public awareness, not just as a people who were living in an isolated part of the world but as a people who had a rich and distinct culture. Kashtin was often regarded with the same acclaim as are teen idols. That the duo's first album sold more than 225,000 copies was an amazing achievement given that it was recorded in a language that has less than 10,000 speakers.

The popularity of performers such as Robbie Robertson, a former member of the 1960s iconic group The Band and a Mohawk from the Six Nations reserve in Ontario, has contributed exceptional talent to Canada's cultural fabric. Robertson is noted for his brilliant soundtrack work, arranging, writing, and performing. Since the late 1980s he has focused on producing Native musicians and music, in addition to his own recordings. He has also worked in television and movies while earning both Juno and Grammy awards.

Tom Jackson, an Anishinabe actor, singer, songwriter, and humanitarian, first gained a reputation as a folk singer of some renown. He has recorded ten albums in the first twenty years of his career, while also working as an award-winning actor. As well, he created the annual Huron Carole Benefit Concert that raises money across Canada for food banks. Jackson generated support for the homeless and disaster relief through benefit albums and concerts.

Susan Aglukark was the first Arctic performer to achieve international commercial success. Some of her material subtly touches on the more negative elements of the Native experience although they are not the primary focus of her work. Her soft melodic approach was widely accepted and earned her many Juno awards and an Aboriginal Achievement Award in Arts and Entertainment.

Over the decades other performers such as country and folk singer Winston Wuttunnee (a Cree from Saskatchewan) or country and western singer Laura Vinson (a Cree-Métis) have been recognized as trail blazers by the Canadian music industry. Wuttunnee has been a prolific musician since the 1960s. He was, and still is, a major figure at many country and folk festivals around the world. He has raised the profile of Native musicians as well through his appearance in radio and television shows and in the movies. In 2003 he received a Canadian Aboriginal Music Award for lifetime contribution to Aboriginal music. Wuttunnee continues his leadership in the Native musical world, and in 2004 he developed a First Nations music course for the classroom. He continues to be a favourite at powwows.

Laura Vinson has blazed her way through the Canadian music industry. By following her Aboriginal roots, she puts a strong Native stamp on the folk and country music scene as she presents traditional music in a contemporary format. She has won major awards such as the Alberta Recording Industry Association's award for Best Roots Album in 1994 and a Lifetime Achievement Award in 2005.

New Directions

Native music has since grown from a cultural symbol or an ethnomusical genre into an industry. It has grown from strength to strength. In the late 1980s Gilles Chaumel wrote, 'The new aboriginal music is precisely about building an identity. This new music is alive because it is constantly changing. It reflects aboriginal society ... which itself is being transformed' (1989). Today Native musicians are found in nearly every type of popular music from hip hop and country and western to reggae, from folk music to blues, from New Age to world music. The collaboration between mainstream artists, Native artists, and Native music has created an evolutionary relationship accompanied by boundless creativity.

Breach of Trust, which signed with EMI Music in 2001, issued its message from a canon of heavy-metal verse. This group and other artists of the new millennium seem to focus as much on image as on content and embrace a wide span of influences including hip hop. Rap has been characterized as the perfect vehicle of rebellion for Native musicians, noting that it was an extension of Native oral tradition. This new generation of Native talent is determined to tell its story from its own perspective – no matter what people think of it. For example, the rap group Reddnation, established in 2000 in Alberta, is a notable group, that won the 2006 Aboriginal Music Award in the best rap or hip hop category. Other hip hop or rap groups, such as War Party and DogSoldierz, are also bringing some of the hard realities of life on First Nations' reserves to their audiences.

Armed with greater social and political consciousness, many Native artists have included traditional music in their work but on its own terms, rather than just lifting tracks from old recordings. For example, powwow groups, such as Red Bull, recorded with the Barenaked Ladies on their song 'Spider in My Room' from the album *Born on a Pirate Ship*. The Whitefish Juniors performed live with Nelly Furtado during the 2004 Juno Awards telecast.

In club DJ styles, the mixing involves a variety of pieces from obscure, unaccredited, vinyl-recorded music to the most popular forms. Quite often, styles and genres converge in an effervescence of creative exploration. Samples of 'world' or 'tribal' music and beats have enjoyed a long relationship in this area. More and more elements of North American Native style, samples, and influence continue to be used.

The inclusion and recognition of Native composers continues. A recent, high-profile example was the choice of west coast Native musician Russell Wallace to create a composition for the Dalai Lama's Vancouver visit in spring 2004. This electronic artist was perhaps the first and only contemporary composer of Native ancestry to be asked to create such work for a distinct purpose.

Awards and Support

As Native musicians slowly began finding commercial recognition by the mid-1980s, networks of Aboriginal musicians enjoyed a rise to prominence. Native promotional agencies, such as the Association for Native Development in the Performing and Visual Arts, encouraged training for Aboriginal musicians. A few Native-owned recording and distribution companies were founded, such as Saskatchewan's Sweet Grass Records, created in 1993 (Wright-McLeod 2005). As well, the Canada Council's Aboriginal Peoples Music Program, established in the late 1990s, has supported the development of Native musicians. It awards grants to support activities, such as travel and workshop presentations, that contribute to the career and artistic development of Native musicians.

One of the strongest factors in bringing a wider audience to Native musicians was the rise in the early 1990s of independently operated Native radio stations on reserves. For example, CFWE, Alberta's Aboriginal radio network, founded in the late 1980s, was an early influence in the west (Canadian Communications Foundation 2005). Native radio stations continue to mix some powwow music with country styles and Native musicians' recordings in all genres (Wright-McLeod 2005).

New technologies, such as satellite communications, have brought Native musicians to even larger audiences. In 1999 the Aboriginal Peoples Television Network (APTN) was founded, which provides a forum for Native music (Canadian Communications Foundation 2005). Today, the Internet has given all musicians, Native and non-Native alike, the potential of a global audience.

Native music festivals, such as the Dreamspeakers Film Festival or the Indian Summer Festival, increased in popularity in the early 1990s. These and other festivals continue to provide another outlet for Native music.

Although the Juno Awards began in 1970 to honour Canadian musicians, an awards category for Aboriginal Canadian music did not appear until 1994. Ten years later, Prime Minister Paul Martin would write: 'The Juno Awards represent the best in Canadian music and it is exciting to see so many First Nations artists recognized for their achievements. As Canadians come together to celebrate, it is wonderful to see Aboriginal musicians sharing in that accomplishment. Not only have they been competitive in the Canadian music industry, but are in fact leading, winning and setting a new standard of excellence ... Canada's unique musical perspective is due in part to the contributions of First Nations' (2004).

The Canadian Aboriginal Music Awards, established in 1999, continues to be a significant, high-profile event in the Native music industry. Each year it honours the keepers and teachers, as well as the promoters, creators, and performers of Aboriginal music.

Conclusion

What Native music has contributed to Canadian society has been subtle and continuous since the time of first contact. Native music has captured imaginations and has resonated deeply with those who have heard and understood the music. This distinct musical form exhibits the spirit of resilience by simply surviving. Its evolution offers a history of experiences that chronicle the last five hundred years and more. Native music and the collaborative process have reminded Canadians that Native peoples are a part of this land and have a long historical relationship with it. The interaction between cultures continues to help build understanding of not only a national identity but also a Native identity.

The image of Canada's Native peoples has become synonymous with a particular aspect of Canada's national identity in a very positive way. Ultimately, at a subconscious level, Native music has sensitized the people to the spirit of the land and a unique identity in the world as Canadians.

Notes

1 See http://www.cfweradio.ca for more details on this radio network.

2 For example, Buffy Sainte-Marie's poignant single 'Universal Soldier,' released
in 1964, drew immediate criticism. This anthem of the anti-war movement was
banned from airplay in some places.

Bibliography

Canada. 1920. Department of Indian Affairs. Deputy Superintendent Duncan
Campbell-Scott (15 December) to Thos. Graham, Esq., Indian Agent, Brocket,
Alberta.

Canadian Communications Foundation. 2005. History of Aboriginal broadcasting
in Canada. http://www.broadcasting-history.ca/programming/History_of_
Aboriginal_Broadcasting.html.

– 2006. Radio – from crystal sets to satellites. http://www.broadcasting-history.ca/
stations/radio/Crystal_Sets_to_Satellites.html.

Chaumel, Gilles. 1989. Music, a cry from the heart. *Recontre* 1989 (September).
Quoted in B. Diamond, et al. (2009).

Diamond, B., A. Kolstee, N. Beaudry, R. Whitmer, K. Peacock, M.S. Cronk, and F.
von Rosen. 2009. Native North Americans in Canada. In *Encyclopedia of Music in
Canada*, ed. H. Kallman and G. Potvin. http://www.thecanadianencyclopedia.
com/index.cfm?PgNm=TCE&Params=U1ARTU0002542.

Dickason, Olive Patricia. 2002. *Canada's First Nations: A History of Founding Peoples
from Earliest Times*. Don Mills, ON: Oxford University Press.

DiManno, Rosie. 2002. Through rain and protest, this Queen is a trouper. *Toronto
Star*, 14 October, p. A3.

Keillor, E., J.M.H. Kelly Cle-alls, and F. von Rosen, eds. n.d. Native Drums online.

Martin, Paul. 2004. Letter to the Juno CARAS BMAC committee and nominees.
Edmonton, AB.

Nakai, R. Carlos. 2003. Interview by Brian Wright-McLeod. *Renegade Radio*, CKLN
88.1 FM, Toronto, 1 December.

Whidden, Lynn. 2009. Powwow singers. In *Encyclopedia of Music in Canada*, ed.
H. Kallman and G. Potvin. http://www.thecanadianencyclopedia.com/index.
cfm?PgNm=TCE&Params=U1ARTU0002845.

Wright-McLeod, Brian. 2005. *The Encyclopedia of Native Music*. Tucson, AZ: University of Arizona Press.

Profile of Gilbert (Gil) Cardinal (1950–)

Métis, Film-maker, Director, and Producer

Gilbert (Gil) Cardinal is a man known to many in the Aboriginal community and in the film industry. He has written, produced, and directed movies, documentaries, and television shows since the beginning of his career in the media industry in the 1970s. His focus on Aboriginal issues and the Aboriginal experience has helped to increase Canadian society's awareness of Aboriginal issues.

Gil Cardinal is a Métis who was raised in Edmonton, Alberta. At the age of two he was ordered into a foster home by the courts. He was raised by a non-Aboriginal family, the Wilsons, and was not exposed to other Métis or Aboriginal people while he was growing up.[1] This would be significant in his later life.

Cardinal started his career in the film industry after taking the advice of a social worker who told him that he should enrol in the Radio and Television Arts Technology program at the Northern Alberta Institute of Technology in Edmonton.[2] After graduating from the program, he began work as a cameraman for the Access Network in the same city. In the early 1970s Gil Cardinal made his first documentary, *A Portrait of the Pianist Mark Joblonski*. He was then hired to direct the television series *Come Alive*. By the 1980s he was freelancing for the National Film Board of Canada. It was here that Cardinal began to focus on Native issues. Some of his earlier work included *Children of Alcohol* (1984), *The Courage of One's Convictions* (1985), *Hotwalker* (1986), and *Foster Child* (1987).

A poignant documentary about his upbringing, *Foster Child* follows Cardinal's search for his birth mother. In it he learns that she, Lucy Cardinal, had passed away in 1974 and that she had battled with alcohol and poverty most of her life. As a result of this production he was able to find more answers about his family background and to meet and connect with many of his relatives.[3]

After producing *Foster Child*, Gil Cardinal went on to make many more

Gil Cardinal.

documentary films including *The Spirit Within* (1990), *Tikinagan* (1991), *David with F.A.S.* (1997), and *Totem: The Return of the G'psgolox Pole* (2003).[4] He has also directed episodes for the television show *North of 60*. He co-wrote and directed several mini-series, such as *Big Bear* (1998), *Chiefs* (2002), and *Indian Summer: The Oka Crisis* (2006).[5] Cardinal has done work for the British Broadcasting Corporation, Canadian Broadcasting Corporation, and Atlantis Films.[6]

Cardinal's films on Aboriginal themes and issues have been showcased at numerous international film festivals and have won him a number of awards. He won a Gemini Award for Best Director for *Foster Child* and in 1997 received a National Aboriginal Achievement Award for Film and Television.[7] Cardinal received an honorary diploma from the Northern Alberta Institute of Technology in 2001.[8]

JEFF MOULTON

Notes

1 Gil Cardinal, *Foster Child*, National Film Board of Canada, 1987.
2 *Windspeaker*, 'Gil Cardinal: Alberta director gets film and television award,' Aboriginal Multi-Media Society, http://www.ammsa.com (accessed 14 June 2003).
3 Cardinal, *Foster Child*.
4 National Film Board of Canada, http://www.nfb.ca/explore-by/director/Gil-Cardinal/ (accessed 29 March 2009).
5 http://www.cineteleaction.com/en/pages/OKA.html (accessed 29 March 2009).
6 National Aboriginal Achievement Awards Recipients, '1997 – Arts: Gil Cardinal,' http://www.naaf.ca/program/92.
7 Ibid.
8 Northern Alberta Institute of Technology, http://www.nait.ab.ca/about/honourarydiploma2001pdf (accessed 7 May 2003).

Profile of Maria Campbell (1940–)

Métis, Writer, and Educator

Maria Campbell is one of Canada's most popular Métis authors. Her literary works have helped to both create a voice for the Métis people and enable them to be understood. She was the eldest of seven children born to the 'Road Allowance People'[1] at Park Valley, Saskatchewan, in April 1940.[2] Her parents were of Scottish, First Nation, and French descent. She felt that owing to this lineage she faced discrimination and rejection from both mainstream Canadians and First Nations people.[3]

Her mother died when Campbell was twelve years old; soon afterwards, her father was imprisoned.[4] Consequently she quit school to care for her siblings.[5] In an effort to escape her unhappy circumstances, when she was fifteen years old she married a non-Aboriginal man, who she hoped would help change her life for the better.[6] The couple moved to Vancouver, and her problems escalated. Campbell's new husband became physically and mentally abusive and eventually abandoned her.[7] She found herself pulled into a life of alcohol, drugs, and prostitution.[8] While she was in the depths of despair, Campbell was able to regain strength by remembering her beloved great-grandmother, Cheechum.[9] She then moved to Edmonton, where she involved herself in the Indian rights movement.

In Edmonton Maria Campbell started to write as a means to healing herself. Her best-selling autobiographical book, *Halfbreed*,[10] begins with a letter to herself. However, *Halfbreed* proved to be only the beginning of her creative endeavours. For example, the lack of culturally relevant Aboriginal-themed literature inspired her to write several children's books including *People of the Buffalo: How the Plains Indians Lived* (1976), *Little Badger and the Fire Spirit* (1977), and *Riel's People* (1978).[11] In 1985 she edited a short fiction book entitled *Achimoona*, and in 1989 she co-wrote *The Book of Jessica: A Theatrical Transformation* with Linda Griffiths. Other works penned by Campbell include the screenplay *The Red Dress* (1977) and the play *Jessica* (1982). She was the editor of the newspaper *New Breed*.[12] She has produced seven

Maria Campbell. Photo courtesy of Terry Lusty.

documentaries and the first Aboriginal television series, entitled *My Part-ners, My People*.[13] Campbell was the writer-in-residence at the University of Alberta (1980) and the University of Regina (1982).[14] Her energies have not all been taken up by literary or artistic pursuits. She is also an ardent sup-porter of human rights.[15] Her community activism and interest in women's advocacy led her to help establish the Edmonton Women's Halfway House and Women's Emergency Shelter.[16]

Campbell has received many awards for her writing, including honor-ary doctorates from the University of Regina (1985), York University (1992), Athabasca University (2001), and the University of Ottawa (2008).[17] She received the Gabriel Dumont Medal of Merit from Saskatchewan's Gabriel Dumont Institute and was awarded an Aboriginal Achievement Award in 1996.[18] In 2004 she won the Canada Council for the Arts Molson Prize.[19] Campbell was made an Officer of the Order of Canada by Governor Gen-eral Michaëlle Jean in 2008.[20]

Today Maria Campbell is a Native studies professor at the University of Saskatchewan in Saskatoon.[21] She continues to write and is considered an important voice in Native and feminist literary circles.[22]

SHERRY BURGAR

Notes

1 The Métis were sometimes referred to as the *Road Allowance People* because, not having their own land, they lived as squatters on public land.

2 Bernard Selinger, 'Maria Campbell,' in *Encyclopedia of Saskatchewan*, http://esask. uregina.ca/entry/campbell_maria_1940-.html (accessed 27 January 2011).

3 Harmut Lutz and Konrad Gross, 'Maria Campbell,' in *Conversations with Cana-dian Native Authors* (Farmington Hills, MI: Fifth House Publishers, 1999), 41–65.

4 Gretchen M. Bataille and Kathleen Mullen Sands, 'The long road back: Maria Campbell,' in *American Indian Women: Telling Their Lives* (Lincoln: University of Nebraska Press, 1984), 113–26.

5 Maria Campbell, *Halfbreed* (Lincoln: University of Nebraska Press, 1973).

6 Ibid.

7 Ibid.

8 Lutz and Gross, 'Maria Campbell.'

9 Rebecca Tsosie, 'Changing women: The cross-currents of American Indian feminine identity,' *American Indian Culture and Research Journal* 12 (1): 1–37.

10 Gale Group, *Maria Campbell: Discovering* (Farmington Hills, MI: Gale Group, 2001).

11 Susan M. Gorman, 'Maria Campbell,' in *Contemporary Literary Criticism* (Farmington Hills, MI: Gale Group, 1995), 95.

12 Ibid.

13 Joan Paulson, 'Campbell wins arts prize,' *Star Phoenix*, 19 May 2004, http:// mmf.mb.ca/index.php?option=com_content&task=view&id=370&Itemid=2 (accessed 1 April 2009).

14 Harmut Lutz and Konrad Gross (1991), in an interview with Maria Campbell, in *Contemporary Challenges: Conversations with Canadian Native Authors* (Fifth House Publishers, 1991), 41–65. Reproduced by the Gale Group in the *Discovering* collection.

15 Gale Group, *Maria Campbell*.

16 Gorman, 'Maria Campbell.'

17 Campbell, *Halfbreed*.

18 Ibid.

19 Canada Council for the Arts, 'Molson Prize cumulative list of winners,' http:// www.canadacouncil.ca/prizes/molson/nw127237760511562500.htm (accessed 19 November 2009).

20 Staff Writer, 'Confidential: Maria Campbell,' *Windspeaker*, 1 July 2004.

21 Department of English, University of Saskatchewan, http://www.usask.ca/ english/fac/bio.html (accessed 15 June 2004).

22 Gale Group, 'Maria Campbell,' in Contemporary Authors Online.

Profile of Alanis Obomsawin (1932–)

Abenaki and Film-maker

Alanis Obomsawin is a singer, a writer, and an activist. However, she is best known for her documentary films on Aboriginal Canadians.[1] Her artistic accomplishments promote Aboriginal rights and highlight Aboriginal concerns.

Alanis Obomsawin was born in Lebanon, New Hampshire, on 31 August 1932.[2] At six months old, she was taken to her mother's reserve of Odanak on the Saint-François River, north of Montreal.[3] Here Obomsawin learned the stories, songs, and legends of the Abenaki.[4] When she was nine years old, her family moved to Trois-Rivières, Quebec, where they were the community's only Aboriginal family.[5] Her time spent there was filled with racism and injustice as, like Native women elsewhere, she suffered from the stigma associated with her heritage.[6] Rather than become a victim of these experiences, Obomsawin held fast to the Aboriginal songs and stories she had learned, and was motivated to raise public awareness in order to help alleviate the injustice facing Native people.[7]

In the late 1950s Obomsawin moved to Montreal, where she worked as a singer and storyteller in schools and prisons, on television, and in music festivals. She wanted the educational system to be better equipped to deal with Aboriginal children, and thus she wanted to make people more aware of the injustices suffered by Aboriginal people. Obomsawin made her first national public appearance in 1967, on the CBC program *Ron Kelley's Profile*.[8] Later, the National Film Board of Canada hired her as a Native consultant. In 1971 she wrote and directed her first film, *Christmas at Moose Factory*. She has continued to make more than twenty documentaries of Canadian Aboriginal peoples, including *Kahnesatake: 270 Years of Resistance* (1993), *My Name Is Kahentiiosta* (1995), *Rocks at Whiskey Trench* (2000), *Is the Crown at War with Us* (2002), *Waban-Aki: People from Where the Sun Rises* (2006), and *Gene Boy Came Home* (2007).[9]

Obomsawin has gained worldwide acclaim and received many awards

Film-maker Alanis Obomsawin (right), director of *Is the Crown at War with Us?*, is shown in Toronto, Thursday, 12 September, 2002. Photo by CP (Frank Gunn).

for her work. In 1983 she was made an Officer of the Order of Canada and won the Governor General's Award.[10] In 1994 she received an Aboriginal Achievement Award.[11] In 2001 she obtained the Governor General's Visual and Media Arts Award.[12] Obomsawin has also been awarded the Outstanding Achievement Award in Direction from Toronto Women in Film and Television, the National Achievement Award from the Canadian Native Arts Foundation, and the Outstanding Contributions Award from the Canadian Sociology and Anthropology Association. Alanis Obomsawin has received honorary doctorates from York University, Concordia University, Carleton University, and the University of Western Ontario.[13] In 2009 she won the Outstanding Achievement Award from both the imagineNATIVE Film + Media Festival and the HotDocs International Documentary Festival.[14]

Obomsawin continues to preserve First Nations cultural heritage. She serves on the board of directors for the Aboriginal Peoples Television Network and the Public Broadcasting Association of Quebec. She also works with Concordia University as a member of the Advisory Committee on Multiculturalism and Issues of Equity.[15]

JOCELYN OBREITER

Notes

1 Hugo Bourque, 'Alanis Obomsawin,' National Film Board of Canada, http://films.nfb.ca/alanis-obomsawin (accessed 22 January 2011).

2 'Obomsawin, Alanis,' in *Historica: The Canadian Encyclopedia*, http://thecanadianencyclopedia.com.

3 Ibid.

4 Government of Canada, 'National gathering on Aboriginal artistic expression: Alanis Obomsawin,' http://www.lac-bac.gc.ca/women/030001-1259-e.html.

5 National Film Board, 'Alanis Obomsawin.'

6 Ibid.

7 Government of Canada, 'National gathering.'

8 National Film Board, 'Alanis Obomsawin.'

9 Government of Canada, 'Obomsawin, Alanis,' http://collectionscanada.ca/women/002026-709.e.html.

10 'Obomsawin, Alanis,' in *Historica.*

11 Ibid.

12 National Film Board, 'Alanis Obomsawin.'

13 Government of Canada (accessed 22 January 2011).

14 http://archives.cbc.ca/society/native_issues/clips/16720/.

15 'Obomsawin, Alanis,' in *Historica.*

PART 6

CONCLUSION

Our Aboriginal Vision for Canada

CORA J. VOYAGEUR, DAVID R. NEWHOUSE,
AND DAN BEAVON

In a world darkened by ethnic conflicts that tear nations apart, Canada stands
as a model of how people of different cultures can live and work together in
peace, prosperity and mutual respect.
    – Bill Clinton, President, United States of America
    Address to Canadian Parliament, 23 February 1995

The 1996 report of the Royal Commission on Aboriginal Peoples contains an
Aboriginal vision of Canada and the principles for the conduct of a mutually beneficial relationship between Aboriginal peoples and the Canadian
state. It argues for changes to the fundamental structure of the Canadian
nation state to accommodate Aboriginal peoples and to restore their right
to govern themselves within Canada. Aboriginal people must be present in
all aspects of the Canadian state and the life within it. This presence should
be based upon a notion of contribution rather than problem. It means a shift
of the societal paradigm regarding Aboriginal peoples.

This change has begun. Aboriginal people have made tremendous contributions to Canadian society and its people. The historical and contemporary contributions range from the geographic and political creation of
Canada to the ongoing debate as to what is Canadian identity. One example
is the treaty process, as we saw in Volume 1, which led to the evolution of
Canada.

First Nations peoples contributed much of the country's land mass
through a series of treaties. These treaties made it possible for Canada to
be what it is today. Based in the Royal Proclamation of 1763, the treaty process continues. In fact, much of Canada's land mass is demarcated by treaties. It is fair to say that without the long history of treaty making, Canada
probably would not have the geographic borders it has today. This treaty-
making process between Aboriginal and non-Aboriginal people in Canada

has evolved over more than three hundred and fifty years. Treaty making has its origins in the diplomatic relationship developed between Aboriginal peoples. This was a relationship based in reciprocity. Agreement between the parties was a cooperative process during which interests, protection, and well-being were negotiated.

Later Aboriginal and European treaties led to economic and military alliances, and Canada began to take form. These diplomatic proceedings were the first steps in a long process that has led to today's comprehensive claims agreements between the Crown and Aboriginal groups.[1] Canadians must recognize that they too are treaty partners and beneficiaries.

The contemporary treaty process is a continuation of Confederation. For example, Canada remains involved in negotiating treaties in British Columbia and in interpreting historic treaties in Saskatchewan. The land claims process is rewriting the map of Canada and creating Aboriginal territories and other forms of government in our federation. The ongoing treaty process continues to reshape the political landscape by transferring lands back to Aboriginal control and creating sites where Aboriginal and non-Aboriginal peoples share stewardship and jurisdiction. Over the last four decades Canada and Aboriginal peoples have signed a number of treaties, land claims agreements, and final agreements.[2] The accompanying table sets out these modern-day treaties and land claim agreements.

In a speech to the British Columbia legislature in 1998 the Nisga'a Tribal Council president, Chief Joseph Gosnell, spoke of the positive aspects of land claims when he stated:

> Today marks a turning point in the history of British Columbia. Today, aboriginal and non-aboriginal people are coming together to decide the future of this province.
>
> I am talking about the Nisga'a Treaty – a triumph for all British Columbians – and a beacon of hope for aboriginal people around the world.
>
> A triumph, I believe, which proves to the world that reasonable people can sit down and settle historical wrongs. It proves that a modern society can correct the mistakes of the past. As British Columbians, as Canadians, we should all be very proud.[3]

The establishment of the Nunavut Territory in 1999 was a historic event. Those who negotiated its birth were referred to by their communities as 'fathers and mothers of Confederation.' More of these sorts of events are needed for Canada to continue to build a confederation that is genuinely based on inclusion and reciprocity. Perhaps the reconciliation approach will help to move this project forward. The presence of Aboriginal peoples in

Modern-Day Treaties and Land Claim Agreements

Year	Land Claim Agreement or Treaty
2010	Eeyou Marine Region Land Claims Agreement (EMRLCA); 7 July
2009	Maa-nulth First Nation Agreement; 18 June
2008	Seton Lake Indian Band Agreement; 4 November
	Gitwangak Band Council Agreement; 4 November
	Metlakatla Band Agreement; 4 November
	Lax Kw'alaams Indian Band Agreement; 4 November
	Madawaska Maliseet First Nation Agreement
	Indian Reserve No. 23 Specific Claim Final Agreement; 22 April
2007	Metepenagiag Mi'kmaq Nation Hosford Lot and Indian Reserve No. 7; 30 November
	Nunavik Inuit Land Claims Agreement Act; 29 October
	Maa-nulth First Nations Final Agreement*; 18 June
	Songhees First Nation Agreement; 29 March
	Esquimalt First Nation Agreement; 29 March
2006	Tsawwassen First Nation Final Agreement
	Lheidli T'enneh Final Agreement*; 29 October
2005	Carcross/Tagish First Nation Final Agreement and Carcross/Tagish First Nation Self-Government Agreement*; 22 October
	Kwanlin Dun First Nation Final Agreement and the Kwanlin Dun First Nation Self-Government Agreement*; 19 February
	Nunavik Inuit Land Claims Agreement
	Inuit of Labrador Land Claims Agreement
2004	Anishnaabe Government Agreement*; 7 December
2003	Westbank First Nation Self-Government Agreement*; 3 October
	Kluane First Nation Final Agreement and Kluane First Nation Self-Government Agreement
	Tlicho Agreement
2002	The Ta'an Kwach'an Council Final Agreement and Ta'an Kwach'an Council Self-Government Agreement
1999	Nisga'a Final Agreement
1998	Tr'ondëk Hwëch'in Final Agreement and Tr'ondëk Hwëch'in Self-Government Agreement
1997	Little Salmon/Carmacks First Nation Final Agreement and Little Salmon/Carmacks First Nation Self-Government Agreement
	Selkirk First Nation Final Agreement and Selkirk First Nation Self-Government Agreement
1993	Sahtu Dene and Metis Comprehensive Land Claim Agreement, Volume I, and Sahtu Dene and Metis Comprehensive Land Claim Agreement, Volume II (effective date 1994)
	Umbrella Final Agreement between the Government of Canada, the Council for Yukon Indians, and the Government of the Yukon
	Vuntut Gwitchin First Nation Final Agreement and Vuntut Gwitchin First Nation Self-Government Agreement (effective date 1995)
	Champagne and Aishihik First Nations Final Agreement and Champagne and Aishihik First Nations Self-Government Agreement (effective date 1995)
	Teslin Tlingit Council Final Agreement and Teslin Tlingit Council Self-Government Agreement (effective date 1995)
	Nacho Nyak Dun First Nation Final Agreement and Nacho Nyak Dun First Nation Self-Government Agreement (effective date 1995)
	Nunavut Land Claims Agreement
1992	Gwich'in Comprehensive Land Claim Agreement
1984	Western Arctic Claim – The Inuvialuit Final Agreement
1978	The Northeastern Quebec Agreement
1975	James Bay and Northern Quebec Agreement and Complementary Agreements (effective date 1977)

*Pending parliamentary ratification.

the Canadian constitution has shaped and continues to shape aspects of Canadian politics and law. Both the debate over Aboriginal governments and their emergence are shaping federal institutions and creating a new level of government. A new Canada, perhaps more amicable to Aboriginal peoples, is starting to emerge after almost four decades of intense political activity.

The political activities of Aboriginal peoples are forcing Canada to confront its colonial legacy and to live up to its values of tolerance and understanding. Canadian society is coming to terms with its Aboriginal heritage; it is starting to address the continued and increasing presence of Aboriginal people within its boundaries and the desire for distinctiveness and visibility in the cultural and body politic of the country. John Ralston Saul goes further and argues in *A Fair Country: Telling Truths about Canada* (2008) that Canada is a Métis nation with a political culture comprising Aboriginal and European political thinking. His argument is a remarkable one that could not have been conceived of in 1969. It is a visible demonstration of the changes in public scholarship about Canada, which is slowly challenging old orthodoxies.

The issues of mutual respect and mutual benefit are the driving forces behind Aboriginal politics, in particular to maintain the distinct identity of Aboriginal peoples, to have that identity represented in real and significant ways in the daily life of the country and in its institutions, and to derive benefits from the Confederation. Traditional Aboriginal cultural, social, and political philosophies are based upon a respect for diversity and distinctiveness within a complex community or nation – a sense that one is both an individual and a part of the collective. Distinctiveness has more than just social and cultural aspects. Part of the desire for distinctiveness is a desire to act upon one's own ideas about the social and the political. It is inherently political, as Canada has come to understand. It does not, however, have to cause division or conflict. Mutual benefit is derived from finding ways to accommodate each other's distinctiveness. Mutual respect can lead to mutual benefit.

The desire for Aboriginal distinctiveness has led to debate about who *is* and who *is not* Indian, Aboriginal, First Nation, Original People, or Métis. This debate is perplexing to many non-Aboriginals. This debate should not be surprising nor should we be frightened by it. We now live in a world where the lines around identity for the sake of inclusion or exclusion are blurred and are drawn in different ways by different forces for different purposes. The Canadian state plays a large role in these debates because the outcomes affect access to and the allocation of state resources. Some argue that the state itself, through its legislative regime such as the Indian Act and associated regulations, has set up Aboriginal identity as a site of continual contestation. As an Aboriginal person, one can have multiple identities, culturally, socially, and legally, sometimes serially and sometimes simultaneously. It is also possible to be Aboriginal and Canadian at the same time. But for an Aboriginal person to be able to say this with pride will require more substantive recognition of Aboriginality by Canada and Canadians.

Although Aboriginal culture and traditional values continue to have a significant impact, Aboriginal people are also products of the times in which they live. For example, contemporary Aboriginal leaders are products of a modern Aboriginality. This Aboriginality is defined by what we call post-colonial Aboriginal consciousness. It is the consciousness of a society that is aware that it has been colonized in many ways, a society that is aware of the implications of colonization and is choosing deliberately, openly, and systematically to deal with the effects of it. It is a society coming to terms with the past and choosing to move forward in full remembrance of what came before.

One example of this post-colonial consciousness sees Indigenous peoples asserting their connection to place by renaming places and objects in the landscape with the original names. One can witness the changes in the territory of Nunavut as Anglo-Saxon place names are replaced by or returned to Inuktitut ones. In a similar but albeit ironic fashion the names of Indian reserves are being changed to reflect historic territories and historic Aboriginal names; the post-colonial necessarily includes elements of the colonial.

It is important to note that Canadian views have changed, and today there is a vigorous discussion, and sometimes debate, about how to rectify the founding error and how to bring Aboriginal peoples (Indians, Métis, and Inuit) into the body politic of Canada. Aboriginal peoples themselves are challenging the place to which they were assigned in the country and are working diligently, conscientiously, and with post-colonial consciousness to move away from the colonial past.

The Canadian state has slowly begun to educate the Canadian public about Aboriginal peoples, their cultures, legal rights, and contributions to Canada. The 1998 Statement of Apology and the 2008 Residential School apology in the House of Commons, and the Truth and Reconciliation Commission, are important aspects of this public education effort. The two public apologies provide a starting point for the creation of a post-colonial consciousness among Canadians. Most provincial public school systems include Aboriginal peoples and their cultures as part of the school curricula for primary- and secondary-level students. Post-secondary institutions have areas of studies focused on Aboriginal peoples, and Indigenous knowledge has emerged as a foundational aspect of most programs in Indigenous studies. It would be safe to conclude that these public efforts may result in a younger generation that holds distinctly different views about Aboriginal peoples than do both its parents and grandparents. *Discovering Canada: The Rights and Responsibilities of Citizenship Study Guide*, produced by Citizenship and Immigration Canada and released in 2009, describes Aboriginal peoples as one of 'our three founding peoples – Aboriginal, French and British.' The guide has continued the debate about the foundations of Canada.

The 1996 report of the Royal Commission on Aboriginal Peoples recognized the need for a large public-education process. The commission viewed this as a means of eliminating the knowledge gap that mainstream Canadians had about Canada's Indigenous peoples. Further, the work of the Centre for Research and Information on Canada over the last several years demonstrates that support for Aboriginal self-government and Aboriginal rights increases dramatically when relevant information is provided, helping Canadians to understand the issues better.

Canada and the provinces can also play a further role in educating children and young adults. The public school curricula can be an effective tool for social change. Much work can be done by accurately portraying Aboriginal history, culture, and tradition. A commitment to include these topics at all education levels would help to dispel many of the myths surrounding Indigenous peoples and lay the foundations for improved social and community relations. For example, presenting First Nations communities and governments as part of political studies courses on the structures and processes of governance in Canada would help to dispel the stereotypes of reserve communities as lacking in governance and laws. The British North America Act, 1867, s. 6 (91), states that the government will 'make laws for the peace, order, and good government of Canada, in relation to all matters not coming within the classes of subjects by this Act assigned exclusively to the Legislatures of the provinces.'[4] Recognizing that First Nations governments have the same long-standing political philosophies that seek peace, order, and good governance would help Canadians see that Aboriginal peoples share their values.

There has been significant work done to improve the material conditions of Aboriginal peoples. We are optimistic for the Aboriginal peoples of Canada because of the foundation of change that has taken place in the past few decades. The following are examples of progress made by Aboriginal people in Canada:

1 Historians over the last two decades have begun to explore aspects of Aboriginal history and examine the agency of Indigenous peoples as they deal with the Canadian state. The roles and contributions of Aboriginal peoples in Canadian society have been highlighted in the work of Olive Dickason, Winona Wheeler, Heather Devine, Sarah Carter, and others. This work has made its way into curricula and public consciousness and makes it easier for Canadians to understand and support Aboriginal peoples' social and political goals.

2 With the constitutional entrenchment of unique Aboriginal rights and the development of case law, the judicial system has provided a solid foundation of legal rights pertaining to Indigenous peoples that force the state to consider Aboriginal interests in its decision-making processes.

3 The state continues the treaty-making process throughout western Canada, particularly in British Columbia. In Saskatchewan, the Office of the Treaty Commission hosted a large public dialogue on treaties. These efforts are educating many people about Aboriginal cultures, political traditions, and goals and helping to demonstrate that the acceptance of Aboriginal interests advances their own interests.

4 A set of Aboriginal institutions has developed over the past twenty years to represent Aboriginal interests, deliver services to Indigenous communities, and interact with mainstream institutions.

5 Over the last thirty years Aboriginal politicians and federal and provincial leaders have engaged in several highly visible discussions such as the First Ministers conferences. Some of these events have been broadcast on national television. These high-profile discussions are easily accessed by Canadians and help to educate them about Aboriginal peoples and their issues.

6 The Aboriginal Peoples Television Network, started in 1999, is required to be carried by all cable companies with a service area of more than 3,500 homes per square kilometre, thus making it available to most Canadian homes with cable television.

7 The National Aboriginal Achievement Awards are broadcast annually on national television, bringing Aboriginal excellence to Canadians' attention. Moreover, the Juno Awards have created a category for Aboriginal music.

8 Several governor generals and lieutenant-governors over the last twenty-five years have made Aboriginal issues a priority during their time in office.

9 Provincial education systems have adjusted curricula to include sections on Aboriginal peoples' history, culture, and contemporary issues.

10 Federal funding has been provided for a variety of Aboriginal interests over the last four decades. Much of this funding has focused upon improving the socio-economic conditions of Aboriginal peoples.

We recognize that not all is well with Aboriginal people in Canada, and a lot more work remains to be done to improve their lives. However, the above-mentioned activities have required considerable discussion, compromise, planning, and effort by all involved. The results of these efforts are benefiting both the Aboriginal community and Canadian society.

Creating a post-colonial country is difficult and emotional work; confronting the past and working to ensure that it does not continue into the future is challenging, and not everyone agrees upon the preferred future. There are still many who believe that Aboriginal peoples ought to assimilate, that the Canadian state spends too much money on them, and that Aboriginal cultures in and of themselves are significant impediments to development. Ending denial, as Wayne Warry argues, means that we ought to ask a set of new questions, not about Aboriginal marginalization but about the nature of the country that we want to live within.[5]

The path forward is to build a national political and social culture that includes Aboriginal ideas and cultural and political traditions – a continuation of Confederation to bring Aboriginal people into the Canadian state in a respectful and dignified way. This was not done in 1867 and remains the country's unfinished business. This is the way forward.

In both volumes of Hidden in Plain Sight we have seen the extent and breadth of the contributions and the sacrifices that Aboriginal peoples have made to Canadian society and identity. We have also seen that reciprocity is a means to social cohesion.

We hope that these two volumes have added a new dimension to the understanding of Aboriginal peoples in Canada. The chapters in Hidden in Plain Sight attest to the multifaceted contributions that Aboriginal peoples have made to Canada, to its culture, to its history, and to its identity.

Our Aboriginal vision of Canada is a society that appreciates and acknowledges the contributions of Aboriginal peoples – our ancestors and our contemporaries – which range from sharing their land to giving their lives. We participated in the treaty-making process that defined Canada through the lands and resources transferred from Aboriginal to Canadian control during the early formative period of the Canadian nation. We gave our lives in defence of this country during the two world wars even though we were exempt from military service. We volunteered for military service in numbers higher in proportion than those in mainstream society. Our skills as marksmen, runners, and interpreters were invaluable to the war effort.

Despite our contributions to this nation some in Canada continue to define Canada's responsibilities to Aboriginal peoples as a burden. Many Canadians, however, view and treat Aboriginals as partners and are attempting to practise a new relationship based on mutual respect and benefit. As editors, we hope that the chapters in this volume will help others understand that Aboriginality has shaped our national life in positive ways and is deserving of a substantive and central place in our Canadian society.

Notes

1 Jean-Pierre Morin, 'Treaties and the evolution of Canada,' in *Hidden in Plain Sight, Volume 1,* edited by David R. Newhouse, Cora J. Voyageur, and Dan Beavon (University of Toronto Press, 2005).

2 A *final agreement* is the outcome of successful land claim negotiations. It details agreements reached between the Aboriginal group, the province or territory, and Canada on all issues at hand, including resources, financial benefits, self-government, and land ownership. The final agreement must be ratified by the parties and signed by the principals. The final step is for the Canadian Parliament to pass legislation that gives effect to the final agreement and renders it valid.

3 Chief Joseph Gosnell, 'Chief Gosnell's historic speech to the British Columbia legislature,' 2 December 1998, http://www.kermode.net/nisgaa/speeches/gosnell4.html (accessed 31 January 2011).

4 'Distribution of legislative powers,' section VI (91), British North America Act, 1867, 30–31 Vict., c.3.

5 Wayne Warry, *Ending Denial: Understanding Aboriginal Issues* (University of Toronto Press, 2008).

Profile of Georges Henry Erasmus (1948–)

Dene and Politician

Credited for bringing Aboriginal issues to prominence in mainstream Canada, Georges Henry Erasmus is a leader and spokesperson who has played a significant role in reshaping the country's politics. He has helped to re-envision the national identity and Canada's relationship to the First Nations.

Erasmus was born in Fort Rae, Northwest Territories, on 8 August 1948. He and his siblings were raised in the territorial capital of Yellowknife. He attended school there, completing Grade 12 in the mid 1960s. Although he did not continue his formal education beyond high school, he later received honorary degrees from several universities in recognition of his contributions to Aboriginal peoples. Erasmus began working in his community in the late 1960s. His roles included chairman of the NWT Community Housing Association, fieldworker for the Company of Young Canadians, a co-founder of the Tree of Peace Friendship Centre in Yellowknife (then as its executive director),[1] and chair of the University of Canada North (1971–5).[2]

Erasmus's entry into politics occurred in the mid 1970s when he was elected president of the Indian Brotherhood of the Northwest Territories (the organizational predecessor to the Dene Nation) He was recognized as an effective and determined leader, gaining national attention for fighting the potentially devastating environmental impacts of the proposed Mackenzie Valley pipeline,[3] which would have run through Dene land. He stepped down as leader in 1983, frustrated by the standstill in land-claims negotiations.[4]

Erasmus did not stay away from politics for long. Later that year he was elected as the Northern vice-chief of the Assembly of First Nations (AFN).[5] He served in this capacity for two years. He then ran for and was elected to the post of national chief,[6] which he held for six years. During his tenure as leader, Erasmus established the AFN as 'the undisputed voice of First Nations people across Canada.'[7] For instance, he was heavily

Georges Erasmus.

involved in the 1983–7 first ministers' conferences that sought constitutional reform.[8]

Erasmus, along with René Dussault, was appointed co-chair of the 1991 Royal Commission on Aboriginal Peoples, which was mandated to address Aboriginal peoples' place in Canadian society following Aboriginal participation in the failure of the Meech Lake Accord and as an attempt to quell unrest within Canada's Aboriginal community following the Oka crisis. By 1996 the commission had issued a five-volume report with more than four hundred recommendations.[9] Although controversial, the report resulted in the federal government releasing the 'Gathering Strength' strategy for addressing Aboriginal peoples' social and economic concerns.[10] Since the disbanding of the commission Erasmus has been involved with various international bodies including the World Council of Indigenous Peoples. He has also served as president and chair of the Aboriginal Healing Foundation.[11]

Erasmus has written many newspaper articles about Aboriginal issues. He co-edited *Drumbeat: Anger and Renewal in Indian Country* (1990) with Boyce Richardson. He delivered the 2002 LaFontaine-Baldwin lecture series entitled 'A Dialogue on Democracy in Canada.' His efforts to improve Aboriginal peoples' condition have not gone unnoticed. In 1987 Erasmus was made a Member of the Order of Canada,[12] and in 1998 he received a National Aboriginal Achievement Award.[13] He also received the Governor General's Northern Medal in 2009.[14] In addition, Erasmus has received honorary doctorates from Queen's University (1989), University of Toronto (1992), York University (1992), University of Winnipeg (1992), University of British Columbia (1993), Dalhousie University (1997), University of Alberta (1997), and University of Western Ontario (2006).[15]

Georges Erasmus has worked throughout his adult life to find livable solutions for Aboriginals, by seeking unity among Aboriginal peoples, advocating for self-determination, and being a strong proponent for the settlement of land claims. He has helped shape a new political landscape in Canada and forged a new direction for Canadian identity – one that takes the rights and concerns of Aboriginal peoples into account.

ONDINE PARK

Notes

1 Paul Barnsley, 'Georges Erasmus: Fighting for his people's rights began at an early age,' *Windspeaker Profiles of Outstanding Aboriginal People*, 9 June 1998, 3.

2 'Georges Henry Erasmus,' in *Who's Who in Canada,* vol. 37, ed. Elizabeth Lumley (Toronto: University of Toronto Press, 2002), 402.

3 Barnsley, 'Georges Erasmus.'

4 Answers.com, 'Biography: Georges Henry Erasmus,' http://www.answers.com/topic/georges-erasmus (accessed 20 November 2009).

5 Ibid.

6 John Ralston Saul, Alain Dubuc, and Georges Erasmus, *The LaFontaine-Baldwin Lectures: A Dialogue on Democracy in Canada,* ed. Rudyard Griffiths (Toronto: Penguin Canada, 2002).

7 National Aboriginal Achievement Foundation, *National Aboriginal Achievement Award's 1998,* http://www.naaf.ca/program/92.

8 Michael Poslums and Anthony J. Hall, 'Assembly of First Nations,' in *Canadian Encyclopedia,* http://www.thecanadianencyclopedia.com/index.cfm?PgNm=TCE&TCE_Version=A&ArticleId=A0000352&MenuClosed=0.

9 Ibid.

10 Ibid

11 Indian and Northern Affairs Canada.

12 Barnsley, 'Georges Erasmus.'

13 National Aboriginal Achievement Foundation.

14 'Northern Medal awarded to Georges Erasmus,' http://turtleisland.org/discussion/viewtopic.php?f= 7&t=6521&start=0 (accessed 26 January).

15 Barnsley, 'Georges Erasmus.'

Appendix:
Recognition of Aboriginal Achievements

PREPARED BY ABBY GABORA AND ANDREW CALLIOU

National Aboriginal Achievement Award

2011 Recipients

Dr Marcia Anderson DeCoteau – Health
Cindy Blackstock – Public Service
Teyotsihstokwathe Dakota Brant – Special Youth Award
Dr Duncan Cree – Technology and Trades
Joseph F. Dion – Business and Commerce
Margo L. Greenwood – Education
Corrine Hunt – Arts
Roger Jones – Law and Justice
Jean LaRose – Media and Communications
Dr Lillian McGregor – Lifetime Achievement Award
Annie Panguit Peterloosie – Culture, Heritage, and Spirituality
Audrey Poitras – Politics
Frederick G. Sasakamoose – Sports
Ronald Edward Sparrow – Environment and Natural Resources

2010 Recipients

Kenneth Atsenhaienton Deer – Media and Communication
Skawenniio Barnes – Special Youth
Danny Beaton – Environment and Natural Resources
Edith Cloutier – Public Service
William Commanda, OC – Lifetime
Tom Crane Bear – Culture, Heritage, and Spirituality
Doug Henry – Technology and Trades
Madeleine Kētēskwew Dion Stout, BN, MA, PhD – Health

Dr Raoul J. McKay – Education
Ellen Melcosky – Business and Commerce
Monica Pinette – Sports
Kananginak Pootoogook – Arts
Hon. Eric Robinson – Politics
Donald Worme, QC, IPC – Law and Justice

2009 Recipients

Stephen J. Augustine – Culture, Heritage, and Spirituality
The Rev. Stan Cuthand, BTh. – Lifetime Achievement
Mervin J. Dewasha – Technology and Trades
Joan Glode – Public Service
Candace Grier-Lowe – Health
Dennis Jackson – Arts
Melanie Jackson – Arts
Cecil King – Education
Chelsea Lavallée – Special Youth
Allan C. McLeod - Business and Commerce
Carol Morin - Media and Communication
Paul Okalik – Politics
Delia Opekokew – Law and Justice
Gordon W. Prest – Environment and Natural Resources
Adam Sioui – Sports

2008 Recipients

Paul Andrew – Media and Communications
Dr Marie Ann Battiste – Education
Boyy Wesley Benjamin – Special Youth
Jim Bioucher – Arts
Shirlely Cheechoo – Arts
Joe Handley – Politics
Reggie Leach – Sports
Sylvia B. Maracle – Public Service
Norval Morrisseau – Lifetime Achievement
David C. Nahwegahbow, IPC – Law and Justice
Elizabeth (Tshaukuesh) Penashue – Environment and Natural Resources
Dr Jeff Reading, MSc, PhD – Health
Hubert Skye – Business and Commerce

2007 Recipients

Alestine Andre – Culture, Heritage, and Spirituality
Hugh Braker – Law and Justice
Lewis Cardinal – Public Service
Joane Cardinal-Schubert – Arts
Fred Carmichael – Politics
Dr Joseph Couture – Health
Wegadesk Gorup-Paul – Sports
Bertha Clark Jones – Lifetime Achievement
James Makokis – Youth Award
Lisa Meeches – Media
Joe Michel – Education
Monica Peters – Technology and Trades
Jack Poole – Business and Commerce
Chief David Walkem – Environment

2006 Recipients

Taiaiake (Gerald) Alfred – Education
Dr Herb Belcourt – Housing
Tony Belcourt – Public Service
Bernd Christmas – Business and Commerce
Gladys Taylor Cook – Heritage and Spirituality
Myra Cree – Media and Communications
Billy Day – Environment
Andrea Dykstra – Youth
Wendy Grant-John – Community Development
James (Sakej) Youngblood Henderson – Law and Justice
Shirley Firth Larsson – Sports
Jane Ash Poitras – Arts and Culture
Jim Sinclair – Lifetime Achievement
George Tuccaro – Media and Communications

2005 Recipients

Bertha Allen – Lifetime Achievement
Lolly Annahatak – Social Services
Andy Carpenter Sr – Environment
Brenda Chambers – Media and Communications

Thomas Dignan – Medicine
Sharon Anne Firth – Sports
Judy Gingell – Community Development
Douglas Golosky – Business and Commerce
Eber Hampton – Education
Joe Jacobs – Arts and Culture
Fauna Kingdon – Youth
Emma LaRocque – Education
Gerald McMaster – Arts and Culture
John Joe Sark – Heritage and Spirituality

2004 Recipients

Pearl Calahasen – Public Service
Andrew T. Delisle Sr – Lifetime Achievement
Kristinn Frederickson – Youth Award
Osuitok Ipeelee – Arts and Culture
Basil Johnston – Heritage and Spirituality
Tina Keeper – Arts and Culture
Clarence Louie – Business and Community Development
Susan Point – Arts and Culture
Suzanne Rochon Burnett – Media and Communications
Muriel Stanley Venne – Law and Justice
Carl Urion – Education
Stanley Vollant – Medicine
Sheila Watt-Cloutier – Environment
Lee Wilson – Science and Technology

2003 Recipients

John Arcand – Arts and Culture
Judith G. Bartlett – Medicine and Health Services
Mel E. Benson – Business and Commerce
Gary Bosgoed – Business and Technology
John J. Burrows – Law and Justice
Matthew Dunn – Youth Award
Thomas King – Arts and Culture
Charles Edward Lennie – Heritage and Sports
Leroy Little Bear – Education
Simon Lucas – Environment
Sophie Pierre – Public Service

Mary Richard – Community Development
Robbie Robertson – Lifetime Achievement
Jay Wortman – Medicine and Health Services

2002 Recipients

Ohito Ashoona – Arts and Culture
Harry Deneron – Business and Commerce
Freda Diesing – Arts and Culture
Leonard (Len) G. Flett – Business and Commerce
Roy Fox – Energy
Gail Guthrie Valaskakis – Media and Communications
Alex Janvier – Lifetime Achievement
Jonah Kelly – Media and Communications
Noel Knockwood – Heritage and Spirituality
George Kurszewski – Community Development
Michael Nepinak – Sports
Joseph Tokwiro Norton – Public Service
Gilles Pinette – Medicine
Jordin Tootoo – Youth Award

2001 Recipients

Freda Ahenakew – Education
Mariano Aupilardjuk – Heritage and Spirituality
Roman Bittman – Media and Communications
Harold Cardinal – Lifetime Achievement
Lindsay Crowshoe – Medicine
Tomson Highway – Arts and Culture
Fred House – Community Development
Zacharias Kunuk – Media and Communications
Leonard S. Marchand – Public Service
Richard Nerysoo – Public Service
Lance Relland – Youth Award
Nicholas Sibbeston – Public Service
Mary Thomas – Environment
Dolly Watts – Business and Commerce

2000 Recipients

Jo-ann Archibald – Education

Simon Baker (Khot-La-Cha) – Heritage and Spirituality
John Charles Bernard – Business and Commerce
Paul J. Birckel (Nashiä) – Community Development
Joseph Arthur Gosnell (Sim-oogit Hleek) – Lifetime Achievement
Fjola Hart-Wasekeesikaw – Health and Medicine
Waneek Horn-Miller – Youth Award
Leetia Ineak – Media and Communications
Edith Josie – Heritage and Spirituality
Steven Point – Law and Justice
Miles G. Richardson (Kilsli Kaji Sting) – Environment
Konrad Haskan Sioui – Public Service
Tsa-qwa-supp (Art Thompson) – Arts and Culture
Roy Albert Whitney (Onespot) – Business and Commerce

1999 Recipients

Howard Adams – Education
James K. Bartleman – Public Service
Dorothy Betz – Community Development
Rose Toodick Boyko – Law and Justice
Edward Kantonkote Cree – Medicine
Lillian Eva Dyck – Science
Dorothy Grant – Business and Commerce
James Igloliorte – Law and Justice
Malcolm King – Medical Research
Alika LaFontaine – Youth Award
Mitiarjuk Attasie Nappaaluk – Heritage and Spirituality
Allen Sapp – Lifetime Achievement
Theresa Stevenson – Community Development
David Gabriel Tuccaro – Business and Commerce

1998 Recipients

John Amagoalik – Public Service
Abel Bosum – Community Development
Wade R. Cachagee – Youth Award
Tantoo Cardinal – Film and Television
Joe Crowshoe – Heritage and Spirituality
Josephine Crowshoe – Heritage and Spirituality
Tagak Curley – Business and Commerce
Georges Erasmus – Public Service

Emily Jane Faries – Education
Dan E. Goodleaf – Public Service
Roberta Jamieson – Law and Justice
Daphne Odjig – Arts and Culture
Buffy Sainte-Marie – Lifetime Achievement
Bryan Trottier – Sports
Cornelia Wieman – Medicine

1997 Recipients

Kiawak Ashoona – Arts and Culture
George Berthe – Youth Award
Gil Cardinal – Film and Television
Chester R. Cunningham – Law and Justice
Billy Diamond – Business and Commerce
Olive P. Dickason – Lifetime Achievement
Graham Greene – Arts and Culture
Rita Joe – Arts and Culture
Stephen Kakfwi – Public Service
Harry S. LaForme – Law and Justice
Stanley John McKay – Heritage and Spirituality
Martin Gale McLoughlin – Medicine
Charlie Watt – Community Development
Darren Zack – Sports

1996 Recipients

Rose Auger – Heritage and Spirituality
Frank Calder – Lifetime Achievement
Maria Campbell – Arts and Culture
Marlene Brant Castellano – Education
W. Yvon Dumont – Public Service
Phil Fontaine – Public Service
Elijah Harper – Public Service
Tom Jackson – Community Service
Robert E. Johnson Jr – Youth Award
Alwyn Morris – Sports
Albert C. Rock – Science and Technology
Mary May Simon – Environment
Mary Two-Axe Earley – Women's Rights
James Watson Walkus – Business and Commerce

1995 Recipients

Kenojuak Ashevak – Lifetime Achievement
Ernest Benedict – Education
Douglas Cardinal – Architecture
Noah Carpenter – Medicine
Angela Chalmers – Sports
Matthew Coon Come – Environment and Public Service
Robert Davidson – Arts and Culture
Frank Hansen – Business and Commerce
Maggie Hodgson – Health Services
Sharla Howard – Youth Award
Marie Smallface Marule – Education
Alfred J. Scow – Law and Justice
Ahab Spence – Education
Louis J. Stevenson – Community Development

1994 Recipients

Susan Aglukark – Performance
Thelma Chalifoux – Community Service
Nellie Cournoyea – Public Service
Cindy Kenny-Gilday – Environment
Jean Cuthand Goodwill – Health Services
Verna Kirkness – Education
Rosemarie Kuptana – Public Service
William Lyall – Business and Commerce
Ted Nolan – Sports
Alanis Obomsawin – Film
Bill Reid – Lifetime Achievement
Murray Sinclair – Law and Justice
Art Soloman – Spiritual Leadership

Members of the Order of Canada

Freda Ahenakew
Etuangat Aksayook
Anahareo
Sarah Anala
Anne Anderson
Mathieu André

Eric Anoee
Simon Baker
Herbert C. Belcourt
Wanda Thomas Bernard
George Blondin
John B. Boucher
Ellen Bruce
Linda Bull
Clara Evelyn Campbell
Tantoo Cardinal
Marlene Brant Castellano
Charlie Peter Charlie Sr
Hwunumetsé-Simon Charlie
Harry Chonkolay
Amy L. Clemons
George C. Clutesi
Janet Cochrane
Dave Courchene, Sr.
Sam Crow
Joe Crow Shoe
Josephine Crow Shoe
Chester R. Cunningham
Tagak Curley
Robert Davidson
Olive Patricia Dickason
Mark Evaluarjuk
Cecil Fielding
Dorothy Maquabeak Francis
Judy Gingell
Lawrence Albert Gladue
Joan Glode
Mildred Gottfriedson
David Georges Greyeyes
Boniface Guimond
Ann Meekitjuk Hanson
Christie Harris
Tomson Highway
Joseph Charles Hill
Christine Wilna Hodgson
Alma G. Houston
Richard Ralph Hunt

Joseph R. Jacobs
Roberta L. Jamieson
Rita Joe
Mary John
Mark Kalluak
Helen Kalvak
John Kaunak
Joseph Irvine Keeper
Thomas King
Verna J. Kirkness
Margaret Pictou LaBillois
Arthur Lamothe
Henry J. Langan, Sr.
Sarah Lavalley
Victor Letendre
Albert Levi
J. Wilton Littlechild
Sandra M. Lovelace-Sappier
Richard Lyons
Helen Mamayaok Maksagak
Annie E. Manning
Helen Manyfingers
Leonard S. Marchand
Médéric Zéphirin McDougall
Hilliard McNab
Angus Merrick
Mildred Milliea
Rufus Ezra Moody
Norval Morrisseau
Corinne Mount Pleasant-Jetté
Mitiarjuk Attasie Nappaaluk
Canon Noah Nasook
Annie Ned
Sybilla Nitsman
Kokom Lena Nottaway
Daphne Odjig
Abe Okpik
Elisapie Killiktee Ootova
Brian N. Orvis
Peter Lewis Paul
Myfanwy Spencer Pavelic

Claude Petit
Ashoona Pitseolak
Taamusi Qumaq
Mildred Redmond
Suzanne Rochon-Burnett
Susan A. Ross
Samuel Sam
Carole V. Sanderson
Polly Sargent
Alfred John Scow
Josephine Sias
Angela Sidney
Mary J. May Simon
Sarah Simon
Robert Smallboy
Elijah E. Smith
Ahab Spence
Percy Starr
Lawrence H. Stevenson
Theresa Marie Stevenson
Florence Adelette Tabobondung
George Terry
Gordon Tootoosis
John B. Tootoosis
Hugh Ungungai
Ida Carlotta Wasacase
Gus Waskewitch
P. David Webster
John Yesno
Isadore Yukon

Officers of the Order of Canada

Susan Aglukark
Kiawak Ashoona
John Kim Bell
Frank Arthur Calder
Sharon Capeling-Alakija
Douglas J. Cardinal
Walter Perry Deiter
Andrew T. Delisle

Georges Henry Erasmus
Dan George
Jean Goodwill
Joseph Gosnell
Tom Jackson
Kenojuak
Zacharias Kunuk
Rosemarie Esther Kuptana
Kyak
Robert Lalonde
George Manuel
Alanis Obomsawin
Jessie Oonark
Roderick A. Robinson
Buffy Sainte-Marie
Allen Sapp
James Sewid
Éléonore Tecumseh Sioui
Ralph G. Steinhauer